THE BLACK
PANTHERS

GINA M. DiNICOLO

THE BLACK PANTHERS

A Story of Race, War, and Courage

THE 761st TANK BATTALION IN WORLD WAR II

WESTHOLME
Yardley

Facing title page: Two members of the 761st Tank Battalion pose in front of their M5 Stuart light tank with a 26th Infantry Division soldier somewhere in Germany in 1945. (*Ellsworth G. McConnell Collection*)

Westholme Publishing, LLC
904 Edgewood Road
Yardley, Pennsylvania 19067
Visit our Web site at www.westholmepublishing.com

First Printing July 2014
10 9 8 7 6 5 4 3 2 1
ISBN: 978-1-59416-195-7
Also available as an eBook.

Printed in the United States of America.

*To the men
of the 761st Tank Battalion and their families
and to my mother*

CONTENTS

List of Illustrations

List of Maps

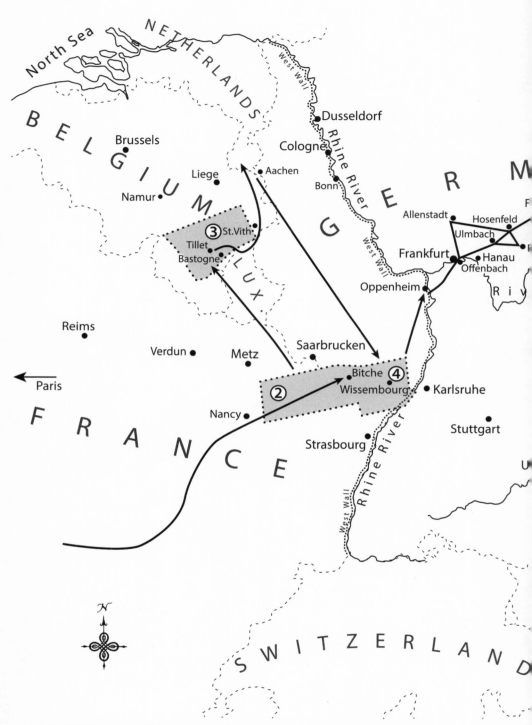

Map 1. The Route of the 761st Tank Battalion, 1944–45. (The shaded areas indicate the locations of detail maps 2, 3, and 4.)

Berlin

M A N Y

Fulda
Flieden
Meiningen
Coburg
Kulmbach
Bayreuth
Lindenhardt
ver Main
Nurnberg
Amberg
Regensburg
Straubing
Landau
Danube River
Isar River
Ulm
Augsburg
Inn River
Munich
Danube River
Wels
Steyr
Salzburg
Enns River

C Z E C H O S L O V A K I A
Prague
Pilsen

A U S T R I A
D

PROLOGUE

HOLLYWOOD IMAGES OF COMBAT BEGAN TO EVAPORATE AS THE men drove deeper into France's Lower Saar Basin. Company by company, the 761st Tank Battalion rolled in support of the 26th Infantry Division, a tactic few armored units had yet to perfect.

The enemy occupied French towns with names like Moyenvic, Vic-sur-Seille, and Morville that the American forces had orders to take. November 8 and 9, 1944, stood as thirty-six hours of confusion and carnage for the green tankers. They fought a battle-hardened enemy and met the mythic German Panzer. The daunting lethality of the enemy's 88 mm rounds awed the Black Panthers and made them question their presence at the European front.

Combat shook the battalion to its core. As the battle raged through the second day, no fewer than fourteen 761st tankers lay dead, with scores more wounded. Smoldering Sherman tank carcasses littered the landscape. Rumors swirled that a German bullet had torn through the Panthers' battalion commander. The men wondered if he had sacrificed himself. How could they continue the fight without him? Would it end for them that day?

Members of the 761st Tank Battalion on Lee Street, Alexandria, Louisiana, in August 1942. Note the military policeman with armband in the center background. (*Yank Magazine*)

Introduction

Order of Battle

I N EARLY 1942 RACIAL TENSIONS SEETHED FOR MILES AROUND
Camp Claiborne, a south-central Louisiana army post. Such acrimony, normally the secret of the army and the remote training regions
that benefited from war's windfall, unexpectedly thrust the nearby
town of Alexandria onto the front pages of the nation's newspapers.

The mounting discord finally erupted in a violent, two-hour,
white-on-black melee in the center of Alexandria's bustling black
business district in the strictly segregated city. It occurred during
January 1942, fewer than three months before the army's 761st Tank
Battalion's activation eighteen miles to the south. Army leadership
contained its outrage and controlled a potentially volatile situation
with brief, well-crafted statements that provided the swarm of interested media with its terse version of the facts. But scores of detailed
"eyewitness" accounts of what became known as the Lee Street Riots
varied wildly, leaving tremendous speculation swirling around what
happened to ignite an apparent race war.[1]

The area's population already had exploded between 1890 and
1930 because of plentiful jobs in the cotton, sugar, and notably timber industries. Rapides Parish, part of a major forestry district in the
state, had longleaf pines awaiting ax-wielding laborers.[2] Logging
companies and sawmills completed the destruction of hundreds of
thousands of acres of old-growth forests at the onset of the Great

Depression, leaving white as well as black workers destitute. But before the end of the 1930s, the prospect of war brought hope through different jobs. Unprecedented growth followed, and the population further swelled from 20,000 to more than twenty times that number, fueled by construction and other defense needs at the surrounding army installations that included camps Claiborne, Livingston, Beauregard, and Polk.[3]

Rambling rows of clapboard homes sprouted across the landscape, filled with hungry workers. Even the lumber company towns overflowed with a new crop of hopeful laborers. Remote logging districts hosted a racially segregated hodgepodge of structures from period bungalows to shotgun and long-pen houses. Black and white tent cities sprouted in what had been a rural sixty-mile radius of Alexandria. Those with cars or trucks lived their own luxury.

The population boom feeding the surrounding army camps' insatiable appetite for workers proved a boon for Alexandria and specifically Lee Street businesses. After sundown, Lee Street hopped like Harlem a decade earlier with all its unabashed freedom. Workers traveled many miles to discuss news, swap tall tales, and fill the many bars and restaurants for their slice of the dream. Soldiers made the almost twenty-mile journey from Camp Claiborne to spend their money in bars and brothels. If a night of love seemed too much to ask, a few minutes would do. Though official accounts maintain that the army had forbidden white soldiers to go in the black enclave, locals said many establishments had entrances for each race, and some noted white servicemen preferred the electrified nightlife up and down the streets of "Little Harlem" to the more staid parts of town.[4]

Some residents said the deadly encounter began as a bar fight between inebriated black and white soldiers. Others swore that a white female driver's angry orders to a black soldier blocking her way started the confrontation. A number of accounts had white Alexandria residents involved in the free-for-all. Yet others pegged military policemen from Camp Claiborne and nearby Camp Livingston wielding fatal blows against black soldiers simply enjoying an evening away from their segregated posts.

Alexandria's newspaper, the *Daily Town Talk*, normally filled with Associated Press accounts of the war, reported the Saturday night incident on its Monday morning front page. The paper highlighted the army's official statement. "None of the 28 Negro troops wounded . . . had died," though it wrote that witnesses flooded the paper with contradictory accounts. Some eyewitnesses counted eighteen blacks killed and twenty-six hurt. Others insisted the death toll stood at twenty-one black soldiers. Stories changed with each passing hour.

The *Town Talk* never clearly addressed what sparked the riot, but Lee Street made the news in other cities. The New Orleans *Times-Picayune* reported the incident in more detail. It noted the trouble began when a white military policeman tried to arrest a black soldier in a black theater. The *New York Times* carried a similar account.[5]

Black MPs typically patrolled Lee Street, but it seems a crowd of black soldiers swarmed both the Wisconsin-raised MP and his prisoner. According to Alexandria chief of police George Gray, the MP called for help, a move that may have pushed a routine arrest across the line. Military police donned "full riot equipment," according to the *Town Talk*. The New Orleans paper reported Alexandria used its entire supply of thirty or so tear gas bombs on the immense crowd estimated at three thousand soldiers and another three thousand civilians. In addition to the sixty MPs involved, twenty city police and ten state officers arrived on the scene. Aside from tear gas, military and state police used "guns, pistols and sticks," to quell what the *Town Talk* called "an outbreak against military authority." Though it gave no details of its mutinous assertion, other than an arrest of a "negro soldier on a disturbance charge," the paper highlighted the army's appreciation "to the *Town Talk* for the way the story has been handled," in what appeared to end with two days' coverage.[6]

Most accounts of what the paper proclaimed the "Lee Street Riots" seemed to describe a one-sided gun battle aimed at the unarmed Lee Street patrons, including members of Camp Claiborne's 758th Tank Battalion, big brother to the yet unknown 761st, as well as hundreds of civilians in the line of fire. Police shot at least four soldiers, whose wounds left them hospitalized in serious condition. The *Louisiana Weekly*, a newspaper that reached a mainly black audience across the southern part of the state, printed an "eyewitness" account and claimed ten dead due to gunslinging MPs shooting up the "Negro part of the city." A stray bullet from marauding officers struck "Miss May Frances Scales in the hip."[7]

The army refused further comment, killing the story in the press but fueling speculation and suspicion among locals and soldiers. Some residents later reported the stench of soldiers' rotting corpses under Alexandria homes. Local officials made no confirmation. Controversy persisted despite a War Department investigation into events that evening.[8] Whatever happened at 8 P.M. on Lee Street in Alexandria, Louisiana, on January 10, 1942, made one thing clear: racial strife thrived inside the army and beyond its borders.

More important, the riots heightened racial distress and mutual distrust. The legend of Lee Street became a cautionary banner and badge of courage for the black tankers of the 761st—a unit that would soon find itself on alert for the threat at home as it prepared for combat abroad.

The issue of race in the military proved daunting to the U.S. military well before World War II. The army of the 1920s understood America's complex and bitterly divided racial landscape, but put its manpower needs foremost. In the event of a full national mobilization, black soldiers would serve the same way as their white counterparts. A 1922 army staff study reported:

> Military realities recognize that the negro is a citizen of the United States, entitled to all of the rights of citizenship and subject to all of the obligations of citizenship; that the negro constitutes an appreciable part of our military manhood; that while not the best military material, he is by no means the worst; that no plan of mobilization for the maximum effort can afford to ignore such a fraction of the manhood, especially in these times when war makes demands upon the physical defectives and the women; and finally, that in a democracy such as ours political and economic conditions must be considered, and that decision must rest these two considerations alone.[9]

Debate raged on exactly how black males would serve. A proud history of black servicemen stood marred in the minds of many, and a number of outrageous and violent events seemed to lend some credibility to white concerns over the military service of black men. At the same time, racial atrocities seemed to justify the sometimes brutal actions of black soldiers on the edge of vigilantism.

The army weighed its options, aware its policies could polarize the public. It flirted with integrating the races. It scoured myriad studies and conducted more of its own and determined the answer to black soldier effectiveness lay in segregated units under white officers. But it soon realized it needed a few black officers to placate the ranks and retain the backing of an entire race. Planners straddled the racial fence: the few black officers the army created would not hold any positions of real influence.

The army on the eve of World War II remained segregated, though the service of black and white had long woven its way through the timeline of the nation's conflicts since the Revolutionary War. The army established four permanent black regiments shortly after the Civil War—the 9th and 10th Cavalry and the 24th and 25th Infantry. Some, mostly northern, members of the new regiments fought as free blacks during the Civil War. Former slaves saw the army's offer of food, shelter, and money superior to their prospects in the racially hateful and war-ravaged South.

Black soldiers served at a variety of isolated posts on the late nineteenth-century frontier. Though townspeople feared armed blacks close to their homes, those in the sparsely populated territories accepted the black soldiers who stood as the first and last line of defense against Indian attacks. Ironically, Comanche Indians dubbed the storied 10th Cavalry Regiment "Buffalo Soldiers" out of respect for the men's fighting ability and because the soldiers' curly hair resembled that of the revered buffalo.[10]

Black soldiers relegated to the frontier kept abreast of news in the east through letters and the occasional newspaper. They formed societies and debated the latest issues affecting African Americans. Favorite topics included contrasting race advocates like the low-profile Booker T. Washington and the fiery W.E.B. DuBois, a founder of the National Association for the Advancement of Colored People.[11] Some, like army Chaplain Allen Allensworth, a Baptist minister with the 24th Infantry Regiment, took a get-along, get-ahead approach. A former slave, he had been sold several times but learned to read and write, escaped to freedom, and served as a Union soldier, the first of his race to attain the rank of lieutenant colonel. His overt deference to white leaders, though criticized, garnered unthinkable advantages such as a school for black students on one post.[12]

Others found violence the great equalizer. As racism worsened in the early 1890s with the advent of Jim Crow, racial policies eradicated freedmen's civil rights and protections under Reconstruction. Many fell under the benignly named practice of "separate but equal," but harassed black soldiers sometimes responded with shocking brutality. In 1892, members of the 9th Cavalry shot up the town of Suggs, Wyoming, as retribution for an alleged racial insult. In 1893,

9th Cavalry soldiers fired into a Texas saloon after a group of Texas Rangers reportedly attacked black soldiers drinking there. In another incident, after rescuing a black veteran from a reported lynch mob in Crawford, Nebraska, again soldiers of the 9th Cavalry, tired of locals targeting their men, warned they would "reduce . . . homes and firesides to ashes and send [the] guilty souls to hell."[13]

Black soldiers fought racial affronts, man-for-man, gun-for-gun. They remained adamant about their value as U.S. soldiers. Upon returning from the politically controversial 1898 U.S. invasion of Cuba, black soldiers met unexplained racial hatred and violent assaults. During the trial of a white soldier accused of a razor attack on a member of the 24th Infantry, the alleged victim, Private George Washington, simply stated, "We did our duty in Cuba, and we don't think we should be insulted because we are black."[14] Deployment to the Philippines in 1899 struck a similar chord. A surprised soldier called to the 24th with some indignity, "What do you think *you're* going to do over here?" Possibly tired of mounting barbs, one black soldier deadpanned, "Well, I don't know, but I rather reckon we're . . . to take up [the] White Man's Burden!"[15]

By 1917, the rich and varied experiences of the four established regiments should have signaled a force ready to fight the threat in Europe. But none of these long-standing units fought in the Great War. With the thousands needed at the front in France, the army considered forming a total of sixteen black regiments.

Horrific events stopped the army cold. Tired of continued mistreatment, soldiers took what some considered unprecedented action. With their veteran black leaders away and a weak, lackluster set of white officers left in charge, at least 100 members of the 24th Infantry Regiment marched on Houston, killing 16 white citizens and wounding a dozen more in a two-hour reign of terror. Of the 155 black soldiers tried, Texas quickly executed 13. The incident underscored the case for racial mistrust at home.[16]

The army recognized black soldiers as an oppressed minority and thus suspected these men as easy prey for an information-starved enemy. The Intelligence Division of the Army War College targeted possible black subversives, chronicling detailed accounts of their activities.[17] Because of the perceived threats posed by black units, the professional soldiers of the 24th and 25th infantries spent World War I in the Pacific and remote outposts on the Mexican border.

Under pressure from a patriotic black community that supported

Members of the 369th Infantry Regiment, the "Harlem Hellfighters," in action during World War I. (*National Archives*)

the war in France and gave to the nation's crucial fund-raising bond drives, the army established the 92nd and 93rd divisions. Not unlike the white units churned out at the time, these divisions suffered from poor training, ineffective leadership, and a dearth of supplies. The contempt some leaders held for their black soldiers proved one of the few and unfortunate differences between hastily created segregated units of the Great War.

Despite contradictory accounts of the brave and cowardly performance of black soldiers during World War I, they proved as fierce as their predecessors on America's frontier. Two men from Company C of the 369th took on a sizable enemy attack during what started as a routine and uneventful evening on guard duty. On the night of May 14, 1918, near a quiet section of No Man's Land, then-Private Henry Lincoln Johnson, twenty-one, and seventeen-year-old Private Needham Roberts heard the quiet clipping of wire cutters as they stood sentry. Johnson recalled, "Somewhere around two o'clock I heard the Germans cutting our wire. I let go with a grenade. There was a yell. . . . A German grenade got Needham in the arm and through the hip. He was too badly wounded to do any fighting so I told him to lie in the trench and hand me up the grenades. 'Keep your nerve' I told him." A morning inspection of the damage revealed the two men fought off more than thirty Germans, by some accounts, with anything immediately available to them—grenades, gunfire, and a bolo knife in hand-to-hand combat. The French hailed the severely wounded Johnson and Roberts as heroes and awarded each the Croix de Guerre, France's award for gallantry. Johnson earned the nickname "Black Death."[18] The incident made the news. *Stars and Stripes* reported on May 24, 1918, "Two Black Yanks Smear 24 Huns; Big Secret Out. Station Porter and Elevator Boy Win Croix de Guerre."

Other units fought with similar fervor. The 370th, called *Schwarze Teufel* or Black Devils by the Germans, continued to harass the enemy. Ten minutes after officials announced the Armistice, a small group of the 370th raided the Germans and captured fifty wagons. The 371th and 372nd enjoyed similar reputations, but at high cost. In September 1918, they advanced to attack a series of objectives, notably Hill 188. They moved forward for eight days without rest. Exhausted, they fought to take and retake French villages against a tenacious German enemy. Casualties mounted, but the Americans remained undeterred.

The *New York Times* published a lengthy retrospective that appeared on February 9, 1919, entitled, "Our Negro Soldiers' Brilliant War Record." "Negro soldiers made a record as fighters in this war as they did in the Spanish American War and civil wars. Fighting for the first time on the soil of the world's most famous battlefields—Europe—and for the first time brought into direct comparison with the best soldiers of Germany, Great Britain, and France, they showed themselves able to hold their own where the tests of courage, endurance, and aggressiveness were most severe."[19]

The Women's Auxiliary of the 15th New York Infantry-turned-federal-369th honored Johnson and Roberts in June 1918 while the young men lay in French hospitals recuperating from their wounds. More than seven hundred gathered at the formal event. Invitee "Colonel" (and former president) Theodore Roosevelt, Sr., a bit of a military legend himself, declined his invitation, but with grace presented the auxiliary with a silk flag. He noted, "Privates Johnson and Roberts have shown themselves to be of the heroic type." His letter abruptly segued into less relevant, but more familiar historic territory for the aging leader. "There are many such men in the 9th and 10th Cavalry with whom I had the honor of serving at Santiago."[20] Though the old warhorse's health had declined, he remained buoyed by the service of young men, including his own sons, abroad. But within three weeks of the Harlem event, Roosevelt would lose his youngest boy, Quentin, in the skies over France.

Black soldiers' combat accomplishments quickly fell into obscurity and the issue of race and battlefield service made postwar planners anxious. Nearly twenty years later, Lesley J. McNair, who rose from brigadier general to lieutenant general in less than a year between the summers of 1940 and 1941, understood the army's crushing manpower needs for the looming war. The army could only be as successful as its training and replacement programs. He believed the army could neglect no asset. Though many officers did not see a need for the widespread service of African Americans, McNair determined black men would fight—despite ongoing concerns over their capabilities. Black soldiers would serve in the Armored Force of the U.S. Ground Forces, placing them in American tanks.

Though the army stood as the most progressive of the services in 1940, Secretary of War Henry L. Stimson, resigned to the fact that blacks would serve, had strong reservations about black soldiers' capabilities in specific areas and echoed, in his diary, what many believed:

> Leadership is not imbedded in the Negro race yet and to try to make commissioned officers to lead the men into battle—colored men—is to work disaster to both. Colored troops do very well under white officers but every time we try to lift them a little bit beyond where they can go, disaster and confusion follows. In the draft, we are preparing to give Negroes a fair shot in every service, however, even in aviation where I doubt if they will not produce disaster there. Nevertheless, they are going to have a try, but I hope to Heaven's sake they won't mix the white and the colored troops together in the same units for then we shall certainly have trouble.[21]

Where McNair found the seventy-five-year-old Stimson adamant, Army Chief of Staff George C. Marshall seemed cautious. In a 1940 note to Massachusetts Senator Henry Cabot Lodge, Jr., Marshall made it clear that treatment of blacks would mirror societal norms as with segregation, and he did not want the army made into some social experiment.[22] McNair as chief of Army Ground Forces faced his own war on four fronts—Europe, the Pacific, a divided homefront, and Washington. The complexities of war, race, and protocol forced him to handle Marshall and Stimson with care. The secretary of war reigned as one of the most powerful men in Washington, even as a Republican in President Franklin D. Roosevelt's Democratic administration. With the War Department placated, McNair acted, determined to defeat enemies in Europe and the Pacific.

McNair's unwavering support of the black soldier bolstered a small but vocal civil rights movement as well as an outspoken black press. Both had gained strength in the 1930s. Men like W.E.B. DuBois held tremendous sway with black citizens across the nation. DuBois reached some influential white political leaders as well. The *Pittsburgh Courier* continued to stoke opinion in the black community. It founded the "Double V" campaign that ran weekly from February 7, 1942, into 1943. With its slogan, "Double V—victory abroad over Nazism and victory at home over racism and inequality," the campaign maintained that blacks risking their lives in war should be afforded full rights as citizens at home. Black papers elsewhere carried the *Courier*'s torch and spread the crusade to black homes across America. Despite a well-thought-out position supported by numerous illustrative articles and editorials, the idea of "Double V" had little impact on policy makers or the average American. Blacks would serve, but equality remained out of reach.[23]

In spite of the hand-wringing that race in the armed forces seemed to inspire, military service equaled opportunity for many families. For some it meant one less mouth to feed as well as a small but steady income. After World War I the permanent black units enjoyed higher reenlistment rates than white units, something that did not go unnoticed by the army. Postwar budget woes and the launch of an army aviation corps all but forced these units to disband during the 1930s, though not without protests from DuBois and others fighting for equality.

No one could predict that after of decades of racial feuding, the German threat abroad would force the army to rethink personnel policies and provide unprecedented prospects for American males, and some females, regardless of race.

One

Why Not Me?

"THEY DON'T TRAIN COLOREDS, BILLY." WILLIAM HAYWOOD McBurney listened as his father punctuated each word as if they told their own story. While he sensed his father's mix of anger and regret, the New York teen clamored to join the army, just like the other young men did each Saturday in the newsreels as he sat fixated at the motion picture matinee. Standing just less than six feet tall, McBurney, sharp, confident, and a self-proclaimed ladies' man, refused to wait to turn eighteen in May 1942, so at seventeen he sought his father's permission to enlist.

Thomas McBurney once harbored an idealism and patriotism much like his son's. As a member of the 369th Infantry Regiment, or the "Harlem Hellfighters," a name the soon-famous unit took on after the war, he fought in a another time under a different tradition, he thought, but as a part of a rich American black heritage—one fraught with pain he did not want Billy to experience.

Originally designated the 15th New York Infantry Regiment, a National Guard outfit, the army drafted the unit into federal service in 1917 and redesignated it the 369th Infantry Regiment. The combat unit shipped to France in late December 1917, but by January 1918 the army relegated the soldiers to duty as laborers. The men's status, with a war roaring, perplexed them. The spirited youth of the regiment, like Thomas McBurney, had come to France for a fight.

Tension mounted and relief for the eager infantrymen seemed to come May 8 when the 369th moved under French control. McBurney donned a French helmet atop his U.S. Army uniform, but as a combat soldier. Despite time in the trenches with the French 16th Division, the black doughboys went on the attack. They fought as a part of the Allied counteroffensive at the Marne. They attacked through Château-Thierry in July. Black soldier prowess in battle came as no surprise. The French recognized the bravest with their Croix de Guerre. The regiment drove through heavy fighting at Meuse-Argonne on the final protracted push against Germany, sustaining heavy losses as did most units at the front.[1] McBurney lay as one of the roughly 1,500 casualties suffered by the unit while battling the enemy. As he grasped his blood-soaked bullet wound in his leg, his pain mixed with pride.

The two generations collided in his son's wish to join the military. Raised at an early age in the hustle of New York City's Hell's Kitchen, William McBurney knew little of the history of blacks' service in the army. Why the recruiter barked, "No Negroes," in the Air Corps remained unclear. McBurney read the army needed thirty-three officer pilots and four hundred ground crew, "all colored," for the new squadron. It had been at least a year since he clipped out the *New York Times* article. Had the army filled the spaces already? He met the qualifications.

The army's body-broker sized up the strapping pick-up football guard, scanned his solid Army General Classification Test scores and figured the aloof and seemingly carefree McBurney would rather ride than walk. "Tanks," he offered, seducing the boy. The recruiter held this invitation in reserve. With 900,000 black soldiers serving in the army during the war, the service could afford to be selective. McBurney snatched the opportunity. He had the aviation article nearly memorized. The last paragraph read, "army officers said that the army was creating Negro units in every branch of the service and it was suggested a Negro tank unit might be formed." Convinced the article spoke directly to him, he concluded a move to tanks could put him well ahead of those aviation boys.

A dapper McBurney strutted out of the recruiter's 39 Whitehall Street office into an April of promise despite a world at war. He caught a glimpse of himself in each plate glass storefront he passed. Standing tall in his only suit, which had grown a bit short in the arms, and high-waisted trousers he tugged toward the exposed rims of his worn leather shoes, his chest puffed beneath his father's white shirt, one of just three garments he had ever ironed.[2] While his African American father buried his combat veteran status from the Great War, his mother, Daisy, took pride as a "reservation-raised Seminole Indian," as he called her. His parents left the hopelessness of Titusville, Florida, looking for better opportunities in the north that the elder McBurney had glimpsed during the war. A photo of the younger McBurney's great-grandfather in traditional Seminole dress hung in his mother's home after his parents separated. But William cared little about

William H. McBurney in his army service uniform. (*William McBurney Family*)

the past. "Dad, I'm turning eighteen soon. I'm all grown now," he recalled saying, cajoling the man who had raised him. Though proud of his decision, he sensed his father's disappointment.[3]

Thomas McBurney knew the realities of war. As he reflected on events twenty-four years past, he saw the army had shipped him off to die and would do the same to his son. But he remained conflicted. He had experienced the excitement of fighting for one's country. He reveled in the camaraderie and the unit's fighting spirit. Fighting under the French with ideal American unit leaders who had little interest in race left him searching for a similar brotherhood after the Armistice. He did not find it. The 369th's well-documented bravery in Europe did not lead to an opening for equality and respect back under American military control or at home. France proved a dream for some and a nightmare for others. Thomas McBurney had never been prouder. But reality had never been more sobering. He marched, albeit uncomfortably, with his unit up Fifth Avenue through Harlem after they returned from the war, February 17, 1919.[4] News reports estimated 1 million lined the streets, screaming and cheering for their doughboys. Now he and Billy lived a few blocks from the site of such fervor. Some days McBurney questioned his memory of events. He admitted to himself the bitterness that dominated him. Despite his honorable service he returned to a nation that judged him not by his sacrifice in battle, but by the color of his skin. He knew the ugliness of America and the lies of the U.S. Army firsthand.

His view now contradicted war's portrayal in the moving pictures that filled Billy's head with myths and misplaced admiration for a nation painfully divided by race.[5] Father and son stood amidst a tenuous détente. The two figures filled the creamy beige kitchen at the front of the rented Madison Avenue railroad flat near 118th Street. Thomas, tall like his son, had made a pleasant life for them well north of West 69th Street and 10th Avenue, where they had once lived and where the Hudson River stood as the only waters inviting his young son to learn to swim. He sometimes found extra work as a dental technician, but his weathered, full-time longshoreman's face told a story different than that of a comfortable city-dweller. He often shifted his weight, still reeling from the enemy bullet that had torn a path through his left thigh. He never talked about the war, dust-covered after nearly a quarter-century, but he could not forget the chaotic exhilaration of France.

The younger McBurney faced the wisest person he knew. Still harboring a glint of hope for a chance at the Air Corps, he told his father he could fly planes in a modern army that wanted men like him. Black men. He carried the worn news article in his pocket as proof.[6] He spoke with the optimism of the child but at that moment he knew he stood as a man.

"They are never going to let us fly," Thomas said, unable to conceal his hostility and concern. He knew their armies, separated by just more than two decades, shared more than a 17-year-old shielded from life's inequities could grasp.

Thomas McBurney probably had read the January 12 *New York Times* article about the army's racial turmoil in Alexandria, Louisiana. The headline, "Negroes Kept in Camp After Louisiana Riot," followed by, "28 Soldiers, Woman, Trooper Hurt in Alexandria Flare-up," grabbed his attention. He read the report more than once and at that moment wished he had shown it to his son. But McBurney knew a writeup about a Southern incident would not deter his determined boy. He thought back and knew it would not have made him any less idealistic about fighting in France. One brief paragraph worried him most: "Almost all of the Negro troops involved were described as from Northern States, principally New York, Pennsylvania and Illinois."[7] City boys from New York, Philadelphia, and Chicago, he deduced. He had witnessed mischievous New York youth having their way with Madison Avenue without destroying local business or getting shot by New York police. He probably wondered about the mention of 6,000 black citizens caught in the four-block area. He would have found that to be quite a crowd, even by New York City standards.

Thomas McBurney probably concluded that if a New York paper carried a story about an incident in Nowhere, Louisiana, something significant must have taken place. Though concerned for his son, the elder McBurney knew he could no longer delay the inevitable. "I am just trying to protect you," came as the only words he could find.

William McBurney looked at his father. He knew nothing of the so-called Lee Street Riots. He sensed his act of patriotism betrayed the gentle-spirited man whom he adored. "I know, Dad, but everyone else is going, so why not me?"

As McBurney took his oath, America fought a war still in its infancy, though a fierce storm had brewed for some time. Japan finally shattered the nation's tenuous neutrality when it crippled the U.S. Navy's seapower at Pearl Harbor. The material damage alone devastated the nation, but the stunning loss of more than 2,400 lives galvanized the resolve of millions.[8]

Darkness and despair filled the first few months of the war. By the time the 761st Tank Battalion officially activated at Camp Claiborne on April 1, 1942, the nation had lost the tiny Pacific island of Wake. An outmanned and outgunned mix of American Marines, sailors, and civilian workers lost an against-all-odds, fifteen-day siege by Japanese imperial forces.[9]

As the slaughter continued in the Pacific, the U.S. looked for hope across the Atlantic. It found little. Adolf Hitler's Germany and Josef Stalin's Soviet Union already had carved up a defeated Poland on October 6, 1939. Germany had moved forward with its invasion of Poland despite a declaration of war by Great Britain as well as France. The Germans cared little about Western opinion. Holland and Belgium surrendered to the Nazis in May 1940. Norway fell on June 10. But France's capitulation in seven weeks proved most shocking. Its June 25 armistice left Germany in control of the continent, the unencumbered platform from which to launch its fight for Britain. America held its collective breath as Great Britain withstood the German Luftwaffe's relentless aerial bombing attacks. Without warning, Britain's vast empire also faced unforeseen challenges.

Italy, specifically its leader, Benito Mussolini, had seemingly remained neutral, at the urging of the French and British to a degree, but in large part to wait and see which nation, and array of personalities, would emerge strongest from this latest European conflict. Mussolini, a World War I veteran, won the approval of Adolf Hitler, and by 1938 the two leaders entered into their military Pact of Steel. Hitler may not have appreciated the weaknesses of his partner and Mussolini may not have understood what Germany would demand of a lesser military power. Nevertheless, the confident Mussolini had plans for his country and latching on to Adolf Hitler would get him the empire he craved.

Mussolini sensed opportunity and declared war on Great Britain and France on June 10, 1940. He planned to attack Britain's colonies in Africa and reroute their supply lines and rich resources to struggling Italy. He had some experience in the region from his invasion of Ethiopia in 1935. Italian forces swept into Somaliland in the Horn of Africa. They attacked Malta as well as Egypt, neighbor to Italian controlled Libya. Italy also invaded Greece on October 28, 1940. On November 11, the British surprised Mussolini and attacked the Italian fleet at Taranto. They pushed the Italians out of Egypt in December. The British had commenced their offensive in North Africa. After the British retook Somaliland during March 1941, the Germans offered assistance. Mussolini accepted.[10]

Notwithstanding the nation's isolationist mood, Congress clearly understood that the threats in Europe, North Africa, and the Pacific placed the nation in peril and passed the Selective Service and Training Act of 1940, the nation's first peacetime draft. As parents panicked, sons sensed an impending metamorphosis not seen since the Civil War, and many wanted in.[11] Some young women saw an inevitable role, too. With the fall of France to Germany, a large-scale mobilization consumed the nation like a tidal wave. Young men, white and black, took their oaths of enlistment in unprecedented numbers. Few complained. Young men stood against tyranny in Hitler's Germany and Hirohito's Japan. They served regardless of race. They served because their nation called.

Germany's presence in Greece and North Africa changed the war. Its forces brought superior arms and innovative tactics. Of most concern, they reversed Allied successes. Despite British suffering from the

Germans' air campaign against the island nation, the U.S. remained neutral and counted on the war-weary Brits to loosen the Führer's grip on North Africa, as it had the Italians', and stem the carnage on the continent. Americans watched the high-stakes prize fight that pitted Britain's Lieutenant General Bernard Montgomery and his Eighth Army against Germany's newly promoted Field Marshal Erwin Rommel and his Afrika Corps.

President Franklin D. Roosevelt took a "Europe First" approach and sought ways to aid Britain without plunging his nation into war. The Lend-Lease Act of 1941 sanctioned an already entrenched U.S. practice. The United States could "sell, transfer title to, exchange, lease, lend, or otherwise dispose of, to any such government [whose defense the President deems vital to the defense of the United States] any defense article."[12] Lend-Lease translated into arms for a hungry friend.

In the face of crumbling neutrality and Rommel's Panzer success, the tug toward North Africa grew stronger especially for the fledgling Armored Force. As the War Department planned for combat, Camp Claiborne's 761st Tank Battalion awaited its chosen few, as the second of the 5th Tank Group's three black tank units filled its ranks.

Paul Bates in his Western Maryland College football uniform, c. 1930. (*McDaniel College, formerly Western Maryland College*)

Two

Smooth and Taffy

W HEN LOS ANGELES NATIVE PAUL LEVERNE BATES RETURNED
to California in 1931, his home state appeared almost unrecognizable from the one he left in 1927 when he headed east for college. The Great Depression had shaken the foundation of the Golden
State. During the 1920s, the population of Southern California mul-
tiplied and Los Angeles moved from tenth most populous city in 1920
to fifth in 1930, behind New York, Chicago, Philadelphia, and
Detroit.[1] Americans flocked to the promise of plentiful jobs in areas
such as manufacturing, oil, aviation, and film. With the 1929 crash
of the stock market, orders slowed for the goods churned out by the
region. Then they stopped. Despite widespread unemployment, yet
another 200,000 migrated to the Los Angeles area in search of survival. Confident the surrounding misfortune targeted the average,
unfortunate sap, Bates snagged a berth on a merchant vessel and
headed to Asia in 1931.

Paul Bates stood just more than 6 feet 1 inch, with broad shoulders on a chiseled frame. Born March 4, 1908, he lived with his parents and two older brothers in a modest Los Angeles home. Like his
brothers, Paul attended Eagle Rock grammar school and Franklin
High School. While at Franklin, his athletic talent, notably on the
football field, vaulted him ahead of his peers and he took on leadership opportunities like other boys consumed milkshakes. Paul under-

stood his abilities from an early age, and most important, he learned how to use them.[2]

Franklin's football coach Frank Hess, a man not yet thirty, had played the game himself as a fullback[3] at Colgate University under the acclaimed Dick Harlow. After Hess left Colgate for California, Harlow moved on to coach Western Maryland College (now McDaniel College), where he found an alumni network that understood the power of top-tier athletics and hungered to join its ranks. The school's athletic association started with Harlow's 1925 arrival to "sell" athletes from around the country on Western Maryland and take its sports program to heretofore unknown heights. To that end, the athletic association entered into its own contract with Harlow and provided the new football coach with $3,000 per year to "sell."[4]

A man like Frank Hess understood loyalty and passed this trait on to his players. Whether Harlow contacted Hess on the search for talent remains unknown, but Hess talked about his former coach to his players. After his graduation from Franklin in 1927, Bates reviewed his collegiate options. His status as a football star opened doors, and Bates chose the school possibly farthest from his home—Western Maryland College in rural Westminster, Maryland.

Philadelphia native Dick Harlow had coached at Penn State before his years at Colgate, and later coached at Harvard. The College Football Hall of Fame immortalized him in 1954. Harlow took undersized teams and made them champions through stunts, deception, and timing. He used lateral passes, shifts, and reverses to outwit opponents, knowing his underdogs could not overpower them. He had the perfect "Harlow player" in Paul Bates—a loyal young man who not only possessed skills on the gridiron, but more important had a dogged determination to win—no matter the odds.

Bates memorized each lesson from the master, knowledge that he thought would later serve him. His rare and acquired talents dominated and drove him. United Press sports writers named him as a third-team All-American in 1929 and he garnered at least an All-American honorable mention in 1930. As football team captain of the "Green Terror" his senior year, Bates led Western Maryland to its second undefeated season in a row, placing the little-known school on the collegiate powerhouse map. Storied rivals like Georgetown and Carnegie Tech fell easily to Bates and his teammates.

Paul Bates orchestrated his rise to the top of his college class. A head turner, he flourished at the school and reached beyond the relative celebrity his athletic scholarship afforded him. He sought leadership roles and rose to the rank of cadet captain in his Reserve Officer Training Corps unit. Members of all four classes elected him student council vice president and president of his Alpha Gamma Tau fraternity.[5]

Bates became a staple in the the *Gold Bug*, Western Maryland's campus newspaper. He appeared on the masthead as the paper's business manager. After any ROTC event, one could find Bates's name in a story. And as football team captain with a championship within reach, the name "Paul Bates" covered the paper almost as completely as he covered the field as a left end.[6] A mix of admiration and envy with a touch of good-natured sarcasm prompted classmates to write: "For four years we have turned to Paul. We have turned to follow him in the athletic field, we have turned to ask his advice, and we have turned to listen intently to his suggestions. It has always been worthwhile. 'Smooth' always knows the latest ideas—in clothes, in football plays, in everything. He is always a leader."[7]

In 1931, bursting with optimism and consumed with himself, Bates, unaware how hard the Depression had hit California, took his diploma, an officer's commission in the army reserve, and wealth of experience and headed home to Los Angeles, fixed on his next adventure.

Paul Bates's interest lay in Paul Bates, but "Smooth" also possessed one weakness: women. With his leading-man good looks and charisma, he attracted the notice of many, but he gravitated toward independent, passionate, and eccentric women. Oblivious to matters of little consequence to him, he probably took no notice as Gwendolyn Mann chased him from Maryland back to the West Coast. If he did, he did not care. Mann, who hailed from a prominent Boonton, New Jersey, family, had a penchant for Harvard men while at college in Boston, but chose a position far from the refined circles befitting her social status. The Emerson Auditory (now Emerson College) graduate accepted an offer from Western Maryland College president Dr. A. N. Ward to teach literary interpretation, speech, and theater at the school beginning in the fall of 1929, Paul Bates's junior year.

Her family's standing may have compensated for her less-than-flattering recommendations for the Western Maryland position.[8] One former professor wrote: "Always puts off till tomorrow what should

Paul Bates in front of an M3 Light Tank. (*Baron Bates*)

have been done today. (Procrastinates.) Fine type girl but as a student she has been a great disappointment to me." Another observed: "very sweet influences—always ladylike. Not outstanding in ability but a faithful worker."[9] Her activities as student council president, the ethereal Queen of the May, and Kappa Gamma Chi sister may have given Western Maryland a better glimpse into the complexities of its candidate.

A salary of $1,200 per academic year plus room and board as well as laundry suited the independent twenty-two-year-old Mann. Of her other duties as a faculty member, outlined by Nannie Lease, the Western Maryland speech professor and fellow Emerson graduate who recommended her to Ward, wrote that she, "would be glad to help in chaperoning and help in any way to hold high the character-building standards of your college."[10] Western Maryland thought it had found its ideal young professor. But the well-bred academic shifted her priorities and set a new goal: Paul Bates. Though their schedules shared no classes or extracurricular activities, Mann fell under Smooth's spell. This single-minded woman abruptly left her position at the college soon after Bates's 1931 graduation.

Mann arrived in California and remained in Los Angeles, undeterred by Bates's sudden maritime junket across the Pacific. With the Golden Age of Hollywood aglow and an endearing but inflated sense of self, Gwendolyn Mann saw opportunity in motion pictures and brimmed with dreams for her future—with or without the elusive Paul Bates. Mann immersed herself in a bohemian lifestyle and cavorted with other young hopefuls. Impressionist Mel Blanc, later known to generations as the voice of Bugs Bunny and other beloved Looney Tunes characters, befriended her.[11]

Gwendolyn's Hollywood fortunes faded as Paul Bates returned from Asia nine months later. Some say she published news of their engagement-that-wasn't in the *New York Times*, unknown to Bates, on January 31, 1932.

Upon reading the announcement, reportedly Bates said of marriage, "Oh, why not? Everyone else is doing it."[12] They married in March 1933. Son Baron arrived in 1934.

The couple shared only brief happiness—if they shared any. As Bates worked in "sales" for Standard Oil, as he liked to term pumping gas in Long Beach, Gwen spent lavishly. Her insensitivity to her new husband's economic struggles caused tremendous strain. Possibly in search of financial stability or the personal and professional fulfillment he had known at Western Maryland, he snapped up a chance to coach high school football—courtesy of Gwen's father, the superintendent of schools—near her girlhood home.[13]

The family moved to Madison, New Jersey, ten miles south of Boonton and less than forty miles west of New York City. Madison High School officials, though pleased with Bates as a coach, found his Western Maryland credentials lacking for his added duties as a history teacher. They required additional coursework, which Bates completed at nearby Rutgers University.[14] Paul Bates reveled in his role as teacher, coach, and leader, despite continued dissatisfaction in his marriage.

But the army activated the reserve infantry officer on January 22, 1941, nearly a year before the attack on Pearl Harbor. Bates left Madison and made good on his military commitment.[15] A world away from the wealth and crush of Madison students and the Mann family, Bates trained as an infantry second lieutenant at Fort Benning, Georgia. Promotion to first lieutenant came four short months later on May 16. Orders from Headquarters Fourth Corps Area, Atlanta, slated Bates for duty at Camp Claiborne, December 2, 1941. The army promoted him to captain on December 29.[16]

Barrie, as his parents came to call young Baron, recalled a Sunday brunch like many he and his parents shared while at Camp Claiborne. He and his mother lived north of the installation in Alexandria while

Paul Bates chose to reside on post. That Sunday the calendar read
December 7, 1941. A man rushed into the crowded dining room and
announced the grim news from Pearl Harbor. Amidst gasps and mur-
murs, a uniformed Bates stood up and walked out of the restaurant
without uttering a word.[17]

Paul Bates found himself in an army of change and opportunity.
Given the need for armor officers, Bates sidestepped his infantry roots
and trained at Fort Knox's Armored Force School, first completing
the Gunnery Instructor Course in October 1941. He attended the
Basic Course from February 7 through April 7, 1942.[18] The graduating tankers from his class went to a variety of armor units, including
the 1st, 3rd, and 4th armored divisions, as well as a number of stand-
alone, separate (independent) tank battalions.

The headquarters of the Armored Force School ordered Bates and
classmate First Lieutenant Lawrence A. Martin to the separate 758th
Tank Battalion, Camp Claiborne, Louisiana, "having completed the
required course of instruction (Basic Tactics Course No. 1) in the
Armored Force School."[19] Bates's paperwork made no mention of the
758th and its designation as a "Colored" unit. According to Bates,
the army first sought volunteers to serve as officers in black units.
Many officers saw service with a black unit as a career-ending event.
Most white officers serving in black outfits moved on to higher positions in white units following promotion, or sooner if they could find
transfers out.

Bates seemed unaware of the effort George Marshall and the commanding general of Army Ground Forces, Lieutenant General Lesley
J. McNair, put into finding the correct officers to lead black units. In
1942, much to the generals' horror, they found those outfits packed
with inexperienced, mediocre white officers, many just out of officer
candidate school. The officers' performance was abysmal, and low
morale plagued these units. McNair insisted on older, more mature
officers, with high leadership ratings, but many army leaders fought
losing their commissioned talent. At the same time, McNair faced a
severe officer shortage. Manpower challenges notwithstanding,
Marshall's office published a list of prerequisites for candidates needed in black units: "a. A primary requirement of demonstrated leadership ability in a command assignment. [No rating below
"Excellent."] b. Mature judgment and common sense. c. Even disposition and patience. d. Demonstrated stability under pressure and
ability to handle emergency situations. e. Ability to organize and fos-

ter athletic and recreational programs."[20] The five criteria described Paul L. Bates precisely. Upon hearing of his assignment to the 758th Tank Battalion, Bates could not find a reason to balk. He had little experience with black men in Southern California or at Western Maryland and had not developed an opinion on race. Camp Claiborne soon welcomed the 758th's newest company commander.

But Bates's stay lasted just four months. Despite high ratings, he moved to the 5th Tank Group Headquarters on July 7, 1942, as the assistant S-3 or operations and training officer. Though far from his dream job, he escaped the racial discord he found in the 758th and moved a step closer to the intriguing 761st. His talents as a tactician proved a plus.

By December 1942, Bates made his move to the 761st, taking over both intelligence as well as operations and training as the unit's S-2 and S-3 officer for a brief period. Promotion to major arrived April 8, 1943. Paul Bates sensed he had found his purpose in the 761st. He knew Camp Claiborne's uneven fields held great challenge as well as promise. Despite his circuitous route, he knew he would command the 761st and train these men as champions.[21] He eyed the fresh tankers and saw an unencumbered future. His memories flashed back to himself in his youth; he and the armor neophytes had much in common. Bates did not need the threat of a German opponent to shape the 761st Tank Battalion (Light) as Dick Harlow had done with his title-holding college team. He knew he faced a far more lethal adversary in a racially volatile army.

Barrie Bates found his father "engrossed" with his work. The growing boy longed for another family trip to Mammoth Cave, Kentucky, a memorable outing for the eight-year-old in early 1942 when Bates trained as a tanker at Fort Knox. Barrie recalled the signs above the restrooms. He already knew what a "White" bathroom looked like; he had one at home. But he wanted to see the colors chosen for the "Colored" restroom. He could not understand why the men in the bathroom laughed.[22]

Barrie missed the lighter and loving moments with his father. When living in Long Beach, three-year-old Barrie would wrap his arms around his father's neck as the elder Bates moved through the Pacific like a mighty sea creature. Paul Bates would roll around the living room floor in New Jersey with his toddler son and developed a special whistle to call him home for dinner. But as Barrie witnessed his parents' disintegrating marriage, fights with Gwen replaced the whistle. He would hear them through the wall when they thought he slept. He believed his mother loved his father as deeply as the day she first decided she wanted to marry him at Western Maryland. He had picked up bits and pieces of their history and knew more than either realized.[23]

Alone and despondent in Alexandria, Gwen packed up Barrie and moved every few months—sometimes out of town, other times out of state as they did for their several-month stay in Sewanee, Tennessee. Barrie's first-grade experience included seven schools, and the second grade improved little. He longed for the days when his father thrilled him with a ride in his tank, but the family had fallen in tatters. The 761st and Camp Claiborne now mattered to Paul Bates. Gwen and Barrie sought refuge in New Jersey, though the boy remained hopeful his father would reunite with them.[24]

Paul Bates learned to enjoy Camp Claiborne life and the entertainment, albeit limited, that the post offered. Given his California roots and collegiate pedigree, surrounding towns like Alexandria and Pineville had little to offer him. A number of installations had their own "Boomtown," like the one that sat just beyond Camp Claiborne's main entrance. The shanty town offered bad food, overpriced alcohol, and sex for every budget and taste.

Bates took in the relatively rich offerings of the remote post. One evening he walked up the Art Deco styled steps into the main post theater. Immaculately groomed, tall and striking in his "pinks and greens," he stood out from the other officers. That night in December 1942, Bates watched as a Russian musical troupe filled the stage. During intermission in the lobby, he eyed an army lieutenant, a nurse, stumbling through an interpretation of a complex move the Russians flawlessly performed minutes before. While endearing, she looked utterly inept. Bates took a drag from his cigarette and contained his amusement. Be careful or you'll fall, he called to her.

Melanie, though not surprised by the comment, gasped when she saw the attractive, tall officer standing feet from her. Her cheeks burned as red as her hair. When Bates queried Melanie about the Russian performers, she said, "Oh, Taffy knows!"[25]

"Who's Taffy?" he asked. Melanie pointed to her friend and smiled. Across the lobby sat an officer, flaxen hair swept back with style and self-assurance. Seemingly unaware of the attention she commanded, she pursed her lips and slowly drew deeply from her cigarette. She exhaled at the same calculated pace, her chin raised, and her lips blew a gentle, smoky kiss across the bar. Bates exhaled with her and approached without hesitation.

Twenty-four-year-old army Lieutenant Helen Rosen had fashioned herself into a self-made Anglo-American woman. As the third child of Russian immigrants loyal to the czar, her heritage disgusted her. She spent a childhood re-creating herself and planning her escape. Her parents named her Helen after the wife of the delivery doctor and at his urging. At age five she recalled removing the pierced earrings she felt had marked her as a dirty gypsy since birth. She renamed herself Taffy, from what she believed as the Russian, *trefenka*, or towhead, for her signature platinum locks.[26]

Taffy Rosen left home at seventeen, embarrassed by her family's very existence. Despite her disdain for them, they loved her. Her older sister Celia adored her and considered the determined Taffy the most remarkable person she had known in her young life. Taffy's mother slipped her money for school, which she accepted, but it did not matter. Rosen buried her family's questionable devotion and past with Helen, the Russian Jew.[27]

With her talent apparent, she found work at New York's Sloan-Kettering Hospital as its institutional health nurse. Soon after Pearl Harbor, she volunteered to serve in the Army's Nurse Corps, though it meant losing a prestigious job she loved. Taffy Rosen wanted to care for sick and wounded soldiers in the cauldron of combat. Unlike some of her peers, she had no interest in a husband. But men fell under the spell of the 14th Evacuation Hospital all-business caregiver.[28] She had her choice of suitors, none of whom held her interest.[29]

Rosen held the "relative rank" of lieutenant, a bizarre parallel structure within the army created in 1920 to recognize the service of army nurses in the Great War. The well-meant but ill-thought-out system afforded nurses like Rosen the rank but not the privileges of a male commissioned officer. Worse, the army paid the nurses less at the time. She bristled at the arbitrary regulations forced on her. She abhorred the nurses' curfew most, an indignity the army had not thrust upon male lieutenants.

She had seen the Cossack show the previous night in Alexandria escorted by yet another attractive but unmemorable young army officer. She attended the second night at Camp Claiborne because the sweet but unsophisticated Melanie did not want to go alone. Bates could not tell, but Rosen stared as he approached. She had never seen a man so captivating.[30] Though momentarily unnerved, she sensed he was worth her time.

Paul Bates sat with Taffy and Melanie for the second half of the Don Cossack Chorus. Fascinated by other cultures, he peppered her with questions about the Russian dancers. Rosen shot back answers as if she danced with the troupe herself. When the show ended, Bates invited his new friends to the officers' club. Melanie, lacking the required uniform, declined. She did not need more trouble from the viperous senior nurses who seemed to lay in wait at the nurses' quarters for the younger and more capable to make a mistake. Rosen did not want her friend to go off alone and also bid good night to the captain. She turned toward Melanie and started toward the exit. Stunned by Taffy's choice, Melanie pulled her friend aside and insisted, "Go! *Look* at him."[31] Paul Bates and Taffy Rosen talked late into the night. She had never met anyone who had been to the Far East, and her curiosity nearly turned the encounter into an interrogation.

Rosen soon discovered the matter of Gwendolyn Bates. Horrified to learn of Bates's marriage, Rosen refused to enter into a scandalous relationship. He led her to believe he and his wife had separated.[32] Despite Rosen's strong misgivings, their accidental meeting soon turned into an illicit affair. Paul Bates hungered for Taffy Rosen, a woman ten years his junior. When separated, he would confess: "Beloved, life will begin again when we are together." But his yearning surpassed his physical desires. Rosen's appearance gave Bates some much-needed relief on the professional front. He had found the companion and confidante he needed.

Three

The Call to Knox

WILLIAM McBURNEY'S EXCITEMENT INFUSED THOSE AROUND him. Fresh from his oath of enlistment, he tucked away his Air Corps disappointment. The adventure he craved was just a bus ride away. But instead of the trip of a lifetime, McBurney and countless others sat in army limbo a few miles from home. The Hell's Kitchen recruit fumed: He heard the army's burgeoning ranks clogged an inadequate training pipeline. Clearing the blockage seemed a simple matter to the young man, but he knew nothing of the racial impediment behind the delay.

Shortly after his May 1942 enlistment, stashed at Camp Upton in Yaphank, New York, at the far eastern end of Long Island, and surrounded by only black soldiers, the new recruit knew little of army segregation. Nothing seemed amiss to McBurney and the buddies he met as debate over the service of black soldiers continued many echelons above him. Years later he recalled, still with a hint of innocence, "Racism? We were all black. We didn't notice anything about racism at Upton."[1]

McBurney and most black recruits at Camp Upton had yet to meet the army of racial polarity. But Upton's uneven history of race made headlines more than once. Camp Upton opened in 1917 as the first stop for thousands of men recruited by the army for the world war. Some famous faces processed through Upton, including composer Irving Berlin.[2]

On September 14, 1917, the *New York Times* led with "Officers
Stop Riot at Camp Upton. Negro Soldiers Clash with White
Workmen . . . Shots in Early Morning Cause Great Excitement."
According to the published account, black soldiers on guard duty
fought with white civilian workers over a routine search that turned
up a large amount of liquor on the white workers. After the soldiers
confiscated the contraband, white officers arrived to stop a potentially deadly incident.[3] That same night, black soldiers returning from a
dance came to blows with white soldiers in the Upton mess hall during the early morning hours. Despite these confrontations, black soldiers became an accepted part of Upton life. New York governor
Charles S. Whitman ensured at least one black battalion marched in
an Upton parade in February 1918.[4]

The army would grow faster between 1941 and 1942 than it ever
had in its 165-year history. But segregation essentially required two
infrastructure systems, which proved costly and a drain on efficiency
in a service gutted after World War I. In the run-up to World War II,
the combat effectiveness of black units remained of concern, although
black outfits had fought valiantly on many occasions in prior conflicts. With soldiers fervently awaiting their call to fight and maybe
die, the volatile issue of segregation could turn lethal without notice.

Housing gave installation administrators fits. Black soldiers could
only occupy an area designated for their race. If a unit proved too
large, progress halted. Similarly, white units could not occupy black
areas unless all black soldiers had vacated the vicinity. A number of
civilian communities complained about plans to post black units near
their homes and sometimes took their concerns to Congress.
Residents of Petersburg, Virginia, opposed stationing black units at
nearby Camp Lee because of alleged racial turmoil during World War
I. In September 1940, Representative Patrick H. Drewry met with
Army Chief of Staff George C. Marshall himself as well as the head
of the War Plans Division, Brigadier General Leonard T. Gerow, to
hammer out a compromise.[5]

Camp Upton had lain dormant since the end of the Great War,
except for the Civilian Conservation Corps, or CCC, one of
Roosevelt's Depression-era New Deal public works entities that promoted environmental conservation efforts to reforest the area. But in
1940 the induction center came back to life and turned into a holding tank for inert soldiers like McBurney. Camp Upton played spigot
for a thirsty army. It also seemed the army of Upton honed the ser-

vice's endless paperwork requirements. Recruits without life insurance signed the papers there. Post information officers regularly released insurance tallies. By November 1941, a month before Pearl Harbor, Upton boasted $26 million in soldier insurance policies as if it had garnered record Victory Bond sales.[6]

McBurney found the posts languid pace suffocating, but he made friends with ease. Early during his stay, he met fellow New Yorker Leonard Smith, who had lived in Brooklyn and later Queens and proved to be McBurney's twin as enthusiastic volunteer. The intelligent teen also had tested well on the AGCT and received the tanker invitation. The young men had no inkling of the size of the black tanker ranks and admittedly had not given the matter much thought. No one explained the army blessed a small fraction of black soldiers to fill the platoons of the eventual three, co-located black tank battalions.

McBurney and Smith befriended Preston McNeil, another New Yorker, but a native of North Carolina and the adult of the group, two years older than McBurney and Smith. McNeil had work experience, spending three years with the Civilian Conservation Corps in Upstate New York. The Roosevelt administration designed the CCC as a work-relief program for single men, aged eighteen to twenty-five. The CCC opened its ranks to all races. It paid blacks and whites equally. McNeil sent $25 of his monthly $30 wage home to his mother each month.[7] Reserve army officers headed the camps, giving the young McNeil an early introduction to regimented life. The CCC may have planted more than two billion trees,[8] but by the time McNeil entered, its army instructors instilled a military discipline in the young men that proved invaluable during the massive call-up in the face of imminent war. McBurney and Smith idolized the sober and mature McNeil. Heaven or luck had spared the younger men starvation and utter hopelessness, a past McNeil kept to himself. Preston McNeil thanked God, the CCC, and now the United States Army. He wondered why good fortune had come his way.

As soldiers grew frustrated waiting at Camp Upton, Irving Berlin's fond memories of his stay on Long Island two decades earlier sparked an idea. His rousing success with *Yip, Yip, Yiphank* in 1918 convinced the patriotic Berlin to compose a World War II revue. Shortly before McBurney arrived at Camp Upton, Berlin began rehearsals for his new musical, *This Is the Army*, on the post. He had written new music at his signature breakneck pace. The army allowed Berlin to cast black soldiers, a victory for Berlin since the army refused his request in 1918. The composer featured them in a sprawling number, "What the Well Dressed Man in Harlem Will Wear," a song McBurney could have thought Berlin had written for him. The famed composer also wrote grand, classic minstrel pieces complete with black-faced performers to the frustration of his colleagues who found them outdated. He donned an army uniform to perform his "Oh! How I Hate to Get Up in the Morning," as he had in 1918. Soldiers went crazy.

After the rehearsals wrapped up, Camp Upton soldiers resumed their waiting game, thrusting the post's morale officers into a role almost as important as any combat commander. Players from the famed New York Giants baseball team thrilled Upton sluggers with a few hours of professional pointers and horsing around, though post officials did not permit blacks at the event or on the Camp Upton baseball team. World heavyweight champion Joe Louis boxed before a crowd of 7,000 at the Long Island post. Well-placed sources maintained Louis insisted on integrated audiences, but organizers and army leaders often did not comply. McBurney felt the thrill of watching Louis up close in the ring at Camp Upton, with the racial component of no import to the young man. "Integrated? We were always segregated. There was not a white man at the exhibition that I saw and I really didn't care," he recalled.[9]

As Camp Upton returned to its routine, Berlin's show, complete with its black soldiers, soon stormed Broadway, raising money and good will for the army. The New York Times summed up opening night: "This is the Army's Rousing Hit; Throng Pays $45,000 at Opening; Soldier Cast Gives Rollicking Performance in Benefit Show—Irving Berlin, Back With Yaphank Tune, Gets Ovation."[10] But Irving Berlin had his detractors. Ralph Warner of the Communist paper the Daily Worker objected that This Is the Army reflected "one of the ancient weaknesses of the song-writing alley in the heart of Broadway—in its out-moded treatment of Negroes."[11] In contrast, others normally skeptical of white culture lauded the show. The Pittsburgh Courier, the nation's leading black newspaper, published a photo of a white and black soldier marching in one of the promotional parades. The caption announced, "No Segregated Ranks Here."[12] Reviews aside, This Is the Army distinguished itself as possibly the only integrated military show during the war.[13]

Few could argue with the finale to This Is the Army: Kate Smith singing "God Bless America." In 1938, with the somber nation clinging to neutrality as war seemed almost certain in Europe, composers avoided patriotic musical fare. Smith needed something to capture the mood of the twentieth anniversary of the Armistice. Irving Berlin updated the 1918 composition that he had created from three words he heard his mother repeat once the Baline family found safety in the United States from Russia's wave of violent anti-Semitism, "God Bless America."[14]

While Berlin and Smith stoked patriotism and morale among the American public, McBurney waited. Worth more dead than alive because of "that waste of an insurance policy" the recruiter "forced" him to buy at Whitehall Street, he stood in the usual gaggle of army hopefuls waiting to hear his name. The faces changed, with new recruits arriving daily and others shipping out to training. The mix of hopelessness and anticipation, punctuated with sarcastic humor, remained unchanged. Two months turned to three and seemed an eternity for the eighteen-year-old. But true to the recruiter's promise, one day the army's list-master read out, "William McBurney." His call for the Armored Force School at Fort Knox, Kentucky, had arrived.

The fall of France in June 1940, reverberated as German aircraft, infantry, and Panzers stormed through the nation's overrated defenses. Germany dominated the European continent, but it was armor that became warfare's darling overnight. The U.S. responded. The Cavalry Branch as well as Infantry Branch ponied up the manpower for the Armored Force, but both Major General George A. Lynch, chief of infantry, a branch on foot, and Major General John K. Herr, chief of cavalry, a branch mainly on horseback,[15] opposed the creation of a separate armor entity. Lynch supported the tank—the larger and more heavily armed the better for his men. Though most linked the tracked combat vehicle to infantry support, a dubious Lynch saw it as a universal weapon and one that would act independently of his infantry forces. Realistic in his expectations, he believed the mechanized cavalry officers who dominated armor would neglect the tactics necessary to help his ground soldiers secure the battlefield. He predicted those who developed tanks would make them unsuitable to fight in concert with his soldiers on the ground.[16]

While Lynch's fears proved accurate due more in part to poor training and organizational issues including the neglect of separate tank battalions, John Herr bore the brunt of the unnerving change overtaking him and his army. It seemed warfare had transformed overnight. Herr, convinced his horse-mounted branch remained essential, commented, "the equipment, training and methods of employment of American horse cavalry in every way fit it to perform a necessary role in the army which no expansion of mechanization, in its present state of development, can hope to replace." But he spoke for a dying breed. His thoughts to better integrate his horses with the mechanized forces and expand horse-mounted cavalry's battlefield duties suddenly turned to salvaging a branch on the brink of extinction.[17]

The army established its Armored Force in 1940 and placed in charge a man who many saw as a brilliant mechanized officer and honored as the "Army's finest horseman." Kansas native Brigadier Adna Romanza Chaffee, Jr., a 1906 West Point graduate, World War I infantry combat veteran, and son of the distinguished Lieutenant General Adna R. Chaffee, Sr., created U.S. armored capabilities to try and at least keep pace with the Germans. Given a blank slate and the urgency of his mission, Chaffee sought to integrate all branches of the army into mechanized warfare.[18]

But first, he had to train the force. In 1940 the Armored Force School prepared to open its doors at Fort Knox.[19] Mechanized cavalry had operated on the site for nearly a decade, almost as an open act of insubordination, circumventing armor restrictions imposed by the National Security Act of 1920. The legislation gutted the army between the two wars and pulled support for an armored branch against protests of army leaders. Brash up-and-comers like George S. Patton, Jr. and Dwight D. Eisenhower advocated for the tank and its broader use as early as the 1920s. With some policy give in 1931, the Cavalry Branch's mechanized cavalry developed a variety of "combat cars," tracked vehicles that looked much like tanks, but legally could not be called such.[20] In a game of armor roulette, tank development outside the infantry violated the law, though the door stood ajar for an anxious army.

Knox, which acquired the more permanent "Fort" status in 1932, had much of the infrastructure that armored training required. The choice of Fort Knox made perfect sense, but it gave the cavalry an edge over the infantry, which looked to Fort Benning, Georgia, as home. With tremendous urgency in the face of what the army believed to be a superior German tank force at the outbreak of World

An M3 Stuart light tank, left, and an M3 Lee medium tank, right, photographed during training sessions at Fort Knox. The Stuart had a 37 mm turret gun as its main weapon while the Lee had both a 37 mm turret gun and a 75 mm gun in a sponson on the right side. The Lee was superseded by the M4 Sherman medium. (*Library of Congress*)

War II, Fort Knox cobbled together its training strategy: tanks on the fly. The U.S. lagged behind much of Europe in both tank development and its associated tactics. To compensate, the Armored Force School took a comprehensive approach. Many of its new students arrived with no military training. Some had not yet attended basic training. Few possessed any technical schooling. Once through the Knox pipeline, these same young men soon could fight abroad without significant supplemental training. Fort Knox instructors labored to publish detailed field training manuals to ensure unit-level instruction met the army doctrine they wrote simultaneously.

Amid the training frenzy that characterized Fort Knox, the first group of black tanker trainees numbered ninety-eight enlisted soldiers. They arrived at Fort Knox during March 1941 from Fort Custer, Michigan, one of few posts at the time with the segregated facilities to handle large numbers of black soldiers. By June, the Knox graduates, many from Chicago, like John S. Weston, laid the base for the first of three battalions of the 5th Tank Group, the only predominantly black tank outfit established by U.S. military service during the war.[21] Established as the 78th Tank Battalion on January 13, 1941, and redesignated as the 758th Tank Battalion (Light) on May 8, the unit known for its elephant's head with jutting tusks insignia and motto, "We Pierce," set up headquarters at Camp Claiborne. Like its sister unit, the 761st, it sometimes carried a "Cld" (Colored) after, or an asterisk before, the unit designation to denote it as a segregated unit.[22]

By April 25, 1942, just more than three weeks after the 761st activation, Fort Knox had eighteen training battalions and could house
15,000 soldiers. The black trainees from no fewer than eight states
and myriad backgrounds added one to their ranks when William
McBurney arrived at Fort Knox.[23] As a New Yorker, the press of the
crowds of trainees did not faze him. The severity and rigidity with
which instructors ruled recruits gave him brief pause. But where most
found discipline, he felt excitement. Twelve-week basic training
included close-order drill, calisthenics, and lectures on first aid. Sore
muscles following long marches with heavy, lung-constricting packs
strapped to their backs discouraged some of Fort Knox's fresh faces.
McBurney marched with the determination of a pack mule.

William McBurney proved a different type of recruit. His trainers
saw him as mature, a description his father, Thomas, might have challenged. They noticed his enthusiasm. At the sixth week the seasoned
recruits pulled guard duty, another new experience for McBurney,
and it went much as he had seen it in the Saturday matinees. Fort
Knox instructors held inspections every Saturday, so each Friday
night McBurney and his barracks brethren scrubbed in the faint hope
the sergeant might dole out passes allowing them a short, off-post
respite. Some weeks, assessors, feigning their dissatisfaction, begrudg-
ingly obliged.

McBurney found his adventure better than he had imagined. He
rarely thought of his father in New York, or his mother a few blocks
away from him, or the railroad flat on Madison Avenue. Fort Knox
succeeded where New York failed him. Optimistic, eager, and still
wedded to his Saturday matinee view of life, William McBurney felt
like he starred in his own Hollywood picture as a recruit at Fort
Knox—and he had not yet touched a tank.

Before William McBurney met his M3 Stuart light tank, the War
Department had agonized on how to best organize its armored force.
Divisions alone afforded few options. But according to army correspondent Private Trezzvant Anderson, "tank groups made up of three
battalions each possessed higher maneuverability and flexibility than
the larger armored divisions and offered greater certainty and security for overseas movement, especially in view of the domination of air
and shipping lanes by German aircraft and submarines."[24] Aside

from its massive armored divisions, the army created five tank groups. The 5th Tank Group included the 758th, the 761st, and the 784th—black tank battalions led by white officers, but the racial mix would soon change.[25]

With armor organization decided by the time McBurney, Smith, McNeil, and others slated for the 761st arrived at Fort Knox, confusion reigned over tank design, not unlike what the Germans experienced several years earlier. The U.S. thought it required light tanks for exploitation and speed, but further innovations by Germany made lighter designs obsolete. The debacles in France and Poland helped prove the argument for heavier tanks, more armor, and an arsenal of onboard fire power. Despite what occurred in battle on either side, debate continued on the optimal mix of machines for maximum combat effectiveness.[26] The army transitioned to a new era.

After basic training, William McBurney finally met his army tank. The months of anticipation faded as he trained in the M3 Stuart. "I got in that tank and did whatever they told me to do," he said, an attribute that made him an ideal soldier. The army had little time and limited assets to develop a training fleet much different from what it sent to U.S. as well as Allied armored units. At the time, the two varients of the M3 medium, the U.S. "General Lee" at more than ten feet tall, and British "General Grant," with its lower-profile turret, ranked as the heaviest weapons the U.S. had to fight the enemy. Engines powering the tanks seemed to change with each update, from the Wright, later Continental, R975-EC2 to the Chrysler A57 and onward.

With the M4 medium tank just entering production, the Grants and Lees became a stopgap until the much-improved Sherman became available. During this lag, units suffered in battle. Aside from increased crews of six or seven depending on the model, the M3 medium proved inferior to enemy armor and thus deadly for Allies in battle. While both M3 variants sported a 37 mm turret gun like the M3 Stuart, they had the added firepower of a 75 mm gun mounted in the hull. But the new gun proved insufficient with weak muzzle velocity and limited traverse. Whereas the Germans could blast an Allied tank at a distance of 1,100 yards in the vast deserts of North Africa, a lucky M3 shot might penetrate enemy armor at 400 yards.[27] Allied combat forces needed the superior M4 Sherman in quantity soon, or the Germans—and what few Italian forces remained, would control North Africa, British supply routes, and much of its empire.

The M4 made its North African debut with the British in late 1942.

Despite the waiting roar of the Stuart, McBurney often found himself in the classroom, but applied his lessons on the army equipment he would use in his unit. Instructors dangled their carrot with desired effect. Soldiers moved from lectures to the hands-on application with the M1 .30 caliber rifle and the 60 mm mortar. They listened closely to classes on the Articles of War as well as military courtesy and discipline. Instructors made it clear: Soldiers with the Articles of War tucked away in their brains stayed out of trouble. William McBurney appreciated the information. He did not want problems at a unit he had yet to join.[28]

McBurney remained excited by the M3 Stuart in which he trained, and had no knowledge of its heavier cousin's combat failures. He and the other hopeful tankers performed as trainers instructed, but improvisation became a tanker staple. The cramped, tracked vehicle with its crew of four had little room for a tall young man like McBurney, but he made it work. "I was skinny, and with practice could move around pretty easily," he recalled. He detailed the steps in learning the positions of driver, assistant or "A"-driver, gunner, and commander/loader as if he had just come off the field. He cared little about tank design evolution, the light-versus-medium debate, or a tank's weight. Speed piqued his interest.

With his height, McBurney preferred the view from the turret as tank commander or gunner. He bonded with the latter position, sighting the 37 mm main gun and firing three-pound training rounds 1,000 yards or more. He could stretch his frame out through the narrow upper steel hatch and survey 360 degrees.[29] But he reveled in the nuances of speed and enjoyed his training as driver. He had heard rumors the British called the Stuarts "Honey" because of how smoothly they drove.[30] He agreed. Sitting low in the belly of the beast had an addiction all its own. The Stuart specs listed its maximum speed at thirty-six miles per hour. McBurney scoffed at the estimate. He still craved the cockpit, but kicking sixteen tons of riveted steel into drive and crashing through the objective delighted him.[31] The Stuart had the added firepower of three Browning .30 caliber machine guns, useful against enemy forces on foot. Handling one made him feel invincible.

The tanks did not roll as often as the soldiers would have liked, but when possible, these hands-on field practicals followed information-packed though sometimes dry and lengthy classroom sessions.

Trainers fought over limited resources with priority given to white students. Training-area scheduling also pitted instructor against instructor, making it difficult to organize the required lessons in armor tactics, tank gunnery, communications, and maintenance for students who seemed to arrive in waves.

But bickering tank instructors agreed on one thing: the men did not listen. Despite explicit direction, the new tankers repeatedly failed to coordinate their efforts with other tanks and would instinctively race to the objective, prematurely ending the exercise. McBurney proved as guilty as his peers. "Phase line," long an important ground tactical control measure of intermediary progress en route to a final objective, simply meant "finish line" to these eager former civilians. To make the training situation seem more hopeless to the besieged instructors, armor students could not mount an effective counterattack against mock aggressor forces. Instructors feared this deficiency would prove lethal for tankers who could soon see combat.[32] Particularly problematic, students often ignored directional changes, potential life-or-death orders to a platoon of five 32,000-pound tanks careening toward the enemy.[33]

The officers who oversaw training reached their breaking point with their joy-riding recruits. Commanders had genuine concern that undisciplined soldiers, especially tank drivers, could place themselves and fellow soldiers at risk in combat. Soldiers like William McBurney knew the rules. Most chose to ignore them. Without warning during one field exercise, officers arranged for military police to apprehend violators. The MPs arrested up to a hundred soldiers a day for speeding. No one pressed charges. Who had the manpower? But for many of the men, this shocking taste of a no-nonsense army remained with them.[34]

Fort Knox training proved effective for a force learning to walk. McBurney and the fewer than one thousand trained tankers who would join the 761st in those early months had taken their important first steps in the world of tanks. They experienced the M3. More important, they could work and live as a four-man team, cycling through each position with ease. They understood the complex machine and could make basic repairs. A Knox-trained tanker could change out a track on a moonless night calf-deep in mud from a bone-chilling rain. Heat reached new heights and some had never known such cold, but they learned to maneuver through such extremes. Those entrenched in the past may have considered Fort Knox training chaotic, but Knox trainers imparted the rudimentary skills and the all-important swagger the tankers needed for a shot at the enemy. The fledgling Armored Force had selected some of the brightest for its costly machines. Level training fields meant talent would determine the kings of battle.

Four

Shiny Gold Bars

S ECOND LIEUTENANT IVAN H. HARRISON GOT OFF THE TRAIN AND
looked at his new surroundings. After months of training and
anticipation at Fort Knox, he had finally arrived at famed Camp
Claiborne. His excitement faded with each step he took. He looked
around at the mishmash of low-rise structures, lack of trees, and plentiful dirt—a dusting of which already covered his freshly shined shoes.
He saw an installation devoid of the excitement he had created in his
mind. During his first five minutes, he determined Claiborne seemed
routine and almost lethargic, the opposite of Fort Knox. Maybe he
would find energy in his unit, if he and traveling companions Charles
H. Barbour and Samuel Brown, fellow Knox Officer Candidate
School graduates, could find the 761st.[1] At that moment he preferred
Fort Knox to Camp Claiborne. To be honest, he would have preferred
Detroit and the poverty of rural Georgia, but he figured that such
foolishness would soon pass.

Harrison looked at Brown and Barbour. Brown, always quick with
the jokes, sensed Harrison's dread as they made their way deeper into
the post. As Brown crowned Camp Claiborne the trio's latest adventure, the three men noticed passing soldiers staring at them.

The new second lieutenants walked past acres of warehouses and
found their way to the 761st Tank Battalion. The unit commander,
Major Edward R. Cruise, another New Yorker, but from upstate,

Poughkeepsie to be exact, greeted them as he would any new officer and assigned them as tank platoon leaders, the most important job for any new tank officer. That day, July 16, 1942, the first black tank officers joined the 761st.[2]

Typical of army efficiency, established units spawned new ones. Trained tankers from the Camp Claibone, Lousiana-based 758th Tank Battalion (Light) provided the base on which the 761st built its battalion. The Armored Force designated both battalions as "Light," an important distinction, determined by the Stuart light tank each drove instead of the heavier, medium M4 Sherman tank. The War Department authorized the unit's activation on March 15, 1942, and by April 1, 27 officers and 313 enlisted men stood in the ranks of the 761st, most courtesy of the 758th.[3]

New soldiers arrived daily. Some came alone, like McBurney. Others arrived by what seemed like phalanx formation. Another 216 soldiers arrived from Fort Knox on May 23. By June, the 761st boasted enlisted rolls of 529 men, just shy of its authorized strength of nearly 36 officers and 593 enlisted soldiers.[4]

In 1940 the regular army counted just five black officers, a number that included three chaplains. The army spent decades planning the optimal service of black soldiers, though it had given officers little consideration and many officials questioned their necessity. But the reality of training of hundreds of thousands of black men and the blunt recommendations made by an early generation of civil rights leaders to the White House regarding the need for increased numbers of black officers forced the army to rewrite its already short-sighted plan for the employment of black soldiers and officers in the war.

Limited manpower planners at the War Department, coupled with the dire challenge to train unready forces to fight in North Africa, presented an opportunity to new black officers, especially tankers. Though white officers dominated the 761st in its early days, Harrison, Brown, and Barbour arrived, shiny gold bars in place and commissions in hand, proof they had completed Officer Candidate School of the Armored Force.

They had an advantage few knew about: Fort Knox integrated its officer training. The army made few exceptions to its policy of racial segregation, but it integrated its officer candidate training across the force, due in large part to Judge William B. Hastie, the civilian aide to the secretary of war.[5] Hastie knew the ways of Washington. In 1937, Roosevelt had appointed him as the first black federal court

judge. Hastie left the prestigious position
two years later to serve as dean at Howard
University. FDR again called on his old
friend for the War Department's civilian
aide position, needing someone who could
cut through bureaucratic wrangling and
work on behalf of the black soldier.
Though the position frustrated Hastie, the
desegregation of officer candidate schools
stood as a milestone in race relations and
for the army.[6]

Ivan H. Harrison. (*U.S.
Army*)

OCS integration made all the more
sense with McNair's tankers. After scrambling in 1940 to establish its Armored
School, 1941 and 1942 witnessed a remarkable influx of manpower.
The Armored School struggled to keep pace. With the army's voracious appetite for trained men, creativity filled the void. With so few
black officers entering the tank force, hardly enough to fill a platoon-
sized unit at any one time, training all officers together regardless of
race became a necessity. Given fast-paced training, a frenzied staff,
and the clash of all-consuming egos, few gave the arrangement much
thought. Though a small step, integration probably helped bolster the
confidence of the officers headed to the 761st.

One can imagine the reaction surrounding their arrival. Soldiers
probably set rumors in motion before the men had a chance to put
down their duffle bags. Black soldiers from around Camp
Claiborne—engineers, truck drivers, supply noncommissioned officers, and others wanted a look. White officers probably found reasons to visit unknown friends in the 761st just to ogle.

The battalion's tankers probably created an imaginary dossier for
each officer. They may have assumed Harrison, the tallest of the
three, as the smartest. If not a Fisk or Atlanta University man, soldiers
probably laid odds 2-1 he attended Howard University in the nation's
capital and had lunch with President Roosevelt himself. "Hell, Mrs.
Roosevelt supported Negro rights. Maybe they had tea in the White
House," the men may have howled.

When McBurney first saw Harrison, he thought he had seen him
on screen. Better looking than that cat, musician Cab Calloway, he
saw a suave, leading man. The kind of guy who gets the girl. The men
did not realize Sam Brown arrived as the elite of the three. The out-

going and natural leader from Charleston, South Carolina, born in 1918, had graduated first in his Buck High School class, not an uncommon accomplishment in the young tank unit. Brown, a renaissance man of sorts, also possessed brawn as well as a gift for music. The oldest of Reverend Samson and Elizabeth Brown's three children, Sam led his football team as well as Sunday services as his father's organist.[7] He and Harrison shared a love for and talent in the boxing ring, another common interest in the growing unit.

Most in the 761st probably felt the excitement, but suspicion and jealously may have tempered the jubilation of some. "Why them and why not me?" Had they turned on their race? The three men probably had no idea of the impact of their arrival. Their presence made soldiers wonder, hope, and fume.

Major Cruise found the three second lieutenants humble, yet filled with the confidence expected from officers. He would keep the gawkers at bay. Regardless, Harrison, Barbour, and Brown had entered a potential riptide. They quickly learned the challenges of a black unit and that all eyes rested on them. Harrison felt the mounting pressure, probably more than Barbour or Brown, but knew when to remain silent. While he saw his commission as well-deserved, the recognition of his potential by the U.S. Army raised his suspicions. Would someone expose the fact that he dropped out of high school?

Barbour, a calm, affable midwesterner, hailed from Junction City, Kansas, hometown of Major General Adna Chaffee, Jr. He went to lead a Baker Company platoon.[8] Brown found his platoon in Able Company. The lanky six-foot three-inch Harrison took his place in Charlie Company.

Ivan Harrison shared little about himself or his family with his new battalion. Paul and Lela Mae Harrison moved their three young boys from rural Lafayette, Georgia, to Detroit when Ivan turned seven. His father had found work with the U.S. Post Office. Like an immigrant at Ellis Island, postal officials recrafted his family name of Haroldson to Harrison. Paul let it go. He had few options and saw little hope for a black family in 1920s Georgia. He took to his new environment and rose to lead the local union. In Detroit, Lela Mae found the St. Paul A.M.E. Zion Church, a passion that remained with her and one she passed to her older boys.[9]

Ivan had other plans. A year shy of high school graduation, Ivan Harrison left Detroit High School College and set out on his own. His

job prospects in the middle of the Great
Depression, like those of Paul Bates,
proved more problematic than he anticipated. Undaunted, Harrison made his way
to Ohio. He met up with an uncle, a local
businessman, and at age seventeen managed a hat shop as well as a cleaning and
tailoring business. Harrison also became a
milliner. Joseph Beil, a salesman for the
Cleveland-based Campus Sweater and
Sportswear Company, hired Harrison as
his driver. Beil, young and eager to begin a
record-breaking sales career, took to the
road. With Harrison at the wheel, the two
logged countless miles across Indiana and

Samuel Brown. (*U.S.
Army*)

Michigan prior to the war. For Harrison, life on the road had become
a grand adventure, one he could not find in Detroit. Aside from real-
world experience few boys his age could claim, he made a tidy sum,
sometimes as much as $100 a month.[10]

A letter dated May 5 from the President of the United States
informed Ivan Harold Harrison: "You have now been selected for
training and service in the army. You will, therefore, report to the
Local Board named above at 3830 E. 131st at 7 a.m. on the 21st day
of May 1941."[11] He studied the letter. Amidst the whispers of war,
the army had drafted him. On the appointed morning, he exited a
Cleveland recruiting office with the faint promise of becoming a warrant officer. After a heartfelt farewell to his friend Beil, he ended up a
private at Fort Leonard Wood, Missouri, that summer, delivering
mail in Company C of the 92nd Engineer Battalion. Apparently he
proved exceptional with letters and packages because the army promoted him from private directly to sergeant in January. In official correspondence dated January 10, 1942, the battalion commander,
Lieutenant Colonel Edwin P. Ketchum, transferred Harrison to
Company B as a private and added the unexpected promotion.[12]

Harrison continued to impress. With an opportunity for Officer
Candidate School, Harrison wrote to Joseph Beil, who responded
immediately with a glowing recommendation. Orders sending the new
sergeant to the Armored Force Officer Candidate School came from
Headquarters Second Army dated March 26. Ivan Harrison packed up
and departed B Company on April 2, 1942, one day after the activa-

tion of the 761st Tank Battalion. He reported to Fort Knox April 7 for "Cl #7," ready for something he could not begin to fathom.

At twenty-four, Harrison typified the age the army targeted. The White House had been clear: No one wanted to take boys from their mothers and put them in the U.S. Army, certainly not the Roosevelt Administration. The army aimed at men twenty-four and older. Roosevelt, though president and aware he needed public support (mothers included), looked fondly on his days as secretary of the navy and maintained an affinity for the sea services. Despite the restrictions on the army, Roosevelt allowed the navy and marine corps to go after seventeen- and eighteen-year-olds. This backroom policy evaporated as the army's need for manpower overwhelmed the senior service.

In Ivan Harrison, the army had chosen a perfectionist who held himself to exacting standards. The unfamiliar military regimen and instruction frustrated Harrison. He possessed none of the benefits of ROTC like Paul Bates and did not hold a high school diploma like William McBurney. He did not think he had the intellect, talent, and likability of his friend Sam Brown. Harrison, the product of rural Georgia and the bustling streets of Detroit, had learned how to make the most of his assets. Some nights at Fort Knox, he would slip from his bunk, tuck his books under his arm, and plant himself under the sole source of light available—the bulb in the latrine.[13] Ivan Harrison, like his father, determined he would reinvent himself as necessary to succeed.

To create Camp Claiborne, the army carved a wide swath of the inhospitable Louisiana wilderness eighteen miles outside the small but bustling town of Alexandria. By the time the Depression loomed large, thousands of acres of forests had been ravaged by the timber industry, leaving a barren apocalyptic-looking region. To everyone's surprise, the vast, clear-cut acreage stretching to the horizon topped the U.S. Army's list of possible installation sites. The area seemed ripe for military growth with no end in sight.

The army built its new post on the government Civilian Conservation Corps land in Rapides Parish. It also established Camp Beauregard, Camp Livingston, and Camp Polk within a sixty-mile radius of Alexandria. But Camp Claiborne took over what had been the CCC's Camp Evangeline, established June 10, 1930, to reforest and reverse forty years of land mismanagement. Evangeline took its name from the local district of the Kisatchie National Forest, so designated by President Herbert Hoover in 1930, a 604,000-acre hodgepodge of army-ready badlands that rambled across seven parishes.[14]

Evangeline meant much more to the people of Evangeline Parish that ran along Rapides' southern border. Louisiana officials named the area in 1901 after Henry Wadsworth Longfellow's tragic poem of love and loss set against the resettlement of the Acadian people from Nova Scotia in 1755.[15] Many of the exiles migrated to the areas surrounding the future army stronghold. But, the army preferred to name its southern installations after southern—often Confederate— military heroes. Officials believed it helped improve local relations. Convinced the lyrical and literary Evangeline proved a poor name for a combat training post, the army decided on "Claiborne," after Louisiana's first governor, a nonnative, finding it a more fitting name.

Born in Virginia in 1775, William Charles Cole Claiborne considered himself a child of the Revolution. The William and Mary graduate moved to New York, took an interest in the law, then established a Tennessee law practice. Claiborne had a gift for assimilating into new surroundings and became the youngest person to serve in the House of Representatives. Claiborne, who represented Tennessee, threw his support behind rumored cousin and fellow Virginian Thomas Jefferson in the disputed presidential election of 1800. In turn, Jefferson appointed the young Claiborne as the territorial governor of Mississippi. By 1804 his duties extended to the neighboring and newly acquired vast territory of Louisiana.[16]

For possibly the first time, the privileged Claiborne found himself at a disadvantage. He governed amidst a French-speaking population with customs different from his genteel Virginia upbringing. But he married a Creole and endeared himself to the Cajun and Creole residents. He established a government representative of both French and English cultures. He fought to keep slavery out of his territory. By a 3-1 margin, voters made him the first elected state governor in 1811. His popularity soared.[17]

The Virginian had military ties, though weaker than those of the famous generals later worshipped by the South. Claiborne established the Militia of the Mississippi Territory and held the rank of brigadier general. He did not flaunt his status, though at least one official portrait showed Claiborne in uniform.[18]

The War of 1812 greeted the newly elected governor with a robust British blockade. At the same time renowned privateer Jean Lafitte brought goods to New Orleans and parishes along the bays and bayous of the Gulf Coast, making him a favorite with locals. But smuggling robbed government coffers, and Claiborne issued a public proclamation against the bandit. After the state legislature denied Claiborne's request for a reward for Lafitte's capture, in late 1813, legend maintained the governor put up $500 from his own purse. The story continued that an amused Lafitte countered with $1,500 on Claiborne's head and advertised his offer on signed posters for the governor to be brought to Laffite's headquarters in a maze of bayous that comprised Barataria.[19] Despite the long-running and laughable feud, Lafitte brought invaluable military intelligence. He warned of British plans to invade New Orleans. Claiborne, an inexperienced military leader, worked with General Andrew Jackson on the defense of the Crescent City, but largely left Jackson to defeat the British at Chalmette, just south of the city, in 1815.[20] Claiborne fell dead within two years at age forty-two. More than a century later, probably not a single worker building Camp Claiborne or its residents had heard of William C. C. Claiborne or gave a damn about the long-deceased governor.

The U.S. Army had its ways. Evangeline and a decade of reforestation vanished as construction of Camp Claiborne started in earnest in 1939. The army had no need for standing trees. It needed warehouses—acres of warehouses, a hospital, headquarters, and training areas as well as gymnasiums, theaters, and stables, too. The army wanted barracks, but if the men had to sleep in tents until contractors completed the structures, they would sleep in a lot worse in combat if they slept at all. When construction began, the army had not yet determined the large number of units that would call Camp Claiborne home. In truth the army had not yet established many of them, including the 5th Tank Group and its three tank battalions, including the 761st.

Camp Claiborne and the surrounding posts arrived like a gift to the region, providing relief and marking an end to a decade of economic devastation. Men and women swarmed the new post in search of work. Even the squatters who had occupied portions of the land now under army control grabbed up the plentiful jobs. Those lucky enough to secure rickety worker housing usually propped a homemade mattress off the ground with a crooked frame made from nailed scraps of wood to help stave off moisture and bugs. These crude sheds kept most of the rain out, but lacked electricity and running water, a situation also typical of local homes.[21] Entire families migrated from places like Texas to find they would have to live out of their cars if they wanted a job. Vehicles and makeshift tents of bedsheets and sticks lined Highway 165, resulting in roadside shantytowns.

Carlton Smith, then a major with the 634th Tank Destroyer Battalion, arrived at Camp Claiborne in the fall of 1940.[22] Much to his surprise, a sprawling construction site greeted him. Though taken aback by the magnitude of the undertaking, he figured the army would finish what it set out to do. But could it finish by 1941? The size of the installation also gave him pause. The post later grew from the 6,195 acres he initially observed, not including the vast training sectors that stretched forty miles to Camp Polk. He looked at the tented areas and other temporary housing and wondered what the army would do when units arrived.

True to the army's word, Camp Claiborne received its first soldiers in January 1941. Early units arrived at the work-in-progress Smith witnessed. The post operated as contractors continued to build, and build. Through a tremendous expenditure of money, men, and natural resources, the army created its own self-sustaining—though segregated—city, soon Louisiana's third largest behind New Orleans and the state's capital at Baton Rouge.

By 1941, no one had yet heard of the 5th Tank Group, and few probably expected an influx of black units including engineers, mechanics, and truck drivers that would call Camp Claiborne home.

Trezzvant William Anderson squeezed out every ounce of what God had given him. With large brown eyes and a flawless complexion, Anderson further improved his looks through meticulous grooming. His close-cropped hair rivaled that of any leading man in Hollywood. His kept his clothes wrinkle-free and tailored to flatter his frame. He stood as the personification of a modern, urbane man.

Two years older than Paul Bates, the North Carolinian attended both John C. Smith University and its attached high school, a common academic pairing for black schools at the time. But after three years in college, Anderson took a job as a railway mail clerk. He knew his talents and planned for that postal paycheck to support his true calling.[23]

Few could deny Anderson's flair for news as well as public relations. He published as contributing editor at the black *Charlotte Post* in 1929. Anderson went after the corrupt leaders and fat cats of any race, who lived large off the little guy, not caring if he risked his personal safety. He exposed racial abuses by the New Deal's Civil Works Administration and Public Works Administration, or CWA-PWA, administrators in four southern states, a risky move for any writer, and a death wish for a black man in the South at the time. After exhaustive investigations and very public trials, corrupt regimes crumbled and men went to prison. In 1940, with the investigation at its peak, the local chapter of the NAACP posted five armed guards at Anderson's home. Anderson saw himself as a leader, as did the Charlotte NAACP, which pushed him as president of the Postal Alliance because of his "excellent and worthy fight for Negros' Rights." Postal officials defended against the threat to their fiefdom, and Anderson his lost postal job in 1941.[24]

Trezzvant Anderson, though a chameleon in many ways, understood the times and served to further the interests of the black men and organizations associated with his race. For much of the 1930s, Anderson served as a mouthpiece for Caesar W. Blake, Potentate of the Shriners, as well as Elks' Grand Exalted Ruler J. Finley Wilson. He would maintain close ties to the Elks.

But his calling as a newsman beckoned. As a young man who railed against injustice, Anderson started the Negro Press Club in 1931 in Washington, D.C., in part as an effort to break the White House Press Corps' race restrictions. He succeeded. Through his dogged investigative reporting, he helped put a husband away for murdering his wife—exonerating the black man accused of the crime against the white couple.

Between his relentless crusading for those who could not speak for themselves and his postal duties, Anderson met Marie, a woman from Louisiana eight years his junior. They married and moved to 1817 Beatty Ford Road in Chadwick-Hoskins, Mecklenburg County, North Carolina. Marriage did not alter Anderson's work ethic or other interests. While traveling for his PR duties and as a newsman, he pursued women with the same intensity he drove himself for other goals. He gravitated toward innocents and those struggling to meet their most basic needs, the prettier and younger the better. Trezzvant Anderson kept this side of his life a secret.[25]

The high-profile image builder understood race and public perception. In 1925 the Army War College commissioned a series of studies on black soldiers. It concluded that the black soldier possessed the capability of serving in all specialties except combat. Researchers reported that the black slavery experience had bred a certain subservience into the race, thus rendering the black man ineffective.[26] Anderson drew other conclusions.

In 1942, at age thirty-six, Anderson approached the army to "volunteer" as a public relations officer, or PRO. With a

Trezzvant W. Anderson. (*U.S. Army*)

birth date rivaling that of the parents of recruits half his age, the army recruiter laughed him out of the office, passing on his offer, the brilliance of which most in the army could not begin to comprehend.[27] Determined that black PROs would serve, Anderson, without specifics other than letters to Washington, lobbied the army for the position. Not one, but two PRO slots popped on the manpower rolls, though the army filled them with other officers.

Without understanding his potential, the army had other plans for Anderson. Drafted in 1943, the kingmaker became an army private and combat correspondent. The army did not expect an independent roving reporter who would answer to one man—Trezzvant Anderson. He knew members of his race would become combat royalty through his chronicles. The 761st Tank Battalion, as yet unknown, would become the crown jewel.

News of the impending activation of the 761st Tank Battalion on April 1, 1942, reached the Office of the Quartermaster General (OQMG), which created the distinctive unit insignia and motto for each unit. The Quartermaster General employed talented artists who could capture the essence of a unit in a simple crest underscored by a few inspirational words—most of the time.

The OQMG based its designs on the history and mission of a unit. The 761st had no history other than its April 1 activation, and the tank and its mission proved too new for Washington to capture accurately. Major Edward Cruise opened the envelope containing the pro-

posed insignia and motto and wailed for his adjutant as if he had just
been gut shot. Cruise stared at two seemingly amputated white limbs
wringing out what appeared to be a dish towel. The suggested motto:
"We wring them out."[28] As the unit's first commander, Cruise had
given the coat of arms no thought. He knew orders soon would move
him out of the black outfit, but he refused to have a dish towel as his
legacy. He probably commanded, "Fix this," with more emphatic language added.

Within a few weeks Cruise had a response for Washington. It
remains unclear who created the design, though Ivan Harrison's name
had been bandied about. Regardless, Cruise liked what he saw and
shot it back at Washington saying, "Shield: . . . a black panther's
head, superimposed in bas relief." "Motto: 'WILCO.'" He justified
their submission:

> The black panther, native of African jungles, vicious and strong,
> characterized by swift, silent attack without warning, is symbolical
> of the functions of the battalion; that of striking swiftly in an unex-
> pected direction from an unexpected location, and carrying to a
> decisive conclusion, its mission, asking no quarter and giving none.
>
> The suggested motto, "Wilco," taken from the Joint Army-
> Navy Radio Telephone Procedure, habitually used by this organi-
> zation, is expressive of the determination of the personnel to
> "carry out orders" in the face of any or all obstacles.
>
> Inasmuch as this organization is composed of colored person-
> nel, the above-suggested Coat of Arms is deemed more appropri-
> ate than the one suggested by your office.[29]

By early October Cruise received word the OQMG agreed with his
panther recommendation, but asked for a list of motto choices
(another organization had snatched "Wilco").[30] The six mottos took
considerable effort to craft. An obvious choice topped the list: the
men chose what they believed to be a quote from their hero, world
heavyweight boxing champion Joe Louis. Many in the unit, including
Ivan Harrison, boxed or fancied themselves as adept in the ring. A
number of the tankers probably contributed to the effort. On
November 5, Cruise forwarded the list to Washington. An exclama-
tion point punctuated one of the six: "Come Out Fighting!" The
unit's preference seemed clear.[31]

The original rendering of the coat of
arms for standard of the 761st Tank
Battalion. (*Institute of Heraldry*)

The list of mottos proved one of Cruise's last official acts. He
turned command over to his executive officer, Major John R. Wright,
Jr., on November 21. Washington approved the black panther
insignia with the motto "Come Out Fighting" on Christmas Eve
1942.[32] The hard-won insignia and motto helped place the men of the
761st Tank Battalion in a position to carry on a proud fighting tradition dating decades before their fathers' service in the Great War.

A column of 761st Tank Battalion M3 Stuart light tanks during training. (*Baron Bates*)

Five

A Good Tempo

O NE THING EVERYONE AGREED ON: PAUL BATES PROVED A taskmaster in the field. From before sunrise to well after dark the battalion trained. But William McBurney, awed by the adventure, noted Major Bates stood over them as they rolled, as they fired, as they repaired their vehicles, and as they sat dozing after dinner in evening classes. He passed by Bates's quarters on more than one evening and saw him working past 2200 hours. He surmised he witnessed the tanker way and adopted it immediately.[1] He mentioned it to Teddy Windsor, his tank commander, whom McBurney looked to as a friend and surrogate father.

Theodore W. Windsor, born in 1909, had lived a lifetime before he joined the army. McBurney knew he had come from Ohio, but a hint of an Alabama lilt remained. Teddy like many of the other tankers had graduated high school, but he found a steady living wage evasive. He swapped his janitorial uniform for that of a U.S. soldier and did not look back.[2] Windsor understood the army and soldiering. McBurney watched him and learned from him, with each day together better than the last. William McBurney worked to contain his excitement.

After the army established the 761st, training began almost immediately at Camp Claiborne, but the unit's path proved rocky. Uneven leadership forced it into a perpetual state of awkward and detrimental change. Ivan Harrison watched as members of the original core of white officers transferred from the battalion to other duties, though such upheaval characterized an army in the throes of explosive expansion. Some officers considered any position in a black unit a professional dead end. Regardless, Harrison realized the 761st required stable leaders to harness talented and eager young men racing for glory.

Shortly before Bates's arrival, to Harrison's surprise, Major Cruise ordered his three new second lieutenants back to Fort Knox for the Tank Maintenance #60 course that began August 21, 1942.[3] The three officers hardly had time to gain a foothold in their platoons. Brown probably joked with Harrison that the army mistakenly commissioned them in the first place. Feigning disgust with Brown's cavalier position, Harrison believed additional training would increase his value to the unit as well as the army. He had learned the importance of broadening one's skills while working in Ohio and as he watched his father's difficult climb through the postal ranks.

By late November 1942, with the three lieutenants back in place at Camp Claiborne and the battalion near full strength, Cruise left the unit as a recently promoted lieutenant colonel. Major John R. Wright, Jr., his executive officer who called Beverly Hills, California, home, replaced Cruise.[4] By the time Wright took command of the 761st, Paul Bates had almost slipped from the 5th Group headquarters into the 761st as the battalion operations and training head, S-3, as well as the intelligence officer, S-2, for a time.[5]

When Bates arrived, he observed competent junior officers, though relative neophytes, supervising a battalion that could perform rudimentary tanker skills. They had squandered precious training opportunities. In Bates's opinion the 761st needed one man: Paul Bates. He brought an intensity that seduced soldiers. From the day he appeared, McBurney felt Bates stood as the most powerful man in the 761st and gravitated toward him.

Even as a new battalion commander, Wright's sole interest lay in a transfer out of the 761st. The arrival of an experienced officer like Bates brought him closer to his goal. The two men understood one another and Bates moved forward untethered in training the battalion. Soon after he wrote, "Work goes along and at a good tempo."[6]

Paul Bates impressed Ivan Harrison, but the platoon leader had grown dubious of unit leadership. Cruise's priorities, though unstated, clearly showed. Harrison had no time for the disinguous, or for two-faced liars, as his men would say. Men like Cruise aside, Harrison marveled as the ranks for the 761st swelled with men like him, mostly black men from varied backgrounds across the country.

No one knew how long Paul Bates would remain with the 761st. He piqued interest as an officer shrouded in mystery. But Bates had a simple plan: With his career tied to the unit, he determined he would train this group of underdogs as the best combat tank outfit in the army and the battalion would fight in Europe. Bates seized his opportunity.

Myriad army studies had shown unit training programs made the difference between success and failure in black outfits,[7] though Bates and probably many army leaders believed the correlation held regardless of race. With Fort Knox struggling to keep pace with the fast-changing battlefields of North Africa and feed its new armored force with tactical and technological life-saving fare, units devoured the field and technical manuals the Armored Force School fed them. Bates approved. Armored leadership had determined if its officers kept the field trained as the school had designed, this system of Knox-to-unit-to-combat could mean survival in battle. But dare they say victory?

Before they touched their tanks, the men had to be fit. To his surprise, Bates found a battalion of out-of-shape soldiers. Older members like Paul Bates himself and Charles G. "Pop" Gates, who enlisted at age twenty-nine and served as a cavalry soldier during the months leading to Pearl Harbor, far surpassed the conditioning of most of the men half their age.[8] Any combat soldier, be he on foot in the infantry, fighting in a tank, or flying through the skies needed to be in top physical form to fight and defeat the enemy. Frustrated, Bates, still a natural athlete, wrote: "How are they going to fight if they're winded after 40 yards?"[9] Intense physical training became each day's first scheduled event.

Outsiders began to take an interest in the unit. Inspections started sooner than Bates anticipated. With the battalion not yet ready for such close scrutiny, Bates grew sullen, though unsurprised by the lackluster results. He wrote early on as the training officer, "The battalion has been having a rather sad time. Many inspections have been made by ranking officers with only severe criticism landing on the two colonels' heads. They have welcomed me enthusiastically and of course there is much work to do."[10] Bates found the disappointing results unacceptable and impressed the need for urgency upon his officers.

Bates's commanders soon seemed on fire, but he feared he would leave the battalion before he had the results he knew possible. One inspecting Armored Force officer fueled Bates's concerns, saying, "Any officer [that] has been with colored troops over one year should be transferred at the end of the maneuvers." Bates had served as a company commander with the 758th, the assistant S-3 at 5th Tank Group, and now an officer in the 761st. Uncharacteristically resigned to what appeared inevitable, he wrote, this "looks like the beginning of my move."[11]

After some reflection, Paul Bates decided he would remain with the 761st regardless of baseless rumors from officers hardly worth his time. He studied current training methods and designed a twenty-four-hour training schedule around daylight, a commander's only friend, as he would say. He and his officers squeezed every ounce of instruction possible from first light to the waning twilight of Camp Claiborne.

McBurney, enthralled by the prospect of yet another adventure, snapped out of his rack at the required 0600 hours, though his early-morning enthusiasm waned with time. The training at the 761st mirrored that of similar units, like the 758th, in many ways, but surpassed others' standards and intensity. To McBurney, their training day seemed longer, but as a tank gunner, he noticed his aim becoming deadlier with the 37 mm main gun of his M5A1 Stuart light tank, the upgrade to the M3 Stuart in which he trained at Fort Knox.

William McBurney, Leonard Smith, Ellsworth G. McConnell, and the rest of the battalion dressed, formed by platoon, and marched to the physical training field. The boyish McConnell, another native New Yorker, quickly adopted the name "E.G." He enlisted at age sixteen with his parents' consent, making him one of the youngest "men" in the unit. But as far as the army knew from his enlistment record, McConnell joined its ranks at nineteen, which must have left boot camp instructors slack-jawed. The teen stood less than five feet seven inches and weighed 140 pounds after a big meal.[12] His angelic face and hazel eyes that sparkled with innocence and wonder probably helped him navigate the army's cruelties as well as win friends.[13] McConnell told McBurney that his parents immigrated from the British West Indies to the Jamaica section of Queens where his father drove a cab. McBurney thought McConnell yapped just to talk, but his stories of non-English-speaking European immigrants had every-

Ellsworth McConnell and his Boy Scout troop during a field trip in New York state in the late 1930s. (*Ellsworth G. McConnell Collection*)

one howling with laughter. But he could never understand the name "Ellsworth."[14]

Daily physical training affected each tanker in his own way. William McBurney grew stronger and less winded. He gained confidence beyond his awkward teen bravado. He felt he could stand man-to-man with Lieutenant Harrison. He started to recover from the "Dear John" letter from Sarah, the girl he loved—and who no longer waited for him—in New York.[15]

After a quick shower, a close shave, and a lingering glance in the mirror, the soldiers slipped on the mandated uniform of the day. It seemed the army updated uniform items more often than its combat weapons. At Camp Claiborne, often they wore the comfortable ODs or olive drab shirts and trousers. Depending on the weather, McBurney might lace up his boots, but often he strapped on his leggings and service shoes. Regardless of attire, a few hearty slurps in the mess tent had them at the tanks by mid-morning. Each platoon or company might receive a class on gunnery or other tank skill. The information came straight from the Fort Knox training manuals. Except for rare additional training opportunities back at Fort Knox, platoon leaders like Ivan Harrison had as much—or as little—tank experience as the men they trained. As they grew as tankers and soldiers, they grew closer.

The men formed their own ties. At first, geographic region seemed to determine one's entourage. William McBurney and fellow New Yorkers Leonard Smith, Preston McNeil, the young E. G. McConnell, and others fell into familiar, home-style rhythms. But self-segregation gave way to unit camaraderie. McBurney, still close to his New York brothers, formed a unique bond with his tank crew brethren, especially Teddy Windsor. Harrison found a special kinship with the funny and talented South Carolinian Sam Brown. The men noted the soft-spoken, polite teen and Texas volunteer Warren G. H. (for "Gamaliel Harding") Crecy and Massachusetts draftee Horatio Scott found a closeness normally shared by brothers. Fellow tankers maintained the two had agreed that each would refuse a promotion if the other had not been similarly advanced in rank. Harding, as his sweetheart Margaret and soon the other tankers called him, came to the 761st as another high school standout but he did not judge Scott by his eighth-grade education.[16] Circles widened and McBurney could feel the unit "just clicked."[17]

Friendships could not have come at a better time. The final letter from Sarah robbed William McBurney of much of his spirit. He thought of tearing up a bar or two in Alexandria, but friends, knowing what had happened, helped him through the shock and disappointment. But Smitty, Preston, and E.G. did not know McBurney had fathered a child with Sarah and a son with another girl back home.[18] It had played a factor in his eagerness to enlist and leave New York.[19] He knew the army documented Sarah's child in his record, but the boy's birth occurred after he left for Camp Upton.

Another tanker who came to the unit with a secret was Russell Guthrie. Guthrie had lost his way as a twelve-year-old boy when his mother, Helen, died giving birth to her ninth child. The young Buffalo, New York, native found the 761st almost by accident. A friend planned to enlist in the army and it seemed the answer to Guthrie's problem. In 1940, recruiters eager to sign up future soldiers had guidelines to follow. Sixteen-year-old Guthrie handed the recruiter a birth certificate. He knew the age requirements. The recruiter looked at the young boy and the piece of paper in his hand. With Russell standing just five feet, five inches and weighing a tad more than 150 pounds, the recruiter did not appear convinced, but he had all the proof he needed. A nervous Guthrie hurriedly confessed he understood he would need his father's permission. The recruiter shook his head and said, "No you don't," and asked Guthrie his age. Russell had no idea what the birth certificate said; he never thought to look. Guthrie laughed to gloss over his mistake and pointed to the certificate. While a mentally incapacitated Norman George Guthrie remained in their Buffalo home, Russell had absconded with the nineteen-year-old's birth certificate and enlisted under his brother's name.

Russell Guthrie. (*Russell Guthrie*)

With eight children filling his home, their father Leon Guthrie still noticed his son missing. The elder Guthrie, a World War I artilleryman and combat veteran of the mainly black 349th Field Artillery Regiment, became the single father of nine. He had traveled the rails as a railroad chef, but with Helen's death, the authorities wanted him closer to home if he expected to keep his family together. Leon left the excitement of the railway and worked a number of close-by stationary jobs including one at Lackawana Steel. Young Russell shoveled coal and ice and picked up odd jobs to help his father, though Leon refused to take the boy's money as he held it out, bills crumpled and change falling from his small hands. He could see the heartbreak in his son's eyes. Leon Guthrie missed Helen, too.

The father's week-long agonizing search for his son ended. Russell had mentioned his enlistment plan to a friend. Leon tracked down his child, but not before the teen had made it to basic training at Fort Dix, New Jersey, the same post the elder Guthrie's 349th had formed. Word of Russell's fraudulent feat stunned staff members, who prepared to send him back to Buffalo, but Leon had witnessed his son's pain and lack of purpose over the past four years. He gave his permission for Russell to remain.[20]

Guthrie with his prewar experience in the 9th and 10th cavalries stood as one of the most experienced soldiers in the 761st. He had known Lieutenant Charles A. "Pop" Gates back as a fellow cavalryman. Russell Guthrie, now a gunner like McBurney, thought he found a place and a family at the 761st. Nothing could fill the void left by his mother, but this tank unit came "pretty darn close."[21]

Tank crews had solidified by the spring of 1943. Skills improved weekly. William McBurney sat high in the turret, one of the perks as tank gunner. With his height, his station seemed a blessing in the cramped Stuart. Tank commander Teddy Windsor positioned himself to McBurney's left. Windsor often stood up through his hatch, taking full advantage of his 360-degree view.

Willy Devore later drove their Stuart. The South Carolina farmer with a grammar school education remained a favorite with his fellow tankers. McBurney grew as close to Devore as any two soldiers could, a surprise to him because as every bit the New Yorker, he thought little of southerners. His own prejudices broke down as he became aware of the value of each man. Harry Tyree, twenty-two, a West Virginia miner with one year of high school, rounded out the crew as assistant driver.[22]

Though McBurney sang the praises of driving the tank, Guthrie had heard that drivers sustained heavy combat casualties. Cradled low in the Stuart, they sat closest to an exploding enemy mine. Fort Knox instructors warned if they hit a German tank mine, it would tear out the bottom of the tank, possibly ending their war. Trainers could not overemphasize the need for nimble drivers. In the best case, a mine explosion would take a driver's legs, but if they laid odds on the driver's survival or the mine impact, they would put their money on the mine. Guthrie hung on every word and stayed up in his turret.[23]

After a few months' training on the endless fields behind Camp Claiborne, Russell Guthrie determined that the "farm boys" made the best drivers. The "sharecroppers," as he called them, had a knack for maneuvering machinery and reading terrain, two talents they acquired as youngsters working the fields at home. Guthrie figured they also had some gift to steer clear of mines like rocks on their farmland, but he had yet to see an enemy mine in Louisiana.[24]

At Fort Knox, the soldiers had trained by position. They learned to sight and fire the tank's main gun in the Gunnery Department. Some men acquired their "land legs" standing on "wobble plates," discs that simulated the tank's movement teaching the students to fire with accuracy on an unpredictable surface. Time on the wobble plates provided much needed comic relief for students and instructors alike, but the randomness of movement prepared the new tankers for trials they could not yet imagine.[25]

All tankers learned basic vehicle maintenance, from changing tracks, to maintaining the engine's air cleaners, to a daily check of the oil. The technical manual for the General Motors-built M5 Stuart detailed all aspects of maintenance. Tankers referred to it as the "TM," and anyone in the 761st knew this stood as the source of all information for the Stuart—operating the tank as well as maintaining it. Windsor and McBurney consumed it. At Camp Claiborne, whether the crew performed a repair or it fell to the company's maintenance section depended on time, necessary materials, and skill level required. If the repair exceeded the battalion's capability, the unit would have to ship the tank out to the next maintenance echelon for repair. Paul Bates disliked losing his tanks for any reason, especially maintenance. The Stuarts had to be in top condition, just like the men inside. McBurney and fellow crew members performed a pre-operation inspection, a checklist of no fewer than twenty-four items, each time they trained in the tank.[26] McBurney walked around studying his tank the way he saw film star Fred MacMurray check his airplane during a Saturday matinee. Though wedded to the ground in his Stuart, over time, it became his personal P-40 Warhawk, the plane flown by the Tuskegee Field-trained 99th Pursuit Squadron, and his closely held fantasy.

After inspecting the Stuart, the four tankers climbed in, each through his narrow designated hatch, which grew easier with practice. Like the rest of the crew, the driver lowered himself feet first through the tight opening in front of his driver's seat, handy for quick entry and exit. He sat low on the left and started his two Cadillac V-8 engines, roaring with 100 horsepower each. Just as the TM instructed, he pulled down two steering levers from their horizontal position above his head. Once they pointed vertically, the driver pulled the lever to the side he wanted the tank to turn, like the reins of a horse. Pulling back on both levers simultaneously equated to "Whoa," and the tank would come to a stop.

With a combination of artistry and skill the man who sat in the driver's seat manipulated the Stuart's two drive shafts as well as eight forward and two reverse gears, whose controls sat to his right between him and the assistant driver. The driver monitored the tank's gauges displayed on a dashboard of sorts in front of him. Windsor stole a glance more than once. If the Stuart had an oil level issue or other mishap, engineers designed the gauges to indicate the problem. Bates drilled into the tankers that impending trouble in a tank meant certain doom in combat. A disabled Stuart left a crew vulnerable to enemy attack.[27] No one wanted to face Bates for losing a tank to negligence.

Teddy Windsor often acted as the eyes for the rest of the crew, three men with a limited field of vision. Sometimes they trained with hatches open, offering a refreshing breeze and broad view of their operating environment. But many days they maneuvered with hatches closed, a situation worse than wearing blinders at first, in McBurney's opinion. Windsor compensated for his driver's and gunner's awkward view of the action outside the tank.

From his turret vantage Windsor ordered driving maneuvers and warned of hazardous terrain, tank obstacles, opposing forces, or other tanks. Willy Devore soon complied by instinct. At the same time, he used what amounted to little more than peep holes to view his interpretation of the field. He trusted Windsor as a second set of eyes, understanding they could mean the difference between a successful operation and an out-of-commission tank.

Windsor directed McBurney's targets. With sight adjustment crucial, McBurney cared for his sights as instructed by the technical manual. He used aiming points and testing targets when possible to ensure accuracy, and he had a periscope. Despite state-of-the-art optics and Windsor's assistance, McBurney at first felt blindfolded when firing the main gun in the Stuart. In time, what had felt awkward came naturally. With mandated cross-training, each tanker kicked the Stuart into gear, loaded the main gun, fired rounds at fixed and moving targets, and took command of the tank.[28] McBurney, even as one of the top gunners, became equally proficient as a driver and loader. He relished his time in the turret as tank commander, with tank helmet and goggles firmly in place. When possible, he would leave hatches open. The stiff breeze lifted everyone's spirits.

After a day training in the tanks, Windsor led the crew through a lengthy post-operation inspection. They rechecked the oil level, "inspect[ed] lights, siren, and windshield wipers [and] check[ed] for loss or damage of exhaust mufflers and accessories." The TM required an additional inspection after two to five hours of operation or 250 miles, whichever came first.[29] Bates added to their exhaustive responsibilities and made sure the 761st had the cleanest tanks. The tanks gleamed before a crew dispersed for a much-needed evening meal.

While platoon leaders and tank commanders with TM in hand taught the tankers how to operate the Stuarts, the field manuals burst with maneuver instructions from platoon through the battalion level. Such training fell under the Armored Forces' grand scheme and for this reason the Armored Force School wrote numerous field manuals like FM 17-30, Armored Force Field Manual Tank Platoon, published in October 1942. Tank orders fell to the platoon leader, and tanks most often trained in groups of five as a full platoon. The 170-page booklet of tank platoon tactics laid out in excruciating detail stood as a step-by-step tutorial and practical application manual. It included hand-drawn diagrams. Page 8, for example, discussed the importance of studying the terrain of the battlefield. Ivan Harrison could point to the drawing of the tank sitting on the crest of a tree-less hill and explain that his crews should avoid such a compromising situation. He could show them that a simple error in combat could, at best, leave the tank and crew vulnerable to enemy attack. The platoon would listen in silence.[30]

Platoons joined and trained as companies, and the eighty-seven-page FM 17-32, "The Tank Company, Light and Medium," addressed both light and medium tank company operations.[31] The heavier medium Sherman tank had begun to make its way into the armor units, with those units headed into combat given priority. According to Armored School doctrine, the light and medium tank units operated similarly.

As Windsor studied the technical manual, tank gunner McBurney made FM-17-12, "Tank Gunnery," his bible.[32] Its 109 pages attested to the complexities of firing a 37 mm main gun while often bouncing around in a fast-moving tank. As he recalled watching rounds head toward the next county, far from where they had been ordered, McBurney had learned firsthand practice made a successful gunner.

Time in the tank proved the path to proficiency and the 761st tankers grew more comfortable with the M5 Stuart light tank. To increase the daylight available for training Bates moved some class work to evening hours. One Plan of the Day listed Ivan Harrison teaching a one-hour class on mine warfare from seven to eight in the evening. Another class followed. The men did not break until after nine P.M.[33]

As a six-foot three-inch platoon commander, Harrison had his own training challenges. His slim build proved a blessing, but he exceeded the ideal height of a Stuart tanker by seven inches. Repetition eased the burden for all the tankers; interior spaces seemed to grow and narrow sights through the armor appeared to broaden each man's window on the world.

Bates stood as pleased as Harrison with the men's progress over the nearly six months he pulled and prodded. He saw better results than he expected. To Bates's surprise, the battalion received a coveted invitation to "the big-time maneuvers," so named by Trezzvant Anderson,[34] but they coincided with another milestone: the unit's organization day or first anniversary.

Six

Organization Day

WILLIAM MCBURNEY AND THE NEW YORK SOLDIERS PROBABLY saw themselves as the most capable to plan a party that few might survive and no one would forget. The unit had thrived despite twelve months of controversy and upheaval. The junior officers probably first discussed their vision of Organization Day, or maybe "birthday bash" in their former civilian parlance. Neither Ivan Harrison nor Sam Brown had interest in some solemn occasion. Maybe a parade? Weapons demonstration? Athletic competition?

The mention of speeches torpedoed enthusiasm and upped the tension. Even a calm Harrison threw up his arms, tired of the bickering. The men finally designed a full day of varied events with something for everyone. Senior officers expected certain opportunities. Most liked to talk. Speeches would allow them time to take credit for the unit's success. Afternoon athletic events would follow. A fancy dinner would cap off the day. Harrison knew as well as anyone what they had achieved during a challenging year. But stability had replaced turmoil. Hundreds of former civilians-turned-soldiers now stood in the 761st as competent tankers.

Paul Bates remained focused on the Louisiana Maneuvers. The battalion belonged to Wright, whose apathy permeated the unit—and all of Camp Claiborne for that matter. The men had control of the events. The officers would keep the day within reason.

The battalion gathered on April 1, 1943, to celebrate its hard-won milestone. Fifth Tank Group also planned to recognize its third and probably final battalion, the 784th. Lieutenant Richard English, slated as the Service Company officer in the new battalion, had watched the 761st since his arrival at Camp Claiborne. While his battalion expected his focus on the 784th's big debut, Dick English held a copy of the day's "programme," as spelled by its 761st creators, reflected on his unlikely path, and looked ahead.[1]

English, unlike the other officers, seemed to grow stockier with each passing day.[2] He had thought the draft would skip him. Given his age—he looked older than his thirty-four tired years[3]—his vocation as an educator, and his growing family,[4] he saw himself as a man who had more to offer molding the minds of the young men who would serve. English lived to teach, not to kill. The army saw the matter differently.

Richard Walter English possessed a life-long love of learning. When he first arrived at Camp Claiborne, he would hike the clapboard walkways that connected platoons to companies and companies to the battalion. He looked with curiosity on the hutment, popular with the post and the army because the hybrid shelter provided cheap and easily built housing. Most soldiers hated the stuffy, confining "structures" that blazed in the summer and shook with occupants' misery during the colder months. Hutments had a base skirted of construction-grade plywood, and the upper half's canvas sagged like the mood of the times.

Hutments proved popular with workers off post, and English noted Camp Claiborne had no real barriers to keep anyone—military or otherwise—in or out. The post and its hodgepodge of buildings melted into surrounding acreage. The vast, remote training areas did not belong to Camp Claiborne. English knew dense, old-growth forests had populated the area. Now an array of hastily built warehouses stretched in every direction. He could tell the warehouses from their quantity and better-quality construction. The army had made its countless storage facilities a priority. The post's elevation kept foundations dry, but the lack of foliage left buildings and soldiers encrusted with a film of grime in near year-round humidity.[5]

Richard English understood dust and filth on several levels. Young Richard, born June 9, 1909, had enjoyed a life of some privilege. He marveled as his father, James English, a famed jockey with a storied career that spanned nearly fifteen years, made his money training and

breeding championship horses. He read
about his exploits, including sleeping next
to his steeds the night before a big race and
a fine for "$300 for chewing gum while
going to the post." It seemed Jim English
often made the papers, and his son carried
a well-worn article in his wallet about his
outlandish father even as an officer at
Camp Claiborne.[6]

Richard W. English. (*U.S.
Army*)

English thought he inherited his father's
work ethic and his imagined penchant for
adventure. But memories of El Paso and
his father had grown fuzzy. As a young boy
in El Paso he glimpsed Mexican revolu-
tionary Pancho Villa cross the ever-changing Rio Grande. His French
mother, Irene de Lacepps, tired of her husband's wandering eye, gathered the bewildered ten-year-old Richard plus her jewels (a lady's
insurance) and stole away to her family's compound of homes in New
Orleans. There, seven blocks from the Mississippi River in a corner
of the city's lower Ninth Ward, Richard adjusted with ease, learning
the ways of a people different from El Paso families and the Mexican
servants from whom he first learned Spanish.

After McDonough No. 35, the first black high school in New
Orleans, he graduated from Straight University (now Dillard).
Richard, who spoke five languages,[7] hungered for knowledge. But
even a city with a complex cultural and racial heritage like New
Orleans stood segregated. Opportunities for English remained limited.
He sold insurance for a few years after college and found the energy
to own and manage a bar and restaurant, the Arabi Club, a little
south of Flood Street in St. Bernard Parish, which abutted New
Orleans. Later he owned The Snack in New Orleans. Supervising thirty-seven employees and keeping the establishment stocked and the
books balanced gave him a unique understanding that transferred
well to outfitting an army unit.[8]

He may have packed on a few pounds at Camp Claiborne, but
English considered himself a gentleman sportsman. He favored ping-
pong, volleyball, boxing, basketball, and baseball. At the same time,
he enjoyed reading, "theatre," music, and a rollicking game of cards.[9]
But he soon found his passion lay in strengthening the minds of New
Orleans' children. From 1932 until the army called him to serve in

1942, he taught in the classroom and watched over other teachers as vice principal. As an administrator he supervised personnel records. He agreed to take on the headaches as the school paper's business manager. He chaired the science department. The busy educator married Loretta M. Thomas in 1935. They planned a large family with sons Richard, Ernest, and Elliot born in 1936, 1937, and 1939.[10]

The irony of Flood Street struck him as he wrapped himself in his current surroundings. He felt at home. Camp Claiborne hutments rivaled some New Orleans ramshackle, Caribbean-style "shotgun" structures and those of surrounding parishes for habitability. He wanted to lead a tank platoon like the ones already formed in the 761st, or better yet, a company of young men. His fantasy harkened back to childhood adventures. Even at age thirty-four, he could be Pancho Villa or anyone he wanted.

But breaking with the classroom proved more difficult than he had envisioned. While at his first post, Camp Polk, Louisiana, not far from Camp Claiborne, English organized literacy classes for soldiers who could not read or write.[11] Always the teacher, he probably swelled with pride as he held the white office paper Organization Day "programme" folded in four. The soldiers had typed it, probably on the administrative section's typewriter. Their work would garner a solid "A" in any of his classes.

On April 1 the platoon leaders gathered their soldiers. They looked forward to an ideal day with temperatures ranging between sixty-six and eighty degrees according to Alexandria's *Town Talk*.[12] As promised, planners packed the day with events. The schedule began early that morning. English felt the tension and excitement, yet it did not seem much different from proctoring a New Orleans schoolyard as he had for the past ten years. He found the similarities between the young men and his high school boys remarkable and a welcome bit of home. He pushed away his worries and tried to immerse himself in the joy surrounding him.

The war did not stop for the 761st celebration and recognition of the 784th. April 1 headlines brought welcome news on the fight for North Africa. The *Berkeley Daily Gazette* led with "Bomb Axis Ports." Allied bombers made their most potent attack to date, according to the report, with a "smashing bombardment of Calgliari, on the Italian island of Sardinia, an area crucial to supplying Rommel's Afrika Corps." The 761st tankers followed the news out of Africa with great interest.[13]

Lieutenant Dave Williams, who had transferred from the 758th, heard that the fight against Rommel had inspired a group of men from the unit to write the War Department that the 761st stood ready to do its part in the war effort. Samuel J. Turley, the unit's first sergeant and fellow 758th alum, appeared to lead the charge. It seemed odd a straight arrow like Turley would skip the officers and ignore the chain of command.

April 1 also brought bittersweet news that probably filled most black servicemen with pride. The navy awarded Mess Attendant First Class Leonard R. Harmon the Navy Cross for his actions on the heavy cruiser USS *San Francisco* (CA 38) during the fight for the Pacific island of Guadalcanal, November 12–13, 1942. Harmon rescued countless shipmates and the ship's executive officer while under heavy Japanese fire. He died shielding another sailor from enemy gunfire. Texas could count two black native sons honored by the navy: Harmon and Pearl Harbor hero and Mess Attendant First Class Doris "Dorie" Miller.

At 9 A.M. sharp, Colonel Fay Smith, 5th Tank Group commander, addressed the assembled 761st as well as the new 784th Tank Battalion. The hours of speeches and pleasantries seemed to drag. But by 11 A.M. the 761st drill squads stood ready to face off, brothers against brothers. English looked at the determined faces. It had been a year of growth, change, and adjustment for each man. That included the urbane English, though he had arrived via a different path.[14]

The flow of guests began at 1 P.M. They had invited leaders as well as loved ones. English noted wives and some children. Little boys and girls squealed, giggled, and clapped as they took turns riding in jeeps and other battalion vehicles. A few lucky ones commanded a Stuart tank. Gwendolyn and Barrie Bates did not visit on April 1, 1943, as Bates and his wife continued to grow apart. Paul Bates kept the matter to himself.

That afternoon, the tankers met on their battleground—the physical training field. Onlookers filled the sidelines. Contenders for each event took their places at the field's far end. They ran the 100-, 220-, and 440-yard dashes.[15]

They raced the mile and ran the mile relay. The taller members or those blessed with long legs had "a leg up," said McBurney, on the competition in the high jump and broad jump. The potato race and "shoe race" probably had spectators as well as participants doubled over in laughter. But they picked themselves up in time for the late afternoon parade and awards ceremony.[16]

Following a day of fun, camaraderie, and pageantry, each tanker dressed for the elegant celebratory dinner scheduled for 6 P.M. Guests sat with programs in hand, the same four-folded sheet of white office paper English admired that morning. They whispered, abuzz about the well-drawn head of the handsome black panther that graced the cover. They approved of the unit's motto, "Come out Fighting," a nod to boxer Joe Louis.[17] The unit's admiration for the world champion went beyond the ring. The lethal cat and boxer's words marked departed battalion commander Edward Cruise's final victory over Washington and an unintentional parting gift to the unit.[18]

Few outside the unit knew the men's talents reached well beyond the Stuart tank. The 761st had its own "fine orchestra," as Trezzvant Anderson later called it.[19] The men had formed a large ensemble with brass and strings. Musicians ranked from private to first lieutenant. They represented most of the battalion's companies and their homes stretched from the Bronx, New York City, to Los Angeles, California. As one of the first teams to form in the 761st, these men played like they could have headlined the shuttered Cotton Club in its prime. They would complete a sweet song that had couples gently swaying to the soft melody and then launch full-force into a jazzed frenzy that had the dance floor hopping.[20] Tankers and guests danced into the night. Concerned this anniversary might stand as the unit's first and last, English took it all in.

Seven

Big-Time Maneuvers

THE LOUISIANA MANEUVERS OF 1941 HAD BEEN CROWNED "THE Big One." In just two years, a massive, pull-out-all-the-stops strategic event and its players had taken on a rare, celebrity status. Louisiana lit up like fireworks on the 4th of July for some, the burning of Atlanta for others. Paul Bates had his concerns about debuting the men too soon, but he still stood as the S-3, not the battalion commander. Wright, though eager to relinquish command, probably thought the maneuvers a good move if he gave it any thought at all. Bates figured Wright saw the exercise as his ticket out of the unit. Participation would look good in his official record, if nothing else.

With war imminent, the army had needed to re-create the military tactical exercise into something that would benefit the service like nothing before in its long history. It already had designed the maneuver concept, but drunkenness "in bayou honky-tonks and fraternization between officers and enlisted men in the army reached a modern peacetime highpoint and discipline in the army reached its low point,"[1] reported the *New York Times* on the prewar maneuvers.

The array of unpleasant challenges facing the army proved an even lower point for uniformed leaders planning how to make the maneuver concept work. The army of George C. Marshall and Lesley J.

McNair needed large-scale, complex, combat arms extravaganzas to ferret out the weak (or drunk) division and corps commanders. If a colonel, brigadier, or similarly senior officer could not meet the tactical and strategic challenges before him on U.S. soil, the army did not need his service in combat to get men killed. Marshall, as the army's chief of staff, plainly stated, "I want the mistakes [made] down in Louisiana, not over in Europe, and the only way to do this thing is to try it out, and if it doesn't work, find out what we need to make it work."[2] While McNair agreed with Marshall, his vision went further. Though the U.S. had not yet entered the war, rumors grew about German armor success, something that worried McNair. He determined the Louisiana Maneuvers would be "a test of tank warfare and antitank defense . . . we are definitely out to see . . . if and how we can crush a modern tank offensive."[3]

Dubious that they would succeed, the army assembled nearly a half-million men across nineteen divisions and assorted other units for the August-September 1941 event, the largest exercise to date, to fulfill Marshall's and McNair's respective goals. Second Army, commanded by Lieutenant General Ben Lear, led the Red Forces and Third Army under Prussian-born Lieutenant General Walter Krueger comprised the Blue Army. They fought over 3,400 square miles of Louisiana and eastern Texas between the Sabine and Calcasieu rivers and north to the Red River. They battled over control of navigation on the strategic Mississippi. The ferocity of the maneuvers riveted onlookers as well as reporters, while results shocked officers all around the army.

Soldiers took over the countryside. Many occupied family homes and farms. During earlier maneuvers, the army paid thousands to compensate civilians for "stolen melons, rutted yards, wrecked barrooms [and] buildings damaged by errant tanks," as well as accidental human fatalities and drowned sheep.[4] This relationship changed and locals became an unanticipated part of the maneuvers. Despite damage to crops, few civilians complained, possibly because of the unexpected windfall from selling food and laundry services to soldiers.[5]

The 1941 Louisiana Maneuvers proved a professional bloodbath as Marshall had anticipated. He and McNair dealt with command deficiencies swiftly and ruthlessly. Final reports read that Marshall relieved or reassigned thirty-one of forty-two corps and division commanders. Nearly all negative actions proved career-ending.[6]

As a tired breed faded, new blood stepped in with bold strategies and unorthodox leadership and Major General George S. Patton, Jr., and his 2nd Armored Division commanded attention. Though outwitted by old friend and Krueger's chief of staff, infantry Lieutenant Colonel Dwight D. Eisenhower, during Phase I, organizers moved Patton and his division to the Red Army to keep armor on the offensive. Patton wrote to his former commander, John Pershing, now a retired general but viewed as the nation's beloved senior army officer, telling him of taking at least ten objectives in quick succession. He boasted, "I am quite sure this is a unique record both as to success and as to number of operations."[7] Free to maneuver as he determined, Patton's daring assault of Shreveport, Louisiana, shut down the exercise days early and secured his reputation as a rising star.

Others of this new generation found themselves on the fast track with names like Omar Bradley and Matthew Ridgway. The aging Walter Krueger saw something in Dwight Eisenhower. Marshall had doubts about Krueger's hand-picked chief of staff, but Krueger assured the general "Ike" stood as both a brilliant tactician and tough soldier.[8] Eisenhower's imaginative and inspired defeat of Lear's Red forces stunned Marshall, and pleased his boss who knew at age sixty he would probably leave the battlefield for the last time. But he helped set Eisenhower on his deserved trajectory. Dwight Eisenhower shot straight to brigadier general, his first star, closing in on his old cohort, George Patton.

The lessons of 1941 loomed large over the men tested in 1943. Otherwise confident senior leaders still approached the maneuvers with more than a little trepidation. Ridding the force of weak and failing commanders remained a goal, though training and identifying competent units that could fight when called proved equally important. The tactical as well as strategic lessons learned would prove invaluable to a new crop of frontline fighters. Regardless, no commander sold the unforgiving army short. Futures remained uncertain.

Paul Bates clamored for realism in training. The stand-alone tank battalion like the 761st rolled in support of infantry. Fifth Group aside, Bates explained to his officers, possibly at the maneuvers, but certainly during combat, the battalion would attach to an army corps, which would detail the tankers to an infantry division. His officers understood the importance of the maneuvers, but the privates, and even some of the sergeants, could not grasp the bloodletting of war and that soon they would fight the enemy. The 761st had participated in smaller, local exercises beyond Camp Claiborne's liquid boundary. But Bates saw the maneuvers as an event, albeit lengthy, that could secure the 761st's reputation, sterling or otherwise. He had backed away from erasing the men's Hollywood images of war. Conflicted, Bates took the gamble. Their fantasies might just prove the push they needed to get them considered for combat in the European Theater or North Africa, with its heavy fighting and reported Allied progress against Rommel.

Bates faced more pressing problems shortly before the maneuvers. Since he arrived at the 761st, he worked to harness tanker energy and direct it across the killing fields—before soldiers wound up killing themselves. He watched the unit bleed out its experience due to carelessness and stupidity. Accidents and training mishaps had accounted for an unacceptable number of casualties. He ranted when his men used a unit weapon for transportation because of the predictable and tragic results. He wrote, "A new colored officer and a sergeant took it upon themselves to drive to Claiborne in one of the self-propelled guns. . . . Lt Harris chanced to see the [vehicle] upside down off the road. The sergeant was against a tree but alive. The officer, dead."9

Major Wright seemed more of a hazard than the men. As battalion commander, Bates found him anything but a leader. He could not get along with the new 5th Group commander and his preoccupation with a long-term skin condition rendered him useless. The battalion medical officer, Captain Sydney Storch, told Bates that Wright would use the malady to escape the battalion.

The 761st finally rolled to Phase II of the 1943 Louisiana Maneuvers on April 8, just a week after the unit's celebration. The mounted march took the 35 officers and 504 enlisted men forty-five miles. Because of orders from 5th Tank Group (L), Bates sent 75 of his enlisted soldiers to Fort Knox. The move left him below manpower strength.10

As the majestic steel weapons moved, tank commanders ensured they kept their speed and position. They traveled slowly at first. After they cleared Camp Claiborne's rear bounds, drivers shifted gears as they gently gave the tank more gas with their right foot. With the tank hatches open, the tank commanders stood tall (some taller than others), surveying the route before them. Though not quite the perfection Bates demanded, he rode with pride in his tank like a combat leader going to war, even with Wright still in command.

As the tanks clicked one mile after another, Bates wondered if anyone cared about a black tank unit. If not, they soon would. He understood their support role, but Bates planned a performance that would have every general officer and officiating umpire eyeing his unit. Though still well short of its full potential, he knew the 761st could match most any other army tank battalion stateside, tank for tank, platoon for platoon, company for company. Their presence at the maneuvers trumped even their best day at Claiborne and a good showing could put them in the combat queue.

The army had an added interest in each unit at the maneuvers. Attention had shifted back to training because of bloody and uneven operations in North Africa and the Pacific. At the same time, the U.S. Army faced a manpower shortage and could overlook no unit. The day the 761st made its way to the maneuvers, news came from the Selective Service in Washington. "Exemptions Slashed in New Draft Order," read national headlines. Congress had already widened the draft pool in 1942 from males ages twenty-one to thirty-six to those between eighteen and thirty-seven years of age. But those making the change placated the opposition with a large number of exemptions from service. The latest move allowed exemptions in just three areas: "Men employed full-time in essential farming. Men irreplaceable in essential, nonagricultural jobs. Men whose induction would mean 'extreme hardship and privation' on dependents." Controversy reigned and the revision brought much debate to the Capitol. Congressmen caterwauled for exemptions for married men with families, but Selective Service stood firm. Publicly, the army remained mum about its dire personnel situation.[11]

Even with fewer soldiers, one army fought another during the exercise. As a separate tank battalion, the 761st attached to III Armored Corps commanded by then-Major General Willis D. Crittenberger, Sr. Pitted against the Blue Army, the Red Army maneuvered in a high-stakes war game of cat-and-mouse. Trezzvant Anderson noted the 100th Infantry Battalion, composed of Japanese-American soldiers, or Nisei, from Hawaii, attached to the 85th Infantry Division. The 85th and its units had come to Louisiana expecting to soon deploy to fight the Germans. Commanders saw this as one last readiness check. A series of tactical problems had the 93rd Infantry Division face off against the 85th Infantry Division making it "a dress rehearsal for the big show" for both sprawling units.[12]

While the military officials and maneuver umpires studied the
761st and other units, the media shied away from the 1943 maneuvers. Alexandria's *Town Talk*, with its continued fawning over the
army and its surrounding installations, especially Camp Claiborne,
skipped the gathering of units. The *New Orleans Times-Picayune*
showed little interest.

The *Pittsburgh Courier*, with a rapidly growing readership, saw
the 1943 exposition ideal for its audience. Readers could count on
consistent and often lively reporting. The paper assigned folksy war
correspondent Edward W. Baker to follow the unprecedented number
of "race soldiers," as the paper often termed black servicemen, taking part.[13] His interest: the black 93rd Infantry Division.

Baker set the mood with the 93rd's journey. He detailed the massive unit's four-day April train ride from its post at Fort Huachuca,
Arizona, to "somewhere in Louisiana." He found moving 14,000
men and equipment no small undertaking. With some degree of security mandated by the army, Baker wrote in generalities and gave little
information of interest to enemy eyes and Axis sympathizers.[14]

The *Courier* announced, "Thousands of Race Soldiers on
Maneuvers in Louisiana." Baker noted the maneuvers stood as, "the
first time in history that such a large number of colored combat
troops with many varied weapons have gone into the southern
states."[15] While such hyperbole may have played well for Baker and
his editors, men like McBurney and Harrison saw this as a rare
opportunity to showcase their skills. Bates had ingrained this idea.
William McBurney would show them his near-perfect aim with the 37
mm, and if he could snatch the driver's seat, he would demonstrate a
Stuart's speed potential, as well as his array of skills.[16]

Though Baker concentrated on the 93rd, the infantry division and
the 761st faced nearly identical challenges. On April 22 Baker's headline read, "Soldiers Undergo Toughest Maneuvers In Louisiana." Still
reporting from "Somewhere in Louisiana," he continued, "maneuvers for Negro troops in this area apparently on their way overseas,
which began April 12, are going to be the toughest and most extensive they have had yet and field training will more nearly approximate combat training than in any previous period. Stress is being
placed on that high state of discipline which is required for success on
the battlefield."[17]

Baker's report could only make George Marshall and Lesley
McNair sigh with some relief. Not far removed from a series of Allied

debacles in North Africa, the army leaders hammered away for realistic combat training so the units could fight and not freeze in the face of the enemy. Though Baker did not write of the 761st, the tank battalion's participation with top units en route to the front allowed the battalion to experience combat training in ways not possible at claustrophobic, race-panicked Camp Claiborne. Trezzvant Anderson wrote, "Many angles of mechanized warfare were revealed in the field under varying conditions, which served to acclimate the members of the 761st to armored field operations in a far more definite manner than could ever have been achieved through the routine training program."[18]

By the time the 761st took its place in the Louisiana Maneuvers, the future of Lieutenant David Williams seemed uncertain. He had come to the 761st from the 758th Tank Battalion under curious circumstances. By all accounts, Williams had the pedigree and the mind to be a superb officer. He had graduated at the top of his Fort Knox OCS class. The Pittsburgh native hailed from a prominent and socially progressive family, one that believed with status came responsibility. Williams worked from a young age and later enjoyed the benefits of a premier prep school and an education at Yale, until he and several classmates left school in early 1941 "for a 6 month vacation." His father, Alvin, suggested Williams get his one year of military service in at that time.[19] Williams enlisted March 12, and served for a period as a private in the 70th Tank Battalion at Camp Meade, Maryland.[20] War changed Williams's plans for a speedy return to Yale. Instead he looked at an army commission. He held his father's views on duty and worried about a misstep as an officer.

Soon after Williams's arrival at the 758th, the Charlie Company commander, a Captain Charles M. Barnes, Jr.,[21] called for Williams so he could meet his newest officer. Williams's stomach tightened and his feelings of dread permeated the thick Louisiana air. He saw himself as too new to have to cross paths with any commander. To his surprise, Barnes seemed a little too gray for his rank and position. His blue eyes stood out from his weathered face. Though Barnes seemed affable, Williams wrote of a conversation heavy on the topic of race. Barnes confessed, "I think we're just marking time down here. Personally I don't think these people belong in tanks. They don't learn fast enough." Barnes continued on about politics and his surprise that someone with Williams's background would end up at Camp Claiborne. Williams said little, self-conscious of a voice he described as befitting a Boy Scout. Barnes seemed genuinely happy to have Williams in his company and made it no secret he looked forward to retirement. The two officers seemed to settle in and Williams thought his assignment with the 758th might go smoothly.

As Barnes talked, one of the company's top enlisted leaders, First Sergeant Samuel J. Turley, entered. Williams recalled observing the self-assured man, one of a handful of African American soldiers whose service predated the war. He expected such a seasoned professional from the regular army, but the rough-looking Turley possessed an intense confidence. Williams knew he had little understanding of tanks and the soldiers who operated them, but he knew people and placed Turley above many he had met. Maybe his Bronx, New York, lineage gave Turley his edge. Williams watched as Turley outlined the men's schedule with Barnes. According to Williams, as Turley turned to leave, it seemed natural to acknowledge their introduction.

Williams rose and reached to shake Turley's hand. "I'm glad to meet you, sergeant." Taken aback, Barnes admonished Williams after Turley's departure.[22] The taboo of greeting between men of differing races may have prompted what seemed to be the spiteful and short-sighted transfer of both men to the 761st a short time later.

After leaving the 758th, Williams looked for an escape. He wrote that he thought he found his purpose as a paratrooper, then as an aviator.[23] Paul Bates told him no combat battalion needed an officer with one foot out the door. But Bates could use the help and felt uncomfortable rejecting the troubled but loyal Williams. Dave Williams understood the perceptions others had of him. He graciously took on the assignment as billeting officer for the maneuvers with the same energy he had shown arranging an earlier successful tanker boxing event, known to the men as "Bloody Wednesday."[24] Few knew Williams captained Yale's freshman boxing team. Williams scouted suitable bivouac sites for the battalion. Though other officers shunned the job, he found it the ideal task at a personally difficult time. With a career in shambles, he could only begin to fathom his father's displeasure.[25]

Typical of a unit on the move, the men gave up the comfort of their cots, three squares, and the advantages of the predictable and mundane. They slept beneath the clear night sky dotted with countless stars. McBurney, who rarely saw stars in skies over New York City, proved this theory—he tried counting them. In the warm rain, the men curled up uncomfortably inside their tanks, though some always devised a way to make the less-than-pleasant a little more like the comforts of home. Adversity brought them closer to their machines and to one another.

Baker described how the soldiers he observed combined their shelter halves and slept. He talked about the monotony of the rations but praised the culinary delights served by the mobile kitchens' "dedicated mess sergeants." He described the incessant attacks from the air—mosquitoes and the like, and assaults from the ground— snakes measuring from six inches to five and a half feet in length.[26] McBurney obsessively inspected his blanket, boots, and other gear for hidden, reptilian surprises.

David Williams. (*U.S. Army*)

As daytime temperatures continued to climb through the seventies, the tankers learned to work with other units and in support of infantry to take assigned objectives—a necessity neither Knox nor Claiborne could accomplish. They faced off with tank destroyers. Morale climbed. McBurney noticed any issue of race seemed to vanish, but dared not comment for fear of ending their run of good fortune.

The tankers communicated with radios and silent hand and arm signals when necessary. Some reverted to shouting above the engine's roar. Tank commander Teddy Windsor would slap McBurney's or another crew member's shoulder to get his attention, even when he could use the tank's intercom system. The battalion communications section knew its business and ensured the 761st could concentrate on operations with clear and continuous contact assured.

They rolled in the pitch of night along uncertain paths to surprise the enemy. They learned lessons more quickly through myriad tactical problems outside the schoolhouse and training environments, with technical manuals closed. In contrast, Lieutenant Williams, still an afterthought, would head out each day with the billeting party to find a new suitable bivouac site. He guided the battalion, under radio silence, to the area. He worked with each company to position the tanks outward in a circle around the battalion headquarters and service company, the textbook procedure for bivouacking in a hostile area.

The tankers often dined on canned K-rations, meals initially issued to army airborne units, though ideal for tank crews. Packaged as three meals and billed as a full day's worth of sustenance for each soldier, K-rations piqued tanker tastes for a brief period. The evening repast included a pack of four cigarettes. Soon soldiers like McBurney went from viewing the army's and industry's prepackaged invention as better than nothing to considering hunger a more attractive option. The meals proved insufficient for the dietary needs of soldiers on the move; the men needed more calories. McBurney and other soldiers hoarded the rations' more useful items like cigarettes and gum. Chesterfields and Wrigley's took some of the edge off their hunger. Tank commanders like Teddy Windsor ordered their crews to eat the daily, 2,800-calorie allowance.[27] With mess trailers a rarity for the 761st, the men quickly learned another lesson of combat tankers on the move: prepacking their tanks with their selection of store-bought delicacies and other comforts.

Bates penned his unique view of the exercise in letters that sometimes ran for pages. He often noted the day of the week or time of day, catching what few moments he could at the maneuvers. While he reported events, his letters acted as a window into Paul Bates, or the man he wanted someone to see. He meant them for one person— Taffy Rosen.

For Paul Bates, the maneuvers meant facing enemies like countless ticks, snakes, mosquitoes and, as he wrote, pigs, the uninvited but protected guests of the U.S. Army. What a nuisance, he complained, as his driver maneuvered around a mock battlefield overrun by pigs. Dead pigs meant angry farmers and compensation to the wronged locals for the destruction of their property. Given the opportunity, Bates probably would have used his sidearm to "move" a pig or two. But to his dismay, organizers had forbidden live ammunition at the maneuvers. One thing worse than a pig in Bates's mind: "the endless chain of inspecting officers." "For the past two days the battalion has had a series of inspections by civilian technicians." Tired of the incessant onlookers, Bates wrote, "The results about have me jabbering like an ape."[28]

Some vehicles did not pass and their deficiencies relegated them as "unsafe," according to Bates.[29] More frustrating for him, the same vehicles deemed unsafe by the civilian technicians had passed an earlier inspection. Despite Bates's embarrassment over the failed tanks, he figured inspectors found deficiencies in most other units. Bad news upped the maneuver ante and made commanders anxious. Thanks to his Western Maryland football coach, Dick Harlow, Bates could take

Lt. Gen. Lesley J. McNair, right, commanding general of U.S. Army ground forces, discussing a point with an umpire during the Louisiana Maneuvers in 1943. (*Library of Congress*)

whatever inspectors or higher headquarters handed him and use it to the battalion's advantage.

One Sunday organizers scheduled two intense hours of aerial bombing demonstrations. Bates marched the battalion five miles, only to wait three and a half hours for the demo to start. The bombing then proved brief, leaving Bates fuming at the wasted training time.[30]

Though he kept his opinion to himself, Bates thought the unit performed well past expectations. He wondered what the maneuver chiefs thought. To his surprise, it seemed top army leaders agreed. Lieutenant General McNair closely watched the maneuvers as he had in the past. On May 29, he and several other senior officers made a personal visit to the battalion and inspected the 761st soldiers and their vehicles. Bates held his breath but appeared as smooth as usual. Never sure what surprise his tankers might have waiting, he tried to think more pleasant thoughts with little success. The battalion's reputation and future lay with each scrutinizing officer. McNair, despite his top-flight reputation, made Bates uneasy. But he may have misread the general. Impressed by his visit to the battalion, McNair reported, "Vehicles and weapons of the 761st Tank Battalion were in excellent condition and well-disposed in bivouac." Bates welcomed the accolades with relief.[31]

Earlier in the month, on May 6, the popular Brigadier General Benjamin O. Davis, Sr., arrived from the War Department's Inspector

General's office for an eight-day inspection tour of the maneuvers. He addressed some of the units. McBurney, staring at the first black general officer and father of the man commanding the 99th Pursuit Squadron, found the elder Davis more distinguished than he had imagined. "There is no racial side to soldiering," Davis said to those gathered. "One becomes a first-class fighting man or he has no place in the armed forces. When an enemy projectile comes over it has no color prejudice and is not going to stop in mid-air to see what is the tint of your skin before plugging you."[32]

Major Wright had spent the maneuvers wandering the fields with no interest in command.[33] At best he proved inert as a stone. Bates watched as he waited in misery for letters and food from his wife. Wright's skin condition proved his salvation and he successfully left the battalion. Bates wasted no time and in a May 16 memorandum to the unit announced he had temporary command of the 761st.[34]

At the end of the maneuvers, *Pittsburgh Courier* headlines declared "93rd Division Ready to Fight!"[35] Bates had not seen the *Courier* and cared little about other units. Much work lay ahead. The unit fought well, but unevenly. At times the men hesitated, at others they moved too aggressively. Bates led a tank battalion, not a sprawling foot patrol. The tankers' skills would improve with time and repetition, as would tactical armor movement.

Despite its inconsistent performance, Bates enjoyed the unit. He wrote how well the officers worked together. His mood lightened when an inspecting colonel congratulated him. As one scenario played out, the 761st faced off with the 634th Tank Destroyer Battalion. Bates listened with some surprise as the colonel told him the 761st "outfoxed and outmaneuvered" McNair's much-favored 634th.[36] Over the course of nearly two months the 761st performed as a combat unit fighting a hostile force. The unit never faced off muzzle-to-muzzle with another tank nor would they. Fort Knox instructors and the battalion officers made sure each tanker understood that U.S. tanks did not engage in tank-on-tank warfare. A Stuart and its 37 mm main gun might buzz like an annoying gnat in the sights of the Panzer IV and the even more lethal Mk V Panther. The Germans saw armored combat otherwise, and reports chronicling their punishing strategy had just started making their way from North Africa.

The Louisiana Maneuvers proved a morale boost for the unit's 43 officers and 593 enlisted men, but feelings of triumph sunk to deep disappointment following the return to Camp Claiborne on June 6. Bates ensured that the training schedule remained robust, but it paled compared to their experience in the maneuvers. Boredom set in, as Bates had feared. Accolades from the maneuvers made matters worse. Even McBurney found the days tedious, but he held fast to the adventure and promise of the maneuvers that renewed his commitment to the 761st.

More so than before the maneuvers, the men scoured the pages of the post newspaper, the *Camp Claiborne News*, for stories and advertisements of interest. The April 8 edition of the post weekly ran a detailed story under the headline "The First Anniversary of the Illustrious 761st Tank Battalion." It wrote of the unit's future plans, "Having reached the final stages of its stationary training the 761st is now ready to embark upon the broader phase of its duty, the job of concretely aiding in the winning of this war."[37]

The *Camp Claiborne News* also aided the tankers in navigating the subtle as well as blatant ways of segregation. They studied the advertisements to find restaurants, tailors, cleaners, and cab companies that served black soldiers. At worst, they could head to the USO on Casson Street that catered to their race. Soldiers like 761st tanker Private Willis Rice raved about the club's new jukebox.[38] On the rare occasions McBurney would agree to head to Alexandria, he scanned each newspaper column looking for "colored" friendly businesses. Black soldiers could count on Community Taxi Line for transportation. They found refreshment at the OK Saloon or the Ritz Grill. But if some men went to great trouble to make a trip to Alexandria, others preferred the relative certainty of Camp Claiborne. Aside from local ads that informed and enticed, the paper listed upcoming entertainment opportunities making life at the post a bit more bearable. As the unit departed for the maneuvers the paper announced an "all-colored USO review" called "Shuffle Along." While at the Louisiana Maneuvers, Blackstone the Magician appeared at Camp Claiborne. The post paper announced he would "entertain the colored soldiers in the recreation hall." Even with a race-friendly taxi service and military vehicles traveling Highway 165 that could transport the black tankers, many like William McBurney preferred to stay put on post.[39]

McBurney and a number of the men tried to reconcile their eupho-
ria from the maneuvers with the despair of Claiborne. The racial acrimony at the sprawling, multiracial camp made little sense. Russell
Guthrie, who had grown up in a Buffalo neighborhood of Dutch and
German immigrants and attended the same local schools as the other
neighborhood youngsters, had no inkling of racial differences
throughout most of his childhood and teen years. As far as Guthrie
knew, he came into the world the same as his friendly neighbors. He
explained, "I had no idea I was black."[40]

Leaders in Washington had long expected clashes over race.
Roosevelt's choice for civilian aide to Secretary of War Henry
Stimson, Judge William H. Hastie, commenced his contentious tenure
on November 1, 1940. Despite strained relations on many fronts,
Hastie remained determined to open the way for black men and
improve their lot in spite of a segregated army. Hastie's stay at the
War Department rivaled his judgeship and posting at Howard in
brevity. Less than three years into his prestigious War Department
appointment, in early January 1943, he publicly stated he thought he
could do more good on the outside than in his current position. But
to Stimson and close associates, including his assistant, Truman K.
Gibson, Hastie bluntly stated his outrage over the tremendous
inequities in Air Corps training facilities and flight training, as well as
assignment distribution. Specifically, the Army Air Force had decided
to establish a segregated training installation, something that caught
Hastie by surprise, since such matters passed across his desk for comment before anyone made a final decision. His tenure ended January
31.[41]

Units like the 761st lost their primary policy advocate when Hastie
stormed out of the War Department. He had pressed for advances
that soldiers like Harrison and McBurney never gave much thought
to. Aside from desegregating officer candidate training and increasing
the numbers of black officer candidates, Hastie pushed for improvements to conditions for black soldiers on posts and in surrounding
and often racially hostile communities. He increased the number of
black medical officers. Few considered Camp Claiborne a showcase
for Hastie's achievements, but Harrison and some of his peers probably directly benefited.

Hastie considered George Marshall a personal friend and support-
er of the black soldier's plight, despite Marshall's reservations about
the unrest racial upheaval might cause at a time when the nation

needed a stable army. The army chief of staff acted on his concerns by routinely addressing race and how to best lead black soldiers. The two men had weathered the racial debate together, and Marshall seemed troubled at the loss of the judge. Hastie, amidst the tension of his break with a divided War Department and legislature, wrote to assure his unlikely ally on January 30, 1943: "While I have avoided imposing upon you personally the detail of various specific problems with which this office has been concerned, I have been aware at all times of your concern that the

Judge William H. Hastie. (*Library of Congress*)

Negro be equitably treated in the armed services. Although I have come to the conclusion that the greater good is to be accomplished by my withdrawal from the War Department at this time, I am keenly aware that your good will has been an all important factor in those things which this office has been able to accomplish during the past two years."[42]

Marshall responded to a man for whom he held tremendous respect. Like Hastie he believed the two had become close partners, both desperate to obtain the best for the soldier and the nation: "I appreciate very much that you saw fit to write me as you did. It is a great satisfaction to me to know that you have felt that we have done our best to meet an exceedingly difficult problem. I was not aware of your prospective withdrawal from the War Department nor of your reasons, but I hope that your influence will be continued to bring about a better understanding in our successive steps in the solution of this great problem."[43] George Marshall knew the army suffered racial strife, which he had hoped to avoid. Regardless of his feelings on race, such turmoil could adversely impact an army's fighting capability.

On January 31, released from the confines of his position, Hastie publicly confirmed rumors and lashed out, accusing the Army Air Forces of "reactionary policies and discriminatory practices" against its black servicemen. He fought the same army he had worked to serve. The Baltimore *Afro-American* highlighted Hastie's departure on February 2, 1943: "Discrimination in Air Forces Caused Dr. Hastie to resign from War Dept."[44]

Mirroring Hastie's frustration, reports of racial unrest seemed on the rise across the nation. The same day the 761st celebrated its organization day, in California the *Berkeley Daily Gazette* ran a front-page story, "200 Colored Soldiers Mix in Stockton Riot." What reportedly started as a bar fight the prior evening "spread over three blocks in the Negro district." It took the entire Stockton police force aided by military police to quell the fighting, firing shots over the heads of the "battlers" and using "their clubs to break up gang fights." Police chief Captain C. C. Smith described the outbreak as the "biggest disturbance so far in Stockton's Negro district." Other than the barroom fight and "scores of soldiers converg[ing] on the area and join[ing] in the brawling," the paper gave no other cause for the immense melee.[45] The *Pittsburgh Courier* reported a similar scenario in Nashville the night of April 3.[46]

The return to Camp Claiborne proved difficult for everyone. While their accomplishments as a unit did not go unnoticed, training at the post after the maneuvers seemed a large step backward. The tankers craved challenge. They wanted war.

Eight

The Case for Tanks

T HE UNIT RECOMMENCED ITS PACKED TRAINING ROUTINE, BUT talented platoon leaders pulled lessons learned from the Louisiana Maneuvers, not contained in the field manuals, and incorporated them into their daily drills. Formerly unsure officers now discussed innovation in the field. Once timid, awestruck soldiers like William McBurney peppered their teachers with technical questions regarding the Stuart tank as well as tactical queries. McBurney even asked about the Stuart's robust cousin the Sherman, every tanker's dream battle wagon. Warren Crecy, who could have reminded his fellow tankers of Paul Bates, asserted himself more often. Evening class fare expanded and included information on tank history. The battalionwide interest in the past and all things armor impressed the teacher in Bates. Between Wright's extended illness and protracted disinterest, the men already had looked to Bates's leadership for many months. The army officially made Bates commander of the 761st on July 1, 1943.[1]

Despite the men's devotion to the tank as well as their mission, few understood that Winston Churchill, George Patton, and the civil rights pioneers of the 1930s paved the way for the 761st Tank Battalion. But Adolf Hitler gave them their raison d'être, a fact all tankers understood. By 1942, tanks entered their formative years in modern warfare, though the idea of an enclosed fighting vehicle had bounced around for centuries. Wheeled siege towers with battering rams rolled through the Middle Ages. Leonardo de Vinci sketched his vision of such the mobile platform in the late fifteen century,[2] and James Cowan patented an armored fighting vehicle in Britain in 1855 modeled after the steam tractor.[3]

A small group of armored-vehicle innovators rode into the twentieth century debating such details as wheels versus tracks and other questions crucial to fighting vehicle design. As Europe plunged deeper into the Great War static trenches stretched across France, underscoring the need for tracked armor to break the stalemate. Though some considered it a questionable venture, Britain's First Lord of the Admiralty Winston Churchill backed the idea.[4] The first British tanks went into action in September 1916. Unfortunately, the small number and sluggish nature of these early tanks failed to garner significant tactical gains. When employed in much larger numbers at Cambrai the following year, they proved much more effective. When the U.S. entered the war and established its own Tank Corps, it employed both the heavy tank design favored by the British and the lighter Renault design of France.[5]

Rapid mobilization put 4 million Americans in uniform during World War I.[6] Of the more than 23 million registered for the draft[7] and roughly 2 million who served overseas,[8] just a smattering experienced combat with the Tank Corps. Some of the men who survived the slaughter in France would lead what remained of the U.S. Army over the next two decades. A few entered World War II entrenched in the previous war, but others studied the hard-earned lessons of the U.S. and European armies and penned warfare's next chapter.

George S. Patton knew those lessons firsthand. Born in California in 1885, George Smith Patton, Jr.'s military lineage dated to the Revolutionary War. A litany of male relatives served the Confederacy on the battlefield and at sea. After a year at the Virginia Military Institute, Patton went to the U.S. Military Academy at West Point, New York. His poor grasp of math delayed his graduation, a rare setback for the fierce competitor. As a member of 1912 Olympic team, Patton traveled to Stockholm and placed a respectable fifth in the first-ever modern pentathlon. Some believe he should have ranked higher, but his prowess with a .38 instead of the smaller caliber .22 that his competitors used may have proved his unintentional undoing. Judges unfamiliar with the formidable .38 may have counted one or more rounds as misses that probably pierced the gaping shot group Patton had already created with the first bullets.[9]

As the U.S. prepared to head to France in 1917, Patton asked Major General John J. Pershing, who soon would lead American forces abroad, for a combat command. Pershing instead insisted the newly promoted cavalry captain take over the Light Tank Training School for U.S. forces in France. But soon after, Patton commanded his first tank brigade. The war ended for Patton as he left the battlefield on a stretcher during the Meuse-Argonne offensive.[10]

Those who had experienced armor's might may have believed they had seen warfare's future firsthand and expected that the army would establish a separate branch to house its horses of steel. However, the National Security Act of 1920 turned on the new armor force, shelving tanks under the Infantry Branch, Paul Bates's designation upon college graduation.[11] The move reflected the infantry support role that tanks had performed in the war and a vision of their mission in future conflicts.[12]

The National Security Act of 1920 not only gutted the armed forces, but it detailed how they could operate. It "laid out the structure of the army for the interwar years, based upon input from a cross section of military leaders, the combat experience of World War I, and expectations of what the army would be required to do in the years to come. It carefully delineated responsibility among the branches, reinforced by force of law, and it established the end strength of the army at 280,000 commensurate with its expected postwar duties."[13] A step outside the law could mean expulsion of an officer and further restrictions on an already hollow corps.

The postwar army suffered a protracted period of genteel poverty. Severe defense cuts followed the war to end all wars. Fast-rising stars who attained rank at lightning speed reverted to humbler, more affordable stations. Patton had raced to a wartime temporary rank of colonel, but settled for captain in 1920. The army promoted him to major soon after, where he would remain for fourteen years.

As the army atrophied around him, Patton grew impatient. While at Camp George G. Meade near Baltimore, he and infantry Major Dwight D. Eisenhower wrote about "tank doctrine and tactics, and the value of armored fighting vehicles in battle."[14] Both men published on the topic. Patton published his article "Tanks in Future Wars," in *Cavalry Journal* in May 1920. He had credibility and could claim hands-on armor combat experience. Patton knew the British solution to the trench held vast promise for the U.S. forces of the future. He opened his typed soliloquy with an apology, then made his case with brash confidence. He grew frustrated with the army's inability to articulate the armor mission beyond infantry support. The British moved tanks to broader roles that the Americans rejected. The army could not produce a clear mission statement for its armored innovation.[15] Short-sighted senior officers and Congress had doomed his beloved tank corps. He understood the prevailing view but his disdain for the institutional army's also-rans underscored his written words: "To the casual observer the tank of 1918 is the last word. It is the tank, a feeble, blind, lumbering affair, 'half devil and half child.' He forgets that this machine, defective as it was, was never stopped unaided by one of the best infantries ever developed, and his frame of mind is identical with that which caused the astute military critic of the early sixteenth century, upon viewing Mons Meg, to declare, 'This is a cannon. It is too clumsy. Therefore, all cannons are, and will be useless.'"[16]

Eisenhower's "A Tank Discussion" appeared in the November 1920 issue of *Infantry Journal*. The article stressed the tank's potential for speed, reliability, and firepower. He predicted, "tanks will be called upon to use their ability of swift movement and great firepower against the flanks of attacking forces."[17]

The ill-timed articles equated to heresy for a cash-starved army. In two short years the war had not faded from memory, and the civilian public distrusted an armed military, an overriding sentiment dating to the Revolutionary War. Despite Patton's experience, his ideas and enthusiasm for the tank and its possibilities threatened an army fighting for its life.

For many the future of combat lay more in its dynamic past. All sides wanted war on the move. Despite the agony in the trenches, a number of World War I clashes drove the point home. The Germans also wanted a return to offensive warfare and developed innovative tactics in the spring offensive of 1918. The successful infiltration of enemy lines relied on speed and surprise, the antithesis of the static trench. Dubbed "Hutier" after Germany's head of the infantry General Oskar von Hutier, this method of warfare became the light-infantry precursor to Germany's highly effective blitzkrieg in its next world war.[18]

But Patton's call for action did find an audience. The U.S. Army, also eager for the offense, wanted to learn more about armor's advantages. Intrigued cavalry leaders saw a potential role for armor in support of the cavalry mission as well as with their horses, and in 1931 established a home for the new mechanized cavalry at Camp Knox, Kentucky, a move in the wake of a long-hoped for revision to mechanized policy, due in large part to Army Chief of Staff General Douglas MacArthur.[19] Though not perfect, it allowed latitude for exploration. Similarly, the Infantry Branch visualized the powerful tank maneuvering in combat in support of its vulnerable foot soldiers, but with a limited budget, and lacking the mechanized cavalry option open to its rival branch, chose to neglect its development.[20]

Caught in the middle of an ever-shrinking army, Patton and Eisenhower quietly abandoned their prophetic enthusiasm for the tank to salvage their futures in uniform. The tank would have to find its way without George Patton.

As the uneasy peace following the World War unraveled and changes on the other side of the Atlantic increased tensions in Europe, U.S. leaders grew concerned. Most nations considered France the premier army in Europe, if not the world, a belief undisputed by the French. Their assumed status assuaged some fears. After all, the French had built their Maginot Line, a complex and varied border of resistance against invasion from Germany. A similar 1914 incursion led to four years of carnage at a cost of 16 million dead with more than 116,000 of those American lives lost during the last year of the war.[21] Undeterred by the intricate French defenses, the Germans sidestepped the three-million-franc inconvenience en route to Paris in 1940. France fell in a matter of weeks.[22]

Credit for the stunning German success went in large part to its tanks. Though the French possessed a tank superior to Germany's at the time, eyewitness accounts embellished the capabilities of the German Panzer, the German word for "armor," in part to mask the shame of the French military and to compel foreign support for their occupied plight. German tactics and its army's aggressive approach to warfare made the invading force appear indestructible. Image translated into success and the French unwittingly assisted the invaders. The Panzer and stories of the German blitzkrieg sent U.S. planners scrambling for their version of lightning warfare.

Though many feigned ignorance, the German achievement should have come as little surprise. U.S. military officers had reported developments inside the German arsenal for several years. Aside from the presence of the military attaché, a number of U.S. officers attended German military schools. Those traveling through Germany availed themselves a chance to peek at the German's growing military, a mounting concern that flouted the Treaty of Versailles prohibitions. Despite its parade of capabilities for its foreign guests, the Germans developed the Panzer in secret for a time.

Major Truman Smith served as military attaché to Germany from 1935 to 1939 after having held the assistant attaché slot a decade earlier. From 1920 to 1924 he witnessed a young Adolf Hitler coaxing a defeated and dishonored nation from the rubble.[23] Smith had a deep understanding of the Germans. More important, he had long-standing contacts that aided him in his clandestine activities. Crucial to Smith unmasking Germany's most guarded military secrets was his friendship with Colonel Adolf von Schell, dating back to when the two officers served at Fort Benning, Georgia. Von Schell influenced German mechanization during Smith's tenure as attaché, but he had gained an understanding of Americans during his time at Benning. He attended the U.S. Infantry School at the Georgia post, headed by Colonel George C. Marshall, the same school Paul Bates would attend a decade later. The German officer took on a cult celebrity status by lecturing on his grueling World War I experiences as a company commander in the frigid and punishing east. Captivated by the German, Benning officials recorded and published his lectures in 1933 as a slim volume simply entitled "Battle Leadership," credited to von Schell. The book acknowledged several officers, including Truman Smith, with its publication.[24] As infantry leaders gushed over the wise lessons of their foreign colleague, one would never have guessed the U.S. and Germany had fought a bloody war twelve years earlier and would battle one another again in less than a decade.

Now a colonel back in Germany, von Schell had few concerns about Smith as the U.S. military attaché, but German military intelligence suspicion of the American grew. Smith sensed tension mounting as he and his staff set to work compiling sensitive information on tank unit organization. The spies guessed at Germany's war-ready doctrine. By 1937 the German Panzer I appeared in the Spanish Civil War for all nations to see.[25] The tank's surprising reprieve from secrecy revealed a robust Germany not just eager to fight, but with an arms industry ready to sell its wares. Smith determined the German war economy "stood without precedent in history" and "was unequivocal proof that Germany intended to be the strongest military state in Europe."[26] The U.S. tasked Smith to report on developments in the Luftwaffe, the German air force. In May 1936, Smith arranged for Colonel Charles A. Lindbergh to review the German aircraft industry and its reorganized aviation forces. Germany, thrilled with the attention from the famous pilot, paved the way for at least five additional visits during which Lindbergh saw the secret and lethal Messerschmitt. He found the fighter aircraft bearing its chief designer's name nothing short of remarkable. He sent detailed intelligence back to the United States and, fearing war, made urgent entreaties regarding U.S. policy.[27]

For Germany and its tanks, eagerness did not translate into success. With troubling substandard performance in Spain, German armor went through a period of confusion, emerging strengthened by its early missteps. Germany had clamored for light tanks, just as the U.S. Army would a few years later. But encounters with the superior Russian T-26 in Spain sent the Germans rushing back to the Fatherland. With Russia so certain of its capable tanks, the colorful, and possibly mythic, commander of a reinforced company, Pavel Arman, a purported Latvian, standing outnumbered with a supposed Republican Spanish general, reportedly said, "The situation is not so hopeless. They have fifteen thousand soldiers, we have fifteen tanks, so the strengths are equal!" Truth or fable, Arman embodied the essence of the strength of Russian armor. Cables extolled the seemingly indestructible Russian machine, and Arman's annihilation of possibly two Nationalist infantry battalions added to German concern. Germany shifted production to the medium tank and took a different path.[28]

Despite its armored success in Spain, the Russians worked to improve their tank. The T-34 entered production in 1940 using the best of what Russian military leaders had seen from other nations. American ingenuity played a part, notably the suspension system designed by engineer J. Walter Christie, an innovation embraced by the U.S. War Department, developed by a man it found insufferable. Christie caught the attention of then-Major George Patton with his M1919 prototype that could "climb a two-and-a-half foot wall and leap a seven-foot-wide ditch." It reached speeds of sixty miles per hour.[29] Christie's unique ergonomic design and suspension system allowed a tank to achieve high speeds across a variety of terrain. He developed the unusual, interchangeable option of wheels and tracks.

The T3E2 experimental tank with Christie suspension system undergoing rigorous testing by the U.S. Army. (*Library of Congress*)

Though the National Security Act of 1920 limited what the army could do with his innovative offerings, the Army Ordnance Department kept in close contact with Christie, who continued to design tanks. Patton remained an advocate.[30]

As Christie's testing and prototypes costs surpassed a staggering $300,000, he needed to sell his work. Despite design shortcomings with the turretless M1928 tank—like its lack of sufficient armor—its speed, range, wheel and track options, and masterful suspension system garnered Christie an Army Ordnance contract in 1930, the same year the army clocked his M1928 reaching a speed of 104 miles per hour.[31] They agreed on a September 1 delivery. But lucrative foreign opportunities diverted Christie's attention. He fulfilled a Russian agreement for two of his tanks, and later delivered the army's order on January 19, 1931, more than four months behind schedule. Though angered and alarmed, the army wanted what J. Walter Christie had.[32] But competition increased, and the army saw designs that better met its evolving needs. By 1932 the army concluded that Christie went with the highest bidder. Having gone from darling to pariah, when Christie could not sell his tank to the army, he parked it in the courtyard connecting the War, Navy, and State buildings.[33] Christie later approached the War Department with his M1937 tank.

The army had long found Christie's "disposition atrocious" and waved him off. Despite the rejection, he remained outside Washington, in Falls Church, Virginia, just a few miles from the Fort Myer army post where he performed some of his most breathtaking feats. He died a broken, penniless man before the end of the war.[34] Unknown to the rest of the world, the Christie suspension system, improved by the Russians, would keep Russian armor formidable in a war that America feared and Smith and Lindbergh saw as inevitable.

The U.S. heaped the detailed reports of Smith and Lindbergh on the "defeatist propaganda" pile. Their accuracy had fueled suspicion of the American messengers instead of action at the highest levels at home. Despite his public vilification, Smith watched and warned, "The German kindergarten period for playing with the tank is over," yet the larger army did not share his alarm. Thanks to the attaché, the U.S. Army possessed detailed information on Germany's tank development. It understood to some degree how the Germans planned to employ their potent weapon. But this knowledge coupled with the proven capability of the Panzer II in the 1938 annexation of Austria, did little to invigorate U.S. training standards. It took the collapse of France to kick the U.S. tank program into gear.

The 761st training program received a much-needed jolt. The unit's time at Camp Claiborne would draw to a close. Fifth Tank Group (L) ordered its headquarters, the 761st, as well the youngest tank battalion in the group, the 784th, westward to Camp Hood in Texas.

The promise of Texas left Bates stunned. The move would place him closer to Taffy Rosen. The army transferred Rosen to the 34th Evacuation Hospital, Camp Barkeley, near Abilene, Texas, in June.[35] Bates calculated that a move to Camp Hood would bring them within two hundred miles of one another. Weekends together seemed a certainty. Going to Camp Hood also meant leaving the familiar, no matter the challenges Camp Claiborne had presented. But Bates knew that if the battalion's situation did not change, his men would become discouraged and find trouble.[36] After an extended period at Camp Claiborne, Bates needed new horizons, too.

Nine

Aggressors in the West

THE WAR DEPARTMENT ORDERED THE 761ST TO OPERATE AS AN aggressor unit at the Tank Destroyer Tactical and Firing Center. The battalion would pit itself as an enemy force against tank destroyer outfits, many in their final training stages before shipping out to fight abroad. On September 13, 1943, the battalion bid an overdue though anticlimactic farewell to Louisiana.[1] Packing up the unit with its 42 officers and 601 enlisted men proved no small task.[2] The optimistic believed Texas stood as their final test before Europe. A minority theorized that the Texas move gave the army the means to snuff out the unit, or at least banish it into obscurity. Regardless, eager for new opportunities, most of the men seemed glad to leave Camp Claiborne.

Paul Bates prepared his battalion for the move to Texas, but had some unfinished business. On July 14 he awarded eight officers, including himself, Harrison, and Barbour, and twenty-eight enlisted men the American Defense Service Medal. To qualify, the individual had to have twelve months of honorable service sometime between September 8, 1939, and December 7, 1941.[3] On July 23, Bates awarded 239 Good Conduct medals to his enlisted soldiers. Harrison, familiar with Bates's incessant muttering about tanker behavior, noticed the battalion commander's surprise that so many met the criteria, but let the matter go.[4] McBurney knew his father would be surprised.

Camp Claiborne held good memories and signaled a bright future for Ivan Harrison. Life had changed for him in ways the savvy, but soft-spoken officer could never have predicted. During the 1943 maneuvers, a letter from the War Department declared that Harrison would replace his gold bars with the silver ones of a first lieutenant, his promotion effective May 7.[5] Word traveled through the unit, but a surprised Harrison said nothing, maintaining the decorum of the best the army had. He thought his commendation from 5th Group for his tactical performance may have played a factor.

While on furlough in Detroit around Christmas 1942,[6] Ivan Harrison met the beautiful Juanita Edwards. The Detroit native possessed a scorched past that engulfed her.[7] Edwards, the daughter of a loving father and graceful mother with a rich heritage claiming French as well as American Indian blood, enjoyed only brief childhood happiness. As an adult, Juanita favored her mother's smooth complexion and stood four feet eleven inches tall. She spoke in captivating sweet, soft tones that drove men to distraction—including Ivan Harrison.[8] The army officer had developed a taste for Hollywood-style sirens,[9] hazardous shoals for most men. Officers with money proved ideal prey. Harrison soon tired of their game. He could not resist Detroit's pure Juanita Edwards.

According to some, Ivan and Juanita had known one another as children in the neighborhood. He recalled giving the little girl candy. In one of his last memories he could see her sitting in a wagon, looking up at him, beaming. It struck him as a rare moment because sadness seemed to shroud the girl. He never thought he would see her again.[10] Few knew the tragedy that had befallen Juanita and her four siblings. Their parents, James and Flossie Edwards, a couple very much in love, enjoyed an uncommon closeness with their four children. They soon expected their fifth child, a thrill for all. James labored long hours building the new family home with a store below. Without notice, he fell ill, contracted pneumonia, and died suddenly. Flossie's happiness passed with him. In 1923, two months after James's death the three-year-old Juanita watched her despondent mother give birth to their final child. She named the healthy girl Wesley, her dead husband's middle name.

Flossie remarried soon after, possibly prompted by loneliness, maybe desperate for help with the house, store, and five little children.[11] The marriage proved a mistake. Her inept alcoholic husband further burdened her. Flossie, still grief-stricken over the loss of

James, took her own life. Six-year-old Juanita heard rumors of an apparent pill overdose in the whispers that follow unspeakable tragedies. As the alcoholic lost their home and all James had worked for, family stepped in and planned to separate the two brothers and three sisters. In an unexpected move, Juanita's mother's brother, James Doss, and his wife, Silvia, scooped up the young brood to keep the family intact. But the Dosses panicked, unsure if a childless couple could care for so many little ones. They packed up the five Edwards children and sent them to live with relatives in the South. Silvia Doss could not reconcile their decision and brought the youngsters back to Detroit. Though the children reunited, Juanita never felt secure. Where would they send her next? Would she wake up one day to find her aunt and uncle gone, too, she would wonder. She stayed close to her family and kept a watch over her siblings, especially the fearless and outspoken Wesley.[12]

Gregarious yet demure, Juanita Edwards dated many young men and had a large number of male friends. But the night the twenty-two-year-old reconnected with Ivan Harrison, she stepped out from the safety her aunt and uncle had provided. In her easy style, she slipped out to meet friends, wearing an unfussy evening frock with cheeks, lids, and lips colored simply, but to perfection. She rolled her long, black hair to rival any Hollywood coif. Harrison saw Edwards. Smitten with the young woman still cloaked in some measure of mystery, Harrison ratcheted up his charm. He made her laugh unlike the other boys. Edwards studied his uniform and found herself taken by not just the handsome and charismatic man making a fool of himself, but by the buttons and bars on the well-tailored jacket on Ivan's slim but muscled frame. A military man and officer, no less, she thought.

Love seemed certain. Their brief courtship continued via postal carrier and soon turned more permanent. Juanita traveled south to marry Ivan, escorted by Silvia as any proper surrogate mother would. When they married on March 8, 1943, Ivan wore his army pinks and greens and Juanita stood by him, calm and self-assured, in a tailored suit. With nowhere suitable to stay near Camp Claiborne, the couple decided Juanita would return to Detroit with Silvia.[13] The dashing six-foot-three Harrison took his tiny bride in his arms. They lingered on the train platform. As Harrison readied for this trip to Texas by rail, no one realized the one-day train ride would change their lives.

It seemed a massive undertaking to move a tank battalion from Camp Claiborne to Camp Hood, but Bates saw it as their last ring of fire before combat. As Harrison prepared his platoon, he tried to imagine warfare. How did one fight his way through foreign lands firing at a concealed enemy while he unleashed his arsenal at the invaders? He remained dubious of the sanitized version of war presented by the papers. He understood they would fight side-by-side with white units, which they had done with surprising success in the maneuvers. But the fighting in Italy seemed surreal. Hollywood's rendition failed to convince him of bloodless conflict. He had an idea of war's true character. If a round scored a direct hit on a tank, the crew could be blown apart or, worse, burned to death. He dared tell no one of his concerns, but figured others found themselves in the same quandary.

Harrison and much of the battalion had kept abreast of world events while at Camp Claiborne. Paperboys covered the post selling the *Chicago Sun-Times* and other major newspapers like the *Houston Chronicle* and the New Orleans *Times-Picayune*.[14] With paper boys an improbable occurrence in an area occupied by black soldiers,[15] a discarded broadsheet would suffice. Harrison, a voracious reader, consumed every word. He would press the importance to stay informed with his peers and his men. He followed the Marines from Guadalcanal and read about their movements from bloody island to bloody island. They seemed destined to take Japan itself, though given the blood-letting on both sides, it would not be anytime soon. He knew the men worried about the army sending the 761st to the Pacific, but did not share their concern.

The fight for Europe entranced everyone. As their Claiborne departure approached, Italy grabbed everyone's attention. The Associated Press reported heavy fighting, as excitement filled the post. Following Mussolini's fall from power on July 25, 1943, Germany continued to fight alongside Italian forces. Axis units heavily opposed the Allied landings at Sicily. The invasion and move toward the mainland proved costly for both sides, though headlines remained optimistic. The *New York Times* bolstered yet cautioned the home front proclaiming "Finest Allied Army Leads Invasion of Sicily; Five Hundred Thousand Tough, Skilled and Confident Troops Were Ready."[16] Neither the 761st nor Americans at home read about the tough lessons learned in the aftermath of the flawed amphibious landing and the fierce fighting that followed.

Bates liked that his men fed their minds and curiosities with area news and papers from some of the nation's greatest cities. Yet he did not like the array of black papers that made their way onto post and into his men's hands. He found the headlines sensationalized. They made his men anxious and he could see why. Some reports disrupted their training. Though some content intrigued him, pointless hyperbole angered him. Bates decided to rid the battalion of the black press—no small feat. He told Taffy Rosen about taking the papers. "You can't do that," she said. "I have to do it. Let them catch me," he responded. They dropped the matter.[17]

Hard-won success in Africa and an attempt to enter the European continent through the back door suggested considerable Allied action in Europe. The 761st, save for Bates, had no idea the army had little more than the units still training stateside to throw at Germany and Japan. Most available units waited on alert for pending operations or had already shipped out. As of December 31, 1943, the U.S. Army projected seven available tank battalions, three of which belonged to the 5th Tank Group. According to an Army Ground Forces memorandum dated January 18, 1943, "It is believed this pool is not sufficient to meet possible requirements."[18]

Bates assigned his logistics officer, First Lieutenant Philip W. Latimer, as the battalion advance agent. Latimer left for Camp Hood September 9 to coordinate final arrangements for the main body. Latimer, a life-long Texan, gave Bates hope for the battalion's future at Hood.[19] Latimer had only been the battalion's logistician for a brief time. The math prodigy came from a small town in north Texas called Detroit. At first, the scholar corrected people's pronunciation. "DEE-troit," he would say, slowly, only to hear, "Yeah, Detroit." Despite his unmistakable accent, soldiers from his first day at basic training through his arrival at Camp Claiborne assumed the fair-haired young man had come from Michigan.

Latimer graduated from Baylor University. As a student, what Latimer lacked in money, he made up for in hard work. He had a job in the women's dormitory where he met Louise Stringer, an only child from Lumberton, Texas.[20] The campus newspaper the *Daily Lariat* had something for everyone at Baylor, including a gossip column. The February 14, 1939, Valentine's Day issue, revealed a budding romance between Latimer and Stringer. On December 10, 1940, the paper announced the planned union of the math major and music major.[21]

After his 1940 graduation, Latimer considered himself fortunate to secure a teaching position at Streetman High School. He
recalled his lean teen years. Philip's father
had managed a large farm, but his employ-
er cut his poistion as the economy ground
to a halt. Philip Latimer kept the family's
struggles to himself, but his experience
served as the foundation of his good-
natured generosity.22

Philip Latimer. (*Joe
Wilson, Jr.*)

Philip and Louise married in her parents' living room in 1941. They took their
vows, side-by-side. She stood in a fitted,
elegant navy blue suit. War still seemed a
European matter to those in rural Texas, but the army drafted Philip
in one of the first groups called to serve. It granted the teacher, football coach, and girls' basketball coach time to wrap up the school
year before he reported for duty. Despite his degree and status as an
educator, Latimer served as a private in the 3rd Armored Division
and as a sergeant in the 7th Armored Division. The army reviewed his
educational background and test scores and sped him through Armor
OCS at Fort Knox. After commissioning in October 1942, he served
as the mortar platoon leader at the 12th Armored Division. He
enjoyed his work. But by early 1943, the army sought to get officers
in the correct assignments, and interviewed lieutenants to serve with
black armored units. Latimer considered himself a "patriotic person"
and saw himself as "extremely qualified to do this." He had grown
up around black families and had no negative views regarding race.
As the fifth of six children and a college graduate, Philip Latimer of
DEE-troit, Texas, arrived at the 761st open-minded, confident, and
thankful.23

The 5th Tank Group and its three battalions vacated Camp
Claiborne. Bates handpicked his men for the transit and assigned
Harrison as the train quartermaster for the first of two trains.
Harrison's train also carried the 5th Tank Group Headquarters and
Headquarters detachment, the Headquarters and Headquarters
Company for the 761st as well as the 761st Service Company. The
second train carried the three lettered tank companies, Able, Baker,
and Charlie, as well as the medical detachment.24

Richard English moved with the 761st. Between the unit's Organization Day and late June, English left the 784th and moved to his coveted tank battalion.[25] He saw himself as the luckiest guy at Camp Claiborne. Bates remained dubious of English and his appearance, but welcomed him, assigned him, and left the effective officer to work as he saw fit. Age and leadership skills summed up the common ground between the two men. They spoke when necessary. While the other officers avoided Dick English, the enlisted men flocked to the approachable lieutenant. Los Angeles native Bates could not decipher the man. Maybe the controversial academic wanted to establish an educational program for the soldiers.[26] Maybe he just did not trust white men. Bates did not trust many white men, either. Maybe they had more in common than he had thought.

If Camp Claiborne had not nailed it down, it went to Texas. The battalion loaded completely—all personnel, gear, weapons, vehicles, and the battalion's full complement of Stuart tanks. Tank transportation had improved since George Patton backed his tanks off the rails himself to get his unit to the fight during World War I. Bates ordered the loading of personnel and equipment completed by 1 P.M. September 13. Along with the tanks, the unit loaded half-tracks and all other tactical vehicles with "all armament in place, with covers."[27] Soldiers placed antiaircraft and machine guns inside the tanks. Bates wanted the tanks fully loaded to conserve space and time. The intricate plan made for an easier transition once in Texas. The men would move their gear, roll the tanks and other vehicles off the cars, and occupy their new area quickly and easily, ready for their first assignment.

Paul Bates directed the move as if he had done it many times before. He probably thought moving all of Camp Claiborne or the city of Los Angeles could not have been much more difficult. With the locomotive ready to leave, Camp Claiborne's transportation officer halted their departure and told Bates it appeared they would reroute the train. Before Bates could act, word came from Washington ordering the train to proceed to Camp Hood as planned.[28]

Frank Mayhorn saw opportunity where others saw dust. As editor of the *Temple Daily Telegram* in Temple, Texas, he created the War Projects Committee of the Temple Chamber of Commerce with the sole, albeit veiled, purpose of pulling the army into central Texas. The thirty-seven-year-old Mayhorn's interest lay in Bell County, an agricultural region with a smattering of disjointed towns like Temple and Killeen, which had teetered on economic collapse throughout the 1930s. In February 1941, the army had more than forty new camps under construction, though none in Texas. At the same time, Mayhorn learned through his Washington, D.C., contacts that the army had plans for a massive undertaking—a camp of at least 75,000 acres where four or five divisions could train.[29]

Given the installation's proposed size and Bell County's terrain and weather, Mayhorn figured central Texas topped any list. The army had enjoyed the advantages of building on federal land as it had in central Louisiana with Camp Claiborne and a host of other posts, but Bell County had more than enough cheap land to accommodate the army's needs. The army made its choice during the fall of 1941: Valley Hills, northwest of Waco and nowhere near Bell County.[30]

Mayhorn received the news and wasted no time. He jumped in his vehicle and sped to Fort Sam Houston in San Antonio to meet with Major General Richard Donovan, commander of the army's Eighth Corps area. The men greeted one another, with Donovan ready to spar. The general scowled, "You don't think much of the United States Army, do you?" Mayhorn tossed the army's site study choosing Valley Hills on Donovan's desk. "I don't think much of this report. But if I weren't thinking a lot about the United States, I wouldn't be down here," he retorted. Mayhorn had Donovan's attention and made his case.[31] On January 15, the site moved to tiny Killeen.

Mayhorn may have had big dreams, but he did not have a patch of dirt to sell a determined army. Most of Bell County belonged to families that had farmed the lands for generations. Like a snake oil salesman Mayhorn planned to get them to sell their land. Those who sold did so with painful hesitation and nowhere to go.[32] For as little as $33 per acre, families left behind their homes with the faint promise the new camp would pack up and leave at war's end.[33]

With the unfortunate task soon completed, 832 tracts of land changed hands: the army purchased 525 outright, while the remaining owners stood fast. The taking of private land by federal authority increased as war drew nearer. The passage of the Second War Powers Act strengthened the government's position on eminent domain, allowing the army to acquire the remaining parcels. Mayhorn's promise of a bright future displaced three hundred families, taking 108,000 acres of ancestral land.[34] Local families believed they had lost a way of life. Soon after Mayhorn had the land he needed, the army and thousands of workers descended on the area to build the new training camp.

As the train arrived, the tracks ran some distance above the post. Paul Bates took in the panoramic view and liked what he saw.[35] As he looked down, he felt reinvigorated by the possibilities that had become somewhat stagnant at Camp Claiborne. When the 761st stepped off the train on September 15, 1943, one year after Camp Hood's official debut, they arrived on a well-established post that had grown to 160,000 acres and hummed with efficiency.[36] Ivan Harrison looked around as he did the day he arrived at Camp Claiborne. He saw the army and its engineers had learned valuable lessons in installation construction. The tankers stepped into a virtual military city of 95,000, Camp Hood's peak population. Harrison noted the occasional tent, but soldiers would live in their respective wooden longhouse-style barracks. Officers bedded in smaller framed structures.

In addition to operating as an aggressor force for training tank destroyers, the battalion reported to Camp Hood for "advance armor training." The term seemed to imply the army would school the unit in higher-echelon tank tactics. But no advanced armor school existed anywhere and Hood had no tank training, the post's world revolved around the tank destroyer. It had no other mission. The 761st would gain additional experience through its role as aggressor—for tank destroyer units.

For the 761st, Camp Hood stood for a bright future. Bates first noted the "excellent" battalion area and gravitated toward the vast and gently rolling training fields. The installation's senior leadership welcomed Bates. It seemed the battalion now held a position of import and top officers included him and his staff in meetings and decision making. But Bates optimism waned within the first few days. Whereas Camp Claiborne allowed for unit autonomy, Bates grew frustrated by the "endless" "Camp Regulations" and "Training Brigade Regulations."[37]

Some of the men of the 761st seemed to have a better if not more sardonic outlook than their commander. The weekly *Mad Tanker* appeared during October 1943. Edited by "The Frantic One" and published by the Special Services Office, this wacky news sheet reported everything of interest to the men. Sports took the lead with the 761st trouncing the 614th Tank Destroyer Battalion, 71–20 on the basketball court. The Frantic One relayed the talent search for the current stage play under Pop Gates's watchful eye. The internal news source also discussed an upcoming reorganization. According to The Frantic One, "Well, chums, you know what that means too. It means more and more maintenance."[38]

What Bates and his men may not have realized, Headquarters Army Ground Forces had a great deal of interest in tank destroyer training and in the aggressors units helping to provide that training. Lieutenant General Lesley McNair directed Army Ground Force inspectors to scrutinize what seemed every aspect of maneuvering units at Camp Hood, sometimes without telling the unit commander. Soon after the 761st arrived, inspectors observed a platoon leader in Baker Company "who failed to take advantage of the tactical situation as a means of furthering the training of his platoon." In contrast, they observed a class given by Bates, where they noted interested and enthusiastic officers and reported that Bates "left no error uncorrected."[39] Paul Bates understood the battalion could improve, but the inspection of his men without his knowledge angered him.

Battalion operations kept Bates busy. "So much happiness for me, the days seem like a few hours," he wrote. The matter of Taffy Rosen boosted yet drained him and placed more than the two lovers in jeopardy. She insisted on abstinence until he resolved the matter of his marriage, but relented.[40] He wrote to her faithfully and incessantly. He repeated his appreciation of her role as confidante. She saw love's promise. He showered her with sweet words and in the same sentence spoke to her as his most trusted lieutenant. Letters remained undated with a simple day of the week or time at the top right. Where Rosen proved brief, Bates wrote pages of his love, their future together, and always his work. "I want you to be happy, to share my day when it ends and my nite."[41]

Rosen had started to refer to Paul Bates as her husband, something he implored her not to do. Though Bates often complimented Rosen on the beauty of her feelings, he knew the extramarital affair, if it became public, would end his army career. He grew concerned about a court-martial and asked for Rosen's discretion. Other officers had been disciplined for similar acts. At best, he would lose his precious 761st.[42]

Rosen's passion for Bates, as well as drama, coupled with his marriage often proved too much for her to handle alone. Passages describing their stolen time together probably made matters worse for the young nurse. The distance left her despondent. She let loose with written tirades of varying intensity. He calmly reassured her of their future together, but worried Rosen's hopelessness might lead to suicide or a turn to drugs or alcohol.[43] Bates referred to her as his "one and only" and encouraged her to do the same with little effect. Rosen understood his words, but as Bates continued to write of his work, she saw his happiness lay with the 761st. Embittered, she detested an army she saw as a lie and remained dependent on a mar-

Paul Bates and Taffy Rosen. (*Taffy Bates*)

ried man ten years her senior, two hundred miles away, with a mission that seemed to move him more than his love for her. Rosen had not planned on a Paul Bates. Her dreams as a battlefield nurse, saving soldiers as shells exploded around her, faded as her confusion over Bates intensified.[44]

While the 761st looked to him as the man who would lead them to Europe, few realized his indiscretion posed more of a threat to their collective future than the backward Camp Hood or an enemy overseas.

Ten

Big Gun, More Steel

OCTOBER 1943 BROUGHT COOLER WEATHER AND A CHANGE that would forever impact the 761st. By a War Department Order dated October 27, the army reorganized the battalion, as the *Mad Tanker* reported three days earlier. The 761st lost its "light" designation when it took on three companies of the top-grade medium M4 Sherman tanks.[1] Crews increased to five men from four and the battalion gained a company. In addition to Able, Baker, and Charlie companies in their new Shermans, the battalion added "D" or Dog Company that retained the lighter M5 Stuarts and became the battalion's main reconnaissance arm.[2] The authorized strength of the 761st increased to 39 officers, 3 warrant officers, and 713 enlisted men. Bates watched as new soldiers poured in to fill the vacancies, but many lacked the training of Bates's core battalion.[3]

German advances already had made the U.S. tanks obsolescent. American updates improved the platform, but the U.S. continued to seem a step behind the enemy. The army designated the Sherman a medium tank with a weight of more than thirty tons, whereas the light Stuart tipped the scales at just more than sixteen tons.[4]

For Paul Bates, a battalion of Shermans could compete on the battlefields of Europe and a company of M5 Stuarts for reconnaissance gave him versatility and speed. He saw the 761st as yet another step closer to a combat assignment.

William McBurney marveled at the new tank, knowing the 75 mm gun belonged to him. He felt great pride, as did the other soldiers, that the army entrusted them with such an exquisite weapon. He practiced his pitch to Teddy Windsor to get extra time in the driver's seat. After all, the army had first trained him as a driver, and he saw himself as good a tank driver as gunner and for McBurney that meant superior. Windsor could handle egos. He needed a versatile, likeable, and loyal man like McBurney, underscoring why the two had been together so long.

McBurney scaled the new vehicle. As he climbed around the Sherman's hull and weaved his way in and out of the hatches the tank seemed much larger than the Stuart. The medium Sherman stood nearly two feet taller and a foot wider. The length increased a little more than four feet. The interior seemed almost spacious by comparison. McBurney rapped on the hull with his knuckles. He could hear the additional steel as the sound echoed. Frontal armor ranged from about two and a half to three inches thick and dropped to fewer than two inches on the less vulnerable sides, top, and rear. This vastly improved the tank's last line of defense. Many Stuarts carried just one and a half armored inches at their exposed front and the veneer on their turret, often the enemy's primary target, he had heard.[5]

The firepower excited the gunner. Whereas the Stuart carried three Browning .30 caliber machine guns, the Sherman had two .30s and a .50 caliber capable of fending off aircraft or buzzsawing through woods and walls. As McBurney stood in the tank's turret by the 75 mm main gun, he studied the commander's hatch with its added rings of rectangular glass above him. Vision blocks, Teddy told him, to help them see outside a buttoned-up tank. Hatch. Deck. Bulkhead. The Sherman even had five periscopes for the crew. The army adopted naval parlance for its tanks because of their roots with Britain's then-First Lord of the Admiralty Winston Churchill. McBurney's ring of glass stood as his porthole on the world when fighting inside their steel craft.[6]

The battalion had surpassed the Stuart's reported maximum speed of 36 mph and pushed it closer to 45 mph with a range of 70 miles. The Sherman, despite its added weight, had an improved range over the Stuart of 120 miles, but a rated speed of a sluggish 24 mph, an estimate in McBurney's opinion. Given its mission in support of infantry on foot, the army deemed the speed acceptable. William McBurney figured they could kick up the pace. He wanted to fly across European

A 761st Battalion M4A3 Sherman in France in 1944. The 75 mm main gun is clearly shown, along with the .50 machine gun mounted on top of the turret and the .30 machine gun in a ball mount in the hull. (*National Archives*)

battlefields, still unaware of the hazards that awaited American tanks. Depending on the tank, a Continental R975-C1 motor more than doubled the 200 horsepower of the Stuart's twin Cadillac engines. Those lucky enough to secure an M4A3 found a Ford GAA V8, the first dual overhead cam with four valves per cylinder. The engine roared with 500 horsepower (gross) and squeaked out about eight-tenths of a mile per gallon. For the war, a number of companies manufactured engines to power U.S. tanks. McBurney heard that Ford modified an aircraft engine for his Sherman.

If the tank took a hit—a substantial, disabling blow—and the crew did not have its hatches as an escape option, they would exit through the lowest point of the tank. One by one they would slip out and shimmy under tons of potentially crushing steel. McBurney, though never a fan of the belly hatch, knew a catastrophic event might provide incentive.

Teddy Windsor protected his copy of the Sherman's technical manual. Just like the Stuart's handbook, the TM 9-759 for the Sherman M4A3 contained most, if not all, the information he and his four other crew members needed to keep it fighting. He thumbed through and noted: commander in turret right rear behind the main gunner who sat forward of him; the new loader would sit to his left ready to retrieve shells for McBurney's main gun. The driver sat low in the hull on the front left, with the assistant driver/bow gunner to his right.[7] Windsor found his round padded seat comfortable though he did not have much use for it or the safety belts. He envisioned a smooth transition.

With the tank overhaul came a personnel shake-up. Inbound soldiers rounded out the tank crews. Officers shifted and a number migrated between the 761st and the 784th after it arrived at Camp Hood. In the exchange, the 761st gained its first black staff officer, New Orleans native First Lieutenant Albert J. Leiteau. With experience as the 784th's personnel officer, Leiteau became the 761st S-1, the battalion adjutant. The transfers also altered battalion staffing in a way Harrison had not thought possible. Upon arrival at Camp Hood, of forty-two officer slots,[8] black officers filled fewer than half. While the army battled a shortage of personnel across the force, the 761st emerged from the reassignments with black officers outnumbering their white counterparts (twenty-two to twenty) for the first time. Bates concentrated his trained tanker elite in his line companies, Able, Baker, and Charlie. His technicians and administrative whizzes filled the headquarters and service companies. The new Dog Company, with its intelligence-gathering mission, formed November 2 under Floridian Captain Arthur E. Campbell of St. Augustine.[9]

As he had at Claiborne, Bates met with his company commanders and staff officers. He understood the impact of these meetings. Bates saw these gatherings as a "chief source of self expression. . . . I must out think all others, advise, guide, order."[10] Bates could mold the 761st into anything he desired. His decision to move Ivan Harrison to command Headquarters Company caught the officer by surprise. Snatched from his tank platoon, the new headquarters company commander now headed a 105 mm howitzer assault platoon, an 81 mm mortar platoon, and a reconnaissance platoon.

Bates had made Lieutenant Irvin McHenry of Leavenworth, Kansas, the battalion's first black company commander when he took on Charlie Company on June 20, 1943, shortly after the unit's return from the maneuvers.[11] Bates placed Sam Brown in command of Able Company one month after he promoted Harrison.[12] Ivan Harrison probably offered brotherly congratulations while Brown probably talked circles around his tall, cool-headed friend. He probably chatted away about Harrison's wife, Juanita, and their first baby due in a few months.[13]

The battalion endured more change. To compensate for any manpower shortfall given the added requirements of the new Shermans, smack in the middle of training, 128 enlisted "fillers" arrived from ARTC, or Army Recruit Training Command, as the result of a special order dated December 30, 1943, from Recruit Training Command headquarters. They landed like time travelers from another era. Their numbers upped the 761st's manpower statistics by 18.5 percent. But the new, untrained bodies gave Harrison and Bates headaches they did not need. The battalion worked to absorb the scores of men. Bates met with the staff and looked to Ivan Harrison for a solution to the invading force. With scant understanding of his new duties, Harrison would make 128 unusable soldiers into something the battalion could employ.[14]

Ivan Harrison had kept abreast of his friends in the 93rd Infantry Division. The coverage of the black media darling on its "Big-Time Maneuvers," suggested the army had determined the unit's path. As the 761st moved to Texas, the army sent the 93rd to Camp Young, California, for additional training. Harrison had read what he considered sensitive information in one of the black papers. He recalled the *Pittsburgh Courier* and the *Chicago Defender* had sent reporters to California to report on the unit, whose overseas deployment seemed imminent. Its West Coast location signaled a Pacific destination.[15] "Poor bastards," probably ran through Harrison's mind.

Life as a tank leader ended as Harrison knew it. He traded, or Bates traded on his behalf, the relative autonomy of the training fields and command of his five-tank war machine. While he had combat platoons with complements of weapons under him, he did not command them directly. He had platoon leaders who answered to him, but few knew how little power he wielded. While he found his title intoxicating, he felt alone and isolated. Ivan Harrison saw himself as the Prince of Paper. As Headquarters Company commander, all battalion disciplinary actions fell to him. Harrison thought himself the least likely choice for the job and developed a persona to go with the unenviable task. Tankers like McBurney saw they had a new marshal in town and in no time dubbed him "Court-Martial Slim." The name stuck.[16]

For a commander like Bates, with his eyes on Europe, the robust disciplinary system, while simple, swift, and harsh, "could be arbitrary and capricious." With no appeals, court-martial panels completed a matter and life moved forward. The Articles of War dating to 1920 and the Manual for Courts-Martial, revised in 1943, guided commanders. With military lawyers or judge advocates general

rare—the army required four years of on-the-job lawyering if it permanently designated an attorney to act as such for the army—the system moved as commanders determined.[17] Bates decided if he would
hold a special or summary court-martial, appointed the panel, and
handed it over to Harrison to hold the proceedings, often the next
evening after training. Weekends proved ideal for courts-martial.
Bates wanted transgressions dealt with quickly. He insisted on the
highest standards of good order and discipline. A court-martial might
take an hour or two. The panel often handed down an unforgiving
maximum sentence as a warning to the rest of the battalion.
McBurney saw his friends sent to the guardhouse, but had no idea
Bates and other officers could prearrange outcomes. Harrison, neither conductor nor puppet master, knew what the men thought of
him. He saw McBurney's eyes glower with disdain.[18] While his unde-
served reputation ate at him, he would never betray Bates's trust.

The 93rd's almost certain departure bolstered the 761st. The army
seemed to look past race. McBurney recalled General Benjamin O.
Davis's comment at the maneuvers: There was no race in soldiering
and no one had devised a weapon to detect skin color. He agreed. Did
it matter what race pulled the trigger to kill an enemy?

More in the army asked similar questions, though for differing reasons. The argument over intellect and education, a challenge regardless of race, had been torpedoed by units like the 761st, with its collection of high school and college graduates, valedictorians and high
scorers on the AGCT. The unit's performance in varied training environments had exceeded most expectations. But questions lingered on
the race's ability to match an enemy on the battlefield, though black
soldiers had proved themselves many times in past conflicts—as
William McBurney's and Russell Guthrie's fathers had done with the
Harlem Hellfighters during the Great War. Bates would not allow his
men to fall victim to the doubt of outsiders. For Bates the opportunity to portray an aggressor force would end any debate, at least
regarding the 761st.

Camp Hood existed for the sole purpose of tank destroyer training.
Tank destroyers massed on the battlefield to destroy enemy tanks.[19]
It seemed straightforward to the exacting Lesley McNair.

McNair's roots lay in field artillery, and he retained the perspective
of an artillery officer when he experimented with antitank defenses as

A column of M10 Tank Destroyers responding to the German Ardennes offensive in 1944. The vehicle used the same chassis as the M4 Sherman tank and has a longer-barreled 75 mm main gun. (*National Archives*)

early as 1937.[20] By 1940, despite his fervent urging for an adequate antitank weapon, manpower challenges proved more pressing for the army. McNair, a man who seemed adept at getting his way, unleashed his frustration as the nation moved closer to war. "It is beyond belief that so little could be done on the [antitank] question in view of all that has happened and is happening abroad. I for one have missed no opportunity to hammer for something real in the way of anti-tank defense, but so far have gotten nowhere. I have no reason now to feel encouraged but can only hope this apathy will not continue indefinitely."[21]

Lieutenant Colonel Andrew D. Bruce headed the early antitank planning board for the War Department's office of the Assistant Chief of Staff for Organization and Training, or G-3. He conducted studies and created a prototype weapon, making the best use of the armaments available. His self-propelled M3, a 75 mm gun mounted on a half-track,[22] debuted at the 1941 Louisiana Maneuvers, where tankers accused officials of rigging the rules to favor the tank destroyer. While the battlefield newcomer could score a kill from umpires with ease, a tank had to practically run over a tank destroyer to obtain a similar recognition.[23]

McNair saw what he wanted in Louisiana and pushed the army to move forward with tank destroyer plans. Tank destroyer performance in the Carolina Maneuvers convinced George Marshall. In late 1941 the army chief of staff activated the Tank Destroyer Force and ordered the Tank Destroyer Tactical Firing Center established. He placed Bruce, a rising star, in charge. The War Department ordered the immediate activation of fifty-three tank battalions and placed them directly under the army's General Headquarters reserve and McNair.[24] Tank destroyer units migrated from Fort Meade, Maryland, where Patton and Eisenhower made their armor prophecies in 1920, to Camp Hood, Texas. The 761st would prepare the tank destroyer fleet to destroy enemy armor and survive to fight again. The tank destroyers baffled the new 761st aggressors at first.

McBurney did not know the care designers took in engineering the tank destroyer. In 1942, Buick looked at the Christie suspension but deemed it archaic and chose a torsion bar suspension instead.[25] Engineers in the U.S. agonized over elements that would give a tank destroyer the speed, maneuverability, and firepower it needed. William McBurney saw hatchless, tank-like vehicles. They sat open with no protection from an enemy round or a pelting rain. Some tank destroyer units towed what looked like artillery pieces. Unknown to McBurney and his fellow tankers, Bruce and his colleagues favored the self-propelled destroyer, which the army could drive where needed. It made sense given the strategy under development. McNair, with his artillery roots never far from the surface, favored the towed variety.[26] Marshall sided with Bruce, but acquiesced to McNair. The army permitted roughly half its tank destroyers as towed vehicles.[27]

McBurney had seen more than a few tank destroyers, but nothing like the collection of units at Camp Hood. The army designed a number of self-propelled tank destroyers to look much like a tank. In fact, the M10 with its three-inch gun used a Sherman M4 tank chassis. It could reach speeds of 30 mph, just a hair faster than a fully armored and outfitted Sherman tank. McBurney heard that the army soon determined the M10 too slow for its mission. He eyed the M10's cousin, the M18 Hellcat.[28] He liked the name. It sported a 76 mm gun with an open turret and could race to nearly 60 mph, a swiftness needed for its dangerous duty. Once the tank destroyers fired on enemy tanks, survival depended, in part, on speeding away from the target and beyond the reach of the enemy's accurate, long-range main gun. Maybe they would race to a different firing position from which to engage another hostile objective. Regardless, the strategy seemed crazy even to the lead-footed William McBurney.

Addressing confusion like McBurney's became a part of Andrew Bruce's duties. Some days he felt he spent more time explaining the tank destroyer than preparing them to kill German tanks. To his dismay, one instructor wrote: "Sometimes I think we are somewhat screwy in our thinking. Our tanks are made with thick armor but their prime mission is to destroy personnel. When a slugging match is evident we endeavor to let them slide out and let antitank guns take over. But the tank destroyer built to destroy tanks is comparatively thin skinned with only its agility to protect it. However, we all agree that a high velocity hit against a tank or tank destroyer will penetrate, so armor in many cases is somewhat valueless."[29] Despite Bruce's efforts, the German's 88 mm gun reigned as the unanswered tank killer on the battlefield.

McBurney, like men with much more experience than he, found it difficult to believe lightweight tank destroyer opponents would hunt tanks instead of the better-protected and more experienced armored divisions and separate tank battalions like the 761st. He knew of nothing in the U.S. inventory that could match the power and range of the German 88 mm, but assumed that he would find a way to defeat it. If one 88 mm round could destroy a Sherman, he could not imagine what it could do to the lightly coated tank destroyer fleet, and did not want to be around to find out. The tank destroyer motto, "Seek, Strike, Destroy," lacked the crucial element of survival, "Run like Hell!" in McBurney's opinion. But no one expected annihilation.

Though the army published FM 18-5, the Tank Destroyer Field Manual, it neglected to adequately explain the effective employment of the tank destroyer to battlefield commanders. In 1943, combat in North Africa brought disaster. Instead of massing the tank destroyer battalion's firepower against the enemy, commanders saw guns up for grabs. To them, the advantages of mobile guns in support of their smaller unit formations outweighed a battalion tank blast at a Panzer unit. They broke down the battalions to the basic platoon to support their ground forces, rendering the tank destroyer anything but. Ignorance of the new weapon and improper employment proved deadly. The Germans mauled U.S. units and crushed their tank destroyers in the early battle for Kasserine Pass in Tunisia.[30]

Tank destroyers bore the brunt of the blame for their ineffective performance, but the army could not ignore the command failures. It placed George Patton in charge of II Corps in March 1943 in time for the Battle of El Guettar.[31] Under Patton the 601st Tank Destroyer

Battalion fought as one according to doctrine and repelled a large Panzer contingent. The Germans retreated and suffered heavy losses. But the 601st success came at a steep price: the unit's casualty rate pushed 60 percent. Patton had a war to win and no time for wound-licking. With its unacceptable losses, he saw the 601st engagement as a failure and refused to credit his tank destroyers. He formed his opinion of tank destroyers during that battle, and like many commanders found his units' organic antitank assets more than adequate.[32]

While Kasserine Pass caused McNair concern, the brutality suffered in North Africa might foreshadow what the U.S. could expect when it invaded Europe. No matter what Bruce published, McNair understood the mind of the commander in the field: he would use all available assets to win. Textbook use of a tank destroyer battalion or any unit seemed of little interest to battle-hardened commanders. Reports from the North African front went from demoralizing to shocking. The tumult and confusion of combat so terrified soldiers some refused to leave transports and hid from the carnage wherever they could. Entreaties by commanders had little effect. Such information further underscored the need for redesigned training across all branches, albeit a bit late, forcing army leaders to review methods and mistakes to date.[33]

McNair's frustration grew. On January 8, 1943, he addressed the West Point graduating class—at a time when the army and navy accelerated service academy graduations to pump leadership into their forces. McNair, distressed by the reports, spoke honestly with the young men, many of whom would not live to see the end of the war. "Battle results to date serve to emphasize the well-known fact that our troops, when they arrive overseas, are not hard enough and are far from adequately trained. Pearl Harbor stimulated training, but insufficiently. . . . Experience overseas has shown the great importance of physical condition . . . ability to shoot and use weapons . . . and . . . familiarity with the sounds, sights and sensations of combat. Systematic effort is being made to afford the soldier in training an opportunity to encounter every element of battle so far as it is possible to create them artificially."[34]

William McBurney stood like his generation: Battle realism for many equated what Hollywood offered. Camp Claiborne had not changed that for McBurney and many of his fellow tankers in the 761st. Training, regardless of length or intensity, did not change it for the breed needed to win the war.

The U.S. Army turned to British commandos, whose combat experience and training went beyond what the Americans offered. This ground combat instruction extended to tank destroyers. Captain Gordon T. Kimbrell, a U.S. officer and graduate of the British course in commando tactics, provided commando-style training.[35] Tank destroyer personnel ran through an infiltration course as well as one of the first urban combat training scenarios—dismounted from their tank destroyers. Leaders wanted training "to resemble the battlefield rather than the gymnasium."[36]

Kimbrell added another element to his physical training program—live fire. The army agreed to allow live grazing machine gun fire twelve to eighteen inches off the ground while the soldiers crawled in the searing Texas heat to their objectives. Random explosives detonated around them to simulate battlefield conditions. Gunners learned to fire by ear rather than sight.[37]

The extensive physical challenges as well as classroom training of the tank destroyer soldiers outside their vehicles left stretches during which there was little need for aggressor units like the 761st to operate. Bates had hoped for this freedom. The schedule allowed the men to bond with their Shermans, the way they had come to know their Stuarts. Crews had to learn to work as five, not four. The tankers broke open and studied the new TM 9-759. They examined the Sherman and learned their maintenance roles. Drivers worked to master smooth speed over rough terrain, make life-saving turns, and throw the tank into reverse with no notice when danger lay ahead. McBurney had a new gun beckoning for his touch. With the unit's growth, all 761st veterans had new tankers to train.

As the men became acquainted with their Shermans, Bates could not think of a better place to improve skills and build crew and unit cohesion than the open firing areas. While the men enjoyed working with their hand-held weapons, Bates preferred the vast almost unencumbered range where his tanks could rove like buffalo. Paul Bates treated gunnery training like footballs drills. The 761st men scheduled more gunnery practice to hone their skills at Camp Hood than they had at Camp Claiborne. They followed the Armored Force Field Manual for tank gunnery, FM 17-12, like a playbook. Each tank adhered to no fewer than seventeen steps in gunnery training. Though the Sherman's 75 mm gun procedures matched the Stuart's 37 mm steps, Bates ensured each tank went through the tutorials with speed and precision.[38]

William McBurney worked to perfect his aim with the 75 mm gun. He obsessed, adjusting his sights before they moved to the firing range. He would chortle to himself as he enjoyed the somewhat improved visibility in the Sherman.

As the tankers had at Camp Claiborne, the platoon practiced as a unit. The officer in charge of firing, often the platoon leader, had all safety responsibility. As tank commander, Teddy Windsor stood ready to relay the target, its location, and the type of projectile for the shoot. As the loader placed a fresh round in the gun's breech, McBurney sighted his target through his scope. Concentrating, his lips parted and his jaw dropped each time he waited for the command. He reminded himself not to hold his breath or move his hand to wipe the sweat dripping in his eyes. He blinked hard to keep his vision clear. Windsor gave the command to fire. Shell casings landed in the bin to McBurney's right.

Russell Guthrie sat ready in his tank. He sighted the target. The tank commander's order would come: "Fire over." Guthrie would fire over the top of the target. Then he would adjust. "Fire under!" came next. He fired beneath the target. Bracketing the target helped to assure a hit. Guthrie's favorite followed, "Fire for effect!" meaning, "Kill the bastard." Just like McBurney and the other gunners, Guthrie sat with his foot hovering over the butterfly, as he called it. When the fire order came, he stomped the butterfly, or foot pedal, flipped the fire switch, and watched his round hit as planned.[39] At first he would let out a little grunt of satisfaction, but as he grew seasoned, he critiqued his work in silence, always striving to improve.

Guthrie knew the rule: Never bracket an enemy tank with high-explosive rounds; just destroy the thing. He figured they would never face a German tank. He could see why the tank destroyers fared so poorly, but he did not think a Sherman, even one crewed by the 761st, would come out on the winning end. He kept his thoughts to himself.

McBurney, Guthrie, and the other gunners moaned when it came time to pass a battery of tank gunner proficiency tests, added pressure with which the other tankers did not contend. Compared to these army-mandated ratings, platoon and company range sessions came as a welcome break.[40] The 761st with its Sherman tanks had the benefit of more than a year's experience in tanks—a lifetime for a soldier in 1943.

Eleven

Face-off

THE TANKERS OF THE 761ST LOVED THEIR SHERMANS. PAUL BATES observed that not one member of the 761st had cared as much about his Stuart as the crews did about the Sherman. Constant admonishments about the condition of the tanks disappeared with the M4's arrival. Some of the men named their tanks like air crews named their aircraft and had the names emblazoned in white on the dark hull. Bates named his tank "Taffy." Other names included "Cool Stud," which reportedly shared its name with the rooster procured by Sergeant Dan Cardell for his Charlie Company tank. Charlie claimed "Cool Stud" as its mascot as did the rest of the 761st—the rooster, not the tank. The tankers had gotten to know Warren Crecy, so it came as no surprise when he named his tank "Crecy." No one could leave out "Big Mamma" or "Black Jack." Russell Guthrie got a kick out of tanks sporting names, each rolling with its own personality.[1]

When the 761st faced off against those tasked with destroying the tank battalion, the combat training scenarios came from the Advanced Unit Training Center. The training brigade coordinator determined when the 761st performed and against which unit. Bates, the perennial teacher, shared his knowledge of armor tactics with his rapt tankers. The men applied their lessons to each engagement, often with swift success. Because the unit could face a self-propelled or a

towed battalion, tactical options increased in number and complexi-
ty, giving the 761st training opportunities it had not experienced at
Camp Claiborne. Before Camp Hood opened, McNair envisioned
experts from Fort Riley and other specialized army training posts
assisting the Tank Destroyer Tactical Firing Center in the areas of
infantry, artillery, cavalry, and reconnaissance.[2] But Andrew Bruce,
promoted to brigadier general as well as major general in 1942, took
a home-grown approach.[3] During November 1943, infantry and
artillery units joined the command and worked alongside tank
destroyers as well as the 761st tanks, simulating battlefield conditions. Bates watched as his men learned to operate with infantry, a
skill central to the unit's mission, but lacking for the separate tank
battalion. Bates had found such training, once a rare luxury, became
routine. The opportunities available to an aggressor unit exceeded his
expectations.

The 761st's proficiency piqued the interest of instructors as well as
the tank destroyer commanders. Bates configured his aggressor force
to meet the nuances of each tactical problem. Whereas a tank
destroyer battalion would go after his men with most of its armament, the 761st might attack minus a company. Tanker maneuver
skills exceeded most challengers, no matter the scenario presented by
the training center.

Bates garnered tremendous satisfaction in each tank's ability to
outmaneuver most tank destroyer battalions. Though similarly configured, a tank destroyer battalion often brought more men and
equipment to a face-off than the 761st—and a fraction of the talent,
the tankers would say. A tank destroyer battalion bustled with 35
officers, 5 warrant officers, and more than 800 enlisted soldiers.[4]
Some battalions boasted larger rolls. Though numbers fluctuated, the
761st carried 37 officers, 3 warrant officers, and 677 men. They
fought in fifty-four medium tanks spread over three combat companies and the headquarters company. Bates's reconnaissance arm of
light Stuarts had seventeen tanks. The battalion maintained six
assault guns and three 81 mm mortars. The service company kept five
tanks in reserve in the case of an out of commission tank.[5]

The tank destroyer battalion also carried six assault guns as well
as at least a dozen armored cars. The attached pioneer platoon—a
combat engineer detachment—kept the tank destroyer unit moving
and stopped the enemy through "small construction and demolition
tasks."[6]

A 761st Tank Battalion crew poses with its M4 Sherman, "Cool Studs Inc." (*Ellsworth G. McConnell Collection*)

The tank destroyer had a friend in Harley-Davidson, which produced motorcycles for tank destroyer advance reconnaissance. The motorcyclists armed with Tommy guns had their own training. Harley-Davidson, like other companies, highlighted its contribution to the war effort. It featured army tank destroyer motorcyclists in its May 1943 edition of its *Enthusiast* magazine: "It is the new hard-hitting, fast moving Tank Destroyer, built to seek out enemy tanks, strike at them in sudden, swift fury and destroy them completely."[7]

Though the 761st bested its tank destroyer opponents in nearly every engagement, Bates explained to his men that aggressors never won—officially. Beyond the tank destroyers' opportunities to train with the finest left stateside at Camp Hood, the army expected much-needed confidence building at this last stop for many before battling the enemy abroad. Defeating an aggressor like the 761st did much to instill self-assurance and a combat spirit. Despite these expectations, Bates did not count humility among his men's strengths. Russell Guthrie hollered from his main gun with the rest of his crew. They could brag to one another about an added victory notch on their tanks, understanding that their unsteady opponents would garner the official win. Accolades for their superb performance also came from outside the battalion. Confidence soared. Tank crews grew tighter and the battalion moved in unison. Guthrie believed no one could stop the 761st—no tank destroyer, and no German Panzer.[8] McBurney saw Guthrie as wild but fearless and he took his cue from the teen veteran. Shy but confident, William McBurney peeked out of his shell. He liked what he saw.

While the Shermans possessed a disadvantage in size and weight when it came to facing a battalion of swift tank destroyers, agile drivers like Willy Devore nimbly outmaneuvered the swifter opponent. Whether the tactical scenario called for a platoon, company, or tank battalion, Bates ran a similar ruse. Tanks rolled out in one direction, but after 400 or 500 yards they would change direction and continue to run a zigzag pattern. The baffled tank destroyers could not lock on a reliable target to attack.[9]

Training with tank destroyers had its hazards. During one scenario in which the 761st attacked tank destroyer units in the defense, Able Company Commander Dave Williams, who surprised everyone except himself with his reappearance at the 761st, watched as tanks rolled within yards of a number of tank destroyers. Williams noticed one of his best soldiers in the bow gunner's area with his arm resting on the main gun. As he radioed ordering the sergeant back into the tank, the turret rotated uncontrolled and the 75mm gun slammed him against the open hatch. The tank halted, and so did the scenario. Bates's handpicked executive officer, Major Charles Wingo, radioed Williams and barked for him to move out. Bates, aware of what had just happened, interrupted, and calmly told the shocked lieutenant to try to get the company moving again.[10] Paul Bates later watched as Williams rushed into the hospital looking for the sergeant. Bates's face conveyed the bad news.[11] The gun had crushed the sergeant to death.

Williams blamed the accident on his time out of the battalion. Dave Williams had returned from his brief stint in the Air Corps. He had felt uncomfortable leaving the 761st when he did, in part knowing his father would see it as the selfish and easy path and would warn Williams that he would regret his decision. Soon after Williams arrived at flight training in San Antonio, doctors found he had an irregular heartbeat but still passed him to fly. Finally, after a training flight, he landed the PT-17 so hard it bounced down the runway. His civilian flight instructor, who endured the landing with Williams, stated what seemed obvious— that Williams did not want to fly. The Air

Corps dropped him from the program and he raced back to the 761st where he knew he belonged.[12] Bates left the tank hatch ajar for the prodigal lieutenant. Now Williams wondered if he belonged in a position where he could get men killed.

One of the British officers, whom Williams had noticed observing the training, gently pulled the grieving Williams aside. "Learn one thing now, men get hurt and die in combat. You must keep the tanks moving and firing no matter what happens." Williams may have found Colonel Edwin Burba's manner rather cold, but the Brit had fought in North Africa. Williams worked to internalize a lesson that could keep his men alive.[13]

As the army poured money, assets, and manpower to create McNair's battle-ready tank destroyer force, reports trickled in from Europe that German armor seemed in decline.[14] Hitler's spending spree on state-of-the-art Tiger tanks pulled resources from the rest of his feared Panzer units, which Germany had limited fuel to run. The relentless bombing of Britain early in the war and Hitler's decision to renege on his agreement with the "Reds," as McBurney called them, and invade Russia, set Germany on a path to hell.[15]

The 761st walked into the center of the racial ambush when it moved to Camp Hood. Bates, caught by surprise, had no idea Washington officials knew of the challenges at a post just more than a year old.[16] Camp Hood and the surrounding areas became the collective enemy.

As at Camp Claiborne, transportation loomed as one of the worst aspects of a black soldier's life. With the bus as the primary means of transportation, no trip came without tension. Black soldiers endured stares and insults. Bus drivers reigned over their routes like feudal lords. Policy seemed arbitrary. Some refused to pick up fewer than six black soldiers. Drivers ensured that black soldiers sat in the rear of the bus, if they allowed them to ride at all. Bus operators on their last run often bypassed black soldiers, forcing them to walk alone back to the post.[17] At Camp Hood, Paul Bates, though baffled by the problem, refused to fall victim to a few locals abusing their power. The absurdity of this racial feud could impact his training plan and his unit's readiness. Bates determined the 761st could bypass the bus system and looked at the possibility of using the unit's military vehicles from its own motor pool to circumvent the racial nonsense of central Texas.

Aside from the transportation aristocracy, the other enemy of the 761st remained the military police, as it had been at Camp Claiborne, but with an intensity—on both sides—that defied description even by the articulate Bates. One Sunday at Camp Hood began with a 3:30 A.M. call that a train had killed one of Bates's "good sergeants" in Temple, east of the post. Reports to Bates called the man "drunk" and on a "quarrelsome spree" and said that he made some "wise cracks" to other 761st soldiers about some girls at a black club. It seemed one of the men knocked him down and authorities found him hours later unrecognizable, mangled on the railroad tracks. Bates found the story odd and lacking crucial information, but he had heard much stranger explanations since his activation. He did not find it unusual the man's shoes had been removed and tied together with his service cap placed on top, but the men of the 761st envisioned a different scenario from their uncharacteristically naïve commander. To Bates's surprise, the men blamed "the traditional enemy."[18] For McBurney the only possible explanation pointed to the military police bludgeoning the man and leaving his body on the tracks. The MPs may have beaten the life out of him or let the next train finish him off—it did not matter, really. McBurney had learned over almost two years how race seemed to work, especially when it came to the "authorities." No one cared about a dead black soldier. Bates, satisfied with the story from officials, dropped the matter.

According to some reports and popular lore, after 1941, one out of every three black inductees came from north of the Mason-Dixon Line, a considerable increase from earlier years.[19] Of more significance, a War Department report acknowledged these new recruits' demeanor demonstrably lacked "the appearance of servility traditionally associated with the Southern black male."[20] Such a characterization, if accurate, proved a plus for some, an insult for others. For men within the 761st, such discussions seemed foreign and laughable. But for the people of Bell County, the presence of black soldiers, regardless of the region of origin, pedigree, or educational level, seemed an overt and hostile act directed at residents who had already sacrificed their families and suffered the loss of their land. It appeared they would fight to protect what remained of their way of life against what they considered a black invasion from the north. The army failed to mention this local tempest to the 761st, but knew it had a sizable problem.

Truman K. Gibson, Jr., civilian aide to the secretary of war, Henry L. Stimson, conducting a press conference in 1945. (*National Archives*)

Truman K. Gibson, Jr., a brilliant thirty-one-year-old attorney and assistant to Judge William Hastie, slipped into the departing civilian aide's shoes February 1, 1943, as the "acting" civilian aide. Certain that Stimson and assistant secretary of war John J. McCloy saw him as too young to fill his boss' post permanently, he set out to showcase talents obscured during his predecessor's tenure.[21]

Gibson's lack of experience on the race front seemed to be his strength. The University of Chicago graduate and law school alum[22] proved a patient man, a gifted bureaucrat, and a good pairing with his bosses, McCloy and Stimson. He played a mean game of badminton and enjoyed his regular poker nights with other men of passion and intellect in Washington, like NAACP attorney Thurgood Marshall.[23]

Gibson made fact-based, pragmatic recommendations to the men who occupied the War Munitions Building at 19th Street and Constitution Avenue. He remained unusually aware of matters affecting unit readiness and the black male. He watched as fifty or so "kids" from the Youth Congress picketed the War Department, "chanting, 'Down with Jim Crow.'"[24] Gibson demanded a level of detail beyond what local commanders expected. He watched over the black force with care, but with his eye on the greater good for the race and the nation. Gibson learned the art of compromise, something Stimson liked. When the henchmen within race organizations worked to use baseless rumors to further personal agendas, such as NAACP public relations pit bull James B. LaFourche did with alleged killings at the 1942 Alexandria, Louisiana, riots, Gibson went on the offensive to halt methods he saw as counter to improving race relations within the army.[25]

Truman Gibson learned that the treatment of the black male in uniform tied directly to how black Americans voted. Members of Congress needing the black vote spoke with Gibson frequently. Finally he sent a lengthy memorandum to McCloy, with whom Gibson probably most closely worked. He referred to it as "exceedingly unwise for the army to enter the political arena" but that circumstances forced them into the maelstrom. Gibson knew his position existed solely because of demands from black leaders. He saw tremendous pressure coming their way in the run-up to the 1944 elections if they did not act now. One recommendation he made: "Commit some Negro units to combat." He knew while others already had made the suggestion, most black Americans did not believe their men serving in uniform would be permitted to fight as combat soldiers.

Men like LaFourche created problems and Gibson needed solutions. He had experimented with radio broadcasts to inform the army about the black soldier and had hoped to enlist the help of prominent Americans like Joe Louis, Duke Ellington, Louis Armstrong, and Hattie McDaniel.[26] But he had to reach black Americans outside the army as well. In the early spring of 1944, the War Department released Gibson's brainchild, "The Negro Soldier," a thirty-nine-minute film meant to highlight the war contributions of black servicemembers.[27] Army Colonel (and motion picture director) Frank Capra oversaw the making of the film. With U.S. forces in Europe a reality and the army scraping its manpower pools, additional support from the black community might force the army's hand.

Gibson saw awareness as a way to improve relations between the races. As a member of the Advisory Committee on Special Troop Policies at the War Department, he observed, "Most of the grievances of the Negro soldier are trivial." Gibson saw the veracity of the complaints paled when compared to the true issue: commanders' understanding of the attitudes of the soldiers. Studies showed that lower level officers, those who worked most closely with the men, had the least knowledge of those soldiers. The army had found that black soldiers lacked confidence in these junior white officers, noted one general officer on the committee. The men in the meeting felt confident that they had isolated the most difficult and detrimental situation in black army units. Publication of a pamphlet titled "Attitude of the Negro Soldier" might bridge what seemed a great divide.[28]

A friend of Gibson's commented on Camp Hood as an extreme case. In his letter, he described the post as "one of the worst situations in the whole AUS [Army of the United States]" and went on to remark, "There is hostility between [military police and black personnel] and segregation on interstate buses operating on the post, and segregation in the post facilities and theaters."[29] Gibson found himself swimming in articulate, descriptive letters from Camp Hood soldiers. All told the aide of similar mistreatment. A physician and old Gibson acquaintance told comparable stories. The doctor's concerns escalated as he described the segregation practices at post facilities.[30] Why Camp Hood, Gibson wondered.

Tiny Killeen, which abutted the post's front entrance, grew from a sleepy town of 1,200 to a bustling sprawl of more than 50,000 in what seemed a matter of days. Unlike Alexandria, Louisiana, a city struggling with race, Killeen remained predominantly white and residents determined that would not change with or without Camp Hood. Word of racial strife spread quickly. Gibson monitored the situation from his office in Washington. Black soldiers would travel to the nearby towns of Temple, Lampasas, and Belton for off-post entertainment, though few establishments permitted black soldiers.

Beyond the racial troubles engulfing Camp Hood, some found a city of hope. Eighty miles away lay Austin, with an active black population that attracted the tankers. Austin opened itself to all soldiers and had a robust War Recreation Program. The Negro War Recreation Council personally welcomed the 1,500 or so black service members who came to Austin each weekend and provided for them in the City Market on Eastern Avenue. Austin beckoned to the 761st and other black units, but distance and questionable transportation made such trips rare. McBurney, who saw anything outside New York as hardly worth his time, found Austin a haven for him and his friends. Transportation proved a challenge for all; some estimates said 20,000 white servicemen visited Austin each weekend. Buses filled with eager soldiers often arrived in town around the same time, clogging Austin streets.[31] By 1944, the city's black civic leaders pleaded for more space for visitors of their race. The Austin City Council agreed to fund a new center.[32]

The city dedicated the new facility to Pearl Harbor hero navy Mess Attendant First Class Doris "Dorie" Miller, a decision that probably both surprised and moved Gibson and anyone immersed in the question of race. Miller had much in common with the men of the 761st and probably would have made a superb tanker. The Waco, Texas, native and Moore High School football standout joined the navy as a mess attendant in 1939 to travel and earn money to help his parents and three brothers. Miller served on the battleship *West Virginia* (BB-48) berthed at Pearl Harbor. On December 7, 1941, then-Mess Attendant Second Class Miller carried wounded shipmates to relative safety as Japanese bombs and gunfire targeted his ship. After he attempted to rescue the ship's dying captain high on the bullet-ridden and collapsing bridge, he scrambled toward a .50 caliber machine gun, a weapon he knew little about. To his surprise it fired. Miller took over his adopted station firing at the Japanese aircraft for at least a quarter of an hour as the Japanese continued their attack.[33] He only left his post when ordered to abandon ship. Despite extreme efforts, the crew could not stem the flooding from the aerial bombs and torpedoes that pierced the ship's deck and hull. It settled on the bottom of the harbor as the remaining crew escaped. Of the 1,541-man crew, the *West Virginia* lost 130 killed and 52 wounded.

Admiral Chester Nimitz, commander of the now-scarred Pacific Fleet, personally awarded Miller the Navy Cross on April 1, 1942, the same day the 761st first stood as a unit at Camp Claiborne. Nimitz remarked to those present on Miller's new ship, the aircraft carrier *Enterprise* (CV-6), "This marks the first time in this conflict that such high tribute has been made in the Pacific Fleet to a member of his race and I'm sure that the future will see others similarly honored for brave acts."[34] Like other sailors Miller moved from ship to ship and reported for duty on an escort carrier, the USS *Liscome Bay* (CVE-56). At 5:10 A.M. on November 24, 1943, the Japanese torpedoed the *Liscome Bay* while it supported operations in the Pacific's Gilbert Islands. Its magazine of aircraft bombs exploded and the ship sank in minutes. On November 25, the navy listed Mess Attendant First Class Doris Miller as presumed dead.[35]

During some of the war's darkest days abroad as well as at home, one bright spot on post remained boxing, and the 761st maintained its battalion of amateur champions. "Come Out Fighting" remained the unit's motto and Joe Louis, its hero. The men of the 761st vowed to train like Joe Louis. They would become the tanker version of the widely respected boxer who seemed to bridge any racial divide. Devotees like Ivan Harrison followed army Sergeant Joseph Louis Barrow, his full, formal name, in the papers when possible. The black press also followed Louis and published reports of his upcoming boxing appearances. A four-week swing in late 1943 would bring him and his team to army installations in five states.[36] Louis had penciled in Camp Hood for December 6; he would box at Camp Claiborne on December 15. Sergeant Barrow, twenty-nine, traveled with First Sergeant George Nicholson, Sergeant James Edgar, Private George Wilson (known to boxing fans as Jackie Wilson), and trainer Corporal Robert. J. Payne. One additional boxer rounded out the exhibition crew, twenty-two-year-old Corporal Walker Smith, the welterweight known as Sugar Ray Robinson.[37] In the arena of army morale, this team provided a much-needed one-two punch.

Joe Louis's fights with the German Max Schmeling—at Yankee Stadium in 1936 and 1938—stood as two of the most talked-about events before and during World War II. Louis, the conscientious, hardworking young man, hungered for fame and for funds to support his parents and siblings. Schmeling, a former heavyweight world champion, fought for personal and national pride, though Adolf Hitler's unrelenting admiration unnerved him.[38] In their first meeting, which many considered a tune-up bout before Louis's eventual heavyweight title match, Schmeling stunned thousands of screaming fans when he finished off Louis in twelve rounds.[39]

The two boxers agreed to a second bout in 1938. But the world had changed in two years. The match took on meaning beyond the German and the American boxers. With one of the greatest political matches unfolding between an aggressive Germany and an officially neutral United States, Hitler pressured Schmeling. The stress also mounted for Louis, who had claimed the world heavyweight title in 1937. President Roosevelt gently pressed the case for the United States. He met with Louis and remarked, "Joe, we need muscles like yours to beat Germany."[40]

Not a ticket remained for the Yankee Stadium event. Sales swirled around $1 million. Fans included Hollywood royalty like Clark Gable and up-and-coming stars like Gregory Peck. J. Edgar Hoover watched the bout, too. The *New York Times* pegged the deafening crowd at 80,000 fans.[41] More than 140 radio stations carried the bout and millions hovered over their radios. The Yank-German match-up piqued Great Britain's interest as it did other nations fearing Germany as it drew the world closer to war.[42]

With the bell, Louis charged "with the most furious early assault he has ever exhibited here [Yankee Stadium],"[43] as one *New York Times* reporter noted. His initial barrage of left hooks and body blows knocked Schmeling down for a count of three. Next he connected with a right hook sending the German to the mat. Three clean shots to the jaw sent Louis's opponent back down for the final time. Joe Louis finished off a defenseless Max Schmeling in two minutes and four seconds into the first round.[44]

In his army uniform, Louis had the status of champion as well as seasoned veteran. Instead of a boxing match, William McBurney and the Camp Hood crowd of about five thousand watched a performance. Louis sparred three rounds with Corporal Bob Smith. Robinson danced around the ring with teammate Wilson. The boxers then lectured on physical fitness, an issue with which the army still wrestled.[45] The crowd absorbed every word spoken by Joe Louis, the Brown Bomber.

Louis boxed more than ninety exhibitions for the army. The world champion seemed to transcend the racially troubled military installations and gave hope to a polarized army. But the trouble at Hood would crystallize around another soldier-athlete.

Twelve

Lieutenant Jack
Roosevelt Robinson

A YOUNG INFANTRY LIEUTENANT ARRIVED AT THE 761ST DURING April 1944, the same month the tank battalion marked its second anniversary. Questions remained unanswered about his army future due to a college football injury. Jack Roosevelt Robinson broke his ankle at Pasadena Junior College in 1937 before becoming an All-American football standout at the University of California Los Angeles. He stood as the first in UCLA history to letter in four sports. But Robinson dropped out of school late in his senior year to help support his destitute family. He could never repay his loving mother, Mallie McGriff Robinson, for leaving Georgia behind so her five children could have access to a better life and education. Robinson picked up odd jobs on the sports circuit and played semipro football briefly for the Los Angeles Bulldogs and later for the Honolulu Bears until the army drafted him.[1] He took his oath April 3, 1942, in Los Angeles.

The army posted Robinson at Fort Riley, Kansas. With his quick smile he made friends easily. The astute corporal and accomplished marksman had his eye on Officer Candidate School, but found that Fort Riley blocked black males from OCS—against army policy. Robinson had become friends with boxer and part-time Riley soldier

Joe Louis, and mentioned his concerns. Louis's humility even as world
champion struck Robinson, who kept a close eye on racial practices
and reported his observations to Truman Gibson.[2] He assisted
Robinson during his painful introduction to a racially bitter army.[3]

The Robinson issue stood ripe for War Department intervention.
Gibson, at the time still assistant to Judge William H. Hastie, the
civilian aide to the secretary of war, separated facts from rumor the
way he arranged his well-tailored suits in his cramped Columbia
Road apartment. Louis passed on word to Washington. Robinson
contacted Gibson.[4] For the young attorney, barring black soldiers
from Officer Candidate School mocked army policy. Truman Gibson
worked within the system to correct challenges brought to public
attention by firebrands of the day such as A. Philip Randolph, the
president of the Brotherhood of Sleeping Car Porters, and Walter
White, the NAACP secretary. Gibson, as outraged by racial inequities
as White and Randolph, could resolve this crucial challenge, moving
behind the scenes with tact and grace.[5] Robinson and several other
black soldiers successfully completed a racially integrated Fort Riley
OCS and obtained their commissions during January 1943.

Robinson had long been at odds with post leaders, and his new
status as an officer did not improve the situation. When he first
arrived at Fort Riley, the post commander had learned of Robinson's
All-American status and placed him on the post football team. When
the University of Missouri learned of the move before its upcoming
game against Fort Riley, it refused to play a team with a black man
on the roster. Installation officials gave Robinson some "time off"
around game day, but would not admit to capitulating to Missouri's
threat. Robinson surmised the real reason for his leave, which added
to his resentment.

Jack Robinson quickly learned about the life of a gifted black man
in the U.S. Army. Between the Missouri incident and the refusal to
send black soldiers through OCS, Fort Riley may have proved the
root of Robinson's quiet but mounting activism. As the War
Department prepared to order an end to segregation at army installations,[6] Robinson, an infantry platoon leader, observed continued mistreatment. Fort Riley denied black soldiers' access to the post
exchange. Robinson reported the problem and threatened to with-
hold his athletic ability. Riley officials said they would *make* him play.
Robinson coolly reminded the army that, if ordered to play, he did
not have to play well.[7]

Orders to Camp Hood relieved the increasing pressure on Robinson. He thought no place in the army could be worse than Fort Riley. But the move to a tank unit gave the infantry-trained officer pause. The army attached Robinson to the 761st, though he never became a unit member, probably because of his questionable medical status stemming from his old ankle injury. With the 761st an advanced tank battalion with more than six months in the Sherman tank, Bates thought he had little need for untrained officers. He had seen them before. "Dullards," he called them.[8]

But Bates probably found a kindred spirit in Robinson instantly. Smooth realized he had met a younger version of himself. The battalion could boast two All Americans, though it probably only mattered to Paul Bates. He determined in their first meeting the California athlete who shared his drive and intellect belonged in the 761st. Robinson's limited duty status and lack of a true transfer into the unit appeared as just more higher headquarters' obstacles to a commander trying to run an outfit.

Bates had hidden his mounting weariness over the months. He had grown lonely and ached for Taffy Rosen. Even his adopted cat of several months, Trouble,[9] did little to lift the dark cloud he felt over him. The doctor could not have prescribed a better elixir than Jack Robinson.

Paul Bates, the infantry lieutenant turned tank battalion commander, assigned Robinson as a Baker Company platoon leader and designated him the battalion's morale officer,[10] the slot Dave Williams had filled.[11] Robinson, both thrilled and terrified, thanked Bates.

Robinson understood morale. Where Williams had been timid and unsure, Robinson worked like a bear. Boxing? Yesterday's news. The tank battalion of energetic young men needed football.[12] Robinson kept the pick-up football games informal but competitive. Most of the men had no inkling of Robinson's sports credentials. McBurney recalled in one game, "I caught the pass and this Robinson character came out of nowhere."[13] Airborne, Robinson flew head and shoulders first, grasping McBurney's vulnerable ribcage. The tackle knocked McBurney to the ground and forced a fumble. Robinson scooped up the ball and scored while McBurney lay in pain gasping for air and mouthing, "He broke my ribs!" Robinson, who seemed pleased with the play, helped McBurney to his feet, smiled with an unspoken but understood "Sorry," and both men resumed play.[14]

To McBurney, Robinson seemed happy at the 761st: "He always had a smile."[15] The unit's morale, already among the highest for a black army unit, spiked. Even Bates seemed relieved to share some of the responsibility for the outlook of his more than six hundred men.

Robinson had found a safe haven in the 761st, but began to learn of Camp Hood's solid and well-deserved reputation as a poor posting for black soldiers. Segregation ruled in the surrounding towns and the farming communities that escaped Mayhorn's land grab. Some directed their resentment at the minority of black soldiers. Truman Gibson continued to hear and read about the poor situation at Camp Hood. The hostility over race shocked him. Relations deteriorated. According to Gibson, "White bus drivers in military towns were deputized and armed. That was their approach to handling Southern black soldiers. I tried to put out fires. We were dealing with the killing of black troops."[16]

With some issues within his control, Gibson, and Hastie before him, chipped away at segregation. A frustrated Hastie believed he could do "more good outside the restrictions of the government." He continued to work to end segregation in the armed forces. To him segregation did nothing to improve military readiness. Opponents fought him. Worse, surveys from the field indicated a majority of white and a significant percentage of black soldiers preferred a segregated system.[17] Gibson quickly understood the magnitude of his departed boss's frustration.

With more than eight months at Camp Hood, the 761st continued as the aggressor force for what seemed an endless stream of nameless tank destroyer units bound for combat. April 1, 1944, brought the unit's second anniversary and the first for the 784th, which recently had returned to the Texas post. Bates wrote of plans for a celebration similar to the first organization day with a parade and field meet, and noted "5 bus loads of college girls as guests,"[18] a dream come true for nearly every tanker. Bates followed with another letter to Taffy Rosen, raving about the day's activities and how nice a time the three hundred girls seemed to have.[19]

Training continued through May and into June. Bates felt the pressure from abroad. His opinion of the tank destroyer had not changed, but he figured any added firepower helped the Allies. For Ivan Harrison and a news-savvy 761st, the anticipated yet unimaginable happened: wave upon wave of Allied forces arriving in Normandy,

France, by sea on beaches with code names like Omaha and Utah. They came by air and jumped behind German lines. The British and Canadians landed at Gold, Sword, and Juno. They gained a foothold despite German opposition. Planners had kept Operation Overlord secret. Harrison wondered what lay ahead. He speculated heavy fighting—without the 761st.

Jack R. Robinson. (*Ellsworth G. McConnell Collection*)

McBurney sat on the edge of his bunk. An invasion of France meant one of two things for the unit. Either America needed the tank battalion, or the Germans had already crumbled, and the war in Europe would draw to a quick close without them. He could not imagine after all their work and months of misery it would end for them this way.

The pressure from events abroad became a strong and steady pull on Paul Bates. He stood certain on the evening of June 6, that as the aggressor force in a program with strong War Department interest, the 761st had garnered attention as well as accolades. The unit not only excelled as an independent tank battalion, but had shown it could perform with precision in support of infantry and other arms. Bates rarely missed an opportunity and saw Europe in their future.

Almost at the start of the bloody invasion, the audacious Lieutenant General George Patton, from his position in England commanding Allied deception forces, bellowed for more armor. But Patton knew the second front proved a stretch of resources. The U.S. already had thrown nearly everything it had at both theaters, save for a handful of units still in the states. At Camp Hood, the 761st maneuvered in that handful of trained units, ready to fight Bates thought.

Tension filled the units at Camp Hood. The 761st debated, bickered, and wondered. After three stress-filled days, the men had their answer. The army placed the 761st on alert June 9 for deployment.[20] The battalion brimmed with energy. McBurney had never felt such anticipation. Bates saw much work ahead and found the men's excitement premature, but they would need that energy soon enough.

The army placed Taffy Rosen's 14th Field Hospital on alert as well. Maybe those dreaded medical field exercises had some value, Rosen thought. She packed for Europe.

Deployment preparations took place in secret. August approached. The move to Europe dwarfed their transfer from Camp Claiborne and this time they would leave much of their equipment including "Taffy," "Cool Stud," and the rest of their tanks at Camp Hood. Going to war required Bates's full attention.

Robinson became the favorite of a man who preferred no soldier over another. Bates wanted him to deploy with the battalion to Europe. The unprecedented request meant a commitment from Robinson, whom the army had not marked fit for duty. In the aftermath of his Fort Riley experience, few in Robinson's position would consider Bates's request. But Robinson seemed to connect with Bates and began to think about a career in the army. As a black officer with a bum leg, a career in sports remained questionable. His first task: obtain fit-for-duty status. The ankle remained an obstacle.[21]

With both men short on time, the undertaking drove Robinson. The deployment consumed Bates. Neither officer predicted what came next.

Summer scorched central Texas, but little seemed to change around Camp Hood. Tank destroyers trained in the searing heat. Robinson sweltered in Temple, meeting with doctors about his ankle. He hesitated, but pushed for a fit-for-duty ruling, ready to follow Paul Bates to war.

The evening of July 6 brought little relief as Robinson took his seat on a Southwestern Bus Company bus next to the wife of another member of the 761st. With her light skin, no one questioned where she chose to sit, but the bus driver, Milton Reneger, seeing Robinson seated next to her toward the middle of the long row of benches, told him to move to the rear of the bus. Robinson shot back that he would sit where he wanted and recommended the driver take care of his driving.[22] An angry exchange ensued and the men spilled off the bus at Robinson's stop. The argument continued as a crowd gathered adding to the pressure and spectacle. The MPs arrived and asked Robinson, the senior officer present, to go with them to straighten out the matter. He agreed. With Robinson in tow, the MPs arrived at Camp Hood's provost marshal. A chatty MP greeted them.[23] Enraged by what he heard, Robinson threatened the soldier who had approached them.

The situation deteriorated. Witness statements did not represent the truth, according to Robinson. No fewer than thirteen depositions described Robinson's behavior on the bus as outrageous. Bates got word of the bus incident soon after it happened from the 761st duty officer who heard from a fast-moving Camp Hood staff. Bates received a call from the provost marshal. He figured he had another ugly but standard bus incident on his hands. He heard "one of his best officers" nearly came to blows with a bus driver. Bates knew the regulations and the bus driver had acted improperly, but apparently the officer went "berserk," using obscene language in front of women (he probably thought it no worse than Taffy Rosen's extensive sailor-like vocabulary). The officer also threatened bodily harm to the driver and an MP corporal. Though the uncharacteristic outburst possibly stemmed from a man tired of the treatment received at and around Camp Hood, Bates understood the post's position.[24]

Bates had a clearer view of the incident after he spoke with Robinson. The provost marshal's as well as Robinson's allegations stunned Bates. The charges against Robinson had nothing to do with the heated verbal exchange on the bus over a matter about which Robinson knew he acted well within army regulations. Robinson's troubles stemmed from his interaction with the head of Hood's MP detachment, Captain Gerald M. Bear. Bates found Robinson's version of events credible and backed him, but with the battalion's deployment to the European Theater imminent, according to some, Bates advised Robinson to leave Texas for a while and allow things to cool.

The army took Robinson from the 761st and placed him in the 758th Tank Battalion. Camp Hood moved forward with a general court-martial, more serious than a summary or a special court-martial and a process that gave the command the power to put Robinson out of the army if found guilty.[25] The army charged Robinson with Articles 63 and 64 of the Articles of War, "monstrously serious transgressions—including the show of disrespect toward a superior officer and failure to obey a direct command."[26]

Jack Robinson knew a guilty verdict would ruin a life that had hardly begun. He needed to use the press to get his story out. He and others contacted the NAACP for assistance, and he wrote to Truman Gibson at the War Department. Robinson detailed what he saw as trumped-up charges and reiterated that his interest lay in justice. "I don't mind trouble but I do believe in fair play and justice."[27]

The pragmatic Gibson backed away from the Robinson case, stating nothing could be done until after the proceedings. He advised Robinson against media exposure, warning it would "fan the flames."[28] Gibson had continued to monitor the tensions at Camp

Hood. Robinson's case appeared as yet another racial intimidation tactic. He remained informed, but tread carefully.

Robinson did not believe he had the luxury of allowing the "proceedings" to move forward without action. The civilian sector interceded. Camp Hood fielded inquiries and the *Pittsburgh Courier* and *Chicago Defender* carried the story. Robinson's California congressional representatives and even the War Department's Adjutant General's Office wanted to know about the Robinson business. The attention terrified the army commanders at Camp Hood. Gibson's assessment had been close; flames had been fanned.

Right out of one of McBurney's Saturday matinees, a Texan, Second Lieutenant William A. Cline, met with Robinson to discuss his defense. Cline, a lawyer-cum-artillery officer, understood his client faced a possible dishonorable discharge.[29] Robinson opened up to the Texan about his background. He talked at length about his mother, whom he credited with everything good in his life. Cline noticed he never mentioned his father. Robinson thanked Cline for his time, but believed the NAACP planned to furnish a lawyer. Cline thought that a grand idea. William Cline heard from Jack Robinson several days later. Though he never learned what transpired with the NAACP, Robinson placed his life in Cline's hands.[30]

In contrast to Robinson's confidence, Camp Hood officials found they had gotten in deep legal waters. By July 17, Colonel Kimball, commander of 5th Armored Group, under which the 761st, 758th, and 784th still fell, recommended a general court-martial to the commanding general of XXIII Corps in his letter dated July 24, nearly three weeks after the incident. Kimball later contacted Colonel Walter D. Buie, chief of staff for Headquarters XXIII Corps and Camp Hood's higher headquarters. Kimball described the Robinson case as "full of dynamite." He explained it needed delicate handling, preferably "by someone off the post." He continued: "This bus situation here is not at all good, and I am afraid that any officer in charge of troops at this post might be prejudiced."[31]

Buie had no intention of tossing a lifeline to Kimball or anyone at Camp Hood. He probably agreed with Kimball—all the more reason for the Robinson matter to remain squarely with the post. It did not help that two days after the Robinson flare-up, the army released War Department Directive No. 97, stating it would tolerate no discrimination on the basis of race for transportation, recreational facilities, theaters, and the like.[32]

Through July, the 761st continued to prepare for its August 9 departure. Bates chose the advance party. He knew he had lost Robinson, but continued to support him.[33] Lieutenant Jack Robinson's court-martial kicked off at 10 A.M. sharp August 2, seven days before the army scheduled the 761st to leave for the European Theater. While the unit dealt with the general tumult of a deploying outfit, the army's system of justice had its own challenges that did not bode well for a defendant like Robinson.[34] Robinson maintained his innocence.

Though the army had many lawyers in uniform, few practiced law. Like a labor union, the Judge Advocate General's Corps restricted JAGs to those officers with at least four years of civilian law practice. Most young men entering the service could not meet the requirement. Robinson had a trained lawyer in artillery officer Cline. When the NAACP attorney did not materialize, Robinson considered hiring outside counsel. The financial burden on a man from a poor family may have had more of an impact on Robinson than the very real threat from the charges he faced.

Army Lieutenant Colonel Richard E. Kyle, a JAG officer, presided over the proceedings. A board of nine officers ranging in rank from captain to colonel, most from field artillery units and tank destroyer battalions, sat in judgment. Second Lieutenant Milton Gordon from the 665th Tank Destroyer Battalion served as the trial judge advocate or prosecutor. Cline, listed from the 658th Tank Destroyer Battalion, stood as Robinson's last line of defense.[35]

After the court read the formal charges of disrespect and disobedience, Captain Gerald Bear, the senior MP and Robinson's accuser, took the stand. Led by the prosecutor, Bear described Robinson's behavior the evening in the guard shack. "On several occasions, I told him to go away from the door and as I told him to go away, he bowed in this manner and said, 'OK, sir. OK, sir. OK, sir.' . . . Each time I told him to go away he bowed in that same manner with the same form of salute and would say, 'OK, sir. OK, sir. OK, sir,' in the same facetious manner." In Bear's opinion, Robinson mocked him and the system with his series of sloppy salutes, bows from the waist, and repeated "grimaces," actions disrespectful to a senior officer. Bear critiqued Robinson's rapid manner of speech. "He continued to raise and lower his voice and continued to act in a contemptuous and disrespectful manner. In fact I had lost control of this Lieutenant."

Cline gave Bear as much rope as he would take. He had had enough of Bear's opinions and objected to the MP's litany of thoughts and descriptions and insisted on facts. The court agreed with Cline, following an objection by the prosecution. Cline went to work like a surgeon. He separated the case's few facts from the preponderance of emotional conjecture. He methodically demonstrated how Bear's personal opinions and interpretation of Robinson drove his testimony.

Cline: Your answer is that you did consider it improper for the accused to ask such questions.

Bear: Yes. In the way that he did it.

Cline: In what way?

Bear found Robinson argumentative when he asked if he had to answer certain questions. Robinson questioned most of Bear's moves that evening and Bear stated he saw this as a loss of control. He explained Robinson's manner proved problematic. He admitted Robinson asked reasonable questions.

Cline: Captain, do you recall if he asked if he was under arrest at that time?

Bear: Yes, I do recall.

Cline: Did you give him answer?

Cline patiently wrestled Bear until he pried an answer similar to what Robinson had received.

Bear: We have arranged the transportation back [to McClosky Hospital in Temple] and you are to go back over there and we will consider that you will be in arrest in quarters and taken over there.

Neither Bear nor the duty officer that day, Captain Peelor L. Wigginton, the Camp Hood laundry officer, could give the court a yes or no answer as to whether Robinson had been placed under arrest. A flurry of questions from the panel of officers followed regarding the arrest status and the perception of sloppiness when a soldier—Robinson—had been placed "at ease."[36]

Cline brought out additional inconsistencies with the witnesses that followed. After an objection from a panel member Cline explained his motive. He would show "whether or not there was an atmosphere there. The background of this whole case should be before the court." Cline pressed Wigginton on the matter of the stenographer with whom Robinson had difficulty in taking his statement accurately. At one point, the stenographer grabbed her bag and left the room. Cline pushed: "I am trying to determine the bias and prejudice of the witness."[37]

Cline had the prosecution's witnesses against the wall. Biases had been stripped and laid before the panel. Facts as far as disrespect toward Bear and disobedience of orders-that-weren't thinned, leaving Robinson an ideal opening in which to tell his version of events.

The court instructed Robinson he had no obligation to testify, but he chose to take the stand. For the first time the court heard Lieutenant Robinson's story. A nervous Jack Robinson sat on edge, eager to talk. He spoke quickly. No one could mistake the tension in his voice. Cline asked his client on more than one occasion to slow down, a scenario similar to what Bear described.

Robinson revealed the flashpoint of the night in question. When Robinson arrived at Camp Hood with the MPs, Private First Class Ben W. Mucklerath, the third MP in question that evening, came up to the vehicle, peered in and asked, "Did you get that nigger lieutenant?" Robinson testified he told Mucklerath, "If you ever call me a nigger again, I will break you in two."[38]

The tension reached a crescendo. The panel waited for Robinson's next words. But Cline stopped his client. "Let me interrupt you, Lieutenant. Do you know what a nigger is?" All eyes fixed on Robinson.

Jack Robinson related that his grandmother had been a slave. She had told him "it meant a low, uncouth person and it applied to no one in particular." Robinson told the court, "I looked it up in the dictionary." He found it pertained to someone of the "Negroid" race. It also referred to a machine in a sawmill. Robinson said the word had been used at other times that evening, each time directed at him. He spoke of the stenographer who had walked out while he asked questions and tried to get her to correct his statement. He recalled only the facts, but without saying so, it seemed she may have left abruptly because of racial discomfort. Fact or conjecture, the human degradation of Lieutenant Jack Robinson seemed to stand as the only issue. Robinson continued, "I am a negro but not a nigger. Captain Bear said I was insolent."[39]

The defense probably could have rested. Cline drew out Robinson's heartfelt testimony that shocked the court and surprised himself a little. He built a case to show the atmosphere of that evening. Lieutenant Jack Robinson seemed to face a general court-martial because he ran into some people one evening who did not like black men in uniform.

The court called Bates. Lieutenant Colonel Paul Bates, a senior officer and commander soon on his way to combat, presented himself to support Robinson. Bates stated, "I command the 761st Tank Battalion"[40] in a way that only Paul Bates could. His position probably trumped that of post laundry officer. In a brief session with Cline, Bates described Robinson's excellent reputation, especially among the enlisted men. He mentioned his status as a known athlete, which brought immediate objections from the prosecution. Bates described his abilities as a soldier and said he wanted Robinson permanently assigned to the 761st, to which the prosecution objected, but the court overruled. Bates said he had rated Robinson as "excellent" and that he would go into combat with him.[41] Bates strode out of the courtroom.

Captain James R. Lawson, the Baker Company commander for the 761st, followed and echoed Bates's responses. Robinson worked under Lawson until his sudden move July 6. Lawson also could only refer to the second lieutenant as "excellent."[42] Others followed and the defense rested.

The army completed the general court-martial of Lieutenant Jack Robinson. Two-thirds of the panel found him not guilty of the charges. The court acquitted him.[43]

Though free, Robinson knew he would never find freedom in the army. He missed his chance to follow Paul Bates overseas. Robinson already had sought a medical discharge from the Adjutant General in Washington. In his August 25 letter, he explained that a July 21 board recommended permanent limited duty. He wrote he would be of more use in defense outside of a unit already over its 100 percent end strength in officers.[44] Robinson probably left the courtroom bitter and alone. He knew he had served the army well, but he had not anticipated spending his brief time in uniform fighting for respect and dignity.

Thirteen

Patton's Welcome

"I COMMAND THE 761ST TANK BATTALION," DECLARED PAUL BATES for the record at Jack Roosevelt Robinson's court-martial. Neither the panel members nor his nearly seven hundred soldiers had any doubt after he marched out of the courtroom. Any dignity of the proceedings, aside from Robinson's and his lawyer William Cline's, followed Bates out the door.

With the trial over, Bates now would lead the 761st to war. After his August 2 testimony, he had one week before the army scheduled the 761st to begin its move to the European Theater of Operations, or ETO, as William McBurney and the others frenetically discussed.

Hurdles remained between Bates and his precious fields of battle. He still worked to get men like McBurney to believe the realities of war. He preferred for them to understand fact over myth before they had a tank blasted from under them and watched their fellow soldiers die in ways that defied imagination. But McBurney stuck with his version of conflict. He saw it on the motion picture screen with his own eyes. He watched the newsreels. How could war be any different?

The clock ticked down. Bates would go to war with the unit he had trained—regardless of what his men believed. Aside from brief film clips, the tankers kept abreast of the news in Europe in newspaper and radio reports. Most ignored the Pacific, still fearful that army leaders would ship them to fight in death traps like Saipan.

With Europe on the horizon, some recalled a chilling report. The Germans had made no secret of their intentions in the event of an Allied invasion beyond Italy. They postured for reporters, boldly displayed their defenses, and promised a fight to the finish. On February 15, 1944, the *New York Times* reported: "Rundstedt Bares Invasion Defenses; Fight to Finish Against Allied Assault on France Pledged."[1] Allied deception surrounding Overlord went just so far. The Germans figured the enemy would hit France hard. But they still doubted the Allies, especially the Americans, had the stomach for the type of warfare the Germans had fought for centuries.

The European deployment for the 761st Tank Battalion would come just as another classified unit movement.[2] Ivan Harrison, buoyed by the news and ready to give the Germans a fight, knew the path ahead remained uncertain. He subscribed to Bates's belief in the unit. Suddenly it fell to the headquarters company commander to keep the men out of trouble, unharmed, and alive to make it to Europe. First order: Avoid bus drivers and MPs.

For Harrison, going to war had taken on a magnitude unknown to him when he enlisted. Europe meant leaving behind his sweet Juanita, who remained in Detroit with their infant son, Ivan, Jr. When he could get a furlough, he would hop the rails bound for Detroit. As the deployment drew closer, he wrapped himself around her one last time. Love against war's uncertainty deepened their passion. He wanted her to remember him and what they shared. He promised to return. Instead of uplifting her, he terrified her.

Until that point, Juanita worried little about her husband's safety. Ivan, Jr. had become her comfort, her peace. Though still scarred by the sudden deaths of her parents at such a young age and the near loss of her siblings, she had hope as Ivan, Jr. squirmed and giggled as her future. She loved Ivan, Sr., but she would survive—regardless of what war brought. Ivan Harrison felt the change in Juanita. Each understood the other's newfound commitment and did not say a word.

Taffy Rosen had felt she moved farther from Paul and Europe, for a period. The army sent her to Camp Gruber, Oklahoma, during late January. She raced to the 14th Field Hospital at Camp Bowie, Texas, in July with the promise of the battlefields of Europe. It seemed odd to her how close two people could remain in such a very large war. Who would cross the Atlantic first, she wondered. Rosen challenged Paul Bates to keep an eye out for her en route to England. She would not be far behind.[3]

Though the 761st's advanced detachment left Camp Hood August 1 for Camp Kilmer, New Jersey, the main body left the evening of August 9 for New York's Camp Shanks.[4] The army created Shanks as it had Hood—through eminent domain. It displaced 130 families with two weeks' notice to vacate their homes.[5] Camp Shanks sat about twenty-five miles up the deep Hudson River from New York City in bucolic Orangeburg. The segregated camp had seven staging areas. Women had their own area, as did black units. Shanks stood as "Last Stop, USA" for more than 1 million soldiers as they made their way to Europe. Outfits like the 761st arrived by train and departed by ship.[6]

Camp Shanks served a number of needs. Doctors performed final medical and dental checkups to ensure each soldier's fitness for combat. They issued immunizations. Soldiers watched training and familiarization films about the enemy they soon would face. McBurney watched the army's moving pictures closely. He learned a few words of French and German. Richard English kept a close eye on their final classroom training.[7] Bates's company commanders and platoon leaders ensured their men prepped their gear for the voyage. They made repairs as necessary, ridded themselves of the unserviceable, and received new items as needed. What lay on the other side of the voyage remained as unknown to Bates as it did to his battalion. They had to be ready.

Paul Bates wanted a tight hold on the reins. No joyriding. No alcohol. No ladies. Everyone would sail. With what little free time Bates permitted, he allowed the tankers visits to the recreation facilities. McBurney could take in one of his precious picture shows. The men had little latitude. Final preparations stood as their primary mission.

At some point McBurney grabbed his gear and stood on the pier looking up at the most imposing seagoing vessel he had ever seen. The HMS *Esperance Bay* had served as a troop transport ship since 1941.[8] Its crew knew its business and had crossed the Atlantic during the height of the German wolf packs that hunted merchant vessels as well as ships carrying combat-ready soldiers like McBurney. The British Navy deemed a German U-boat attack during this crossing with the 761st highly unlikely.

Though New York native William McBurney had a father who worked the docks, he could not describe the thrill and sense of accomplishment boarding the vessel with his fellow tankers. Getting underway August 27 proved surreal. Many of the tankers had never set foot on a boat, let alone a British ship. The passing sites over-whelmed Russell Guthrie as he floated by the Statue of Liberty at a smooth, calculated pace. How he wished his mother could see him.

Guthrie heard the chances of an enemy submarine attack stood near zero, but he had none of it. One brief trip below decks to where the 761st berthed told him an attack would wipe out the unit. He grabbed his belongings and found a main deck cubby just big enough for his five-foot six-inch frame and gear for the duration of the voy-age—if no one kicked him out first. He kept his find a secret. He made required musters and kept to himself during the voyage. He looked to the guys as his salvation, but in some ways not much had changed since he lost his mother. He missed her more on that ship that he had in some time.[9] Eleven days later, September 8, the *Esperance Bay* safely disgorged its charges in Avonmouth, England.[10]

Arrival in Britain probably did more for morale than it did for readiness. Army correspondent and Private First Class Trezzvant Anderson found the young Englishwomen quite friendly during his stay in England.[11] McBurney finally found a place that rivaled New York. The bars, well, pubs, as he had to correct himself, welcomed him and his buddies. Each young lady seemed nicer and prettier than the last. The tankers marveled as the English girls flocked to the black venues. Russell Guthrie, who, despite his age, knew his way around the music scene and understood the young ladies, thanks to his favorite girl, let his fellow tankers in on one fact. "They like the way we dance."[12] McBurney and the other soldiers would accept the attention of the delicate beauties anyway they could get it.

William McBurney found it difficult to move back into a combat focus coming from his English fantasy. But he and the 761st crossed the English Channel one night and stepped ashore in France the next day. They landed at Omaha Beach, to be exact, October 10, 1944, already assigned to Patton's Third Army.[13] The men liked their big talk, but the reality of fighting under General Patton hushed them with a reverence reserved for solemn occasions.

Instead of the carnage of the French coast four months earlier, Bates found a bustling supply hub. To his relief, the army had the 761st's tanks and other gear ready. Though briefed otherwise, McBurney thought a German or two might pop their heads up and take a shot at the battalion.

Company commanders of the 761st Tank Battalion meeting in England before their deployment in France. Clockwise from left: David Williams, Able Company; J. B. Lawson, Baker Company (he would soon be replaced by John D. Long); Irvin McHenry, Charlie Company; Richard English, Dog Company; Ivan Harrison, Headquarters Company; August Bremer, Service Company. (*National Archives*)

The front had shifted four hundred miles inland since June. Their next destination beckoned. Bates ordered the battalion packed and ready to move. The 761st bivouacked at La Pieux, France, October 12, waiting for the order to roll to the front.[14]

Bates and his battalion covered the distance with a battalion of new, untested tanks in just six days, arriving near Nancy on October 28.[15] Tension increased when one company commander discreetly challenged Bates's refusal to stop in off-limits villages to afford the men some rest and entertainment. Despite the heated exchange, neither man held the other's contentious position against him. Paul Bates could have easily removed Richard English, Dog Company commander. Acrimony aside, both men sensed larger challenges lay ahead.[16] Bates established his headquarters in a bombed-out chemical plant complete with a maze of underground passages.[17] McBurney felt as if they had flown across France. Still on alert, he kept an eye out for Germans.

The battalion assumed its combat status October 31. Paul Bates had already met with the Major General Willard S. Paul, commanding general of the 26th Infantry Division, the unit the 761st would support. Known as the "Yankee Division" because of its New

England National Guard roots, the 26th had been in combat since
October 12. Despite its experiences at the Louisiana Maneuvers,
Camp Claiborne exercises, and tank destroyer aggressor problems
with infantry units, the 761st had not supported an outfit this large.
Bates assured his men they would support regiments and smaller
units. They had the skills and training to succeed in any scenario, he
reminded them.[18] All felt they had arrived at a very big game.

Major General Willard Paul and the 26th Infantry Division
answered to XII Corps as did the 35th and 80th infantry divisions
and the 4th and 6th armored divisions. Early November proved quite
a change from September 15 when the rapid advance of much of
Patton's Third Army ground to a halt. Tanks ran on fumes and units
lacked the supplies necessary to sustain the fight.[19] Paul's sprawling
outfit of more than 14,000 men dwarfed Bates's battalion of 700.
Even Paul Bates found the numbers unnerving, but remained confident his men would click where they belonged. Infantry divisions
depended on firepower from attached units. Aside from the 761st,
these included the 602nd and the 691st tank destroyer battalions, the
945th, 255th, and 243rd field artillery battalions, and the 165th
Combat Engineer Battalion.[20] It seemed clear the tank destroyers
might not mass for too many tank engagements, but would provide
General Paul and his commanders the guns and extra muscle their
men lacked.

Bates had one eye on Paul and his staff and the other on the all-
important infantry regiments. The division had three, the 101st,
104th, and 328th. General Paul had engineers, a medical detachment,
and more artillery than Bates could ever use.

To McBurney's and Guthrie's surprise the charismatic division
commander welcomed them to the Lorraine campaign of northeast-
ern France soon after the 761st arrived. Paul greeted the tankers with
a tone reminiscent of a carnival barker. Standing on a half-track,
looking every bit the hardened combat commander, he addressed the
men as if he spoke to each as an individual. "I'm delighted you're
here. I've got a little work for you to do. Your outfit and mine have
trained a hell of a long time. We were itching for battle and we're in
it." Paul knew the exact words to spur the men on to victory. "I hear
you're itching for battle and I'm sure you'll get it right soon. You are
the first colored tank battalion in this Third Army, and I can tell you
I'm proud as hell to have you supporting my division.[21]

"I am damned glad to have you with us. We have been expecting you for a long time, and I am sure you are going to give a good account of yourselves." Paul continued to build excitement, "I've got a big hill up there I want you to take and I believe you are going to do a great job of it."[22] The men went crazy. A general officer, preparing for battle, took time to talk to them. McBurney determined he would do anything for General Paul, though he doubted his tank would take any hills. Russell Guthrie saw a stern, no-nonsense man and considered the general as straight-up and honest.[23]

A short time later, Guthrie heard rumors Patton had arrived in the area. The tankers knew from talking to Guthrie that he admired the man and claimed a large number of General Patton sightings.[24] Most tossed his latest report on the pile with his others. Lieutenant General George Patton had become many things to many people over the years and most were fraught with controversy. Some hated the man. His foul moods and unrealistic demands endeared him to few, but he won battles. Junior commanders cringed when he addressed their outfits. His coarse language made many young men uncomfortable.[25] As the Allies pushed toward Germany, leaders in Washington and his old friend and rival General Dwight Eisenhower looked to him to win the war in Europe—and the 761st clamored to assist. Eisenhower, now Supreme Commander of Allied Expeditionary Forces, outranked Patton by a star. In Patton's opinion, Eisenhower had become "a damn politician," a crime of which no one would accuse George Patton. While Eisenhower commanded echelons above Patton, he depended on "Ol' Blood and Guts" to finish off Germany.

McBurney, who tended to read news on the aviation front, had skimmed stories about Patton, as had Harrison, English, and most of the men of the 761st. They knew little of the political wrangling of men they had come to see as gods. Bates probably saw a future for himself like George Patton. To catch a glimpse of the three-star general in Nancy, France, seemed an absurd notion.

For once, Guthrie had accurate information. Lieutenant General George Patton had arrived. Patton first rallied the men of the 26th Infantry Division on November 3, 1944, with a mix of enthusiasm and realism. He imparted his decades of knowledge about how to fight and live to the young men fixed on him. "The keynote of any attack is speed and aggressiveness. . . . Most casualties are caused by the enemy in the last four or five hundred yards—cross that area in a hurry. Don't stay there and let him shoot you. . . . You can't see the enemy but can shoot into the area where he is, make him keep his head down and he won't be shooting back." Most important, "Keep shooting, closing and kill him."[26]

He decided he would address the soldiers of the 761st. The commanding general of the Third Army wished to talk one-on-one with the tank battalion. He pulled Paul Bates aside and asked the battalion commander what he wanted him to say. Bates felt comfortable with Patton. He told the general the unit stood well-trained with the best equipment the army had. But his men needed one thing from the general—"the needle so they would kill."[27] Patton understood.

For McBurney, Patton's appearance exceeded any expectation he had of armed conflict. He did not think a moving picture could adequately portray what unfolded. Trezzvant Anderson quoted Patton standing atop a half-track addressing the 761st: "Men you are the first Negro tankers to ever fight in the American Army. I would never have asked for you if you weren't good. I don't care what color you are so long as you go up there and kill those Kraut sons of bitches. Everyone has their eyes on you and is expecting great things from you." He continued, his voice higher in pitch than Harrison expected. "Most of all, your race is looking forward to you. Don't let them down, and damn you, don't let me down."[28]

There. "Kill those Kraut sons of bitches." An impressed and relieved Bates could not have said it better.[29] The general's bravado worried Harrison. McBurney wanted to follow Patton, no matter where. Guthrie, taken by Patton's sternness, thought the general also reminded him of his father, a man he loved and trusted. People misunderstood Leon Guthrie as they did George Patton. Leon, the hard-working widower with nine children, could outcook anyone in the neighborhood, even as he labored full-time at Lackawanna Steel. Russell saw his father as stern, indicating an honest man who meant what he said. Russell Guthrie trusted the unyielding George Patton and believed in the man that would lead them to victory.[30]

Overall, Patton's brief but stirring remarks did exactly what he wanted them to do. The men would kill as many "Krauts" as possible for Patton and a few extra for their families back home. Bates hoped the encounter injected some realism into the unit. Looking at his star-struck tankers, he had his doubts. Patton had a way of telling people what they needed to hear to elicit his desired response. He did the same with the 761st. Patton had seen the War Department reports—the army had few tank units left in the States. He did not have much choice. If a unit killed Germans and did not sustain the unacceptable casualty rate the 603rd Tank Destroyer Battalion did in Africa, he cared little about color. At this point, he probably would take higher casualties as long as they killed more Germans and units could push themselves to the final victory.

During their days before kick-off, Bates ordered his officers to get as close to the front as possible. This perplexed Able Company commander Dave Williams, but once he arrived he understood. Though combat action had lain dormant in their area for more than a month, the Germans remained busy. What he did not see unnerved him. The enemy remained unseen yet Williams felt an undeniable presence. Williams sensed he could only move so far forward or risk a bullet from the invisible force. The Germans had taken the land on which he stood and the Allies had pushed the enemy back to this point. He looked at a No Man's Land before him that he and his men would soon enter. He had many questions, but realized two items mattered: Keep his men moving and kill the "sons of bitches." Williams had made more mistakes with the 761st than anyone should have allowed, but if he followed his two principles, he should lead Able Company with relative ease.

As he grew aware of his simplistic and immature vision, the experience transformed Williams. His fear of an unknown enemy evaporated, but could he lead in battle? The calm of the front worried him, yet it seduced him. He sensed the waiting storm. Except for some senior NCOs, his men remained none the wiser about what awaited, and he thought he would keep it that way. They would learn the truth soon enough.[31]

Bates gave Williams his orders along with a stack of maps. Williams appeared less than enthused. He figured Bates probably chose to ignore his lackluster reaction. He had not been the most reliable officer. That Bates had let him return to the battalion gave Williams some confidence. Bates told Williams he would move in support of the 104th Infantry Regiment and would receive further orders from its commander, Colonel Dwight Colley.[32] It hit Williams that Able Company would maneuver alone, without the rest of the battalion. Panic set in. Bates reassured him, emphasizing his faith in the officer's abilities. Williams believed him because he had nothing else to grasp at that moment except the self-assured battalion commander. Bates gave the young captain a few tactical hints on placement of tanks to reduce engine roar, an unmistakable noise that tended to attract enemy fire.

Williams thought it would have been nice to have had this invaluable information a little sooner, but his primary concern lay in lack of contact with Bates when he met the enemy.[33] Williams and his company would operate on their own with the 104th.

Dave Williams felt ill.

Fourteen

The Battle for Lorraine

T HE NEXT DAY, NOVEMBER 7, 1944, A FRIENDLY AND RELAXED
Colonel Dwight T. Colley handed a cup of hot coffee to the
Able Company commander. Just as Dave Williams began to breathe a
bit easier, Colley dropped what seemed to him to be a high-explosive
round in his lap. The 104th Infantry would keep two of Williams's platoons. He would send his remaining platoon to the 101st Infantry
Regiment, though the two regiments comprised one task force.[1]

Williams thought this had to be a cruel, new-guy joke, but Colley
explained the "big picture," as Bates said he would. The colonel
seemed adept at combined arms operations. Williams hung on every
word—where to go, with whom to talk, where to place his tanks, and
when to commence his attack. He nodded, trying to keep his jaw
from dropping open.

Dave Williams, "D.J." to his company,[2] chose the strong and confident Charlie Barbour and his platoon to go with the 101st. He mentioned it to Barbour in the course of conversation. Barbour stopped,
unable to grasp that his platoon would not be with the rest of the
company. Williams trusted Barbour more than any of his well-heeled
family in Pittsburgh, but had some concern about the 101st's ability
to employ Barbour's platoon. He did not share those thoughts with
Barbour. Everything would proceed just as they had trained. They
would meet up a little later. Williams appreciated Barbour's coopera-

tion, but sensed his unspoken protests. They had to move forward. He recalled Texas: Keep moving and the men will survive.[3]

As Bates met with his fellow commanders, he learned the front would become a tough slog for the Allies. German resistance had proved fierce. He figured it would only get worse as they closed on Germany's Westwall, the Siegfried Line in Allied parlance, purported as the most heavily defended line in the theater. Bates knew they would have to cross it at some point if they expected to defeat Germany.

Williams spent the day in meetings with Colley and officers of the 104th. The sheer number of lieutenants proved quite a sight. The closely held information piqued his interest. Relieve the stress on Metz. Attack Château-Salins and Morville-lès-Vic with the first platoon. Ford rivers. Bypass blown bridges.[4] Williams had not given much thought to the enemy blowing up their route, but it made sense. He would have his men cross a river if it proved shallow enough. He could lead his tanks. Bates never mentioned blown bridges.

Patton and the Third Army did not go it alone. Combat support surrounded Willard Paul and his new tank unit. No fewer than three army divisions continued to pound the French city of Metz, nearly sixty miles north of Nancy, Lorraine's ruling city over the centuries. During October 1944, war raged for the German Westwall city of Aachen, which stood as one stronghold the Germans did not intend to lose. Aachen fell to the First Army and the Allies October 21 and may have been a kick to the German hornet's nest. Headlines billed the German defeat as "the first of Hitler's doomed cities." The victory bolstered soldier morale as well as spirits at home.[5] Where a bustling urban center once stood, shells of incinerated buildings remained. As pockets of fighting continued, the Seventh Army dispatched XV Corps to hold the front to the south.[6]

With the north and south engaged, it fell to the 26th Infantry Division to take the towns and roads in Lorraine near the Lower Saar Basin to cut off all supply routes into and escape routes out of Metz. It seemed clear the Germans had no intention of leaving Metz and were confident of their superior position. Forty-three "intercommunicating forts on both sides of the Moselle [River] ringed the city" from which the Germans could rain hell on the 5th, 90th, and the 95th infantry divisions.[7]

The German Army had grown stronger during October when orders from General Dwight Eisenhower forced Patton to abandon his offensive. It had become apparent to the commander of the Supreme Headquarters Allied Expeditionary Forces, or SHAEF, that current supply lines could not support a full Allied attack into Germany. Eisenhower needed a port in the north. He needed Antwerp.[8] The offensive would recommence once the Allies had the German-controlled Belgian port. But the lull allowed the enemy time to entrench and fortify. The Germans built concrete barriers reinforced with steel. No advance route appeared vulnerable for Allied penetration. The enemy concealed artillery positions around themselves as well as along avenues of Allied approach. Few armies stood as well-acquainted with the power of armor than the German Army. Limited in what they had available, Hitler's forces laid mines by the thousands as a major defense against the American tank. The Germans maintained reserve infantry, armor, and ordnance. Luftwaffe planes sporadically flew overhead.[9]

As the Third Army planned and prepared for the renewed offensive, Patton extolled the advantages of armor at every opportunity. But some in his larger armor units quietly disagreed. While he maintained his beast of battle could breach the Westwall, the final obstacle to blitzing across Germany, experienced junior officers with strong opinions reminiscent of the brash Patton of 1920 believed German tank defenses would destroy Allied armor.[10] As November arrived, these officers believed the mud too much for the tanks to move through and remain combat effective. The continued rain made the situation worse. Of more concern, Patton faced restarting a Third Army that a month earlier epitomized success and morale. Marking time for logistical support went against the Patton grain. They had given the enemy a month to refortify. Regardless, Patton and his army stood ready, laden with supplies and a system of resupply to reach their final objective. Allied gains such as Aachen relieved some frustration, but Patton wanted to move and take the fight deeper into Germany.

Willard Paul waited with the rest of the Third Army and gave the 761st time to prepare its tanks. Soldiers checked parts, oiled guns, and stocked and positioned ammunition. Teddy Windsor patted William McBurney on the back as he inspected every inch of his main gun, running his hand along the exterior like he did with the armor of each new tank. He checked the barrel and breech. He adjusted his sights. He checked the .30 and the .50 caliber machine guns, too. Windsor and McBurney had been together since Camp Claiborne.

William McBurney stood as one of the best gunners in the battalion, something the tank commander rarely told him. This seemed like a good time to mention it, but as he watched McBurney work, studying each piece of the weaponry, he did not want to disrupt the kid's rhythm.

The army had attached Trezzvant Anderson to the Third Army as a private first class combat correspondent and a self-described "Army War Correspondent."[11] He stood as possibly the oldest private in all of Europe. Anderson raced around the theater with an energy and enthusiasm of a soldier half his age, writing and filing stories about the Red Ball Express, the Allied mobile supply line that derived its name from the red balls that marked the vehicles' routes.[12] Aside from proving a favorite for the veteran journalist, the Red Ball Express provided a choice target for the Luftwaffe.

The Third Army excelled at distributing information. Its intelligence section published "Morning Headlines" to keep at least its field commanders informed. News from the States indicated Roosevelt ahead in the presidential election vote count. "Morning Headlines" summarized Allied newscasts over the previous twenty-four hours, reporting on the attacks on Nancy and Metz, two towns of great interest to anyone serving under George Patton. The repackaged news covered the Eastern Front, Italian Front, the Air War, and Pacific Theater as well. It gave updates on Germany. Harrison probably nabbed his copy from the 761st intelligence section. Though published by the psychological warfare people and a bit optimistic for those facing the enemy, Harrison figured it gave them an overview beyond the tankers' bit role in the unfolding drama.[13]

Trezzvant Anderson hungered for information. He drove to the edges of the often lonely resupply routes of the Red Ball Express. His exhaustive search for the best stories in the predominantly African American-manned logistic train paid off. In his easy, folksy way he talked to countless soldiers. He cajoled their names, their parents' names, maybe a home address. He noted something distinctive about each soldier, maybe his successful high school football career, but always something that made the man special.[14]

But despite his freedom to prowl theaterwide, Anderson grew impatient. He needed more. He wanted to write about the unique. He demanded the cream of the black outfits. He discovered the army placed the 761st on alert soon after the order came from Washington. The tank battalion stood foremost on his mind, but he did not know the unit's arrival date. Eager to cover the battalion, he scribbled messages in his reporter's notebook anticipating the men's appearance.[15] He verified their status daily like he checked the time on his watch. He caught up to the 761st the day before the men expected to go into battle. The battalion of black combat tankers proved more intriguing than he had imagined. His mind raced. He had big plans. First, he needed photographs and had two signal corps photographers snap a number of pictures of the tankers. The images appeared sharp, clear, but unnatural and staged.[16] He talked to the men and watched as the tanks rolled to Athienville, the line of departure. He began his series of articles on the 761st before the new unit had fired a shot.[17]

Willard Paul planned to take the Lower Saar Basin with three regiments abreast, left to right, the 104th, the 101st, and the 328th.[18] As Colley had explained, the plan attached Williams and two Able Company platoons to the 104th. Ivan Harrison's buddy, now-First Lieutenant Charlie Barbour, one of the first three black officers in the 761st, commanded the platoon placed with the 101st Infantry. The rest of the force included the remaining 761st tanks, notably Charlie Company, moved to support the 328th Infantry Regiment.[19]

Barbour grew more concerned. It seemed that the 101st Infantry Regiment did not understand that if the enemy had dug in with gun emplacements, no tank could barrel down the main road to attack the village and expect to make it farther than the well-concealed enemy allowed. His tanks would get to the exact point the Germans planned and hit them hard with their waiting arsenal of machine guns and array of antitank weaponry. Any German soldier with this shoulder-launched panzerfaust—an antitank weapon similar to the American bazooka—could inflict damage if not destroy a tank and crew.

At the same time, Williams learned the commander of the first battalion of the 104th Infantry had expected more tanks than Williams's two platoons.[20] Williams looked at him and shrugged, wondering, *Don't these guys talk to each other?* Williams knew what Bates expected and kept the information to himself. He had not envisioned tension, confusion, and arguing independent of the German enemy to characterize his prelude to combat. He remained certain that two platoons would support the 104th Infantry Regiment and one would fight with the 101st. Williams, Barbour, and their infantry regiments moved into position on November 7, and waited for the order to attack.

The second force had a variety of units. The 328th Infantry Regiment seemed the most robust, with the 602nd Tank Destroyer Battalion, elements of the 165th Engineer Battalion, and the remainder of the 761st in support. The force had air support on call. Heavy artillery stood in question. Depleted ammunition stocks gave commanders fits, but tanks and tank destroyers still held enough rounds to provide significant firepower.[21]

At H-hour, November 8, Charlie Company under Captain Irvin McHenry headed off into combat supporting the 328th Infantry.[22] During their first moments, little had changed for most of the tankers. The briefings through which some dozed and films they saw made combat no more real than a Hollywood picture. The tanks had not changed nor had the tankers. The 761st happened to be in a different location deviating little from a maneuver in the States. William McBurney disregarded the uneasiness that filled the air.

Paul Bates remained with the largest force, Charlie and the 328th, his attention fixed on the movement of his tanks and the supported units. He enjoyed some solace with Williams and Barbour in position. They could handle their missions and their men, allowing Bates to concentrate on his tanks as well as the infantrymen they supported.

The units waited for the attack. Williams and his two platoons held at Bezange-la-Grande. He moved one of his platoons to the area of the MLR, or main line of resistance, to support the attack until they could cross the Seille River, as planned.[23] Barbour held just north of Arracourt. Russell Guthrie tensed in his gunner's position, face pressed to his sight. He closed his eyes anticipating the unknown. Able Company sat breathless, but ready. The Germans also waited, equally prepared. Certain of the attack, they surmised the Americans would move toward Dieuze. They guessed wrong.

Williams, Barbour, and their supported regiments instead headed toward Moyenvic, Hill 310, and Vic-sur-Seille, following Willard Paul's order.[24] Given a close review of his maps and the available intelligence, this option would give Paul's forces their best chance of success. Williams could tell success stood as the only option with men like General Paul. Dave Williams ordered hatches open for the first attack, despite the chilly rain. He developed the preference at Camp Hood. If an enemy round pierced the armor of one of his tanks, the men would have to exit. Hatches sometimes would stick, trapping tankers. If his crews survived a hit, their chances decreased with a sec-

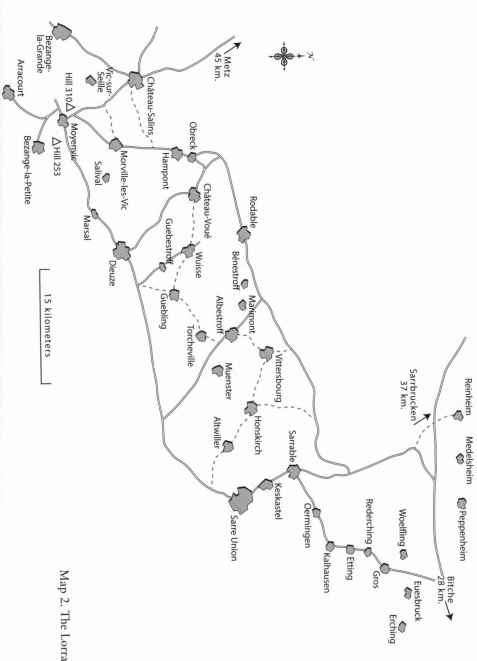

Map 2. The Lorraine Region.

ond and third strike. The tankers understood they might not escape a fire in a buttoned-up tank.[25]

The 104th and Williams's platoons made the first enemy contact in their attack on Vic-sur-Seille. Lieutenant Joseph O. Kahoe, Jr., moved his platoon. Lieutenant Robert Hammond had his tanks in place. With men like Kahoe, Hammond, and Barbour, Williams appreciated his good fortune. His sometimes unpredictable senior enlisted leaders gave him fits, but they stood as some of the best men in the 761st. This first day of combat proved no different. Williams ordered Staff Sergeant Ruben Rivers's section into town first. Rivers operated on his own rules, infuriating Williams. But the company commander trusted Rivers and knew he would get results. Williams needed a Ruben Rivers this day and stood prepared for the consequences.

As much as Rivers liked to talk, he said little about his family. Williams could understand and had tired of references to his father. Their paths to the 761st differed, but the brutality of combat joined them. Williams reminded himself he could handle the well-meaning and fearless staff sergeant. Ruben Rivers, a native of Tecumseh, Oklahoma, and the oldest of ten children, completed two years of high school and made his way toward the army through the Civilian Conservation Corps. His CCC paycheck and wages as a soldier helped his father, Will, a farmer, and his mother, Lillian, keep the family fed.[26]

The enemy welcomed the 761st and the infantrymen it supported with heavy fire. Williams cared little about the machine gun bullets that bounced off his Shermans. While he watched for the monstrous 88s, he remained most concerned with German mines, the outlines of which he could see from his position. The enemy probably hid a large number during October's fighting lull, but others appeared placed in haste.

He received updates from Kahoe and Hammond as they moved into Vic-sur-Seille. His tanks continued to take heavy fire from every direction. He had placed the battle in their hands. The infantry fared little better. Pre-attack fire on the town and tank rounds seemed to have little effect on the unseen enemy. With slight protection a barrage of enemy fire forced the 104th to take cover in roadside ditches, precisely where the Germans had aimed their weapons. The tanks fought off the invisible enemy as it fired to cover the Americans on foot. Williams thought the situation could only worsen for his men as they sat motionless in the open and directed his tanks to move down the road. He knew he risked an 88 hit no matter his decision. As drivers tried to maneuver their tanks out of the range of the enemy guns, they tripped mines. Enemy explosives disabled three Able Company tanks. They sat vulnerable to whatever the Germans threw at them. Williams watched his men, including those wounded by the blasts, scramble from their tanks. As Corporal Floyd Humphrey lay injured, medic Private Clifford Adams rushed to his aid. German rounds flew above the men. An exploding enemy shell hit Adams as he crouched, shielding Humphrey. The impact mortally wounded the medic.[27] Williams again recalled the harsh and tragic lessons from Hood: Take the loss and move forward.

The 104th Infantry and Williams continued to take fire in the vicinity of Vic-sur-Seille. His platoons maneuvered a mere 2,500 yards from Charlie Barbour's position. Williams still directed his tanks via radio. In an attempt to wipe out the Americans, the Germans had blocked the road, forcing the tanks to roll to a halt in the middle of the attack. Regimental intelligence reported Panzer activity, but Williams had seen no indication of German tanks. Staff Sergeant Ruben Rivers had a clear view of the situation from his lead tank. He understood the column had to move or the Germans soon would destroy the Able Company tanks with a few well-placed, high-explosive rounds. He reported the situation to Williams. Before the company commander could respond, Rivers had scrambled out of his tank lugging a heavy cable. Bullets whizzed by the unprotected tank commander. He attached the cable to the road block, an apparent tree, and connected the other end to his tank. He climbed unharmed back into his tank and moved the obstacle, allowing the column to move forward before the enemy could end Able's war just as it began.[28]

Dave Williams learned of Rivers's actions after Rivers finished the job. Williams knew something like this might happen. He dutifully expressed his anger at Rivers's recklessness, but Rivers knew the truth.

After the attack on Vic-sur-Seille commenced, poor weather, limited visibility, and the unanticipated challenges posed by the narrow and crooked village streets forced the infantry battalions to break down into smaller and smaller elements. Groups of soldiers exclaimed, "Don't shoot, we're Americans." Some sorted out the situation by giving the names of squad leaders and company officers, in lieu of code words that seemed not to exist.[29] Despite the confusion, the first battalion "root[ed] out the Germans in house-to-house fighting."[30]

Barbour's platoon and the 101st Infantry moved toward Moyenvic, the smaller of the two rural towns, and one offering the Germans less concealment in the way of structures. The mission had its challenges. The primary objective stood as Hill 310, the high ground soaring 110 meters above the Seille River and just two kilometers from Moyenvic.[31] The river had crested and slipped past its banks, hampering the American attack. One rifleman from F Company of the second battalion tried to wade across, but it proved too deep for the unit to move swiftly and effectively with the enemy in the area.[32] One bridge spanning the Seille remained intact, a fortunate fact crucial to the Americans' advance, though leaders hesitated to put their men on a bridge exposed to enemy fire.

The Germans had no plan to relinquish control of the area. They continued their barrage on Hill 310 and challenged the American invaders in the village. Barbour's platoon in support of the 101st Infantry took positions on the high ground north of Bois de Piamont. While his location seemed ideal, Barbour had not received any firing missions. He watched as the doughs, a common reference to doughboys, or infantry soldiers, fought for any gains. Companies E and F in position on top of the hill received direct and unexpected fire from the town of Marsal, a moated city to their rear. Additional fire came from enemy positions to the southeast. German automatic weapons flanked routes in and out of the area, making duty as a messenger, medic, or ammunition carrier a deadly proposition. Barbour awaited fire missions. Casualties mounted on the high ground and the regiment lost increasing numbers of officers to small arms and mortar fire in town. Charlie Barbour could do little to stave off the multipronged attack, but the 101st seemed to push back the enemy. By the next day, F Company counted all its officers among the casualties.[33]

The weather turned colder and the rain continued. Some infantry soldiers found themselves shivering in foxholes with six inches of standing water. An enemy sniper shot the F Company first sergeant-cum-company commander in the leg as he stood to relieve himself.

As the force pushed and success seemed imminent, noncombat casualties mounted. The long hours in cold pools that few could escape brought on the dreaded trench foot. Men who could, hobbled to aid stations on frozen stumps. The units evacuated the rest.[34]

Despite dwindling U.S. fighters, the town fell that morning to the Americans.

It became obvious that no one controlled the tank support. Though Barbour's tanks fired, they had no designated targets and did not fire in support of any specific infantry actions. In the confusion, leaders of the 101st believed such decisions should have come from the 761st unit commanders[35]—Barbour, Williams, or Bates. Barbour, who had expressed his concerns about the 101st, could not understand why he had no targets from the infantry. He chose to fire as he saw fit to best support the men on the ground.

Ruben Rivers. The staff sergeant would be posthumously awarded the Medal of Honor. (*761st Members Album, courtesy of Dale Wilson*)

From Barbour's position north of Bois de Piamont, "as the artillery preparation reached its height their [the tankers'] enthusiasm began to exceed their discretion and they began to fire with their main armament and their machine guns in the general direction of the town."[36] Barbour kept the platoon firing with everything it had on what he determined as the target, ignoring the principles of fire discipline, until after the town fell. During the siege, he turned his guns on Salival Farm to support I Company.[37] When the order came from the regimental commander for the tanks to move forward, Barbour realized his error in expending more than his allotted ammunition and ordered an immediate resupply. He fell behind the 101st Infantry. The platoon moved forward once it had its ammunition.[38]

Despite German resistance, the Americans unknowingly benefited from the element of surprise for which they originally had planned. Major General Friedrich F. von Mellenthin, the chief of staff for Army Group G, wrote, after his capture, that in spite of German intelligence and reconnaissance, "the enemy had made his final preparations with such cleverness and with such excellent deception, that our local forces were taken by surprise."[39]

Dave Williams sat exhausted. Maybe he faced poor timing, but it struck him he did not fully control his company, though Rivers and Russell Guthrie saw otherwise. While relieved by Rivers's quick action removing the road block, Williams knew the Oklahoma native well enough to realize that he would act before Williams gave the order. This had been a source of tension between the two men for some time. Rivers's penchant for operating on his own order seemed well-known and Trezzvant Anderson heard of Rivers's tank crews' "wild escapades."[40] Dave Williams considered this Rivers's flaw and saw that he, no matter how well-meaning, potentially endangered each man in the company. Though Williams understood that as company commander he protected or endangered his men, he allowed Rivers to anticipate his decisions. Somehow Rivers made the correct move each time before Williams barked out the command. Dave Williams envied Ruben Rivers.

The 104th took Vic-sur-Seille in a little more than an hour of fighting, though it seemed much longer to Williams, who agonized with every inch of mine-riddled ground his men's tracks covered. The battle did not end quickly enough. The German's 361st Volksgrenadier Division destroyed two of the three bridges and left the third in ruins, but with enough large debris that the engineers could make it passable by laying timbers.[41] Though the town stood in U.S. hands, German soldiers remained holed up within.

Williams pushed for further orders from regiment, but Colonel Dwight Colley had sustained serious injuries while coordinating the infantry and tank attack. Lieutenant Colonel Ralph A. Palladino, Colley's executive officer, assumed command with nothing more than the words "Château-Salins."[42] Williams nodded and got his tanks moving.

With Williams firmly with the 104th and Barbour's platoon securely with the 101st, their tanks rolled in support of the infantry while making mistakes that unknown to the two officers stood as typical of one's first combat engagement. They helped drive off the enemy in two towns, cleared roads, and rolled across bridges they now controlled.

Dave Williams felt a growing sense of dread. He prepared his two platoons to cross the stone bridge in daylight and without cover into Château-Salins. Before he could calculate the odds of the Germans blowing the bridge, he received the news: Lieutenant Colonel Bates had been killed.[43]

With the battle surrounding Able Company and each regiment moving in its designated sector, most of the 761st had no idea it had suffered its first combat death minutes into battle. That lack of information probably proved a blessing.

But who stood as the first casualty, Bates or the medic Adams?

A 761st Able Company Sherman crossing the only passable bridge in Vic-sur-Seille. The retreating Germans destroyed two of the town's three bridges and left the third in ruins but engineers were able to make it passable. (*National Archives*)

Earlier, Paul Bates watched as his tanks eased toward the enemy. He had concerns about tank defenses, hidden gun emplacements, and most of all—mines. As the tanks moved forward, Bates grabbed his driver. The two set out alone. Bates felt compelled to stand unprotected and direct his tanks. He went so far forward that he lost contact with his headquarters. For Bates, the area seemed unusually quiet. Calm. Intelligence reports did not place the enemy near his position, though he had seen the spot where he stood crawling with patrols each previous night. He left his driver in the jeep and set out alone on foot. Satisfied his men moved down the correct path, Paul Bates made his way back. He climbed in his vehicle. As he watched the last tank rumble its way down the muddy road he heard the unmistakable sound of gunfire.[44]

The operations report for the 328th Infantry Regiment included information the operations officer received on the newly attached 761st Tank Battalion. For the twenty-four-hour period between 11 A.M. November 7 and 11 A.M. November 8, the operations officer Goldsmith reported, "f. 'C' Co, 761st Tk Bn—At 0700 vic Rechicourt commenced fighting among themselves knocking out one (1) of own tanks. Fired on friendly troops in Rechicourt and ground to immediate front. C.O. Tk Bn. Wounded in ankle by own men. Tanks recalled and remained W of Rechicourt. Inf attack minus tanks."[45] The 328th believed Paul Bates's men shot him, delaying any further combat action of Charlie Company tanks that day.

With a battalion commander struck down at the beginning of battle, "eyewitness" reports abounded. One maintained that Bates moved onto the battlefield to arrest a Frenchman he suspected as a spy and who held up the movement of his tanks. Others believed a last-minute change in the tank route forced him to personally direct each tank. Others swore a German patrol got lucky and closed in on Bates and his jeep, ignoring the large collection of tanks for some unknown reason. An enemy machine gunner popped over the hill and riddled Bates's vehicle with bullets. Such an attack would have come from Bates's right. The bullet struck him in the lower left leg. No matter the cause, the fact remained: Bates had been shot.

Losing contact with Paul Bates came as no surprise to Ed Reynolds, given his commander's penchant for breaking his own rules and sacrificing his safety. He knew Bates well enough that he would just have to wait on the man. But as time passed, Reynolds grew concerned. He nudged Captain Russell Geist, Bates's other operations officer, and slipped away without a word. He did not want to cause alarm. Reynolds soon found Bates, who babbled something about an armed German patrol, but Reynolds heard little of what he had to say. Ed Reynolds focused on the gravity of the situation as he helped load Paul Bates into the ambulance. Reynolds had come to the 761st on a promise from Bates.[46] Paul Bates had delivered the crack tank battalion, but could his men perform without their leader? No one stood ready to take his place, not his executive officer, Major Charles Wingo, next in line of succession, and not Reynolds.

Most of the men heading into battle remained unaware of Bates's situation. Following the delay, Captain Irvin McHenry continued his Charlie Company tanks forward in support of the 328th Infantry Regiment. The regiment planned to penetrate enemy lines to Rodalbe and aimed for Bezange-la-Petite, Moncourt, and Hill 253. As feared, they hit considerable German resistance. McHenry, new to combat like the rest of the 761st, could not understand how he lost three tanks in the attack. The blood rushed from his head when he learned he had five men killed in action and two wounded. The battalion evacuated the casualties. Disabled tanks sat until Allied forces secured an area. McHenry hoped maintenance crews might salvage his tanks and get them back in the fight, but the damage pushed them beyond repair. He tried to conceal his shock from his battle losses, but his men felt the day left their commander numb.[47]

The perplexed tankers arrived at the front like millions of other young men. General McNair, killed July 25 near St. Lô, France, by an errant U.S. aerial bomb, had worked to increase the realism of combat training across the army. Live-fire courses designed by the British commandos helped the tank destroyer battalions at Camp Hood en route to the ETO. But McNair understood that training, no matter how realistic, could only come so close to actual combat. Soldiers had to get in the water and swim. They might go under a few times, but enough would make it to the other side.

The suddenness and cruelty of combat shook Charlie Company. McHenry, one of the strongest leaders in the battalion, held the men together, but if they had another day like November 8, he might see his unit crumble. Combat's truths held varied meanings. Each tanker, crew, and unit began to sort out what they had experienced from what they had envisioned. They could not reconcile the two.

Fifteen

The Ordeal of Company C

From Major General Paul's perspective at the 26th Infantry Division headquarters, despite the losses, and with a green unit like the 761st in support, the men had taken a handful of towns and one hill. Willard Paul had hoped for more, but they had to start somewhere.

Paul Bates's body contorted from the pain. Medical personnel determined the wound needed attention in a hospital. Bates looked at the medic. He had raced four hundred miles with his battalion to turn around for a stay in an English hospital and possibly a trip back to the States? He looked at his bleeding, broken leg. He had few options.

Bates remained optimistic. An unlucky shot delayed his part in the war, but no one would deny his unit its moment. It might have been a rough start, but he had trained them and knew his men as the best the army had to offer. They carried him from the battlefield. A day later he scribbled his first note to Taffy Rosen across the center of a V-Mail sheet, dated 9 November 1944: "Beloved: Was hit by Machine gun fire yesterday. Was unbelievably lucky. A broken leg about 10 inches above the ankle; small bone only, and a puncture of the leg, Am being evacuated to England by air now. All my love, Paul."[1]

Bates went over the past days and hours in his mind to determine if an error or fate forced his evacuation. Night after night, meetings had gone well past midnight, egos apparent. Plans for tank deployment changed many times, forcing Bates to note "it nearly drove me crazy."[2] At 2 A.M., hours before he was shot, Bates went to see Willard Paul, recommending he call off a part of the attack. The rain had made it impossible for his tanks to maneuver. Bates's news, so close to the H-hour, angered Paul, who immediately called his regimental commander for the part of the attack in question. At 3:45, the regimental commander called Bates to meet with him immediately. Sheets of rain forced Bates to have his driver transport him the two or so miles to the regiment instead of Bates's characteristic travel on foot.[3]

The regimental command post sat a thousand yards from the front. Despite the darkness, Bates noticed a number of enemy patrols. The regimental commander had made his decision: The attack would commence at 7 A.M. with Bates's tanks in the lead.[4] Bates in his later letter explained to Taffy Rosen that just before the attack, other vehicles mixed in with his platoons', slowing his tanks' movement. Bates jumped in the quarter ton, unraveled the tangle, and sent the last of his tanks on its way. An enemy machine gun fixed on the last armored Sherman. Bates watched as its bullets bounced off. At 6:45 A.M., the Germans spotted Bates in the soft, predawn light and opened fire. Bates sat exposed in his vehicle. The enemy riddled the vehicle with bullets. The only injury seemed to be a single shot to his left leg. Though grateful to be alive, Bates wrote, "wishing like hell I was with the unit for knowing their assignment know how badly they need me. Doctor says that I will take six weeks [to recuperate]."[5]

Word about Bates made its way to a few. Harrison found out soon after it happened. As headquarters company commander, he held the command post when Bates went to battle. He also took the headquarters tanks into combat. Ed Reynolds said little after putting Bates in the ambulance. Most in the unit continued with no idea of what had happened to their commander. Bates's status did not affect McBurney and he had no information on his battalion commander's location. He focused on his gun.

Harrison, in a rare moment to himself, pondered a 761st without Bates. Paul Bates had trained them, led them, and given men like himself a chance to learn and lead. Harrison wondered if he left them ready to fight without him. Apprehensive, he figured he soon would have an answer about Bates's prognosis. He may have linked his future and that of the 761st to Paul Bates's fate. Had they worked these many months, two years, really, to be hoodwinked at the threshold of glory? He planned to keep news of Bates restricted until he had more information.

Early on November 9, Williams's two platoons and the 104th attacked Château-Salins. The town fell with relative ease in four hours. The 101st "moved out toward the northeast in the valley along the road to Dieuze."[6] Barbour appeared to move to meet Charlie Company tanks. The 761st S-3, Captain Russell Geist, kept abreast of operations across the 700-man tank battalion. Geist, junior to Reynolds and the aviation S-3, thought he had it easy. In contrast, General Willard Paul answered to XII Corps for his sprawling 14,000-man division. Geist knew Bates found reports a nuisance and a logjam to combat leadership and had chosen an exceptional staff, in Geist's opinion, to accomplish the important but unenviable task. Geist maintained and organized records of daily actions for the 761st as well as myriad reports that went to higher headquarters. The operations officer prepared a monthly after-action report for the War Department's Adjutant General in Washington, D.C. Bates, a former 761st S-3 himself, selected Geist as the sole man in the 761st capable of doing the detailed job to Bates's standards. As the 761st fought, Russ Geist chronicled the operational action: "with one (1) Company of Infantry mounted on tanks crossed IP at Arracourt 0900. Moved through Infantry at Moyenvic (Q137205) proceeded north."[7] He may not have worn the director's hat, but he wrote the combat story of the 761st upfront, by the minute, and as it happened. Geist had no set hours. When the battalion fought, he worked. When the men slept, he caught up his backlog. Russ Geist chronicled the operations of a unit some said would never exist, let alone fight against Germany. Not even Ivan Harrison had an inkling as to the nonstop workings of the Geist mind.

Two platoons from Baker Company took up positions to the south. With their main guns sighted and loaders busy jamming in round after round, they pummeled the village of Salival with such intensity they set it ablaze, clearing the area for infantry to enter as the inferno subsided.[8]

From the moment they stepped off, it proved a different war for each soldier during those first two days. Bates headed to Britain leaving his battalion leaderless and divided. Able Company remained split in support of the 104th and the 101st. The remaining combat companies continued in support of their regiments. Harrison remained in reserve with a few Headquarters Company tanks. Between him, Geist, and the S-4 Phil Latimer, whom Harrison saw as the best supply man and logistician around but annoying as hell with his Texas optimism, he knew they stood as the very few who maintained a view of overall operations, albeit from differing vantages. Harrison dealt only in facts. He and the staff received reports from the companies as the battle unfolded. Bates had taught them enough so he could figure out how to lead a headquarters and a posse of tanks with a hostile enemy always a threat.

But Harrison remained concerned. The glue keeping the companies and platoons together and performing seemed to be the men's belief that they fought on a Hollywood set or as the cocky, care-free Camp Hood aggressor force, outmaneuvering the larger and more nimble tank destroyer battalions at will. Harrison waited. Save for Charlie Company's losses, the tankers had not yet witnessed war's full impact.

Baker Company commander Lieutenant John D. Long, not surprised by his tankers' success at Salival, glimpsed the effects of his guns for the first time. In a few seconds they pushed through smoldering ruins littered with grotesque, charred remains of what appeared to have been German soldiers. But any impact passed without comment. Their minds had moved to the next objective. [9]

Despite taking Vic-sur-Seille and Moyenvic, fighting continued in the area. Someone at a higher headquarters had learned of Bates's fate. A new commanding officer, Lieutenant Colonel Hollis A. Hunt, took control of the battalion. Major John F. George arrived as his executive officer.[10] Ed Reynolds's heart sank as he slinked back to his operations job from his hours leading the 761st. The opportunity to command arrived much to Reynolds's surprise after Charles Wingo seemed to flee the battlefield. Reynolds later wryly recounted to Bates the series of whirlwind transitions while the 761st and 26th Infantry Division fought the enemy.[11] The quiet command transition went unnoticed by the embroiled tankers.

With Able Company in Château-Salins, and Baker's destruction of Salival, the 761st moved toward Morville-les-Vic, but before they could reach their objective, they came under heavy enemy mortar and artillery fire. Adrenaline pumped through the battalion. Its effect seemed especially strong on the gunners, who fired shell after shell on the town. A number of infantry and tank elements converged on Morville for the attack. Baker Company had its mission to move up the middle and into the village. It moved forward without giving the enemy much thought, but roadblocks and panzerfaust fire halted its advance. One look at the enemy's antitank capability and Long knew he had to get his tanks out.[12]

A roadblock supported with enemy antitank weapons seemed like a page out of one of the tankers' myriad manuals, labeled "Do not let this happen to you." McBurney and most of the tankers learned to fear the panzerfaust most of all the German antitank weapons. A lone German with a cheap, disposable panzerfaust on his shoulder could move on foot within sixty meters of a tank and blast through the hull with its preloaded 150 mm high-explosive shaped charge. It could penetrate nearly eight inches of armor with ease, more steel than U.S. tanks carried.

Though the U.S. had invented the one-man antitank weapon, gunners like McBurney and Guthrie could see the enemy won this contest with its improvements. The lethality of the panzerfaust trumped the bazooka, which could only penetrate about four inches of armor, although the bazooka did have an effective range that averaged twice to three times that of its German cousin.[13]

As Baker Company faced its challenges, the force commander fell wounded. Hunt, new to the 761st but not to combat, took command. The well-trained cavalry officer pushed for the attack to continue.

McHenry and his men had regained their confidence the second morning of battle, November 9. They had done their jobs and most survived. Their first day seemed a fluke, a bit of bad luck. Most agreed combat could be no worse than it had been the first day. McHenry and his tanks swept northwest from Bezange-la-Petite toward Moyenvic. Barbour made his way back to meet McHenry and form a pincer movement. McHenry advanced toward higher ground overlooking the other force at Morville.[14] U.S. forces converged for the attack. Able Company remained to the left, while Baker again fought its way up the center into Morville, aware of possible roadblocks and antitank fire.[15]

Charlie Company continued northwest, while Dog Company, the reconnaissance arm of the 761st under Richard English, engaged, moving from Salival.[16] English's men, working with a patrol from the 3rd Battalion, 101st Infantry Regiment, fought off an enemy unit ready to counterattack Salival.[17] German forces that had taken up positions at a German artillery officer candidate school at Marsal surprised the Americans and fired on them with every available weapon.

Baker broke through the trap the enemy set and pushed toward the center of Morville, only to be greeted by another barrage of anti-tank and machine gun fire from second-story and cellar windows. The Germans dominated and knocked out the Baker tanks of their choosing. Sergeant Roy King, who commanded the second Baker tank to make it past the enemy obstacles, pulled his tank into position to destroy one building, a suspected lair for several German gun posts. An enemy panzerfaust returned the favor and destroyed his tank in seconds. With his Sherman in flames he ordered his crew to evacuate. The Germans hit King with machine gun fire, killing him as he exited the tank. The panzerfaust blast badly wounded Corporal Herbert Porter. He slumped in the Sherman. Private Nathaniel Ross, Jr., scurried out the turret hatch opposite King, unscathed.[18]

Private John McNeil and Technician Fifth Grade James I. Whitby saw little chance of survival in the disabled tank, yet an escape attempt through the turret hatch looked like suicide. They exited through the hatch in the deck of the tank, crawling out with their sub-machine guns. They dreaded the belly hatch, but the tankers had rehearsed the harrowing exit so often that slipping out came almost naturally. With forty-four tons of steel for cover, McNeil gunned down Germans as they raced for their antitank weapons. He took out at least one second-story machine gun nest.[19]

Whitby slid back in their burning tank the same way he had exited, manned a .30 cal and took out several machine gun nests and a panzerfaust. The battle seesawed for three hours between the rag-tag tankers and what appeared to be a superior German force. Enemy fire hit McNeil's disabled tank at least two more times, but he and Whitby kept firing. The rest of the Baker Company column and the infantry soldiers continued to fight their way through the village.[20]

With machine gun fire the enemy pinned down the infantry tasked with clearing Morville. Tankers like Warren Crecy covered their escape with .30 cal fire from the tanks.

Despite the heavy antitank attack, Baker Company fought off the enemy and seven tanks passed through Morville-les-Vic. The bruised tankers assisted the infantry in gaining ground in Bois de la Géline. At the same time, Richard English and his light Stuarts found heavy combat, but they broke through as well and maneuvered to the north-east, to the high ground flanking the woods, and broke up a German counterattack. Instincts forged in training took over their movements, but a determined enemy force continued to challenge the tankers and infantry. After losses to both sides, the Germans seemed to disappear. The tankers claimed Private First Class Obie J. Smith knocked out twenty German soldiers with his machine gun.[21]

While his Stuarts engaged the enemy, English, the New Orleans educator, performed the company's reconnaissance mission on foot armed with his Tommy gun tucked close by his side. The day proved a new experience for one of the oldest men in the battalion,[22] and English shook just like his teenagers. He recited the periodic table over and over to calm his nerves.[23]

McBurney had stopped thinking after he fired his first round. He acted on instinct and nearly two years' training. He paused for a moment to take a breath and realized he and the others had made it through one hell of a first day. The second day left him nervous as he allowed himself to consider the prior day's actions. The Germans' weapon fire terrified him, though he had not really noticed his fear the previous day. A deep drag on a cigarette calmed him. No shaky hands for the gunner, said Teddy Windsor, whose tone seemed less than convincing, but the slap on the back reassured him as it always had. McBurney thought for a moment maybe he had rushed to judgment. He would give war another chance. He had no choice and it could be no worse than the first day.

McHenry waited. He paced. He cursed to himself, his men none the wiser. He had heard about Bates, but could not be sure if he had been killed. Regardless, he felt as if he had lost his right arm. For the briefest moment he thought the battalion would collapse and go to hell. But as Bates-trained men, they would make it.[24] They had to. They would succeed or end up guests in some German prisoner-of-war camp.

Charlie Company held the high ground that day and would hold the area until "doughs," could make their way to relieve McHenry and his men. Word had spread to the commanders that a hellacious tank ditch might greet some unlucky unit around Morville.[25] McHenry would have appreciated more information as to its exact location, but he would take whatever intelligence he could get. Any tank obstacle could mean trouble, but a tank ditch just the right size could disable the lead tank in a way that the other tanks could not maneuver around. Throwing each tank in reverse probably would do no good, since the enemy would have disabled the last tank. The trapped column would sit ripe for an enemy attack.

McHenry's tanks found the ditch. Captain Irvin McHenry, startled by the German trap, halted the column. The enemy made no attempt to camouflage the enormous trench because whoever encountered it could not escape. It ran from the wood line and across the road, completely cutting off anyone who dared approach. McHenry had never seen anything like it. As the company ground to a halt, some of the tanks hit the mines the Germans had set forward of the ditch's edge. The column had also come to rest within range of the concrete pillboxes less than fifty yards on the other side of the ditch, well-concealed

Samuel Turley. (*761st Members Album, courtesy of Charles M. King*)

by the recent snow. McHenry and his company became the unlucky saps. The Germans knocked out seven of Charlie Company's tanks almost immediately.[26]

First Sergeant Sam Turley, who had come to the 761st with Dave Williams from the 758th, rode with Charlie on November 9. At the last minute Turley took the place of one of his jittery drivers and acted as tank commander. Turley and platoon leader Second Lieutenant Kenneth W. Coleman knew the Germans would slaughter the company if the men stayed with the tanks. McHenry gave the order to dismount. The German firepower from the other side of the tank ditch overwhelmed the men attempting to crawl to safety.[27]

Turley and Coleman watched the pathetic scene. Tankers hugged the cold, wet ground in the open as German bullets ended their war. The two tank leaders acted. Coleman gathered the men still in the column. He followed behind, laying fire to cover their evacuation while they struggled to safety in front of him. Turley remained between the enemy and the tankers to cover Coleman and the rest of the company making their escape. Both men moved with automatic weapons and ammunition in hand, firing at the enemy.[28]

Turley and Coleman moved back-to-back, as if they had rehearsed for this moment their whole lives. Coleman tried to hurry the men away from the ditch and out of the range of the German weapons. Tankers continued to fall.

Sam Turley rushed the void that separated enemy from enemy. He let loose with a barrage to cover Charlie's evacuation. The spur-of-the-moment plan, though not ideal, seemed to work better than either Turley or Coleman could have hoped. Some soldiers made it to safety. Turley remained exposed in the middle of the firefight. He may have believed he would rejoin Coleman and Charlie and Captain McHenry that day. Regardless, he knew he would see his men again. He stood, feet planted, and continued to fire across the ditch, suppressing the German machine gun nests.

Help seemed imminent from Baker Company. Baker had arrived on the other side of the woods, forcing the Germans to divide their fire, providing some relief to Charlie Company. But the enemy attack immobilized Baker at the edge of the tree line,[29] a fortuitous situation for the Germans but a deadly one for Charlie. Baker's situation allowed the Germans to divert fire power back to the tank ditch and concentrate on Charlie's complete annihilation.

No one left a tanker behind that day. Those able helped others to safety. Private Dennis A. Osby went back into his burning tank where gunner Autry Fletcher struggled, his feet tangled in a .50 cal ammo belt. Staff Sergeant Frank C. Cochrane pulled Ernest Chatmon and tank commander Technician Fifth Grade George Collier from their disabled tank. Corporal Dwight Simpson rescued Technician Fourth Grade Horatio Scott from his burning tank.[30] Warren Crecy, with his own men to lead, had no idea how his closest friend, Horatio Scott, had fared.

Even with Turley's firing rendering some enemy guns ineffective as they took aim at his men, escaping the Charlie tanks did not equal survival. Exposed tankers belly-crawled hundreds of yards under heavy fire through a cold slurry of snow, ice, and mud. Enemy rounds whizzed by Turley and struck their intended targets. Those who made it to relative safety could only watch as German fire picked off tanker after tanker. The refugees had dragged what weapons they could, but the mud and debris filled the barrels, leaving them inoperable. Some found escape hopeless and pulled their firepower under their tanks and took aim at the enemy, inspired by Coleman and Turley.

The escaping tankers looked back. Sam Turley stood at the edge of the mine-laced precipice, still firing his machine gun. When the Germans recovered from the surprise of the brazen Americans, they killed Coleman. Turley continued until a burst of fire nearly cut him in two. He collapsed, in the slush, weapon in hand.[31] Some said a German 88 landed where he fell. Sam Turley's war had ended.

With some communication remaining between the units, a shaken McHenry called for fire. Harrison dispatched Lieutenant Charles "Pop" Gates, his assault gun platoon leader. Gates gave the order to his M4s equipped with 105 mm howitzers that opened fire, killing an estimated two hundred Germans and destroying twenty of their vehicles. Two air liaison aircraft reported a column of Germans soldiers moving toward the battle area,[32] probably reinforcements for what appeared to be an already robust German force, in McHenry's opinion. Between Gates's howitzers and the rounds that Charlie survivors fired at the Germans, the task force limped forward and cleared the area.

The 328th Infantry Regiment thought little of Charlie's deadly encounter. They had fought enough battles in as many days and lost more men than Charlie had that day. Regimental and infantry battalion S-3s neglected to mention Charlie's challenges. The tankers faced unprecedented losses, something Bates had talked about with his company commanders. He watched them nod as he spoke, but it seemed they did not understand the realities of war. McHenry recalled discussions with Bates, but had not expected this. He got them caught in a German trap. Turley and Coleman and too many soldiers died because of his carelessness. He did not yet know how many men he had lost. He did not deserve these men. If command meant losing his men's lives, maybe Bates had picked the wrong guy.

Charlie Company had to move forward. McHenry still had a mission. He grew concerned his remaining soldiers would turn their heads to the wall and give up the fight, as he had considered more than once that day. Instead, his survivors manned the remaining tanks. New crews formed with no time to mourn those lost, among them best friends.

The men removed the casualties from the field. The death toll mounted—four, seven, fourteen. Coleman and Turley and twelve other enlisted soldiers.[33] McHenry tucked away his shock and numbing sadness. Medics transported the injured. Though each company engaged in its action, tankers like Warren Crecy checked on friends. When the units began to move, Crecy asked about Horatio Scott and found he had been transported for further medical care. Crecy received a message from Scott. He would see him soon.[34]

The technicians reported to McHenry. The Germans damaged three of the seven tanks beyond repair, but they could save four.[35]

The battered battalion had its orders, but the battlefields of France stood as a slaughterhouse. William McBurney had trained to be a tanker, but over two days he learned all those months at Camp Claiborne and Camp Hood had come down to a choice: kill or be killed. He tried to reconcile the combat of France with that portrayed in the moving pictures. He saw men die. He killed the enemy. He now understood why Bates had them move so quickly in training. McBurney had thought Bates worked them to keep them out of trouble. Paul Bates trained them to act on instinct to survive. He learned in a few minutes of combat that the countless days of monotonous drills took over his quivering body when his mind went blank. He fought because that is what Bates trained him to do, regardless of the adversity they faced. Bates handpicked their leaders—men he knew would remain solid. Yet nothing could have prepared him for this.

He had little time to consider what had happened fighting the enemy, not that he saw himself as a deep thinker. Worse, or maybe better, he had no time to grieve.[36] He knew he should feel sadness for friends lost, but he had to look forward to survive and defeat the enemy. His father had been clear and he had been a soldier long enough to know what "they" said about black units like the 761st. He looked around. He saw no sign the 761st would crumble, though he admitted it entered his mind. Fall apart? They worked too hard and he believed they shared the same resolve. It took them a long time to get to Europe. He had no plans of leaving until the 761st completed its mission.

Two days left a changed battalion. The new battalion commander, Hollis Hunt, moved quickly to rebuild his companies, especially Charlie, which had almost been knocked out of the war. He had seen the orders from division. Another match against the enemy appeared imminent. McBurney learned that he, Teddy Windsor, and the whole tank crew now belonged to Charlie Company. He nodded in agreement, knowing he would serve with the best.

Sixteen

A Step Closer to Germany

T HE 761ST WANTED TO ROLL OUT OF MORVILLE MORE THAN IT
had wished to leave Camp Claiborne and Camp Hood, but
work remained. Two platoons from Able Company and the 104th
Infantry Regiment marched through Morville, placing the town firmly in Allied hands.[1] The 4th Armored Division arrived in the area to
support the 26th Infantry Division and attacked in a parallel zone to
A and B companies of the 1st Battalion of the 104th Infantry through
Ham Pont and Obreck.[2] By November 9 the 104th learned it needed
to better communicate with and employ supporting assets like the
761st tank platoons.[3] Regimental leaders also tried to refrain from
judging units on appearance. C Company of the 104th stood as one
of the most ragtag bunch of infantry soldiers some had ever seen.
Their company commander, Major Werner Holz, admitted the
"appearance" of his men "was considerably below the standard
maintained during their training period. Nevertheless morale in the
company was high and all missions were accomplished."[4]

The 104th Infantry moved to the crossroads at Ham Pont and to
Obreck as planned. Williams's two tank platoons rolled in support.
The Germans had anticipated the Americans' move and waited with
added firepower. Regimental intelligence reported elements of the
11th Panzer Division in the area.[5] On November 10 the towns fell
with less resistance than anticipated. Reports made their way back to

headquarters that Staff Sergeant Ruben Rivers had gunned down possibly hundreds of Germans. The 104th cleared Obreck. One of its battalions established its command post in the village. But victory came with cost: Williams lost two tanks with two men killed and three wounded in the fighting.[6]

The morning of November 10 found the 101st Infantry Regiment on the offensive. Barbour remained shaken, but ready to support with his tanks. I Company "resumed its attack on enemy position in the woods to the north."[7] The company planned to send Barbour's tanks "up the ravine to the northeast to blanket the woods with flanking fire."[8] Before Barbour gave the command to move forward, the company received word of a tremendous tank ditch stretching across the ravine and making its way well into the treeline on either side. Charlie's hell the previous day from a duplicate scenario remained unknown to Barbour and the others. The 101st I Company commander remained undeterred. He would send the tanks out "cross-country" with his infantry trailing. Their destination: the corner of the woods where the ditch ended. Barbour gave the order and his platoon moved out. The foot soldiers had not expected such a brisk pace. Barbour pulled ahead and tankers and doughs lost one another. A determined I Company commander regrouped with Barbour, his newfound respect for the tankers apparent. The leaders, both on edge, came to an agreement and mapped out their plan.[9]

Hollis Hunt probably figured he might have to pull McHenry out of Charlie Company after the losses he suffered. Instead, he brought Barbour back to the command post for a few days before he made a final decision. He saw that Barbour performed well, but it seemed the loss of three tanks and two men killed in action shook his spirit. Ed Reynolds thought the losses put Charlie Barbour in shock. Regardless, Hunt sidelined Barbour from his platoon before an error cost more tanker lives.[10]

The 101st Infantry Regiment fought in the area of Dieuze, its flanks exposed. The 3rd Battalion occupied nearby Rodalbe, though it remained vulnerable.[11] Late in the afternoon of November 12, the Germans counterattacked and attempted to take back the town. Enemy tanks and Panzer infantry surrounded Rodalbe and trapped the battalion. Able Company tanks worked to muscle their way to the beleaguered battalion, though they fell short, "unable to bring aid because of roads, mines and enemy antitank action."[12] Heavy enemy artillery fire escalated to robust shelling with 88s.[13] The brazen enemy invaders swarmed the town, shouting to further intimidate the overrun Americans. German Panzers roared and stuck their main gun muzzles point-blank "in cellar doors and windows." The battle subsided as the evening wore on, though no one rested. During the night, small bands of U.S. infantrymen escaped the perimeter. Despite a U.S. counterattack, the Germans nearly wiped out the 3rd Battalion, and the 1st and 2nd battalions took heavy casualties, yet they prevented the German counterattack from spreading. After what became nearly a week-long siege dominated by the Germans, the Americans, with fresh replacement soldiers, recaptured Rodalbe.[14]

McHenry had one Charlie Company platoon working with one Dog Company platoon to flush local woods of enemy infantry. Together they gained ground, moving them closer to the next target.[15]

As the 101st Infantry Regiment ensured that Rodalbe sat firmly under Allied control, Guebling stood as the next main objective, fifteen kilometers west of Ham Pont, but several enemy-occupied towns stood between the two. The Germans expected the Americans in Dedeling and Château-Voué. Unfortunately no place could be overlooked. Leaving even the smallest German foothold meant the enemy controlling a rear position from which it could launch attacks or cut off and surround the Americans, as the 101st learned when the Germans fought to retake Rodalbe. Despite a substantial and prepared enemy, Able and the 104th cleared one town and moved to the next.

The 104th Infantry and its fellow regiments worked to consolidate gains each day, but dwindling manpower hampered their efforts. After the heavy losses suffered at Rodalbe, the operations officer noted future moves by the unit relied in part on replacement infantry. Where possible, regiments looked to exploit gains and learned they must keep their flanks secure.[16]

Dave Williams felt they fought day and night without rest. Could he be any more tired? He marveled at his men who showed few signs of slowing other than the occasional catnap. But next stood the village of Wuisse, and Able Company had fire missions. With little trouble, Able destroyed two enemy tanks and Wuisse fell to the Americans following a battle with one Able Company platoon under Lieutenant Joe Kahoe and the 2nd Battalion of the 104th Infantry.[17] The Americans expected a counterattack and fought off an enemy attempt to retake the village through the night of November 13 and into the next day.[18] But Guebling remained in German hands.

The 104th Infantry Regiment and Captain Dave Williams received word the 4th Armored Division would make the attack on Guebling. Williams certainly did not want the job. The early battle seesawed between the Germans and the Americans. The U.S. tanks of Task Force West found themselves in a tank-on-tank shoot-out with several German Panther tanks from the 15th Panzer Regiment. Both sides took casualties, but Task Force West took Guebling. Or so U.S. forces thought.

A shortage of daylight did not permit the Americans to secure the all-important high ground or knock out the remaining German observation posts. This proved costly. At 3 A.M., U.S. gasoline trucks rolled into Guebling. The Germans had taken up positions, waiting for the Americans to make a move. Once all the trucks had pulled into position and parked, enemy fire resulted in a series of tremendous explosions. Flames engulfed the area. Given the formidable enemy, Task Force McKone arrived at first light to reinforce Task Force West. The Germans beat them back. But the 10th Armored Division made gains on the high ground. By noon the mix of snow and rain had become blinding. The 4th Armored Division commander reviewed his losses of tanks and men. As he received reports of the Guebling gains crumbling, he ordered Lieutenant Colonel Delk M. Oden to withdraw his armor.[19] The Germans had concealed their weapons. Oden's men and vehicles faced a 1,500-yard gauntlet of exploding enemy shells. A smoke screen helped the escape, but Oden described his losses as "severe." The enemy nearly destroyed the 35th Tank Battalion, leaving it with just fifteen operational tanks.[20] The Germans planned to remain in Guebling. It fell to the 104th Infantry's and Williams's tank platoon's task to take it from them.

On November 18, as Dave Williams moved five tanks toward Guebling to prepare for the assault, they came under fire. Williams, seeing Rivers's mangled lead tank, probably damaged by a mine blast, stopped and feared the worst. He climbed inside and, to his relief, found the crew very much alive. Rivers said nothing. Williams saw his arms around the shredded cloth that covered his bloody leg. Rivers at first rebuffed efforts to bandage the deep wound, but relented. Williams watched. He thought he could see the bone but said nothing. The medic intervened. Dave Williams put his arm around a man who at that moment seemed the most important person in his life. Rivers needed a doctor. As he tried to lift Rivers for evacuation, the wounded staff sergeant stood on his own and declared he would not go back to the medical tents, possibly unaware of how much the wound had weakened him. He assured Williams he would need him. Rivers, probably shaken, but hiding his pain, left his damaged tank and climbed in to command another Able Company tank.

With one major attack already repelled by the enemy, Williams thought he invited disaster with the impending Guebling mission. Rivers now may have lacked stamina to lead the mission, but Williams let it go. He did need Ruben Rivers, he thought, no matter his condition.

The town of Guebling sat a step closer to Germany. But the enemy units occupying Guebling already had defeated a sizable U.S. task force and had driven the Americans from the town they had taken— albeit briefly. The Germans often disappeared from threatened towns, but they determined they would hold Guebling, a major communications hub between Château-Salins and Saarburg, and would kill anyone who tried to take it.[21] In a tactic now well known to the Americans, they had heavily mined the town. The large number of hidden explosives concerned Williams more than rumors of German tanks patrolling the area. Disabled 761st tanks did no one any good. While his men might survive the mine blast from below, the tank would suffer enough damage to render it inoperable. The crew could perish in the flames that might engulf the small compartment or find themselves cut down by enemy gunfire as they made their escape. Williams looked for an option.

It had grown colder and snow had fallen, making conditions miserable for the men to live and fight. Coordination and communication between the tank company commanders and the infantry leaders proved a challenge at best. From Obreck, the liaison officer reported enemy action to Geist. One bridge sat blown and a crater stretched across the road between Nancy and Dieuze. Local civilians reported enemy work on "dug-outs, pill boxes & tank traps at Mittersheim." Pilots reported fifty enemy convoys of twenty to thirty vehicles each in the area. The liaison noted on November 18 that one Panzer division headed toward Merzig and Saarbrueken with MK V Panther as well as MK VI Tiger tanks.[22]

At 8:00 A.M. November 19, Able Company attached one platoon to the 101st Infantry Regiment in the vicinity of Wuisse. Baker placed two platoons with the 2nd Battalion of the 104th. Charlie had one platoon and five assault guns with the 328th Infantry, and Dog remained with the 26th Reconnaissance Troop.[23] They had their missions.

Despite his injury, Ruben Rivers rode out ahead in the lead tank toward Guebling with his eyes scanning for the enemy. He knew the Germans already proved deadly. Rivers prepared for the worst. Williams grew nervous. He knew Ruben Rivers belonged in a hospital far from the front. The medic had insisted Rivers move to the rear and get the deep hole in his leg assessed. Williams ordered him to a field hospital. Rivers ignored him. Williams shook his head, frustrated that the young man with such talent proved more stubborn than even Paul Bates. Rivers, in a low, raspy voice, told Williams and the medic that with the extreme cold, he did not feel a thing. At this, the medic's internal alert told him that Rivers had slipped into shock and should be moved immediately. Rivers again declined the offer, reasoning the company would be out for a couple of days, tops, and Williams needed him. Dave Williams stopped arguing. Rivers lived by Rivers's code.[24] Williams did not want to lose his best man. He respected that Rivers fought on his own terms, and Williams, knowing that as the company commander he had used poor judgment when it came to Rivers, allowed it.

They moved through the frigid morning air. The roar of tank engines and the crunching of Sherman tracks broke the silence. The sound of German guns added to the cacophony. The battle had begun. Rivers lost his tank to enemy fire, but scrambled to another M4 and climbed in, joining a crew that included driver Tech 4th Jonathan B. Hall, Private First Class Frank Jowers, Bow Gunner Ivory V. Hillard, and Gunner Private Everett Robinson.[25] He radioed Williams and confirmed he saw the enemy, "D.J., I see them."[26] Williams knew trouble and he felt it. "Ruben, get back. Get back," Williams radioed, his panic evident.

Rivers's tank passed within two hundred yards of a German's position. The enemy fired on his second tank with two high-explosive rounds. The first round penetrated the Sherman. Three men went down. The explosion killed Rivers instantly. Hillard died on the ricochet. Rivers's lifeless body absorbed the second round.[27] The rest of the crew attempted an escape, expecting a third round, maybe more. Before either man could react, Williams heard a horrific static in place of Rivers's voice. Williams shouted, "Hello, Ruben! Hello, Ruben! Ruben!" No response.[28] He felt it. He called again. Nothing.

As more tanks in the platoon met trouble, men evacuated the disabled tanks, but had no way to safety. Platoon leader Second Lieutenant Robert C. Hammond manned a .50 caliber machine gun and covered their escape. He died saving his men. Staff Sergeant Theodore Weston scrambled out of his tank, took Hammond's position, and continued the assault. Guebling fell later that day. Between the mines and the antitank fire, the Germans took out half of Williams's tanks. He still had three tanks positioned west of the river, where they did him no good.[29]

Sergeant Henry Conway made his way to Williams. With tears streaming down his muddy cheeks he confirmed the deaths of Rivers and Hammond. Williams thought maybe Conway had gotten it wrong—possibly confused identities. Williams called for stretchers and men to carry the wounded. His men confirmed the worst.[30] Dave Williams broke down and blamed himself. Rivers had a Silver Star nomination and that gaping hole in his leg. He should have been on his way home, but Williams wanted them to beat Germany together. So damned selfish, he thought. With Rivers's and Hammond's deaths on him, the war changed. He had failed his men. His life meant nothing to him.[31]

In the middle of Guebling, Williams met Hollis Hunt. An angry Hunt could not understand what had happened to Able and pulled the company off the line. Williams announced he planned to nominate Rivers for the Medal of Honor.[32] He rebuffed Hunt's protests. The medal concerned Ruben Rivers and not Hollis Hunt. Through his anger, Dave Williams knew Hunt characterized Williams's mess with accuracy. The battle did not please Williams either. He knew he made mistakes. He would make changes, but he would allow no one, not even Hunt, to block his way when it came to Ruben Rivers. Dave Williams had no way of knowing he would spend the next several decades fighting for the soldier to whom he owed so much.

After the German slaughter of Able Company, the 26th Infantry Division continued to move west and recaptured towns from the enemy. Lieutenant John Long received orders to move Baker Company to Benestroff to support an infantry offensive. Buoyed by his men's performance, Long chalked up their success to training and talent. Luck had nothing to do with his good fortune or Charlie's and Able's troubles. As he moved Baker Company from Rodalbe to St.

Suzanne, Long lost two tanks to enemy mines, jarring the young company commander, who nonetheless kept his men moving forward. Later Long feared the loss of the tanks as a sign of things to come. Baker hit a roadblock and came under heavy antitank fire. Long maneuvered away from the threat and ordered his men out on foot on a reconnaissance mission. They found an alternate route to Benestroff, a not-so-secret one that the Germans had filled with mines.[33]

A new order came for Long and Baker Company to support the 2nd Battalion of the 104th Infantry Regiment in its attack on Marimont. Long decided he would move to Benestroff as planned and race south to join the 2nd Battalion.[34] Clearing the road to Benestroff proved more difficult than anyone anticipated. The engineers failed to clear the route for Baker Company to support the infantry battalion in its attack on Marimont as planned. The tank company assisted the infantry "advance to the edge of the woods northeast of Marimont" and forced German tanks to withdraw from the area. Long saw the company's performance as a good omen: another mission, though altered from the original plan, with no casualties for Baker.[35]

Geist left the confines of the operations shop and joined McHenry and Charlie Company on November 20 to shell Kerprich, Dieuze, Guenestroff, Guebestroff, and Vergaville, still supporting the 2nd Battalion of the 328th Infantry Regiment. A weapon recoil broke McHenry's hand.[36] The shocked Charlie Company commander stared in disbelief, and concealed the mishap as long as possible, probably swearing Geist to secrecy. When Hunt learned of the injury, he sidelined McHenry on November 22, two days after the accident, and ordered his evacuation for treatment. He moved Lieutenant Charles "Pop" Gates from his assault guns to command Charlie.[37] Dog Company shifted in with the 328th and moved on two more towns. For several days the attached tank battalions, 761st assault guns, as well as Willard Paul's infantry regiments moved like a wildfire, occupying town after town. Targets like Bassing, Bidestroff, Inswiller, Torcheville, Nebbing, and Neufvillage fell under U.S. control.

Albestroff proved an enemy stronghold. Major General Willard Paul ordered 761st tanks to support the ongoing attack on the crucial crossroads at Albestroff by the 1st Battalion of the 104th Infantry. Baker Company and Lieutenant Long already had fought with the

The November 27, 1944, *Stars and Stripes* (Paris Edition) featured 761st tankers in Guebling on its front page. (*Library of Congress*)

2nd Battalion. Long found the roads barely passable and riddled with mines.[38] Williams and his men took the mission.

The infantry battalion prepped Albestroff with artillery fire aiming for the center of town. A Company of the 104th attacked on the left, with C Company on the right. Enemy machine guns fixed on the Americans. The Germans had blown the bridges and destroyed the railroad tracks every fifty feet.[39] The 1st Battalion continued its attack, but the powerful enemy forced the Americans to withdraw.

Williams and Kahoe relieved Baker Company, attaching to the 2nd Battalion of the 104th. The fighting continued the next day, November 23. The Germans went on the offensive, assisted by the townspeople. Civilians alerted the Germans which buildings held Americans, specifically C Company. Enemy infantry and civilians set some buildings ablaze. Panzers fired into others, forcing A and C companies to withdraw. Extreme German shelling gave one location the nickname "Dead Man's Hill," where shrapnel had hit a number of officers.[40]

Albestroff remained under German control as doughs, tankers, and engineers took their turn and grabbed what they could of a hot turkey dinner for Thanksgiving. Philip Latimer would not allow any-

Elements of the 4th Armored Division driving through Dieuze, a town first attacked by the 761st Tank Battalion on November 19, 1944. After the engagement, the enemy withdrew and American forces were able to enter the town without resistance. (*National Archives*)

one to overlook his tankers on the day Franklin Roosevelt proclaimed as one of national thanks.[41]

The attack continued, with the U.S. 35th Infantry Division threatening the German stronghold. The enemy withdrew and the town fell to the 2nd Battalion, 104th Infantry. The enemy disappeared, but its mines remained. Once the engineers cleared a wide path, Able Company tanks rolled in to occupy the hard-won village.[42] Infantry regiments and tank companies continued to fight town by town, liberating what the Germans had taken. The 761st tanks and assault guns ready for their fire mission.[43]

Seventeen

Village by Village

WILLIAM McBURNEY'S SHERMAN HAD TAKEN A BEATING NOT just in combat but as it maneuvered through the mud and snow of the cratered roads. The tanks needed maintenance, but the war needed tanks—and his deadly aim, of course. The 761st developed a workable maintenance-combat rotation. As a unit would come back to the command post for maintenance another unit would take its place in support of infantry. Reserve status also rotated allowing for additional maintenance opportunities. On November 25 when Williams and Able Company returned to the battalion for maintenance, Baker went on alert as the Division Reserve. Dog Company remained with the 26th Reconnaissance Troop.

To stave off down time for repairs, Williams and the other company commanders quickly discovered it most effective for their maintenance sections to follow closely as they maneuvered. But unlike Camp Hood where tank mechanics swooped in on a disabled tank and had it running in short order, "enemy artillery fire made it impossible for the company sections to recover immediately those tanks disabled."[1] William O'Dea, the battalion motor officer, ran motor operations in a way that bridged the divide between the technician repairing a tank and a company commander clamoring for his Sherman. Commanders understood the continued roar of a disabled tank engine drew enemy mortar and artillery fire. Recovery vehicles also attracted hostile fire.

Commanders ordered no maintenance work until the enemy had been cleared from an area, a move proving safer and more effective in the long run.

Determined tank crews sometimes attempted repairs under fire, but more often had to leave the task to the maintenance section. Once a repair crew had a tank back in the fight it moved to the next tank, and the next. Badly damaged tanks went to the rear if they could be salvaged. Suspension systems seemed heaviest and most frequently hit probably because of the enemy's penchant for mines, overtaxing maintenance crews.[2]

The 761st evacuated any work beyond second echelon to the 501st Ordnance Company, but battalion technicians held out as long as possible.[3] Even when a Sherman needed attention from the 501st, if the 761st had the parts, time, and expertise in-house to repair the tank, that 761st tank rolled without leaving the battalion. While Hunt liked their dedication, he kept an eye on the section, waiting for the overworked repairmen to slip up or collapse.

With Thanksgiving past, Christmas approached. Williams grieved in private over the men he lost, but found inspiration with those who survived. He knew he had a company to lead and would see this war through with them. After less than a month fighting town by town, one could lose perspective of the ultimate mission to defeat Germany.

To McBurney, Charlie Company drew Germans like a magnet, and he wondered why he followed Teddy Windsor into the line of fire. Though the unit's skills improved each day, where Charlie went, trouble surfaced. Charlie Company, now under Captain Charles Gates's command, with the assault gun and mortar platoons, supported the 328th Infantry, taking Wittersbourg with little resistance.[4] Muenster gave the Americans fits, but somehow, they performed each mission and towns fell under American control. As they moved down the road with orders to take Honskirch, the tankers expected more of the same.

Gates did not like the German fortifications and thought the attack ill-advised. He recalled lessons from Paul Bates, who stood adamant on bad missions—Don't sacrifice your men or tanks on situations better avoided.[5] Division intelligence had confirmed that Honskirch "teemed with enemy armor."[6] "Pop" Gates went to the regimental commander, who had little interest in what the tank company commander thought and continued forward.

Russell Guthrie rode in the lead tank with Charlie Company. With Able at battalion for maintenance, Dave Williams could afford to share some of his best men, like Guthrie, with his fellow company commanders. Guthrie, who had known Gates since their days before the war as cavalry soldiers, could see Gates's frustration in his body language. Guthrie had long put his trust in Gates. The man just had a sense about things. "Stick with 'Pop' and you can't go wrong," Guthrie would say.

The tanks moved forward. At Honskirch, the Germans unleashed their wrath and confirmed Gates's fears. With guns in position, they inflicted heavy infantry casualties. The Charlie tanks did not fare much better, caught in a barrage of antitank fire. The enemy hit Guthrie's tank first, halting the column. German artillery fire quickly disabled another four tanks and one assault gun.[7] Guthrie and the rest of the crew scrambled out of the tank, black smoke billowing.

Guthrie could hear the screams above the roar of the tanks. As he looked for cover he saw another tanker disappear deep inside a smoke-filled Sherman. He reappeared, struggling through the gunner's hatch clutching an injured soldier. He lifted his body out of the tank to gently slide him down the side of the Sherman, just as Guthrie had escaped. Russell Guthrie saw the mangled flesh of what remained of the man's legs. He wanted to dive like a centerfielder to catch him as he hit the ground. Other tankers came running. The man wailed in pain. Unable to quiet him, Guthrie heard someone comment that if the Germans had not already figured out where they were crouched, they knew now. Guthrie and the other men grabbed the bloodied soldier as they looked for a safe place to stash him until help arrived. They laid the pleading and mumbling tanker in a shell hole full of ice water. The frigid pool slowed his bleeding. They pumped him full of morphine.[8]

The tankers continued to take heavy fire. At least one round hit McBurney's Sherman, but tank and crew remained unharmed and rolled forward. Someone, maybe Gates, called for artillery support, but nothing came. As the advantage tipped toward the enemy, matters worsened as some tanks ran out of ammunition. Guthrie heard one officer over the radio, "Why the hell aren't you firing?" The nervous response confirmed that only white phosphorous rounds remained. "Hell! Fire 'em. All of them." Guthrie credited the volley of white phosphorous rounds with getting what remained of Charlie Company out of Honskirch alive. But Charlie lost men. An apoplectic Gates let loose on the reported finance officer who commanded the infantry regiment, an incompetent whom he felt had little regard for his men's survival.[9]

Despite a roughed-up American force, it appeared tanks and infantry would take the town, but the enemy won the battle, repelling the U.S. force. Tankers and infantry attacked again. Honskirch fell.10 The 328th and 761st set the village ablaze, but the damage inflicted by the enemy forced the units to withdraw to Wittersbourg. The day also had ended worse than either Gates or platoon leader First Lieutenant Thomas E. Bruce had imagined. Four tankers lay dead with fourteen wounded. The fighting left another five casualties from the mortar platoon.11 The news of casualties grew worse. On November 26, the 328th reported the infantry ordered to "cease all aggressive action after suffering h[ea]vy casualties in at[tac]k."12 Gates refrained from reminding the commander of his warning before the engagement.

By December, the battalion pieced together companies like a patchwork quilt. Charlie Company had fifty-eight enlisted men for a company that entered with nearly three times that number.13 But it did not experience unique manpower woes. The 761st suffered casualties and needed replacements, trained replacements. Harrison saw none en route.

On December 1, Baker Company rolled in support of the 101st Infantry Regiment with seven of its own tanks, three tanks from Able, and two M4 105 mm assault guns. With them went a liaison section with a number of enlisted soldiers headed by Lieutenant James T. Baker, as well as a half-track with a "508/506 radio," and a quarter-ton truck with a 510 radio.14

The 101st Infantry had big plans that included the tanks of the 761st. The 11th German Panzer Division remained a threat. The enemy lurked, obscured by thick, snow-covered vegetation and assisted by sympathetic villagers. The Reich's tankers kept the Americans at a safe distance from their Panzers, but still within striking range of their lethal 88 mm guns. Unknown to the Americans, the 11th Panzer sputtered with just 3,500 men that included 800 ground soldiers. Since 1943, the German division had fought in France and the Balkans, where it captured Belgrade. It fought in Russia. Depleted by heavy losses in the Soviet Winter Offensive of 1942–43, it moved to France to replenish. Though far short of its its full complement, the Panzer division tracked and harassed Allied units.15

For McBurney, a glimpse of a German tank meant a deadly creature to slay. He shuddered a bit at the thought but had no idea these monsters had very little fire left to breathe, but the "jitters" Trezzvant

Anderson observed the day before the men first met the enemy had disappeared the same way the Germans seemed to vanish from conquered villages. McBurney understood they would probably fight at the front for the duration of the war. Exactly what that duty entailed after recent weeks no one ventured a guess. Acceptance replaced impatience and the tankers lived day-to-day, minute-to-minute, mission-to-mission under fire. Not an optimistic adolescent remained in the battalion. The horror and terror experienced in a brief period transformed men like William McBurney into sober war veterans with all the reverence, reflection, and cynicism that came with the honor.

Few knew, however, that the Germans lacked what they required to sustain an all-out battle, notably fuel. They made their presence known, but remained concealed in the shadows compared with the less discreet 761st Shermans. Reconnaissance and intelligence kept as close a watch as possible on the elusive German tank units.

December also opened with the heavily fortified Sarre-Union daring the Americans to attack. The town stood as the objective for the 101st and 104th infantry regiments. Baker Company tanks supported the 101st.[16] The 101st Infantry had prepared during the final days of November for the attack on Sarre-Union. Units finalized plans on November 30. As the regiment with Baker Company tanks in support moved on the town, the 2nd and 3rd battalions came under heavy fire. The 3rd Battalion continued its advance, covered by a ridgeline. It planned for its three companies to move on a road along the railroad tracks. I and K companies continued as arranged, but L Company took the main road in error. While I Company made it to the center of town unopposed and found the area deserted, the enemy unleashed on L, pinning the unit with heavy fire. As the men of L Company fought their way out of the engagement, all units pulled back to the outskirts of town, since no one knew if the companies could hold the town through the night. Little thought seemed given to any advantage their decision could afford the enemy.[17]

With the 11th Panzer believed close by, Baker had its orders—attack to the north and east, aid infantry, and advance into the wooded area. By 6 P.M. December 1, Baker radioed back to headquarters. Another minefield had halted its advance. Tank commanders probably nearly clawed their way out of their Shermans to remove the mines themselves.[18]

The 761st already had lost men to this effective enemy tactic that halted the column. Baker Company, now with four Able Company tanks and two assault guns, moved in for the battle on December 2. A firefight erupted in Bois de Altenberg. Baker found itself the target of high-velocity fire from the vicinity of Sarre-Union and fought back. Baker Company lost one tank to antitank fire. One quarter-ton truck went down to mortar and heavy machine gun fire. The company evacuated seven soldiers wounded in the battle.[19]

The Germans also had their guns in place in the woods. After hostile fire wounded one assault gun commander, Sergeant Robert A. Johnson took over and fired on the German positions. A minefield halted the advance, but Johnson and his section continued to fire into the woods around Sarre-Union. The gun crew scored at least one direct hit, knocking out a German gun and killing at least two enemy soldiers. The 761st evacuated five wounded motormen.[20]

The 101st Infantry Regiment and Baker Company tanks with the 4th Armored Division recommenced the attack the next morning. To their surprise, Sarre-Union had undergone a metamorphosis overnight. The previous day's actions alerted an enemy at large. An area barracks emptied and rushed to assist in the fighting. Though the 101st thought it had secured the town by noon the second day, the Germans launched a counteroffensive that dwarfed their earlier attacks on the Americans. Well-camouflaged German Panzers came out of hiding and overran the 3rd Battalion. They pressed on to fight the 2nd Battalion, which had taken up positions in the homes lining the streets. German tanks surrounded the 101st's field artillery battalion during the fighting. A call for fire came from the American field artillery battalion on its position in a suicidal effort to kill the enemy and end a battle the Americans seemed close to losing.[21]

The artillery fire proved decisive and forced the enemy to withdraw. The 101st believed I Company killed the commander of the enemy tanks with a well-placed shot to the head. The Germans left, determined to get another chance to take the town. The next several days brought sporadic fighting around Sarre-Union—some heavy, some directed at the 761st tanks—but the Americans held.[22]

Men dozed, but no one slept that night. Worsening weather conditions greeted the task force on December 3. Cold and wet became frigid and icy. Baker Company found itself unable to identify targets because of the poor visibility. Tank commanders and gunners squinted to discern their marks without success. The tank company got off only eight rounds from its 76 mm guns, a larger main weapon cour-

Soldiers of Company I, 101st Infantry Regiment looking for snipers during the attack on Sarre-Union, December 2, 1944. The regiment was supported by the 761st Tank Battalion at this time. (*National Archives*)

tesy of the trickle of the battalion's recent replacement tanks. Those rounds proved the day's highlight, especially when it was discovered the heavy Shermans had bogged down in the mud. Baker sat stuck and an easy target for the weakest of enemies. Johnson and his assault guns continued to fire on what he had determined as the enemy, probably saving Baker Company the loss of more lives and tanks.

While Baker remained with the 101st, Dave Williams took five Able Company tanks and attached to the 104th Infantry Regiment the afternoon of December 3. They moved toward Pistorf. An attack on enemy positions cleared the way for the 104th Infantry to enter the town. Williams moved his tanks farther west and battled a firefight north of Aachen, a major city that had fallen to the First Army on October 21.[23] The prolonged battle for Aachen proved a bitter defeat for the Germans as well as a near direct hit on the German's precious Westwall.

Williams and Gates prepared to press into Germany as a fresh 87th Infantry Division relieved the battle-weary 26th Infantry Division on December 11, to the surprise of the tankers.[24] The 26th had landed on Utah Beach September 7 and entered combat October 7, one month before the 761st. The army pulled it from the line for rest in Metz, though the men believed they might head to Paris instead. No one knew the enemy would cut short their respite.

In a parting gesture, Major General Willard Paul in conjunction with XII Corps Commander Major General Manton S. Eddy issued the 761st a unit commendation. Eddy wrote: "The speed with which they adapted themselves to the front line under the most adverse weather conditions, the gallantry with which they faced some of Germany's finest troops, and the confident spirit with which they emerged from their recent engagements in the vicinity of Dieuze, Morville-les-Vic, and Guebling entitle them surely to consider themselves the veteran 761st." Paul added: "Your battalion has supported this division with great bravery under the most adverse weather and terrain conditions. You have my sincere wish that success may continue to follow your endeavors."[25]

Leadership roles changed and went unnoticed by the men in the tanks. Hollis Hunt returned to the 17th Armored Group. He left with a Silver Star nomination for taking over command on November 9 and continuing the attack after combat wounds forced the initial unit commander from the battle. Major John F. George moved from his position as battalion executive officer to command the 761st Tank Battalion.

As the men performed much needed tank maintenance, the battalion staff officers submitted typed, organized synopses of November's activities to the Adjutant General in Washington, D.C. Reports flowed from Intelligence, Operations, Maintenance, and Medical. Their unemotional, often day-by-day accounts provided factual overviews of the battalion's movements and infantry support capability. They reported numbers killed and wounded and equipment status. The reports left no doubt—the 761st had come to Europe for a fight. William O'Dea, the battalion motor officer, listed November's tank casualties:

Fourteen lost to anti tank guns
Five damaged by artillery fire
Six damaged by "bazookas" [Panzerfausts/Panzerschrecks]
Nine damaged by mines[26]

Of the thirty-four tanks damaged, the battalion classified eleven as combat losses. O'Dea counted repaired tanks shot up a second and even a third time in action as separate incidents.[27]

The battalion surgeon, Medical Corps officer Captain Garland N. Adamson, filed a medical after-action report and had the grim duty to report casualties. In his account covering November, less than one month in combat, the 761st suffered eighty-one combat casualties and forty-four "nonbattle" casualties. He listed twenty-two men killed in action. Two died of wounds.[28] He included Bates as a casualty.

Infantry regiments began to notice tank units for their impressive actions under fire. The 328th reported that Baker Company knocked out two enemy tanks.[29] Together all moved closer to the Reich. By December 14, Dave Williams found himself and Able Company in Germany. He dared think the end neared.

As winter approached, despite German resistance, the Allies, including the 761st, had continued their advance village by village, area by area. They fought and ferreted out the Germans, killing many, taking others prisoner. While the Germans made life hell for the Americans in Lorraine, they lost ground. Their gains from early in the war vanished. By late 1944 the Reich's fifty-five available divisions—albeit depleted—faced approximately ninety-six Allied divisions—some equally manpower starved—on the fast-moving front.

Aside from pushing German ground forces back toward Germany, the Allies had essentially grounded the Luftwaffe, rendering it impotent for crucial intelligence purposes as well as targeted bombing. A string of hard-won victories left the Allies confident they faced a gasping enemy. But the German army found it had gained a surprising advantage. The more of Western Europe it lost, the less territory it had to defend, meaning it could consolidate and reinforce its remaining units. Resupply and communication challenges eased as German units moved closer to the Fatherland. They needed fewer encrypted messages, reducing sensitive information falling into Allied hands, a primary source of frustration for the Führer and his leaders. Hitler determined he must strike back.

German soldiers fighting outside of Bastogne, Belgium, in December 1944. (*Bundesarchiv*)

Eighteen

The German Counteroffensive

S OON AFTER THE ALLIED LANDINGS AT NORMANDY AND
subsequent German losses, Hitler and his generals raised the idea
of a counteroffensive. The Führer looked first to the east. Though the
option had some supporters, the sheer numbers of Russian bodies
Stalin could throw at the German forces made success unlikely. But a
Western offensive had possibilities.[1] Hitler had a low opinion of the
Americans and their fighting abilities and would exploit perceived
infighting among the Allied generals, notably between U.S. General
George C. Patton, Jr. and Great Britain's Field Marshal Bernard
Montgomery. Hitler considered the alliance between the Americans,
British, and French weak, at best, and prone to disintegrate if challenged.[2] Hitler's generals remained cautious. They worked to match
his goal with the means Germany realistically had available, and
advised smaller advances. But Generaloberst Alfred Jodl, chief of staff
of the Wehrmachtführungsstab, or the Supreme Command of the
Armed Forces, a loyal German soldier since 1910, assured the forces
had adequate petrol[3] and presented Hitler with an inflated listing of
his forces.[4]

The Führer had his answer and demanded they overrun anything
in their way en route to the French coast. Hitler decided his army
would make the surprise attack through the Ardennes.[5] The Germans
and their enemies knew the area well and clashes between the two

there dated to World War I. The dense forest and rough terrain would likely retard the speed Hitler hoped for, but he bet the miserable weather conditions for which the weak-willed Americans remained unconditioned, as he believed, and the complete surprise of the Allies more than made up for environmental challenges.[6] Hitler and his generals had a plan in place before the 761st reached the French coast.

As the Allies pushed the enemy back toward Germany, they noticed enemy intelligence dried up. By November 1944, given continued German losses and apparent overall weakness of its forces, Allied leaders determined a German offensive impossible. The lack of intelligence chatter underscored their conclusion.[7] At the same time, of all the areas that had been ravaged by war, the Allies deemed that same sprawling, heavily wooded area that encompassed France, Belgium, Luxembourg, as well as Germany a quiet if not catatonic sector. The U.S. sent its greenest, most inexperienced units to the Ardennes, the 99th and 106th infantry divisions. It sent the war-weary 28th Infantry Division to recuperate in the idyllic setting.[8]

Hitler planned his move for November 25.[9] He saw the Allied advance slowing, tethered to overstretched supply lines. He thought the Russian Army had grown sluggish to the east. While the Allies seemed to disintegrate, his forces appeared as plentiful as he expected, further proved by Jodl's account. Adolf Hitler saw opportunity but failed to fully consider whether Germany could sustain an offensive encompassing hundreds of thousands of soldiers. Simple items like gasoline remained an undisputed challenge for Germany, though Hitler had Jodl's assurances. Since he saw his forces reaching the French coast quickly, resupply would come through captured means. Current rail lines already proved a plus.[10] Hitler studied Frederick the Great and began to emulate the legendary leader.[11] Adolf Hitler again expected to control the future of Europe.

As in the past, Hitler banked on Allied stupidity and laziness. He planned a multipronged attack. The 6th Panzer Army led the counteroffensive, tasked with clearing and capturing the towns leading to the crucial port of Antwerp. Lieutenant General Hasso von Manteuffel's 5th Panzer Army would move up the center, destroy the American forces, and hold the strategic rail hub at St. Vith. From there, it would bypass Brussels and capture Antwerp within a week.[12] The U.S. Third Army already had met von Manteuffel.

During a blinding snowstorm, the Germans began their offensive at 5:30 A.M. on December 16, 1944, committing more than 200,000 soldiers and in excess of 1,000 tanks. But Hitler started three weeks late. The planned November jump-off gave the Führer the hope of wrapping up the counteroffensive before the Soviets began their winter offensive. He would fight on one front and could later commit the western units to the east. Three crucial weeks could limit his options.[13]

The Reich's forces knew their mission: to reverse Allied gains made since Normandy and push to the French coast. The route included a seventy-five-plus-mile front through the Belgian Ardennes. But before recapturing France, they would take the Belgian port of Antwerp.[14] Hitler's obsession with Antwerp perplexed his generals and the move seemed unnecessary and risk-laden. This raised concern, but the generals said nothing to discourage the Führer.

Hitler could have chosen few more arduous routes on all the western front. To the Führer's credit, the road system had improved—a boon for the Germans. The terrain, though not conducive to massive troop movement, would not cause units to pile up, unless they faced an Allied counterattack. Hitler found this unlikely. If his forces hit any resistance, they would find it well past the Ardennes.

Without an inkling of the German plan, Allied operations continued. U.S., English, French, and Canadian forces stretched across the western front. The First and Ninth U.S. armies led the main effort through Bonn and Cologne. Third Army, including the 761st, fought near Nancy, Metz, and the Saar River. Seventh Army fought in the south and west. It had captured Strasbourg and had reached the Rhine. The French and British armies fought along the northern edge of the front.[15]

Eisenhower wanted to knock out more enemy divisions and take Germany more quickly. The Brits and French already had pushed for a December end to the war. It seemed they would fall well short of that goal. With no knowledge of Hitler's plan, Eisenhower ordered an offensive to begin December 19 along the Saar, Third Army's area under George Patton.[16] The Allies in many ways believed their own press. They became overly enamored with their successes evident in the ground they took from the Germans since the landings in France. Their arrogance left little room to question the tenacity of what had once been a much-feared enemy. The Allies pushed forward with no thought of the Ardennes.

U.S. units observed changes in enemy forces that hinted at the German plan. The 28th and 106th infantry divisions, positioned in the Ardennes, noticed increased German traffic in the area. One S-2 reported additional noise from enemy movement, though his commander waived off his head of intelligence. Finally a woman made it to the 28th Infantry Division reporting German activity in the woods surrounding Bitburg. She seemed one of the most credible sources yet. VIII Corps rushed her to First Army, but the German assault already had begun.[17]

Hitler's Operation Watch on the Rhine stretched from southern Belgium to Luxembourg. To some, 5:30 A.M. December 16, 1944, may have seemed like 7:55 A.M., December 7, 1941.

As the Allies operated in their sectors, Germany launched its offensive unnoticed except for the onslaught in the Ardennes. The dazed Americans awoke to waves of Germans pointing their searchlights to find their way as well as hunt the American enemy. The uncharacteristic cold and heavy snow hampered both sides. Visibility proved a rare luxury.

The Germans overran some units, killing the Americans as they went. They circled behind other groups. The Americans who withdrew did so haphazardly and without a plan. The 3rd Battalion of the 393rd Infantry Regiment, 99th Infantry Division pulled together. By 9:30 A.M. the Germans reached the battalion command post. In the confusion, when the battalion gave its companies the order to pull back, it seemed K Company did not receive the crucial information. The company crouched alone with its leadership missing. When the final Panzer passed it seemed a substantial victory for the shaken unit, until trailing enemy infantry cut down the men who remained.[18] The 81 mm mortar crew took aim and fought off the aggressors. Despite the rumored slaughter of K Company, the battalion commander reported he thought they could hold through the night.

The enemy killed or captured all of Company B, save one platoon. The Germans surrounded C Company, but the men nearly fought off the attackers until enemy numbers seemed to magically multiply.[19] A plea went out for help. A mine-laying platoon from the regiment, with "26 riflemen, 13 runners, plus cooks," fixed bayonets. The men pulled together and established a new line of defense. Despite these efforts, losses to the 1st Battalion, which had begun the day near full strength, topped 70 percent. Other units did not fare much better.[20]

Elsewhere the situation further deteriorated. Men reverted to their most basic instincts to save their brothers. The most inexperienced and junior stood their ground. Rumors of the massacre of scores of

American prisoners traveled through the U.S. units. On December 17, the Germans gunned down nearly 100 American prisoners of war at Malmedy.[21] It was hold or die.

December 16 proved a busy and memorable day for Dwight Eisenhower. He had pinned on his fifth star the previous day—two more than George Patton. He decided to throw a party to celebrate his promotion at his Versailles headquarters. He also hosted a wedding for his orderly Sergeant Mickey McKeogh nearby at Marie Antoinette's chapel.[22]

General Omar Bradley happened to be at Versailles on unrelated matters. The two generals spent considerable time talking about the unpredictable Adolf Hitler and a possibility of a German counteroffensive. Soon after, Eisenhower received word of the Ardennes attack.[23] Had Hitler sent 200,000 soldiers? Or 250,000? Maybe half a million? And his tanks, nearly 1,000 or 2,000 gassed and ready?

The stunned Belgians, more familiar with German invasions than they cared to admit, took action. They replaced their Allied flags with those of the Reich. British forces guarded the bridges over the Meuse River, a route Hitler's generals had warned against but one the Führer intended to use to reach his objective.

Eisenhower ordered his commanders from across the theater to meet at Bradley's Verdun headquarters December 19.[24] The Germans had surprised them, but the audacious German counteroffensive should never have gotten past all of them. Eisenhower, who studied Allied prospects after finding out about the offensive, walked into the meeting with ideas and optimism, but no solutions. But he proved "upbeat," addressing the generals: "The present situation is to be regarded as one of opportunity for us and not disaster. There will be only cheerful faces at this conference table."[25]

When the U.S. entered the war, Dwight Eisenhower looked back with some regret at a distinguished but unremarkable career. Certainly he drew attention at the Louisiana Maneuvers in 1941, but the door seemed to slam shut. He had rank but little responsibility. Eisenhower resigned himself to the fact he would retire as an also-ran. But his fortunes turned in 1943, when his talents as an administrator caught notice. His presence commanded respect, but without any air of threat. He got along with the most difficult personalities the Allies could serve and befriended each equally.[26] As Supreme

Commander, Allied Expeditionary Force Europe, he found himself
with the U.S. responsibility in planning Overlord. He interceded in
Patton's and Montgomery's squabbles. In an operational as well as
political move, Eisenhower took over the ground campaign from the
British and old "Monty." Though Montgomery received a "promotion" to Field Marshall as a consolation, he remained embittered, his
disdain for Eisenhower ever present.[27] The U.S. had reached a point
in the war where Americans bled the most men and money of the
Allies, and Eisenhower wanted more of a say in the war's direction.
The European Allies had hoped to end the war by Christmas 1944,
but the American supply lines had been depleted nearly as much as
those of the enemy.[28] It seemed a bit late for that well-worn discussion. Without acknowledgment, both sides fought a war of attrition.
It had come to where the Allies could afford only one force to move
forward. The choice lay between Montgomery and Patton.
Eisenhower refused to choose,[29] possibly knowing either selection
could cause irreparable damage to achieving their ultimate objective:
the unconditional surrender of Germany.

Patton had always found his old cohort Eisenhower quiet and
more diplomatic than he. He saw their careers diverge and found
Eisenhower overly conciliatory to the British. After a decades-long
relationship, as they slugged it out in Europe, many believed he
referred to Eisenhower as "the best damn general the British have
got."[30] But Patton remained fiercely loyal. He met with Eisenhower
and Montgomery in a dilapidated schoolhouse in Verdun that served
as Omar Bradley's 12th Army Group headquarters. Verdun proved an
ironic choice given the blow it dealt the Germans in World War I. The
longest single battle of that war came at tremendous cost to both
sides and, in short, denied Germans victory over France.

Patton had arrived ready to mix things up. The German move
enraged him, possibly more because of its brilliance on the surface
and that they had slipped it by him. As Eisenhower's optimism raised
the spirits in the room, Patton shouted "Bastard," referring to von
Manteuffel, a Prussian aristocrat and highly decorated infantry officer in both the first and second world wars. A young, confident
Panzer army commander, the career officer had success on the eastern
front against Russia as well as in North Africa. Each feat brought
advancement. Now the lieutenant general that gave Patton fits in the
defense of Lorraine with his 5th Panzer Army moved toward
France.[31] He had outwitted the Third Army commander more than

once. George Patton probably attributed the German offensive to the cagey German and wanted his revenge. Regarding von Manteuffel, he stated colorfully, "This bastard has put his cock in a meat grinder and I've got ahold of the handle!"[32]

British army legend Bernard Montgomery proved the voice of dissent, challenging Eisenhower, humiliating him, and insulting the whole of the American war effort. Monty's animosity came as no surprise. Eisenhower coolly offered to kick the decision on Allied military action up a level, a threat that brought Montgomery bleating into the fold. Eisenhower had no doubt Montgomery would do his military duty, but Montgomery singed any trust between the two.[33]

Eisenhower felt emboldened. He and Patton stood as the two in the room who could cut off the Germans and resume the offensive. They began to discuss counterattack options northward, in the vicinity of the crucial town of Bastogne. Eisenhower, juggling timeframes in his mind, asked how soon Patton could be ready. Without hesitation, George Patton looked straight at Eisenhower: "Three divisions, two days." Eisenhower, doubting the feat possible even for the warhorse and man of his word, brushed it off, assuring Patton he would settle for something more reasonable.[34]

Patton excused himself. He had come to Verdun well-prepared. He had briefed his most trusted staff and left them with three options and corresponding code words. If necessary, he would call, give one of the three codes and his forces would be on the move while he jabbered with the generals. After Patton's call, the Third Army turned northward toward the Ardennes and commenced its attack before Patton left that dreary schoolhouse.[35]

The first few days, Hitler's forces clicked down the kilometers into what briefly had been Allied reclaimed territory. For more than a week, the new front moved west. The offensive seemed to work, thanks in large part to General Hasso von Manteuffel. Jodl had planned for an 8:00 A.M. barrage of heavy artillery fire on American positions in the Ardennes. Von Manteuffel vehemently opposed announcing the Germans' arrival and pushed for the early morning attack over and around the sleeping Americans. Hitler agreed.[36] But the offensive slowed. Weather proved more of an impediment than Hitler had predicted. Overall, the Germans achieved their deepest penetration around December 26—about sixty miles from where the forces had begun their assault, but hundreds of miles from the French coast and more than a hundred miles southeast of Antwerp.[37]

The German counteroffensive had fallen short of Hitler's expectations. As warned, the route through the Ardennes forced commanders to push their large units from behind. Though many U.S. units fled the enemy, some remained—either by accident or as a matter of duty, an unanticipated move.

But Operation Watch on the Rhine took back what land it could. The Germans slaughtered whoever stood in their way and created a deep bulge in the Allied line, redefining the new front from which each side would fight. Hitler sensed further success. For him the war had tipped once more in Germany's favor. Many Allied commanders and civilians had thought the Germany of December 1944 would simply continue to protract its inevitable defeat. Its well-planned, ferocious counterattack proved otherwise.

The time to inspire had long passed. Allied victory in this battle into the unknown lay with the moxie of the American soldier. Eisenhower understood he probably had an emotionally defeated Allied force. He had to couch the dire situation in terms that would inspire every soldier. He issued a force-wide order. A large number of news outlets worldwide printed his thrown gauntlet. One December 22 headline read: "Destroy Enemy Gen. Eisenhower Orders Troops."[38] Eisenhower told his forces and the world:

> The enemy is making his supreme effort to break out of the desperate plight into which you forced him by your brilliant victories of the summer and fall. He is fighting savagely to take back all that you have won and is using every treacherous trick to deceive and kill you. He is gambling everything. But already, in this battle, your gallantry has done much to foil his plans. In the face of your proven bravery and fortitude, he will completely fail. But we cannot be content with his mere repulse. By rushing out from his fixed defenses the enemy may give us the chance to turn his great gamble into his worst defeat. So I call upon every man, of all the allies, to rise now to new heights of courage, of resolution and of effort. Let everyone hold before him a single thought—to destroy the enemy on the ground, in the air, everywhere—destroy him.
>
> United in this determination and with unshakable faith in the cause for which we fight, we will, with god's help, go forward to our greatest victory.

Members of an American patrol scouting in Luxembourg on December 30, 1944. (*National Archives*)

Eisenhower's hyperbole proved of no interest to the Reich. Antwerp remained within German grasp, but at a very long reach. Bastogne sat as Germany's gateway. No fewer than seven major roads converged on the Belgian town of Bastogne, lines the Germans needed to control to capture Antwerp.

Unknown to the Americans, the Germans set their sights on Bastogne. In initial planning to repulse the Germans early December 17, Eisenhower's SHAEF staff reviewed its options. The G-3 Major General J. F. M. Whiteley said of the 82nd and 101st airborne, "I think I should put them there," pointing to Bastogne. "That place has the best road net in the area."[39] Bastogne held no special significance to the Allies. The battle-weary 28th Infantry Division rested in the area and from most accounts stood in no shape to repulse a major German attack. At the same time few realized the 101st commander, Major General Maxwell D. Taylor, attended to business in the United States, and many of the unit's soldiers enjoyed some well-deserved, time off in Paris.

The Germans moved quickly. Though well below combat strength, the 28th Infantry Division planned to hold the area and established a command post at Wiltz, Luxembourg, twelve miles from Bastogne. The Germans surrounded it and tore it apart in three days.[40]

Ultimately, the 101st Airborne gained the Bastogne mission. It arrived December 19, low on cold weather gear, food, ammunition, and other items crucial to survival let alone repulsing the aggressors. The Germans wasted no time. Forces, including some of von Manteuffel's commanders, surrounded the town by December 21, ensnaring everyone within its perimeter. Plunging temperatures and blinding snow stood as the worst in memory. The Germans had Bastogne in their tight fist. Between the weather and the strong Germans forces, the 101st found resupply from both the ground and the air impossible. Neither Eisenhower's people at SHAEF nor the 101st itself anticipated this type of swift, aggressive action.[41]

The 761st Tank Battalion knew nothing of Verdun or the apparent resurrection of the German army. The combat-hardened tankers battling frigid temperatures as well as mechanical woes did not know the course of the war had changed and that their unit would soon barrel toward the enemy.

Nineteen

Sergeant McBurney's War

O N DECEMBER 15, 1944, WITH NO IDEA OF CONCURRENT EVENTS
in the Ardennes, the 761st detached from the 87th and moved
to the 17th Armor Group. The tank battalion struggled each day to
keep more than 50 percent of its tanks combat effective, a benchmark
rarely met. The tank situation again had turned grim. The battalion
had just three operational medium tanks, forcing the 761st off the
line. After five intensive maintenance days, that number shot to thirty-one.[1] At the same time, on December 16, the army promoted
Richard English, still in command of Dog Company, to captain. His
men swarmed him with congratulations. Even for his detractors, the
English promotion proved a bright moment during a very dark time.[2]
When Patton's order came, the 761st fielded three medium companies
with ten tanks each. Harrison saw it as an early Christmas gift. The
combat-ready battalion reattached to the 87th Infantry Division.[3]
From what little information trickled into the battalion, company
commanders like Dave Williams heard they might need them to battle Hitler's forces in the Ardennes or where the Germans purportedly
had broken the Allied lines.

At the time of Patton's sudden move of much of the Third Army,
the 87th Infantry Division, with the attached 761st, followed right
along with Ol' Blood and Guts. The division numbered an impressive
15,000 men, dwarfing its manpower-starved tank battalion. No mat-

ter the infantry, division, or the village—French, Belgian, or otherwise—each tanker had developed his unique rhythm. Dave Williams had a manner that gave Able Company some assurance in uncertain combat, something he learned during his turbulent tenure under Paul Bates. William McBurney looked to Teddy Windsor, who ensured tank crew stability in the face of an enemy determined to blast them out of the war. As a matter of routine, the stoic Windsor would receive his orders and he and his men would move out on their next mission. No fuss, no discussion, and McBurney appreciated it, though he never said as much to Windsor. McBurney worked to find his own place without relying on Windsor. The one-time demure New York teen, who abhorred tobacco, now smoked and swore like a longshoreman, but fooled no one in his battalion with his assumed tough-guy persona.

Orders came to turn northward, and the 761st supported the infantry regiments just as it had since its first day in combat. Somehow it seemed easier to McBurney. He never wanted to repeat November. After less than two months in battle, the battalion of tanks and regiments of infantry joined as if there had never been another way of fighting. Charlie Company supported the 346th Infantry Regiment, taking up defensive positions in the vicinity of Obgailbach, France. Baker stood in reserve with the 347th.[4]

By December 22 the situation for the 761st and 87th took an unexpected turn. The terrain prohibited the use of tanks. Though the 761st did not move, it sat ready to fire in support. McBurney paced with impatience in the turret. Windsor's eyes followed his gunner. McBurney did not like the way the battalion had bounced from the 87th to the 17th Armored Group to the 44th Infantry Division for a day and back to the 87th Infantry Division.[5] Windsor listened. Without overt acknowledgment, they rejoined forces and moved forward however they could, pushing through poor weather and increasingly challenging terrain. McBurney shook his head. Maybe he did not have to understand everything.

With Christmas came clarification. SHAEF released the 87th Infantry Division and its supporting units to 12th U.S. Army Group. They would position themselves in VIII Corps sector on Third Army's left flank.[6] Third Army ordered the 87th and its attached units to the vicinity of Neufchateau, Belgium, via a specific route. As they traveled back into familiar territory, no one had thought he would see the conquered towns of the Lorraine again, like Nancy, Château-Salins,

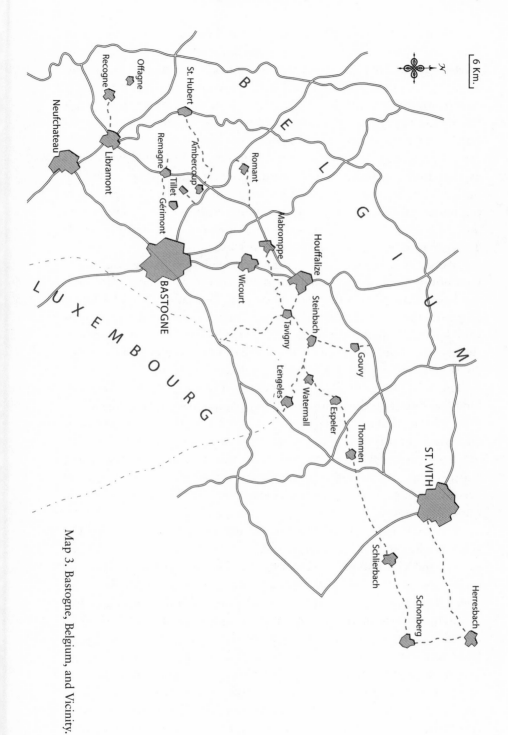

Map 3. Bastogne, Belgium, and Vicinity.

and Wuisse. They had started their war in Lorraine. The province of deceptively picturesque villages proved a deadly place for the 761st. Enemy forces easily concealed machine gun emplacements, tanks, and anything else they possessed to kill the tankers and did so with success. Lorraine and the Lower Saar Basin stood as an enigma and a harrowing experience for most that fought there. The tankers moved quickly past the towns, alert to the unpredictable enemy. McBurney took a long drag from his K-ration cigarette and exhaled with relief as they made some distance without coming under enemy fire. He understood that the Germans attacked from the east, but after hearing Bates had died (he had not) and Wingo suffered battle fatigue (he did not), McBurney put little stock in word from headquarters. But if Teddy Windsor told him, he took it as truth.

The 87th and the 761st pushed through the deepening snow. Conditions proved too much for some of the Shermans. The men worked on their tanks for twelve hours on December 26, determined to get to the fight. They rolled again. The tankers performed additional needed maintenance on the 28th followed by an extensive twenty-four-hour refueling effort in Beine. The 761st closed out 1944 consumed with maintenance outside Offagne, Belgium.[7]

The 87th Infantry Division and the VII Corps' 11th Armored Division swung to the southwest. They planned to attack in the direction of Houffalize. When they jumped off the next morning, December 30, they ran into the flank of two enemy divisions attacking Bastogne from the west. Both sides stood surprised. Though the Allied forces did not remain to fight a protracted engagement, their presence stopped the capture and closure of the Bastogne corridor by the Germans.[8]

McBurney had not seen the enemy angrier. On December 31, the Germans hurled seventeen attacks against the Third Army front. Both sides fought in sub-zero temperatures. Though McBurney felt his tank crew operated from what seemed an icebox, at least they had cover. The doughs, now comprised of a large number of clerks and supplymen reassigned as infantry replacements, could not dig foxholes in the frozen ground. Many resorted to wrapping themselves in bedsheets for some concealment against the white snow.[9]

On New Year's Eve, the tank battalion and its supported infantry division wasted no time and started toward the primary objective. The order had been unambiguous: "Clear Tillet." The word trickled down through the crews. McBurney and some of the other tankers

The 761st Tank Battalion during its drive to assist beleaguered American forces in the winter of 1944–45. (*Ellsworth G. McConnell Collection*)

believed it came straight from General Patton himself. The 761st and the 87th would not just take Tillet, they would clear it of every last German. Major George, who had slipped into the battalion commander slot with relative ease, reviewed maps of the attack on Tillet with his staff officers and company commanders on December 30. They contacted the 87th Infantry Division. As McBurney concentrated on his small piece of the operation, he had no way of knowing the magnitude of the offensive building around him.[10]

Tillet stood as a crucial town, a German necessity because of its east-west road. The battle to reverse the enemy-created bulge surrounded them. Varied and larger units fought a determined German force, reminiscent of the 761st's early enemy encounters. Patton's army faced an ugly task. The Germans in the Ardennes combined strong will with large forces and substantial firepower on all sides. Given the towns the 761st had recently taken with little resistance, McBurney had no idea he faced a reinvigorated and steadfast enemy.

As they rolled the thirty to forty kilometers from Offagne to the objective, intelligence had determined German resistance along the route as somewhat lighter than initially thought, but substantial in important villages. The intelligence shops had not addressed a larger and more immediate problem—the weather.[11]

Deteriorating conditions worked to the enemy's favor. Temperatures continued to drop as the tankers made their way toward Tillet, pushing through heavy snow. Visibility worsened,

negating any possible Allied air support on ground targets. The
Sherman drivers manipulated their tracks and engines in the deep
snow, but progressed slowly. Dog Company's complement of Stuart
tanks again proved invaluable. Their lighter armor allowed them to
almost glide compared to the Shermans' movement. Stuarts sacrificed
armor, but at least they had a better chance of reaching the fight.[12]

Each infantry regiment traveled with its intrinsic assets, including
an attached artillery battalion. Williams had heard that Bastogne
must hold at "all costs." When the 4th Armored Division relieved
Bastogne December 26, the Allies found that Major General Maxwell
D. Taylor and Brigadier General Anthony C. McAuliffe and their men
of the 101st Airborne Division held, but suffered more than 1,600
casualties. Almost every soldier on the ground knew what "all costs"
meant and had seen testimony in truckloads of contorted, frozen
corpses. One hard-fighting soldier wondered how much more he
could do other than die in place, a pointless sacrifice if "at all costs"
failed to deny the Germans their gains and push them back.[13]

While the relief of Bastogne stood a victory, the task of pushing the
enemy back into Germany remained and the 761st stood ready for
the mission. Except for the weather, the move toward Tillet began
with deceptive smoothness. The regiments of the 87th Infantry
Division, the 345th, 346th, and 347th, and their attached units rang
in the year 1945 with a different, but befitting manner given the circumstances. Charlie rolled in support of the 346th Infantry. Baker
pushed through deep snow to fire for the doughs of the 347th. The
345th Infantry Regiment took the Belgian towns of Rondu and
Nimbermont. Resistance seemed unusually light, as predicted, until
the 347th neared its next objective—the enemy stronghold of St.
Hubert. On January 2 the offensive against St. Hubert began almost
thirty-five- kilometers due west of Bastogne. With armor backing the
enemy, the 345th Infantry moved its few Baker tanks "as a backstop
for the eastern flank."[14] Breaking the German grip on St. Hubert
would deny the enemy the important Bastogne–St. Hubert Road, a
step in the defeat of Tillet, an engagement already under way.[15] Baker
Company lost First Lieutenant Elyseo Taylor, Technician 4 Sheridan
H. Murray, Technician 5 Robert L. McDowell, and Private Allen
Jones, all wounded in action.[16] The force pressed on, casualties evacuated. Tankers and doughs engaged more of the enemy as they moved
through reoccupied Belgian towns en route to Tillet. They cleared

once sweet Belgium villages like Bonnerue, Recogne, Remagne, and Jenneville.[17] Men fell on both sides.[18]

The 87th Infantry Division and 761st Tank Battalion maneuvered determined to remove any obstacle between them and Tillet. They understood more Germans would die. They remained equally aware they could lose more of their own men.

Sitting in the buttoned-up tank, the war changed for William McBurney. He felt the tide turn as he prepared for the attack on Tillet. Until Patton turned his army, the fight had been an officers' war—planned by officers, led by officers. The winds had shifted. Even General Eisenhower had said as much. The men and the enlisted leaders of the 761st would take Tillet.

Like Windsor, McBurney watched other tankers, those with the gift to lead and talent to fight, take over for the handful of battered officers who had taken them this far. McBurney looked to these men, some not much older than he. The promise of the hardship of unknown magnitude that lay ahead at the threshold of Tillet called for the uncommon and unconventional. Those who came forward varied in age, vocation, and region, but McBurney and Russell Guthrie had complete faith in these men and entrusted them with their destiny. To Guthrie, who fired on command in his buttoned-up tank, these men appeared as invincible as Tillet at that moment. A war of wills would rage. But who would prove stronger, a group of fearless young Americans or the enemy? Henry Conway, Johnnie Stevens, and Theodore Weston directed their tanks in Able. William Kitt emerged in Baker. Frank Cochrane, Moses Dade, and Teddy Windsor pushed for the bruised Charlie Company. William McBurney wanted to step forward like Teddy, but understood his talents lay with his weapon. Windsor would slap him on the back reassuring his young gunner. McBurney sat ready to fire.[19]

Infantry and 761st tanks, with Company B of the 691st Tank Destroyer Battalion in support, advanced toward the objective on January 1. The weather started "clear and cold" with good visibility at five miles. In less than twenty-four hours conditions deteriorated. A front brought snow and yet colder temperatures. Just as McBurney felt certain he had experienced the lowest temperatures possible more frigid air would arrive. With the weather change, Charlie tanks relieved Able and moved in support of the 1st Battalion of the 347th in the attack to cut the Bastogne–St. Hubert Road at Amberloup.[20]

The 346th Combat Team held the left flank while the 11th Armored Division advanced on the right flank of the 87th Infantry Division. The 87th and the 761st skirted Tillet but did not show their hand as far as an attack on the German-held town.[21]

Units made their way toward Tillet southeast of St. Hubert. Baker Company led an attack with First Lieutenant Harold B. Gary in front.[22] They counted 150 enemy dead at Bonnerue. Charlie Company reported knocking out three machine gun nests and killing fourteen Germans at Recogne. Though impressive, Dog Company reported it knocked out eight guns, killed seventeen of the enemy, and took another seventy prisoner.[23]

Richard English, with his knowledge of European history, understood how these areas had strong French as well as German influence, evident in the town names. Centuries of peace and war kept the area moving between the bordering nations. And so all fought again. English remained in his company commander mode and kept Dog Company busy on all fronts. Ice made roads impassable for 761st resupply trucks. Dog Company kept the supply lines running to the medium tanks. The deeper the snow, the more crucial the battalion found its Stuarts. McBurney liked Richard English, especially when a Stuart appeared with supplies. But he and the other men could tell, despite his work, the officers kept him an outcast. It did not seem right to William McBurney.

As his tanks moved past a town, Dave Williams would check his map. Tillet lay a mere six kilometers from Remagne. Bastogne, which seemed to stand as the center of this conflagration, sat less than fifteen kilomters due east of Tillet. The big boys had already duked it out for Bastogne. The tankers and the 87th's infantry regiments figured they would have their hands full with Tillet.

As they closed on the objective the next day, the enemy hit Able Company hard. Williams approached his breaking point. Reconnaissance told him Tillet looked like a "suicide trap." Williams knew Able had to at least skirt the village and pound the bastards with everything they had, though they did not carry the arsenal he preferred. As Williams, who often discussed plans with his platoon commanders and men, began to give the order for the dangerous mission, his throat tightened and his eyes stung. This gaggle of misfits who did not know any better placed their trust in him. They stood as his reason for being. They believed in him at his lowest and redeemed him. He owed them his life. No doubts today, thought Williams, as he stood composed, commanding like Paul Bates. Able moved out carefully.[24]

Despite Williams's best effort, the Germans continued to pummel the Able tanks. At the end of a very long January 4, Williams lost two more dead and four wounded. His company, though shaken, remained ready. The battalion listed platoon sergeant Staff Sergeant James W. Nelson and "cannoneer" Thomas S. Bragg as killed in action. Bragg's death left the shocked tankers sobbing on the field. Williams recalled Nelson's joy as one of the first in the battalion to roll on German soil less than a month earlier. Dave Williams lost another four men to combat wounds—driver Tech 4 Charles J. Tidwell, and gunners Corporal James H. Jordan, Corporal Walter Lewis, and Private Charles W. Brooks.[25]

The next day found Williams and Able down to two Shermans. Adversity seemed to feed tanker determination. The subzero temperatures, coupled with the ice and deep snow, sent even the best tank drivers skidding off makeshift roads. The slightest grade presented more challenges.[26] Maintenance crews could get few tanks running and had to send them back to the command post for repair. Damn it, thought McBurney, but he saw misfortune as typical for the 761st since the battalion's first battle. McBurney and his tank crew had found it impossible to keep up with required maintenance for one tank, let alone compensate for the stresses of the cold, rain, snow, ice, unpredictable terrain, and the cruelty of combat. Add an armed enemy, he thought, and BAM! Tank down. He saw how few tanks maneuvered during stretches of combat and had heard about reports on the situation out of the command post. He had come to accept a fact of war: on any given day, a tank company will have more tanks down than operational.

With Able Company back on line with six tanks,[27] the 87th and its attached units chose January 5 as their D-Day. But problems struck from the outset. The deep snow and ice made it difficult for the tank drivers to maneuver. The doughs fared worse standing, waiting in the elements. McBurney thought manning a gun inside a block of ice might seem warmer than his Sherman. He did not see the situation improving. As he drew deeply on his cigarette, he cracked his hatch to get some frigid, but fresher air. "Damn Krauts," he muttered, blaming them for the poor timing of their offensive.

McBurney heard that Headquarters Company tank commander Sergeant Robert A. Johnson died a couple of days earlier of wounds suffered in a previous battle.[28] He thought Johnson fought as bravely as any of them, including Crecy. Damn shame and damn bad timing. He knew Court Martial Slim would take it hard, even though he had a new set of worries in Service Company. With his goggles in place, McBurney popped up through the open hatch. He looked straight ahead, envisioning the battle and targets yet to be determined. Standing deep in thought, he did not feel the icy wind against his exposed skin as he pressed his back against the hatch.

Tillet had the aura of a fortress. The Germans owned the town and stood ready to destroy any challenger. Windsor's Charlie tank went in support of Able Company. Windsor, now a staff sergeant leading a platoon, but always McBurney's tank commander, ordered the platoon to lay a base of fire to push out the enemy. Despite their efforts, the Germans again halted the Americans' advance as if it never started. Windsor's actions briefly cleared the area, but not enough to take an inch of ground, let alone nab Tillet.

The Americans' presence proved no surprise to the waiting enemy. Despite the damage inflicted by Windsor's tanks, the Germans hit the unwelcome invaders with a heavy mix of artillery, mortar, and anti-tank fire. For the 761st and the 87th Infantry Division, assaulting Tillet seemed no different from hitting a steel wall—a heavily armed steel wall. Another tank had its track shot out from under it, forcing the crew to evacuate. The attack crumbled. The nearly frozen infantry soldiers bore the brunt of the German onslaught. Those soldiers still in their dark uniforms against the snowy backdrop created ideal targets for German riflemen. Even those who adopted the crude bed sheets and pillowcases fared little better.[29] Soldiers on the ground found themselves further hampered by frozen feet and footwear. The unsuitable shoepacs, cursed by most soldiers because of manufacturer flaws and a lack of training on how to wear the cold-weather boot, forced many ground infantry to don the combat boot with an overshoe, if they could get their hands on the latter.[30] Despite the setbacks, the Americans estimated more than 150 Germans killed, but hardly a dent in the force awaiting them.[31]

On January 6, the Americans tried a different approach. The snow had stopped, but visibility improved little, ranging from poor to limited.[32] The battalion moved to the vicinity of Freux. Able Company shifted into position, taking the high ground a thousand yards northeast of Gerimont, less than two kilometers from Tillet, to support the movement of the 347th Infantry Regiment. Able Company had the unfortunate task of covering a bloodied infantry withdrawal into Gerimont. It later supported the advance of the sister infantry regiment, the 346th, through Bois la Chenaie. As they moved in place for supporting fire, they could find no suitable positions from which to shoot. The density of the Ardennes rendered the tanks ineffective, forcing the men of the 346th to rely on their own weapons. Williams looked at the terrain from every angle and found no solution. He probably saw it as a failure on his part.

The 761st backed the 345th, 346th, and 347th infantry regiments as they fought for Tillet, though the 346th fought through the worst of the battle. Conditions challenged the most hardy. The daily temperature hovered around zero. With little cover and the frozen ground denying them the luxury of an ice-encrusted rifle pit, many infantry fought and died exposed to the enemy. Tanks offered some concealment as the foot soldiers maneuvered. The big main guns and machine guns provided some relief, but the 761st rolled toward Tillet in tatters.

Richard C. Manchester, a communications specialist with K Company of the 345th Infantry, welcomed the firepower and concealment the 761st tanks could provide. But he found they proved no match for the mighty German guns. He watched as the 761st supported the 87th Infantry Division's drive to secure the crossroads. He stared amazed as Panzers' main guns and antitank weapons put Sherman tanks out of commission as if snuffing out a candle. Crews evacuated the four disabled M4 tanks in the snowbound fields. He wondered if anyone would see those tanks again.[33]

Able Company, again with just two tanks in operation, pulled back for maintenance and reorganization on January 7. Baker moved in support of the 3rd Battalion of the 346th, which had stepped in for the 347th. Assault guns from Headquarters Company, each an M4 Sherman chassis with a 105mm howitzer mounted in the turret, attached to the 345th.[34] The enemy shredded the battalion, but the tankers refused to break.[35]

The doughs made gains, only to get hammered back down by German machine gun and mortar fire. Curtis Shoup from I Company of the 346th Infantry, a soldier admired by most in his unit, caught a glimpse of one of the many enemy machine guns, but could not get a good shot at its crew.[36] The twenty-three-year-old from Napenoch, New York, sprung up and sprinted for a position from which he could shoot. He stood and fired, hitting the machine gun nest. The

Germans had him in their sights before he pulled the trigger again and shot him soon after he first hit them. Shoup, still conscious and determined to silence the gun, clawed his way toward the nest. His unit watched as his well-placed grenade finished off the machine gun crew. But the Americans' elation proved short-lived. Seconds later, a German bullet ended Curtis Shoup's war.[37] Shoup's act shifted the battle in the minds of the men who watched in awe. It inspired a regiment of men losing hope. Soon after, the true U.S. attack began.

For the enemy, Shoup's act meant little. The Germans still held the advantage. While their Americans attackers remained in the open, the enemy occupied buildings at will. They fired from secure positions. Reports at the headquarters said the Germans' Panzer Lehr hovered between Bastogne and Tillet. Panzer Lehr held tremendous pride for the Führer and stood as one of his most trusted units. At the time of the Allied invasions of Normandy it had no fewer than 109 tanks and 612 half-tracked vehicles, double the allowance for any other unit. By July heavy fighting against the Allies left it at 22 percent strength. By July 25 the division commander sounded the unit's death knell, but the German command decided to resurrect it to its former glory. It breathed fire into the unit with hundreds of soldiers and seventy-two new Panzers. Allies further bloodied the unit in the fight for Aachen, though it remained combat effective. Like many of its brethren, the Panzer Lehr joined the Ardennes offensive.[38] It spearheaded the southern prong of the attack and suffered heavy losses. The Panzer Lehr stood ready for a fight at Tillet with more than forty tanks, far exceeding what the hardscrabble 761st could cobble together. Tankers and ground soldiers sacrificed much, but gained little. They had to pull back again.

Like Joe Louis coming at Max Schmeling in the ring in 1938, the 761st and the infantry regiments agreed on another run at the village. They had hit a German wall of resistance on each previous attack. On their next attack they would hit Tillet with every asset possible. They spent January 8 preparing and gathering all available firepower. Tankers performed the maintenance necessary to carry them through their most arduous attack. McBurney wanted as much weaponry as possible. Windsor and his fellow tank commanders scavenged for what they could find. The depleted battalion threw everything it had into the mission—eleven Shermans, two assault guns, the mortar platoon with three 81 mm mortars, one platoon of five reliable light tanks—enough battle-hardened tankers to come out fighting.[39]

The battle for Tillet reached a crescendo January 9. Despite the additional firepower of the 761st, the attack again would move forward with the infantry in the lead. On the fifth day of the battle, McBurney watched as the 346th spearheaded the cleansing of Tillet. Temperatures remained near zero during the battle. Men froze in place. The Germans kept the Americans pinned. A frustrated 346th found either the cold slowed their bodies, or the icy air wreaked havoc with their weapons. No one could say why they did not give up.[40]

Theodore Windsor. (*U. S. Army*)

The tankers hit their own challenges. The 346th Infantry had to delay the attack from the northeast one hour because a tank hit a sunken road and threw a track. Heavy German fire rained down. The enemy hit each 761st tank at least twice with mortar, antitank, or artillery fire. Another tank hit by high-explosive fire lost a track. When the seven remaining tanks reached the objective, it appeared they found sixteen German tanks waiting. The tankers found themselves in the situation they had learned to avoid. With no choice, they engaged. Sergeant William Kitt, who possibly fought in every position during those hours, took out one enemy tank, but fired no fewer than eight 76-mm rounds to kill the beast.[41]

Willy Devore drove McBurney's Charlie tank, steady and confident as always, regardless of the chaos and pocked terrain around him. The tank crew never saw the mine that tore out the bottom of the tank, but his commander Teddy Windsor could not mistake the familiar explosion that rocked his tank for the first time. Shaken, Windsor gave the order to evacuate. McBurney knew the procedure, but hesitated and called to Devore, who did not move. Windsor watched McBurney. "Come on! Get out of the damn tank or we're all dead," he barked. McBurney knew he had to exit the tank and leave his friend. "Move!" Windsor needed to save his men.[42] Windsor figured Devore died instantly in the explosion. No time to grieve. Now the tankless crew had to find a way to survive.

Around 5:50 P.M. the 761st withdrew for resupply and refuel, but the Germans pursued them in a surprise counterattack. They caught the tankers off guard, forcing the tank battalion and the infantry regiments to retreat to their line of departure. Without saying as much, the infantry and tankers knew the enemy chased them back to where they had started. Despite the lethal tug of war between the enemies, for the 761st the day's engagement ended with Devore's death and four wounded and the loss of ground.

The next day, an ever-shrinking 761st supported the advance of the 346th. To McBurney's surprise, the area had grown eerily quiet and few targets presented themselves that McBurney could see. But the enemy had inflicted tremendous damage on the 87th Infantry Division overall. During the infantry regiments' assault on Tillet in a week of combat, companies crumbled from the lethal combination of enemy fire, the cold, and the emotional strain of war.[43]

The battle for Tillet ended as suddenly as it began. German resistance vanished as if it had never existed. In an anticlimactic reversal, Tillet landed in the Americans' laps.

With guns silent, McBurney thought about the previous day. "No time to grieve." He watched brave and remarkable men like Frank Cochrane, Moses Dade, and Teddy Windsor out in front doing whatever the situation needed at the moment. Old habits and such put Windsor firmly in McBurney's tank. When Windsor dashed out as he often did, McBurney took over as a shy but capable tank commander. The crew understood how they worked when Windsor ran off. No one uttered a word. McBurney did not want the responsibility. He saw Windsor as special, possessing something he did not have. William McBurney's gun satisfied him. He felt safe in the gunner's chair. Fighting in the Ardennes in January had its challenges, but life in the tank remained close to how Bates had trained them.

McBurney lost his tank at Tillet. He lost his driver and friend Willy Devore. He recalled Devore had made it known to anyone who would listen that he would not survive the war, annoying his fellow tankers with his prediction. Everyone probably had fears and McBurney kept his to himself. Devore's loss showed McBurney his naiveté. Devore faced his fears without embarrassment. He performed his duty without hesitation and remained one of the best drivers in the ETO, in McBurney's opinion. Even after the carnage of November, McBurney saw an enemy determined to cut down the 761st and the U.S. Army if it could. But in William McBurney's world, his buddies lived. He left Willy Devore alone on a frozen battlefield. He needed time to grieve as he made a slow sign of the cross. He begged for God's forgiveness. He asked Him to care for Willy.

Dave Williams, back at the command post with his tanks, sat in silence. He had fought and cried as a commander who loved his men. He swore he would see the war through to the last man. He had prayed for his own mortality the day he lost Ruben Rivers, but now, he had other men who depended on him to survive. Williams remained by their side and led them. He had their backs. The army awarded him a Silver Star on January 8,[44] which held little interest. He wanted to be with the men of Able Company. He remained consumed by guilt over Rivers's death. But the gods of war had final say over the fate of any soldier, including Dave Williams, once a boy-of-a-man who had found his place, albeit by a route strewn with agonizing loss. Dave Williams's war ended with an unceremonious evacuation for a severe case of trench foot.[45] He fought the medical order and held fast to his company. The men of Able Company stared, bewildered, as the medics drove their commander away.

Like campfire stories, the tankers heard rumors that Tillet had not been held by regular German units, as some thought, or SS units, as others believed. Soldiers passed word around it appeared to be Hitler's elite Führer Begleit Brigade, or palace guard,[46] though they had no credible source. After a battle, no one wanted sources. Similarly, no one wanted to talk about the fact the 761st went to Tillet with a mere eleven tanks. Regardless of whom the tankers faced, George and his company commanders turned their attention to the next mission. In the end, they took Tillet with a whimper. Fine, in McBurney's opinion. He wanted to leave that Hell in the past.

SKETCH OF
LT. COL. PAUL BATES
761ST TANK BN

Willard Sunehill
1944
USO CAMP SHOWS
England

A portrait of Paul Bates sketched by a USO artist
while he was recuperating in England. After the
war, Ellsworth McConnell created an album
about the 761st Battalion and beneath a photograph of Bates he wrote, "This man gave us the
dignity, honor, and pride that America wouldn't.
With this we fought on to glory and honor few
men have ever lived to see." (*Baron Bates*)

Twenty

Bates's Return

WITHOUT REST AFTER TILLET, WHAT REMAINED OF THE 761ST continued its race against the Germans. They took up defensive positions in Gerimont with three Shermans, two assault guns, and the mortar platoon, covering a zone assigned by the 87th Infantry Division, a sector to the left of the 345th Infantry Regiment. Baker Company performed a limited objective attack on Pironpie and Bonnerue but the Americans found the towns void of enemy forces. Baker then supported the 3rd Battalion of the 347th Infantry Regiment in already-surrendered territory.[1]

On January 12, Charlie Company moved its four operational tanks with two assault guns to the vicinity of Amberloup in support of the 345th. They met no opposition. At the same time, Baker covered the 347th in St. Hubert. The site of such harsh fighting nearly two weeks earlier had not a single enemy soldier in sight. Americans occupied the village unchallenged.[2]

Trezzvant Anderson believed he served in the Third Army to build the reputation of the 761st Tank Battalion, judging by the coverage he devoted to the outfit. The unit captivated him. As a correspondent in the ETO he had specialized in Red Ball Express stories, but the black tankers had captured his imagination. He could do great things for the people of his race and their fighting men risking their lives. Always the PR front man, Anderson built the unit's status in words, reporting its actions with tension and flair. He combined some actions, no one the wiser. The black press at home republished his stories, and heroes in Anderson's world lived on, despite grave markers bearing their names and empty spaces left by their tragic deaths. November became a blur of dead Germans and medals for valor. He cited Ruben Rivers for the slaughter of two hundred Germans and Private First Class Obie J. Smith with killing twenty. Sergeant Warren Crecy, whom Anderson claimed had gained the reputation as the most fearless man in his company, killed the enemy, rescued fellow tankers, and provided protection for infantry units. He wrote of Lieutenant Richard English and his ability to carry out the reconnaissance mission, Tommy gun in hand, while his men fought the enemy. The action in which the Germans nearly annihilated Charlie Company at the tank ditch and fourteen men lay dead became in Anderson's world a series of heroic tank rescues by First Sergeant Samuel J. Turley. Rivers's death nine days later evaded mention, though Anderson detailed his heroic acts. He would make the 761st famous. Though not accurate when compared to operational reports, the tales of valor served their purpose and may have given a segment of the homefront pride and hope.[3]

On January 14th, the 761st attached to the 17th Airborne Division in the vicinity of Freux-Menil. The division's executive officer took one look at the battle-scarred tankers and dearth of firepower and ordered all into supervised maintenance.[4] McBurney heard that the executive officer told Major George he had a war to fight. He established a rigid inspection schedule to verify the progress on the much-needed work on tanks, weapons, and other equipment.

A week later, brighter news encouraged a tired McBurney. Staff Sergeant Frank Cochrane from battered Charlie Company and Baker's William Kitt, a dependable, one-man tank battalion, received battlefield commissions effective January 20.[5] But what about his own tank commander Teddy Windsor, he wondered. Windsor seemed the most deserving in the battalion to the biased McBurney. Brigadier General John L. Whitelaw, the 17th Airborne assistant division commander, promoted the men to second lieutenant and awarded a Bronze Star to Bravo Company commander and now-Captain Long.

As the tankers pieced themselves back together from the against-the-odds triumph at Tillet, Harrison heard more details about what had been accomplished on the lengthy mission. He saw them as a first-rate tank battalion. They fought as a legitimate partner with the

87th Infantry Division and other supporting units. The 761st not only helped push the Germans from Tillet, but assisted taking many villages before it. Charlie Company and the 345th Infantry kept the Germans off balance and moving out of the vicinity of Fosset and Roumont and closed the Marche-Bastogne Road, a major supply route for the Germans. The 87th claimed the Germans needed it if they had any hope of continuing the present fight.

At the request of the 17th Airborne Division, George, Geist, and the 761st company commanders made their way to the front—a quiet front. After a thorough,[6] hour-long reconnaissance they put together their recommendation for defensive as well as offensive missions. Geist suggested reinforcing Baker Company with the assault gun platoon and one platoon of light tanks and placing them in the vicinity of Wicourt. Good roads would help them move quickly and with relative ease. Division agreed and the tanks planned to move at 1710 that evening, but moved on the 19th instead, while the rest of the battalion still worked to get its tanks and weapons ready for the next engagement.[7]

After much-needed maintenance, gunnery practice, and training with the replacement soldiers while attached to the 17th Airborne, companies prepared to relieve Baker and not too soon. By January 23 after days of dancing with the faceless enemy without any heavy engagement, Baker had had five of its nine tanks mired in mud with no recovery vehicle. As the men struggled to free the tanks, Able took the mission and replaced Baker.[8]

Familiar challenges resurfaced. On January 25 as Able—with just one medium tank, one light tank, and three assault guns operational—moved with the 513th Infantry.[9] Its other three tanks met a fate similar to Baker's the previous day, but the stuck Able tanks sat positioned to fire. The regiment considered the tanks crucial to flushing out German prisoners from a wooded area, coded P798776. The new Able Company commander, First Lieutenant Maxwell Huffman, had the opportunity to lead his men out of the situation. No one could replace Dave Williams, though. And no one could dislodge the tanks. They fired from their positions and good fortune decided the enemy would not fire upon ideal stationary targets. They sat a second day, with no enemy attack. Support vehicles had been down for some time. Able dispatched another tank to tow the disabled tanks out of the mud only to bury its tracks deep in the soupy mess. Despite Able and Baker's problems, Richard English and Dog Company kept the battalion supply train moving with its light Stuarts. Trucks remained unable make it through the mud and the off-road tangle of vines and other foliage.[10] Even with Able's unenviable situation, the force had killed twenty-five Germans the previous day and flushed an enemy unprepared for the fight from the woods and took them prisoner. Charlie supported the 194th Infantry without incident.[11]

Just two weeks after Tillet, the Americans had met a different enemy. The Germans appeared weakened, almost timid. On some days it seemed they had disappeared. The Americans took towns like Watermall, Espeler, and Thommen and pushed the Germans from Gouvy and Hautbillan. During rare engagements, the Americans killed or captured the enemy soldiers.[12] In what felt like a coup, they cut the road from St. Vith to Bastogne, a primary objective of the Allied offensive, and a fact unknown to most of the tankers.[13] Harrison and Service Company had their own challenges during January, running support to fighters at the front. Geist prepared his January S-3 report reflecting on the month. Operations for the 761st had remained eerily quiet since January 10. Maybe they neared victory—or all hell again would break loose.

McBurney heard the battalion would move to support the 101st Airborne Division, but it had been reported in error. While Harrison and the headquarters wondered who next would scoop up the limping battalion, Colonel Latimer (no relation to Captain Phil Latimer) arrived from 12th Armored Division to discuss replacement tanks.[14] Major George probably laid out their desperate need for tanks, obvious to anyone who visited the battalion. Without making any promises the colonel would have tried to say something reassuring, noted the needs of the 761st, and left.

At the end of January, the 761st rejoined the 87th Infantry Division.[15] It seemed they faced a fading enemy, but they found pockets of resistance. The tankers again rolled in the support of the 345th and 346th infantry regiments. February opened with Baker in reserve awaiting the completion of bridges to Schonberg. Charlie moved in support of the 345th Infantry. To their surprise they met an enemy column moving east from Emierscheid. The Americans killed at least 175 enemy soldiers. As the tankers drove off, William McBurney turned around and saw the enemy weapons ablaze. It still seemed a strange sight on a country road. German forces made a stand at Huem, where Baker knocked out several machine gun emplacements, enabling the infantrymen of the 345th to maneuver and take the town.[16]

McBurney, now in a replacement tank, and his fellow Charlie tankers battled strong German resistance in Herresbach and Schonberg. The same occurred the next day in Emierscheid, bringing the Americans back to the German border.

On February 2, the 761st attached to the 95th Infantry Division. Other units assigned to the 95th included its three infantry regiments, the 277th, 278th, 279th; its artillery, the 547th AAA (antiaircraft artillery) Battalion; and the very handy 320th Engineer Battalion, which "cleared snow from roads, sawed wood, conducted road and bridge recon and repaired culverts." The 607th Tank Destroyer Battalion prepared to detach and the 803rd had arrived to take its place.[17]

A number of soldiers told Trezzvant Anderson they found leaving the 17th Airborne difficult. Anderson explained that in their brief time together the men of the two units developed a true camaraderie. The men told Anderson the division commander, Major General William M. Miley, commented he would rather have five tanks from the 761st than a larger number from another armored unit.[18]

They left the area surrounding Gouvy at 0300 February 6. Leaders classified the movement as top secret. They removed all unit identifiers and withheld routes and destinations. McBurney wondered if they expected trouble, but kept his thoughts to himself. The force covered 141 miles and arrived in Hermee just after midnight February 7. In the relative safety of Holland, vehicle maintenance now stood as the battalion's primary mission. In its current state the 761st Tank Battalion stood far below the combat-effective threshold. The tankers took stock of their dismal plight. The battalion listed its February 7 operational tanks: Able had four M4 Shermans up; Baker had three M4s; Charlie, three M4s; Dog, eight M5 Stuarts; Headquarters Company, two assault guns.[19]

As it had in Texas, the Replacement Command pumped fresh soldiers into the 761st, a move the men considered ill-timed and whose presence they resented. McHenry, Harrison, and the grizzled tankers in the trenches, like McBurney, knew they needed bodies, but for some, replacing the fallen seemed a sacrilege. Other tank commanders had recreated their broken crews and devised techniques to compensate for their losses. McBurney did not care about the replacements. Many tankers had little interest in untrained, untested men from what they considered lesser specialties. But the veteran tankers learned the replacements had names and more experience than they realized. Many came from service units, and a number had seen action at the front in the Ardennes and wanted to fight with the 761st.[20]

George pulled the staff together. It seemed they would remain in Holland for more than a few days not just for maintenance but for training and other opportunities. The battalion established a tank training course. In two weeks 761st tankers who now stood as unit cadre had the "fillers" proficient enough to take part in combat missions. They would learn other skills on-the-job. Some of the more seasoned and mature replacements saw tank commander in their future.[21]

Reinforcements continued to pour in faster than they could be trained and placed. The officers never dreamed they would have an excess personnel situation. The influx overwhelmed them. One solution: Establish a new company—E Company—for the recent acquisitions.[22]

To Harrison's surprise, he also found he had an excess of vehicles. Someone saw fit to heap tanks, trucks, and the like on the battalion. Going into Holland, the unit had a clear trend in "loss of vehicles," some because of battalion shortcomings but many because of breaks in supply lines and challenges reaching higher maintenance echelons. Gains or losses, Harrison and Latimer controlled an influx that could have turned chaotic.[23]

The Hermee maintenance respite continued through much of February.[24] Though the men remained at the front and the enemy seemed just over a ridge, the pace eased a bit, and the panic of the personnel and equipment influx subsided. It made for a workable transition against the backdrop of war. As maintenance continued, so did training. Company commanders hoped the extended stay in Holland would bring most of their tanks back on line. They planned to keep their veterans' skills sharp while bringing replacement soldiers to a level of proficiency where they could fight.[25] After the bloodletting at Tillet, Germany still had resolve. The 761st had to be ready.

By February 10, the battalion worked to remove camouflage paint from all vehicles. It turned in a number of its Shermans and much to the battalion's surprise, received new tanks in return. Emotion accompanied the task. The departing tanks had saved their lives and taken the lives of countless enemy soldiers. More than tanks, the Shermans stood proudly as trusted steeds to some, angels from God himself for others. Parting with old friends proved difficult.

In a move just short of rising from the dead, Paul Bates reappeared February 17.[26] Lieutenant Colonel Bates thanked now-Lieutenant Colonel John George and took back his command. George wasted no time and headed back to Third Army the next morning, possibly knowing Bates no longer needed him or sensing Bates did not want him in his battalion.

Bates wished his return to the battalion kept quiet. The men would know soon enough. Many in the 761st expected Bates had been long gone, probably home in the States recovering from his wound. Some had written to him in the hospital and had an idea of his plans and progress. Bates had arrived at the 104th Evacuation Hospital near Southampton, England. To his surprise, further evaluation of his leg revealed a shattered fibula, and doctors said his recuperation might take longer than originally estimated.[27] They worked on Bates's leg and determined he would not walk anytime soon. Paul Bates would slide his leg off the bed and try to stand—on the rare occasion he found the nurses distracted. Much to his horror the doctors correctly evaluated his condition. At first, Bates had little news on his battalion. Rumors whirled up and down the ward about the war. Despite a rough start, he guessed his men gave the Germans hell. He had hand-picked his commanders for just this scenario. Williams, Lawson, McHenry, for Able, Baker, and Charlie. He still could not understand Richard English, but he proved the right man for Dog Company. Bates had trained them all. They knew how to perform, but could they execute in the face of a formidable enemy?

As time went on, Bates kept abreast of the battalion during his much-longer-than-expected recovery. His men sought him out, and their numerous appreciated letters reported the news from the front. He heard of the Charlie Company ambush that second day of combat. He knew of Hollis Hunt and John George and felt confident as Charlie Company continued to jab under its able leadership. The early overall losses concerned him, but he had trained the men to push on no matter the odds. He knew they had listened, judging from what they wrote. One letter fed his pride as a commander, but he felt the sting of guilt. The men depended on him too much, an attachment that could get his tankers killed. His lesson to them stood as self-reliance.

Sergeant R. E. O'Daniels wrote in his November 26 letter to Bates, "It was a . . . blow to all of us when you received your injury and I know I speak for all the fellows. I personally know the EM [enlisted men] had all the confidence in the world in your judgment and ability. We look forward to your speedy recovery and hope you will once again be at the helm."[28] Bates shocked O'Daniels by taking the time to respond. The sergeant wrote again with his perspective of events. Bates, already aware of the disappointing performance of his handpicked executive officer, Major Charles Wingo, read that Wingo commanded the battalion one day—a day longer than he had read from anyone else. The letter noted things became "uncomfortable for him." O'Daniels confessed what the officers and men really thought, "He ran out on us."[29]

It seemed Major Wingo, who probably stood in for Bates at the command post that morning, ran from his duties. As Bates's executive officer, Wingo stood next to command the 761st. Bates remained dubious that Wingo fled as a coward, but as reports made their way to his hospital bed, they told the same story.[30] Charles Wingo made it to the 95th General Hospital. In a letter dated November 19, 1944, Wingo wrote Lieutenant Leonard P. Taylor: "I had hoped I would have been out of here and back with the unit before now."[31] He probably wrote Taylor, figuring that as the battalion adjutant, he best communicated with the other officers and would tell his side of the story. Like others in the unit, Taylor had a background in education and taught mathematics at prestigious Clark University from 1936 through 1938 in his native Atlanta.[32] He would not play Charles Wingo's game.

Wingo explained he had an injury to his foot, but thankfully, no broken bones. He also confessed he suffered from a "nervous condition" that prevented him from keeping food down. He emphasized his worry about the battalion and his interest in news from the unit. At the same time he asked Taylor to forward his mail to the hospital. He sent his regards to Reynolds, Geist, and Nelson.[33] Wingo, alone and seemingly panicked, wrote Taylor no fewer than three times, exasperated his fellow officers, including Reynolds and Bremer, had not responded to him.[34]

Bates had Wingo's letters since Taylor, Reynolds, and his posse of staff officers would have nothing to do with a man they considered a coward. Bates sent Wingo's pleas to Taffy Rosen and asked her to write him, but reminded her not to say the unit wanted him back, "the officers and the men, right or wrong, would not tolerate him," but as a nurse in a field hospital at the front, Taffy Rosen had more important tasks.[35]

Sergeant O'Daniels also told him of the throngs of untrained replacements and gave unvarnished truth on vehicle maintenance. "Too many tanks down and not enough time or equipment to get them up. Maintenance falls farther behind." He noted that the several day rest periods helped them—just to lose more tanks to enemy fire as well as deep snow and slick roads.[36]

Ed Reynolds dashed off a two-page letter to Bates dated December 1. "It's needless to say the B[attalio]n misses you very much and wishes that you were here with us. You have always had the B[attalio]n's backing 100%. It is really 'your' outfit." Reynolds told him of the many mistakes made by both the tankers and the infantry, which "forced all to learn that much faster." Regarding the battalion, he admitted, "I am sorry to say I was one who doubted that would be the case."[37] He shared a positive note with Bates on support tactics. "Sherman companies have attached to the regiments and have a scheme of maneuver that seems to work well for all." But he reiterated O'Daniels's maintenance account: "Fifteen to five tanks in two days, with maintenance times anyone's guess. . . . Never the less, the division would not be where it is today without the support we have given them. We rate big with the division. We are all proud of the outfit and I'm certain you would be."[38]

Corporal Louis N. Phillips saw Bates and his work differently, and found the voice with which to share his thoughts. In his November 28 letter he wrote with aching eloquence, "Forgive me, but I could not hold back the urge any longer to write you. I have always held you in the highest esteem, and always will. . . . The battalion has not only fought for the name, and advancement of the Negro Race, as a whole. They have fought and are still fighting for you."[39]

A number of injured tankers made their way through Bates's hospital and gave him eyewitness accounts of the war. One man from Charlie Company recounted the company's tremendous losses. Turley's and Colemen's deaths hit Bates hard. "They were two of the finest soldiers I have ever known."[40]

Back with his unit, Paul Bates limped with a cane. But the tankers could look past his hobble and see the man who commanded the 761st had returned to lead them. It may have taken days for the battalion to learn of the loss of Bates, but they knew to a man when he returned. Harrison looked up and grinned. The reception took Bates aback. Smiles, cheers, and a reunion with his staff that included champagne supplied by Rosen.[41] With Paul Bates, the air returned to the battalion lungs. McBurney, no longer weary, wanted to go kill a few Germans with the colonel. Despite his absence, Bates still carried their raison d'etre, though most had already internalized it for themselves.

Bates walked through the companies. Not a youngster remained. Quiet, sober, serious contemplative men surrounded him. He wrote Taffy Rosen that they had become the battalion he had hoped they would.[42] No one had a doubt: The 761st had one commander—Paul L. Bates.

March 8, 1945, marked a homecoming of sorts. The 761st received orders back to Third Army. The battalion attached to the 103rd Infantry Division[43] and the men felt a kinship with its commander. Now-Major General Anthony C. McAuliffe had not just fought at the Ardennes, the former deputy commander of the 101st Airborne Division and de facto commander during Major General Maxwell D. Taylor's absence had also stared down thousands of Germans as they surrounded and choked his men in Bastogne.[44]

The war again had shifted. The 761st met an enemy solidly entrenched in a defensive posture. Weeks earlier, the Germans stood like giants, breathed fire, and snacked on the bones of Allied units. Bates bet that dragon lay somewhere, waiting for the Americans to come to him. As the 410th and 411th infantry regiments patrolled, the enemy remained unseen, but automatic and small arms fire from the hidden opponent forced a U.S. patrol to withdraw from the area of Uhrwiller and Niefern, France, on March 14.[45]

The 761st (minus Charlie Company) joined with the 3rd Battalion of the 409th Infantry Regiment as well as one platoon from Company A of the 328th Engineer (C) Battalion and detachments of Divisional Signal Company and Division Artillery. They formed Task Force Cactus, conspicuously named on March 13 in honor of the 103rd, itself nicknamed the Cactus Division.[46] Success seemed predetermined. In the operations instruction, the G-3 announced in his first line: "Enemy is completely disorganized."[47]

As the rest of the 409th Infantry Regiment moved out, attacking to the northeast, the 411th Infantry met little opposition in its sector. The 103rd waited. It held the task force, then unleashed it with little

A 761st M4 Sherman supporting the 103rd Infantry Division at Niefern, France, March 1945. (*National Archives*)

notice to the northeast the afternoon of March 17. It advanced rapidly and maneuvered through Gundershoffen and reached Eberbach ready for orders from division. The next day the division made a sweeping advance toward the Westwall, or Siegfried Line as it was called by the Allies, and fully expected to push through the invisible Germans. Instead, by 2300 hours on March 18, the firehose of closing U.S. infantry turned into a trickle. The enemy nearly halted the advance with a complex series of roadblocks, deep craters, blown bridges, heavily defended pillboxes, and mines. Some divisional elements continued to push forward. They attacked repeatedly and believed they made progress until they met the next line of resistance—the outer defenses of the Siegfried Line.[48] Bates wrote that his men "never caught up with the infantry as the road blocks in the mountains prevented closing with the 'Krauts.'"[49]

On March 19 the 409th and 411th met a well-armed and well-entrenched enemy. The defenders had turned brazen. They slipped from their catacombs and patrolled looking for Americans. They ambushed a vehicle from the 411th south of Bundenthal.[50] The U.S. attempted to repel the enemy, but no matter the intensity or direction, the seasoned U.S. soldiers knew the Germans on the Siegfried Line stood as mostly battlewise combat veterans "interspersed with Volkstrum personnel"—a less formal, but no less devoted hodge-podge of old men, volunteers, and conscripts, armed with whatever the regular army could scrounge for them. These men believed this stood as their duty as Germans. Army and Volkstrum alike shared the goal of saving the Fatherland—and killing anyone who challenged them.[51]

The experienced Germans on the line appreciated defensive terrain and knew how to employ it to their advantage. They used these features in the defense of Nieder Schlettenbach and Reisdorf, Germany.[52] They blew buildings in Westwall towns like Niederbronn to conceal their work from the Americans, denying the Allied invaders useful intelligence in the efforts to raid Germany. But the enemy wavered late on the 20th; maybe the air assaults combined with well-placed mortar and artillery fire proved too much. Able Company, one Charlie platoon, and infantry captured Nieder Schlettenbach.[53] More towns fell, but the Siegfried Line held.

Inspired by the French and their Maginot Line, the Germans constructed a system of defensive positions and obstacles in the late 1930s. The Reich spared no expense, yet the Germans doubted they would need their wall that stretched 630 kilometers, abutting no fewer than four nations. Four miles wide in some places, the fortifications appeared almost medieval in design, despite advanced German technology, relying on large, crude impediments, natural terrain, and a network of bunkers and pillboxes where Germans soldiers would fire from concealed positions. But the Westwall, far from outdated, stood as a tribute to German ingenuity. To defend against units like the 761st, the Germans dug deep tank ditches, erected concrete dragon's teeth, and laced the area with mines. They backed the anti-tank maze with fortified facilities for command and control and reinforcements.[54] In 1940 the last line of defense proved unnecessary and confirmed the opinion of many critics. Germany had no idea France and much of Europe would fall as quickly and easily as they did. But by 1944, the Reich learned it would need its wall as well as its connection to the European nations it once held.[55]

With the 103rd Infantry Division probing the defenses, Germans responded with stiff resistance. The 103rd stood as one in a long line of failed invaders. The Allies made a number of runs at the Siegfried Line during late 1944. Between September 1 and December 16, First

Army bore the brunt of German wrath in its campaign for the Huertgen Forest, suffering 47,000 casualties and losing 550 tanks. Ninth Army's losses tallied 10,000. The overall cost in battling for the Westwall during less than four months stood at nearly 140,000 men. While Siegfried towns and cities like Aachen fell and Allied attempts may have challenged and weakened the Germans, the Allies failed to crack the Siegfried Line.[56]

As Patton and his Third Army, including the 761st, had fought well in the Saar Basin during the success in the Lorraine, Patton prepared for a December 19 assault on the Siegfried Line, but Eisenhower and the Germans' sudden Ardennes offensive changed his plans. By March 1945, with the Ardennes a bloody memory, the Allied return to the Westwall forced Germany to defend against an attack. Resistance increased. Both sides understood the stakes: Crack the Seigfreid Line and open the way to the final defeat of Germany. No other option existed for the Allies. American forces prepared to advance on the enemy.

McBurney heard talk and felt the tension. The Siegfried Line sounded immense, but he did not see how their mission differed from the many gruesome actions of the past months. Could anything rival Tillet? Though he once felt Tillet ushered in the end of the war, it seemed only a successful Siegfried breach would signal what he and the other tankers worked toward, at least from the chatter around the battalion and among the doughs. Did cracking that line signal an end to the war or the beginning of the fight for Germany? McBurney kept his thoughts to himself, but reasoned the latter. As he took a long drag from his last cigarette, he thought Hell probably lay waiting for him on the other side of that line.

Given what seemed insurmountable challenges, Task Force Cactus dissolved, but the 103rd, the 761st, and other attached units continued to battle along the Siegfried Line. Each time a break in the line seemed imminent, Germans poured in like wet cement to fill the fissures. Major General McAuliffe and his commanders reviewed the situation and established another task force, but with a different approach—one neither the Allies nor the Germans expected.

Twenty-One

Task Force Rhine

THOUGH PAUL BATES HAD BEEN BACK WITH HIS UNIT ONLY A little more than a month, McAuliffe saw a fine officer in control of an experienced tank battalion, albeit, a seriously bruised unit. The 761st had come to him filled with battle-hardened veterans driving combat-effective masses of steel that packed a punch second only to the German Panzers and their 88s on this battlefield. The men possessed a certain flair, maybe more spirit than talent, but this mission called for the unconventional. McAuliffe and his men in the 101st Airborne Division survived Bastogne by doing very little by the book. He stood willing to go with the 761st in the lead. He had nothing to lose.

At 2030 on March 21, McAuliffe placed Bates in command of Task Force Rhine.[1] Like Task Force Cactus and innumerable task forces in the war, a task force had a particular mission with a specific organization of short duration. They lessened any impact on the main force and rolled back into the larger unit when dissolved. Task Force Rhine stood as Bates's blitzkrieg; it would move quickly. Paul Bates and his force would assemble in less than twelve hours.[2] The battle for the Siegfried Line presented itself as the pinnacle of the 761st Tank Battalion's journey. Months, years, a lifetime of training came down to this opportunity. It stood as the promise he made to the men of the 761st. If they put their trust in Paul Bates, he would take them all the way.

With little time, he planned and moved in quick succession. He chose Baker as his lead company which included Lieutenant Sam Brown.[3] Lieutenant Harold B. Gary and his tanks would roll as Bates's lead platoon. Able Company would follow Baker. Richard English or "Bulldog," as the men had come to call him, and Dog Company would provide reconnaissance as well as interference as ordered.[4]

In addition to his tankers, less Charlie Company, Bates had the 2nd Battalion of the 409th Infantry Regiment, one platoon from Company A of the 328th Engineer (C) Battalion, and a Signal Detachment from the 103rd Signal Company. The 614th Tank Destroyer Battalion attached a reconnaissance platoon.[5]

Paul Bates had already determined the battalion would maneuver without Charlie Company. From what Bates had read while in England and observed since his return, members of Charlie had proved themselves since they entered combat. The men fought with instinct and cunning, despite their near slaughter. Charlie's experience would have put lesser soldiers out of the war, but they stood on their own and continued to fight. Charlie remained in support of the 103rd "Cactus" Division's 411th and 409th Infantry Regiments, where it would clear the way for Task Force Rhine.[6] Bates watched the company press forward. Pop Gates ensured that Charlie Company took control of its role. The men had proved themselves at Morville, but Task Force Rhine stood as their chance to display their prowess as American tankers. Gates understood and believed in Paul Bates.

McBurney shook with anticipation when he heard his name. Opening the way into Germany seemed a long way from Harlem. He thought of the army recruiter. He wanted his father to see that they do train black men. He would roll with Teddy Windsor like they had since birth, it seemed. Task Force Rhine equated promises kept and hope realized. He and Windsor and Charlie Company would spearhead to clear the way. William McBurney and his fellow tankers now stood as respected combat veterans entrusted with an important mission. Generals in addition to George Patton counted on them. They could change the war. The men believed they had already changed the opinion of their nation. The news sheets said as much. For McBurney, clearing the way for Task Force Rhine offered something in return for endless training and rising expectations as well as the pain and rejection that seemed to come with the distinction as a 761st tanker.

Trezzvant Anderson saw the future of a group of men, a battalion, an army, and a nation—waiting for McBurney and the others.

McAuliffe entrusted Bates and the task force to open the way for the 14th Armored Division. If they cracked the Siegfried Line, they could claim victory; fail . . . Bates understood. The 761st's commander worked through the night, studying any intelligence he could find. Because of the heavy German defenses anticipated in areas along the route, he determined he only could commit a few tanks at a time. By Bates's count, he had 1,200 men in the task force, exceeding his full battalion strength.[7]

The operation turned more fluid than expected. Gates divided his Charlie platoons, a move the companies loathed when they entered the war in November. Separated, Charlie Company could better support the infantry regiments and more quickly clear the towns for Task Force Rhine's advance. One platoon remained with the 411th Infantry, driving the remaining enemy forces from the Siegfried town of Nieder Schlettenbach. It took out thirteen pillboxes and ten machine gun nests. Thirty-five of the enemy died in the fight. The remaining Germans shifted elsewhere. The rest of Charlie Company and the 409th Infantry Regiment attacked the area between Nieder Schlettenbach and Erlenbach. They made another attack on the approach to Reisdorf, still a German stronghold. Tension ruled as they maneuvered closer to face the entrenched enemy. They took aim knocking out "seven pill boxes and 10 machine gun positions surrounding the town." McBurney credited himself with the demise of at least two guns. With twelve enemy killed and sixty-four taken prisoner, the force discovered the Germans had mined the area. Charlie lost one tank to a well-placed mine.[8]

Charlie Company platoons under Lieutenant Frank Cochrane and Staff Sergeant Moses Dade fought hard in the attack and lost tanks to heavy enemy fire. To compensate, the men joined platoons to create a larger unit. Given stiff enemy resistance, the combined unit stood as their best chance at clearing the way for Bates's task force. Dade commanded the first tank. The inseparable Teddy Winsdor and William McBurney followed. Sergeant Warren Crecy's tank drove in the third position. Technician Fourth Grade Isiah Parks trailed Crecy, and Sergeant Daniel Cardell commanded the final tank. Cochrane took the lead.[9]

Despite the new, emboldened ad hoc unit, concern over Reisdorf escalated. Bates and the task force would arrive in Reisdorf in a few

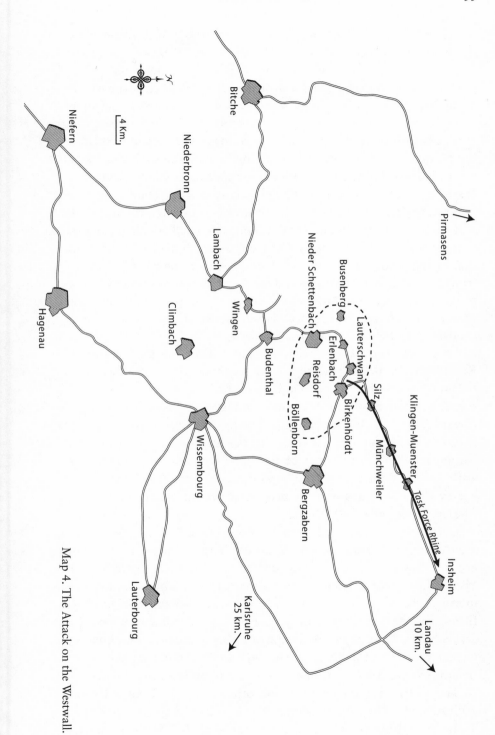

Map 4. The Attack on the Westwall.

hours and the Americans had yet to gain control.[10] At 0615 on March 22, Bates commenced "32 of the wildest hours"[11] he ever wanted to see. As planned, with a platoon of Charlie Company tanks in support, riflemen from the division swarmed the area to clear the way for Task Force Rhine. The enemy responded with violence at the slightest provocation. The 1st Battalion of the 411th Infantry moved three rifle companies to the high ground north of Böllenborn and Reisdorf, but "murderous fire of every description" halted their advance. When the task force pushed toward Reisdorf and assembled south of the enemy-controlled town at 0800, the Cactus Division soldiers engaged in house-to-house fighting much of the day to take the town. The 1st and 2nd battalions of the 411th Infantry, slowed by enemy mortar and automatic fire, received relief from a detachment of 761st tanks that brought "direct fire on enemy casements in the zone."[12] Judging from enemy activity, Bates sensed the German forces surrounding the town—watching the Americans and waiting for some unknown opportunity. Enemy resistance within Reisdorf remained a threat, though Bates held his task force in place.[13]

Paul Bates and Task Force Rhine jumped off and pushed through Reisdorf at 1600. The enemy fired on the task force from the hills to the northeast. After an attack from Bates's men, the pillboxes fell silent. Bates then split his force in two. One section headed northeast toward Birkenhördt and the other east to Böllenborn. Bates believed they had done significant damage to the Siegfried Line's defenses in Reisdorf, but fell just short of the breakthrough they sought. The 14th Armored Division needed a substantial opening cleared of any enemy threat.[14] Bates and his task force would create the opening. The question remained: When?

German patience paid off. As Task Force Rhine's two forces moved out, both soon ground to a halt. The Germans probably did not see the task force as any different from earlier attacks. The "Birkenhördt Force" pushed past a rain of small arms fire, but once in range, the enemy stopped the advance with two antitank guns, one firing from the northeast, the other positioned somewhere west of Birkenhördt. Paul Bates knew he had assets available to him, including air power and artillery.[15] The Birkenhördt Force called for fire from II Corps. Artillery rained down and pummeled the town.

The 103rd Infantry Division and other units like George Patton's 10th Armored Division worked to crush resistance that could impede Task Force Rhine's progress. The 10th Armored Division arrived, tasked with outflanking the Siegfried Line defenses remaining west of the Rhine River. It planned to drive south to Annweiler and threaten "all enemy troops in the Landau pocket."[16]

With fire support in almost all directions, Task Force Rhine could move up the middle. As the task force rolled forward, gunners as well as tankers with their fingers on the triggers of the .30 and .50 caliber machine guns, fired at "any position that might conceal anti-tank guns." Even with the recent artillery fire on target, they found four active machine gun nests remaining. A gun battle ensued with two; the crews of the other two ran. The tankers cleared the village. Infantry moved forward and consolidated its gains. Between the power and precision of the artillery and the work between tanks and foot soldiers, Bates nodded with a simple, "Excellent timing."[17] Birkenhördt had fallen.[18]

By 1700 hours, after his men "jabbed and slugged"[19] the enemy, the task force stood one step closer to its final objective. But McAuliffe seemed less impressed and unusually impatient. Division reiterated the order, Break through the Siegfried Line to the Rhine Plain.[20]

At the same time, the Böllenborn Force had been stopped by anti-tank fire to its front and left flank when attempting to enter that town. With a specific schedule to keep, force leaders chose to withdraw and follow the route of their sister force, bypassing active enemy guns. At 1800, Task Force Rhine received orders from the 103rd Infantry Division to move to the north and east to make contact with the 10th Armored Division in the town of Silz, another Westwall town.[21]

Interrogated prisoners revealed the withdrawal of the 118th Volksgrenadier Regiment from the area. More important, the task force learned that the Reich's 36th Volksgrenadier Division intended to delay the Americans, vanish, and regroup at the Rhine River. The Germans used every remaining man, weapon, and tactic to continue to fight the battle. The commands to the Germans had been clear: Fight to the last man. Counterattack to regain any lost ground. Resist until all ammunition had been exhausted or the Allies surrounded them. Many of the once-proud soldiers, now American captives, had not eaten in five days.[22]

The 409th Infantry Regiment met strong resistance along the Siegfried Line. The enemy fired from pillboxes and crude dugouts. Isolated pockets held. The 409th closed with the enemy. Knowing their defenders' orders from their German headquarters, the

Americans called for their surrender. The Germans instead chose to fight. The 409th understood their decision and fired until they killed the last man.[23]

At 1835, Task Force Rhine moved out again with Birkenhördt in American hands. The task force broke through "numerous road-blocks, craters, and anti tank obstacles," but it did not get far. A large crater in the road outside Birkenhördt halted the force. Bates called for the engineers, who had it filled quickly.[24] Bates and his mix of units moved out again at 1940, but the task force faced treacherous conditions. The Germans used natural terrain as a barrier, and a large portion of the Siegfried Line wound its way through the Hardt Mountains, some of the most rugged landscape Bates had encountered. The task force traveled nearly ten miles over jagged and cratered mountain roads, made all the more harrowing in the uneven shadows cast in the moonlight. Russell Guthrie felt he needed to shift his small body to keep his Sherman from cascading down the mountain. Bates knew the enemy watched in the chilly evening air but he refused to react, concerned any deviation would reveal his plan. Paul Bates had little interest in road conditions and razor-edged cliffs and pushed the tank commanders to move faster.[25]

Eager to meet up with the 10th Armored Division, Bates barked out orders for the capture of Silz. Now rolling on flat land, the task force glowed in the late winter moonlight, making it easy prey in enemy-held territory. No one in the task force heard a sound, yet Bates remained certain the Germans watched and waited. As the task force approached Silz, it met a horse-drawn convoy moving enemy supplies. Guthrie looked through his scope. The moonlight flickered on the majestic animals' smooth coats. He thought of the farms skirting Buffalo and his mother's love of such beauty. He found them handsome and a welcome break from the killing of the past hours.

Bates gave the order. In what seemed a matter of seconds, Guthrie's world filled with some of the worst destruction he had yet witnessed. Indistinguishable supplies, splintered wood, and remains of those that had pulled the simple carts filled the road as far as he could see, rendering it impassible. Bates then gave orders to move the carnage. A tank dozer pushed the bloody and broken like garbage to the side of the road.[26] Guthrie watched in horror.

The Germans waited, and once the force moved on top of them they let loose with their arsenal. Bates saw no sign of the 10th Armored Division. The misinformation about the division concerned him, but the enemy attack required action. With neither the 10th Armored Division nor any Allied unit near Silz that he could determine, Bates gave the order to set the town on fire with the main guns. A cataclysmic explosion of a large ammunition dump increased the tension for the tankers. "Fire for effect" no longer stood as Guthrie's favorite order. Round after round, Guthrie watched through the scope. He had not anticipated creating an inferno. The flames seemed to unnerve the calmest men. Tank rounds continued to burst as they struck a number of homes that exploded like bombs. Bates surmised that most structures along the Siegfried Line had become munitions and supply warehouses. The raging fire reduced Silz to ashes.[27]

The task force and supporting arms pounded their targets without mercy, and Bates's instincts proved accurate. They destroyed the towns of Busenberg, Lauterschwan, Vorder, Weidenthal, and Darstein. More than four hundred vehicles burned along with countless ammunition stores and fuel dumps.[28] McBurney saw the devastation but no longer thought of these as places where people lived. The towns of the Siegfried Line stood as armories for the Reich. The images of the dead strewn about came with the business of war for Bates, but burning a town remained one of his greatest challenges. He confessed to Taffy Rosen, "it stops my mental processes for a bit and a cold, numb feeling holds me."[29] The concussion of the big guns also troubled him, but his men had no need to know his personal struggles. In writing of a battering of 155 mm howitzers, "their firing jars your nerves like finger nails on a black board." The fact that the enemy had a worse time with the 155s served as some consolation.[30]

The Germans continued to leave their mark. American engineers hurried to clear roads, fill in tank ditches, and bridge any other gaps. They made the path for Task Force Rhine as smooth as possible. Allied planes strafed numerous German soldiers. With the flames, no one could tell a corpse from debris, and no one cared.

As they pushed to the final objective, enemy small arms fire continued to annoy the tanks. Bates watched for the next hazard to impede their progress. Well-concealed snipers took aim on the task force with little effect. The enemy had littered the roads to halt the tanks' progress. For the 761st, many saw the obstacles as momentary inconveniences. The Shermans crushed some. Well-placed high-explosive rounds took care of the remainder. Tanks acted as dozers to remove debris when necessary. The engineers swooped in to handle anything the tankers could not take care of on their own.[31]

The growing number of German prisoners held by tankers and infantry alike proved a hindrance. Bates's men placed them in front of their tanks or wherever they had room. The infantry units set a division record, processing 1,321 prisoners in a single day as they fought to break open the Siegfried Line.[32]

The task force picked up its pace. It flew through the darkness and fired on each town. The 761st drove off machine gun crews in Münchweiler shortly after midnight, in the early hours of March 23. The 410th and 411th fought their actions in the vicinity—clearing the area of active enemy pillboxes and taking surrounding villages.[33]

One town lay between Bates and open access to the heart of Germany. The large, heavily fortified town of Klingen-Muenster stood as the task force's last objective before they would blow the Siegfried Line wide open. Klingen-Muenster appeared larger than Bates expected and too much for the task force to occupy. The 409th preceded the tanks and quieted pockets of resistance.[34] Task Force Rhine occupied the outskirts. Bates gave the order and his men "shot the hell out of it."[35]

A number of the enemy survived the barrage, and the task force began to take fire. During the fighting, large numbers of Germans surrendered, adding to Bates's growing challenge and one he had not considered, at least not one of such large numbers of surrendering Germans. He thought back to his discussion with his officers. Any enemy soldier that surrendered would be kept alive and cared for by his men. As the task force loaded prisoners on gas and ammunition trucks and anywhere else they could stash them, the enemy closed and attacked the rear of the column. The tankers opened fire. A second gun battle ensued at the front of the column, and one platoon took up firing positions on the edge of town. Task Force Rhine sat nearly surrounded while holding prisoner a large number of Germans within its perimeter. Tank commanders barked orders. Guthrie knew they had not come all this way to die in some German firepit. Bates gave the signal. Russell Guthrie and the other gunners hit the town with every shell they had. Casings began to overflow the bins that caught them, and no one had time to dump the holders. Loaders heaved the rounds on adrenaline, their strength long spent. Between the firefights outside the tanks and the complete destruction of Klingen-Muenster, the enemy withdrew or surrendered.[36] Satisfied that Charlie Company had opened the way for Task Force Rhine,

McBurney sat back in his seat, perspiration dripping off his chin. Teddy Windsor slapped him on the back. They said nothing.

The task force had yet to achieve its main objective. Bates could see the Rhine Plain, but could not touch it. He called a meeting of his commanders. They decided to push forward fourteen kilometers, leaving no doubt the Siegfried Line lay open for the 14th Armored Division and other Allied units destined for the Rhine Plain.[37] Word reached McAuliffe, who ordered Bates to remain in place guarding the gateway to the Reich. Fourteenth Armor would pass through Task Force Rhine's position in less than a day.

That next evening Paul Bates, working on several days without sleep, and Russell Geist slipped away from the task force to survey the area. Bates looked at the wreckage, proud his men created the chaos "smashing through the Siegfried Line." As they walked among the corpses, he noted a number of "near dead Kraut soldiers." He felt no compassion for the men and no "desire to evacuate them though they had been there for twenty four hours." He felt compelled to put pen to paper and share these feelings with Taffy Rosen.[38] His contempt for the enemy seemed to justify his actions.

McBurney reflected on Charlie Company's part in the operation. In some ways it seemed more harrowing than their earliest engagement and even the five-day siege at Tillet. For the gunner, supporting the task force seemed different from other missions. He knew Task Force Rhine stood as a battalion victory. He watched a few of the tankers react at their accomplishment. For McBurney, it seemed more a solemn moment. He felt solitude in his tank with his main gun. This wild ride to crack the Siegfried Line stood as his most remarkable mission yet. Maybe having Bates back made the difference.

Russell Guthrie also sat in silence. The damn horses. They had to kill the horses. The task force's work entailed high risk with the potential for stupefying cost. The horses. He knew Pop Gates would understand, but he kept his thoughts to himself.

Elements of the 784th Tank Battalion prepare to cross the Rhine River in March 1945. (*National Archives*)

Twenty-Two

We Lived Through It

Now it fell to the 14th Armored Division to exploit the success of the 761st Tank Battalion and commence the final annihilation of Germany. Bates cautioned his men that the war now moved onto the enemy's home territory—Germany.

The 103rd Infantry Division commander lauded Task Force Rhine. Bates felt a kinship to McAuliffe, possibly because of the general's fabled stand at Bastogne during the German counteroffensive through the Ardennes. But Paul Bates remained uncertain what to make of him. McAuliffe, aware he lost several men and a tank dozer during the Task Force Rhine lightning strike,[1] ribbed Bates about the dozer. "Smooth," unsure what to say, apologized and bid the general farewell.

The Daily News Summary from McAuliffe's headquarters credited "elements of the 2nd Battalion of the 409th Infantry and the 761st Tank Battalion." Media reports restated the general's remarks to the 103rd "and attached units."[2] The public oversight, though not McAuliffe's doing, irked Bates. He believed his men deserved more credit. For Bates, the 14th Armored Division rolled safely through what many believed impenetrable terrain thanks to the 761st Tank Battalion. "We will never get the real credit we deserve for it as others won't think it possible to do what we accomplished."[3]

The success of Task Force Rhine brought more change. A few short days later on March 28, the 761st left the 103rd en route to support the 71st Infantry Division, to which the battalion stood attached.[4] It moved the short distance to the Rhine River, like other Allied units, and crossed at Oppenheim March 30. By March 31, the tankers had orders to move 132 miles, securing countless German towns, roads, and the surrounding countryside.[5]

News of Task Force Rhine reached the States. On April 7 the *Chicago Defender* led with the headline "Tank Units Plunge Through Nazi Towns; Blaze Bloody Path for White Infantrymen." The paper's war correspondent Ed Toles wrote of vicious fighting, heavy infantry casualties, and the challenges faced by the task force commander Lieutenant Colonel Paul Bates. In the end, "Task Force Bates" achieved its objective. Readers had no idea of Toles's inaccurate reporting, but the gist remained clear: the task force opened the way for the army units and someone named Bates had something to do with it.[6]

With the slow crumble of Germany came new challenges and unexpected opportunities. Bates became the authority in the areas the battalion occupied. He commanded his unit as well as the German civilians.[7] At night the officers and men bunked in local homes, running townspeople out of their residences with little warning. Bates would listen to them "weep and wail." He showed no compassion. The sight of German civilians brought dead and wounded Americans to Bates's mind. Certainly the German people had no consideration for the men the battalion lost. He made no distinction between the pleading townspeople and armed German soldiers.[8] As the area authority, Bates wrestled with residents whose towns stood untouched by the war. They demanded compensation from the Americans for some phantom grievance. They quoted the Atlantic Charter to press the point. Bates, angered by apparent dishonest opportunists, "put them straight" and moved the unit forward.[9]

The battalion straddled war and its aftermath as it made its way across Germany. The armed enemy remained unseen and the German population brought its own hazards and uncertainties. Geist reported days with "no enemy activity."[10] Yet Bates still commanded soldiers and fighters. With the threat of enemy contact in question, some in the nearly seven-hundred-man battalion grew restless.[11]

A few found trouble. On March 29, Bates reported seven alleged violent crimes in two days by members of the 761st, each incident calling for an investigation, robbing him of irreplaceable time and invaluable manpower. Any courts-martial would steal more hours and people. His frustration peaked when another unit member reportedly entered a home and attempted to assault a woman. He slashed her husband and then cut her head, neck, and arms. Bates, aggravated by the disciplinary problems, noted the troublemakers seemed to come from the 175 replacements they trained in Holland. Two other soldiers threatened to shoot an officer. The small percentage of "bad apples" reflected poorly on his high-quality unit.[12] Bates could not forgive an attack on the hard-won reputation of his men.

After several days of autonomy, the tank battalion joined the 71st Infantry Division around April 1, the 761st's third anniversary.[13] Despite the all-out maneuvering necessary during Task Force Rhine coupled with the mileage the battalion covered, the 761st Shermans and light Stuarts stood in good shape.[14] Bates watched his maintenance crews working almost nonstop to keep the battalion fit for combat. Able had twelve tanks in operation. Baker had seven running. Charlie stood at thirteen operational, as did Dog Company with thirteen Stuarts.[15] The Stuarts had more than proved their worth and resilience since arriving in the European Theater.

The tankers found themselves in combat again against an inconsistent enemy. From April 1 through April 3 the chase continued. The Americans pursued the Germans, but which Germans? The capture of SS Lieutenant General Karl Heindrich Brenner on April 2 gave the Allies their answer. By April 3 the Americans had captured and dismantled the six-thousand-man 6th SS Mountain Division.[16]

The 761st rolled across the grueling miles, day and night, with little sleep. Paul Bates understood himself as a different man after Task Force Rhine, a matter better hidden from the men. He looked at warfare from new and darker vantages. His pace eased, yet his anxiety increased. Few, if any, called him cautious, but when a town capitulated moments before coming under American attack, he confessed to Rosen the tension drained from him. He could breathe and release the uncharacteristic thoughts of his mortality that now dominated him: "Is this the time I get it?"[17]

The continued burning of towns further affected Bates, despite his disdain for the Germans. He could not get used to the smell. Same procedure. Same outcome. Same smell. The stench of musty houses and animal and human flesh. It did not take over just Bates's nose, it permeated his body such that the atrocious acts remained a part of him.[18] "What a way to live," he penned.

McBurney saw their situation as a new sort of war. He had heard about "mop-up" operations. Though unsure what the term meant, he felt reasonably certain the 761st Tank Battalion and 71st Infantry Division still engaged a fanatical enemy at times. On April 4, Dog Company found fully stocked tank supply dumps. In Flieden, reconnaissance soldiers reported 150–200 enemy entrenched ready to attack the much larger American force.[19] A suicide mission.

Few worried, but McBurney could not predict this enemy. The tanks took infrequent fire from every direction. A heavier attack might materialize from an occasional machine gun emplacement. Sometimes Windsor ordered McBurney to fire on a nest, killing the crew. As the tanks rolled, German soldiers simply appeared in the road, surrendering to the tankers as mysteriously as they had once vanished at Tillet.

Captured German letters told yet another story of the peculiar enemy. In one officer's letter home, he wrote he continued to fight, but with few men and dwindling ammunition. Though William McBurney witnessed enemy forces melt away during more than one engagement, Lieutenant Horst Fruefer of the 57th Regiment, 9th VGD (Volksgrenadier Division), wrote of desperate retreats as they watched American numbers swell. After a clever counterattack against the Americans, U.S. forces broke through the German's flank and "annihilated" his unit. Immediately his higher command "promised" him an Iron Cross. Despite his lack of experience, he soon found himself in command. His unit spent its days marching, weaving quietly around the Americans. The prime goal—avoid capture. He hoped to make it to the Rhine, possibly unaware that thousands of Americans had the same orders, but their conditions continued to deteriorate. Fruefer endured lice infestation and longed for some soap.[20]

A top secret memorandum from the 47th Volksgrenadier Division discussed the conservation of ammunition and noted that its soldiers had exceeded current limits by "almost 100%." Though considered suspect by the 761st, such information proved a boost to a unit widely recognized with already high morale.[21]

Despite accounts like that by Horst Fruefer, it struck Bates how war-ready this nation still appeared. The battalion stumbled upon a large, abandoned post that Bates likened in size to Fort Knox. He walked through the rows of new combat equipment, including sixty new 150 mm howitzers. He saw enough gear to outfit at least one division. He marveled at abundant food, not to mention crate stacked on crate of wine and cognac. Dishes, bedding, clothing, and more filled the shelves. Bates surmised the Germans had run out of gasoline, leaving them unable to move the precious supplies.[22] All pointed to proof of a wounded Germany, but possibly stood as verification the enemy remained around them with whatever weapons and provisions he could carry. The threat kept McBurney more on edge than the rip-roaring pace of Task Force Rhine. At night the soldiers secured their equipment. The next day they often found evidence that someone, possibly enemy soldiers, had stolen whatever they could.

The Germany they traversed seemed a nation of contrasts. A poorly supplied enemy struggled in the shadow of warehouses stocked with items to meet any soldier's needs. This vicious yet wheezing army and a nation devastated by war stood against a backdrop of stunning beauty. At the same time Paul Bates observed what the enemy had done to "pervert" the surrounding majesty. It had filled the woods with "pill boxes, slit trenches, caches of supplies and troops."[23]

Despite Bates's misgivings, some tankers took to the woods. The dense forests proved a welcome break from the fighting and sleeping among the dead. One tank company and some of the doughboys bivouacked among the mighty old–growth trees one evening. Later that night, another unit bedded down beside them. As the morning sun rose, the stunned tankers faced an equally shocked and groggy German SS unit. Someone opened fire and the 761st drove the German unit from the area.[24]

Between pristine medieval towns, vast rubble and jagged ruins meant the tankers had come upon what had been a major city. McBurney would not have known they had rolled into places like Ludwigshafen, Offenbach, and Frankfurt if he had not heard their names over the radio. Amid the wreckage of these once bustling and prosperous urban centers, the German people appeared well-dressed and well-fed, but the "slaves'" plight worsened.[25]

The "slave" population increased and grew more desperate as the tankers moved east. Behind the picturesque façade of one small town Bates found eight hundred enslaved "Poles, Russians, Czechs . . . and Italians."[26] They saw slaves in nearly every town. Paul Bates ordered medical attention for their "neglected wounds and the skin diseases"[27] but looked on them with a mix of contempt and deep feelings of helplessness: "They are ragged, hungry and dirty. They eat from our garbage cans."[28]

The past weeks had been difficult on the Shermans and Stuarts. The tankers logged long miles, forfeiting mandated repairs. The push to an undefined end came at a price. That any Sherman could move, let alone roll the distances ordered, seemed a miracle to Bates. By April 16, Able Company, still in support of the 5th Infantry, had twelve tanks, Baker remained with the 14th Infantry and rolled with seven tanks. Charlie Company counted twelve tanks and moved with the 66th.[29] For the first time since his arrival at Camp Claiborne, Paul Bates found genuine respect for his maintenance soldiers. They worked regardless of the weather or the hour to keep his tanks on the road. They worked without thanks. The farther east they traveled, the more difficult it became to obtain repair parts. Shifting tanks to higher echelon maintenance proved a challenge given the battalion's migration. The maintenance chiefs understood they had to fix the tanks with what they had in their magic bins. Bates did not realize they had worked miracles during the worst of the combat. He understood he needed competent maintenance crews more than he needed tank crews at that point. He had to get the tanks (and the men) to the end—whatever form that "end" might take. Paul Bates needed that end to come sooner than anyone realized.

Radio announcers prematurely broadcast, "The war is over except for the shouting," enraging the frustrated commander. The news made his men anxious and the false belief that hostilities had ended could only serve to get men killed. "Wish some of those jerks would spend a few hours against SS troops. They would keep their mouths shut until the last bullet was fired," Bates exploded.[30]

As head of Service Company, Ivan Harrison had contact with every tank company and spoke often with Bates. He and the other officers had observed a change in their commander. Bates seemed angry, vengeful, and tense. He admitted he felt "keyed up," but Harrison saw it lay deeper. They had heard Bates could not sleep and could not relax. Harrison saw he proved merciless with the German people as well as the prisoners kept as workers in the German towns. He heard somehow Bates ended up in some "hovel" that housed a large number of Polish and Russian women and their children. No men, just women and children. He took no pity on the innocent and later ranted about the foul-smelling and ill-behaved lot. It angered him that the women said they were pleased with their appalling accommodations. To him, they had succumbed to Nazi propaganda, making them all the more despicable.[31]

Possibly Geist had told Harrison about the wounded German soldiers Bates left to die their last night as Task Force Rhine. Harrison knew with so many prisoners the battalion did not have the room or the resources to take on more men, let alone large numbers needing medical attention. Geist would have shaken his head. Harrison understood Bates's decision would not sit well with Geist. Without radioing the 103rd for assistance, Bates had few choices, short of putting a bullet in each man to end his suffering. To a discreet few, Bates had seemed to lose his humanity. Had the many and varied challenges of the years with the 761st been too much? Or did men like Harrison witness a combat commander suffering from battle fatigue? Ivan Harrison watched over Paul Bates. The battalion would not lose another man to this war, certainly not the one who got them there, ready to fight.

Daily events proved the enemy's presence: the clash after the bivouac in the woods, the nightly missing supplies, and "Pop" Gates reclaiming one of his OCS classmates who had fallen into enemy hands. Gates "recaptured the officer, now a lieutenant colonel, who remarked, 'My God, am I glad to see you!'"[32]

Bates believed that mostly SS soldiers moved about the area. He reported small units attacking the tanks, firing only their pistols, sacrificing themselves against his men well-protected and well-armed in their Shermans. Bates alleged one soldier ran out in front of a tank just to slit his own throat.[33] Bates did not realize no one else in the battalion witnessed enemy suicidal acts. He also maintained he saw his first "woman soldier" dressed in a man's uniform but her hair flowed sixteen inches by his estimation as he studied her bullet-riddled and lifeless body.[34]

Bates seemed to experience a war separate from his battalion. No other unit member seemed to carry such disdain or bitterness. Harrison, McBurney, and the other men continued with their missions as they crossed the Reich. Ed Reynolds proved a strong and loyal executive officer.

With the mission complete in his mind, yet miles to travel before he could rest, Bates relied on his sole friend and confidante to get him to his predetermined end. He described to Taffy Rosen the unspeakable. He entrusted her with his descent into darkness. He took her to the most painful places he had known in his relatively charmed life. He shared his increasing hopelessness, "Only you can know how much I miss you. . . . There is so much emptiness. . . . For me, now, your goodness is such an inspiration. Now especially in these great times of loneliness. So terribly great. I can feel you near. It helps so much."[35]

The drive across Germany fed Bates's decline. He privately cursed the monotony forced on his battalion of combat veterans. Humor helped keep them from "losing our minds," according to Bates. "We go without sleep, bathing, have limited companionship, and drive our men into taking the necessary chances to accomplish our mission. We capture towns and others come in to leisurely occupy them."[36]

Paul Bates had no doubt he had one of the best units in Germany, but as they moved across the enemy's country, he found he had to "continually sell" their acceptance to officers "whose units are not half as good."[37]

He witnessed an army ready to fight with only sporadic challengers. He saw the ugly underbelly of war. He had become a part of the cruelty. By April 17 he looked at no fewer than seventeen alleged rapes by the men in his battalion.[38] The crumbling forces of many nations trapped him. Rosen alone stood in contrast to the revolting images that surrounded him. She lit his way to escape "all discomforts and turmoil."[39]

As they moved eastward, enemy resistance stiffened. McBurney found engagements brief but potent. Enemy soldiers would vanish as quickly as they appeared. But the Germans failed to impress the 761st. Geist noted little of operational import, save for a few noteworthy battles. The hope of combat seemed to lift Bates's mood. After days of sporadic and pointless enemy encounters, the 761st met a bold force in the area of Bayreuth. Able Company reportedly knocked out several machine gun nests. Baker hit a number of vehicles, killed nearly a hundred enemy soldiers, and took twice that number prisoner. Charlie destroyed almost twenty vehicles and took out more soldiers than Baker. The surprise encounter became an all-out battle for Bayreuth. The 761st Tank Battalion and the 11th Armored Division pummeled the town. The Germans surrendered April 16.[40] The 761st penetrated farther into the country and headed toward Czechoslovakia.

Despite clear indications of a fragile German force and vigilant, well-informed Allies, the enemy caught Baker Company by surprise

One of Dog Company's M5 Stuart light tanks in Coburg, Germany, April 1945. The tankers were waiting in the event they were needed to clear any enemy resistance. (*National Archives*)

on April 19 near Lindenhart. Once the 761st pushed back the attackers, the officers in Baker Company asked about John Long, their company commander, a man no one recalled seeing since 1:30 that afternoon. Similarly, Bates wanted to talk with his executive officer, Ed Reynolds, but his staff told him he had gone to one of the tank companies. The next morning the stunned battalion could not account for four tankers. Major Ed Reynolds, Captain John D. Long—two of Bates's best and most trusted officers—Technician 5th Grade George Sandford, and Technician 5th Grade Freddie Fields had disappeared.[41] Long's Baker Company turned frantic and looked for the dead or wounded commander. As far as anyone could tell, no one had been killed, yet it seemed unfathomable that the men would have been taken prisoner. No member of the 761st had fallen captive during the long and dangerous months at the front.

Search parties combed the area and found the men's two quarter-ton vehicles destroyed in the woods. Bates had his people interrogate the prisoners from the skirmish and learned "two officers and two enlisted men in fact had been captured." Somehow the German prisoners knew the Americans "were still in a large patch of woods, and offered that information around 10 am." With few options Bates reported the situation and received permission to sweep the area. The battalion had moved forward, leaving Bates with a handful of tanks, some half-tracks, and about ninety officers and men. He had asked for volunteers. The men jumped to help find their fellow soldiers. He led a group of mostly cooks, mechanics, and radiomen. Bates also sent armed search parties to find his men, but they found nothing.[42] No one wanted to leave the men behind, but they had to rejoin the battalion. The missing four weighed heavily on everyone, especially Bates. Each hour he wondered if he moved farther from his missing men or did this German unit parallel them. If they had no use for the Americans, maybe the Germans would simply let them go.

While Bates reviewed the situation of his first captured men, Pop Gates and two Charlie platoons supported the 1st and 2nd battalions of the 66th Infantry Regiment in sacking the town of Neuhaus. William McBurney's platoon waited in reserve. McBurney watched from his gunner position, eager to fire. He observed the hidden enemy repel the infantry platoons as they moved to take the town. At the same time, Gates's platoons came under heavy fire. His tanks attacked. The fighting seesawed between the Americans and Germans. McBurney recalled many nameless towns had fallen with less effort, but the enemy seemed determined to hold. The order came across again, more emphatic than the last: The Americans must take Neuhaus. The day's stalemate carried into the evening hours. In an unusual tactical move, at 2030 hours Gates ordered Frank Cochrane to attack the town from one side and moved Moses Dade's platoon to shell from the other. The surprise crossfire proved effective. The tankers pummeled the enemy. The 1st and 2nd battalion soldiers moved in and finished off the dazed German force. Neuhaus fell.

Earlier, the 3rd Battalion of the 66th Infantry Regiment had moved to the high ground. Teddy Windsor pointed. From where McBurney's tank sat, below the bluff that jutted above the town, he could see a soaring stone tower that looked as if it might topple from its foundation. A maze of trees covered the mount supporting the compound. The 3rd Battalion approached the massive structure and came under attack. The soldiers believed they had come upon Hermann Goering's five-hundred-year-old castle. They found about one hundred SS soldiers protecting the impressive fortress. The two sides exchanged fire.

With Goering on the run or at least in hiding, the Germans had little incentive to remain and the Luftwaffe leader's lair fell to the Americans. The soldiers investigated behind the thick stone walls and through the maze of air raid tunnels. Some may have hoped to find his rumored riches.[43]

Bates would have to fill Long's position. Someone had to lead Bravo Company. He spoke openly to the men of the four's speedy return. In truth, aside from what the prisoners told him, he had no idea if his men survived their abduction. He thought back to his "kill or capture" conversation with his officers. The Germans had nothing to lose and had no reason to spare his men. He remained helpless and quietly confessed, "I am very depressed." He watched Russ Geist, probably Ed Reynolds's closest friend, dragging himself around the battalion "trying to be cheerful but is as dead inside as myself."[44] Bates could not bring himself to replace the loyal Reynolds. He would handle Reynolds's duties. If he needed assistance, he could count on Taylor, Geist, Latimer, Harrison, or McHenry.

True to Bates's reassurances, it was a speedy return—but for only three. An American unit encountered the Germans holding Long, Sandford, and Fields, and recaptured them. They returned to the 761st on April 23, unharmed and well-cared for.[45] The still-missing Reynolds surprised even "Smooth." Did he lay dead, forgotten by his captors? Had he escaped and crept through unknown regions searching for the unit? Bates had men patrolling for him as the unit moved east. A mix of patience, cunning, and luck stood as their best chance of finding Reynolds alive. As long as Ed Reynolds did not get caught up in some unfortunate circumstance, he would see his friend again.

Next to Paul Bates, the Germans had captured the most senior officer in the tank battalion. With Reynolds in their control, they separated him from the other three and moved him to an interrogation unit. The enemy pressed for information about the battalion—its name, the commander, other officers' names. Reynolds would not comply. Though the major felt certain the Germans would shoot him, they treated him more as a guest, despite the poor accommodations. The Germans had little interest in American games. No one sat more surprised than Ed Reynolds as the Germans interrupted his pointless responses and named Paul Bates as the battalion commander, the names of each company commander as well as "the names of the infantry divisions and armies the 761st had been with."[46] Reynolds

realized he held no value for his captors and became certain of his
fate.

As the 761st moved eastward, the end of April approached. The
weather turned colder, enemy resistance again stiffened, and Bates's
mood worsened. Referring to several of Rosen's letters he wrote,
almost despondent, "And all [your letters are] saying just what I
wanted to hear. . . . how much you love me and how much I mean to
you. . . . If you only know how terribly important it is to read those
words . . . there are times I have to remind myself there is a reason
for things. That living is worthwhile. And God knows you are my
reason."[47]

By the time the 761st Tank Battalion and 71st Infantry Division
approached the Danube River, supply lines stretched to the thinnest
the men had experienced. The units had moved quickly, eager to finish what they had started, but unsure what form the defeat of
Germany would take. They bypassed small pockets of resistance that
would slow them, but fought off any enemy in the mood for a fight.
Their efficiency left them low on rations and other supplies.[48] And
they faced another river crossing. The Germans had not shown their
hospitality to their Allied guests arriving at the Danube. They left no
bridges intact that Bates could see. On April 25, as the tankers
approached, they spotted two German personnel carriers packed with
enemy soldiers attempting to escape north. The American tanks fired.
The vehicles went up in flames.[49]

That night Major O. Robert Eddy and his 271st Engineer Combat
Battalion found the best site for the main bridge and began work.
They erected four spans, but lost one to flooding and a second to
enemy fire.[50] Fog hampered the crossing, but the two bridges and a
large number of small boats brought the men and equipment to the
other side. Bates and his tanks crossed the Danube by treadway
bridge April 27. After the crossing, as the infantry regiments dispersed, the tank companies followed in support. Able went to
Straubing, Baker to Salching, and Charlie Company remained with
the 66th Infantry Regiment in Perkam. Bates and the command post
followed a day later and set up at Straubing April 29.

As Geist reviewed his April logs for his monthly report to
Washington, the lack of enemy contact, while a relief, seemed to curse
the 761st. The battalion's efforts to move across Germany came at
tremendous cost. Casualties still mounted. The long miles ravaged the
tanks. Keeping the top number of tanks operational proved almost

impossible. Though Geist could recite myriad reasons for their troubles, the battalion's biggest problem stood as a shortage of parts, including essential tracks and motors. Neither he nor the maintenance officer could say whether that battalion would reach the end of the war with its tanks. He did not know how much longer they could roll with the infantry battalions.[51]

May brought the battered battalion and its commander to Austria's gateway. Bates worked to hide his erratic moods. As he reached another breaking point on May 1, Ed Reynolds appeared in front of him as he penned at letter to Taffy. "I can't believe my eyes. There stands Major Reynolds." Like the first three prisoners, Reynolds had been recaptured by an American unit, but he had been missing eight more days than the others. Despite the successful return of his four missing men, Bates saw their capture as his supreme failure.[52]

The 71st Infantry Division and its attached units had orders to move into Austria, then to Steyr, a small strategic city where the Enns and Steyr rivers converged. While the Rhine crossing a month earlier had proved easier than he had expected and the recent Danube experience racked Bates's nerves, they would cross the Inn River. Maybe an end lay in Austria. Bates stared at their only path forward, a narrow dam in poor condition. His Shermans stood 8 feet 7 inches wide. Would his tanks tip and tumble, as he had seen more than one unlucky tank from other units do, or would a crouching enemy blow the structure, ending the war for the 761st? He cleared the first company to cross.

McBurney had watched the invisible enemy blow bridges since their days in France. With hatch open, drawing on his third cigarette in an hour, he ensured ammunition sat ready for the .30 and .50 caliber machine guns. He and the loader checked the rounds for the main gun. His tank would roll, prepared for whatever this enemy had to offer.

Russell Guthrie had lost count of the river crossings. One melded with another and into the last. He worried about the tank's weight. He knew his driver could cross the narrowest span, but could an old, decaying structure hold a Sherman?

Guthrie watched the Sherman roll slow and steady across the rutted span. He could see the tank commander waving off the battalion in disapproval. Guthrie had seen this before. The structure seemed weak to the tank commander. The engineers rushed in and reinforced the dam with thick wooden planks. The tanks of the 761st started across again, creeping one by one, avoiding unnecessary movement.[53] Aside from sporadic enemy resistance, they crossed without incident. Bates ordered his companies to rejoin their regiments. They would fight their way south to Steyr and wait at the Enns River.

The last shot had been fired, in Bates's mind, but still no end to the war. Tankers and doughs engaged what Bates saw as the last gasps of the Reich's army. The tired, tense commander and his battalion had traveled 465 miles in thirty-six days. Exhaustion set in. His body ached. Bates felt as if he had dragged forty tanks and nearly seven hundred men across Germany.

A merciful and inevitable end came and went with little fanfare. When the 761st heard about the German surrender, Bates wrote of the battalion, "[we] all looked at each other speechless." No one had interest in celebration. What would they celebrate? Bates made a brief statement of fact to the men, "We lived through it." Those stood as the 761st's celebratory words of Germany's official surrender. With that, the unit went to bed more tired than usual. Bates surmised each man wanted "to be with his own thoughts."[54]

The end of the war brought a close to what they had worked for over the past three years. They lost men they loved. They realized dreams. Russell Guthrie at twenty-one years old had served in the army longer than most in the battalion. He recognized he probably would leave the service at the same age his father did after the last world war. It surprised him how much he missed Leon Guthrie. Paul Bates had reminded him of his father since the first day he met him. He owed a tremendous debt to both men. He had found a home at the 761st, but he left a home behind with a man waiting for the son whom he adored. Russell Guthrie did not want to admit it to anyone, but he looked forward most to his father's cooking.[55]

They achieved what most had deemed impossible. While they helped defeat Germany, they had realized important, personal victories. For McBurney and most of the men, blending in with the other units and fighting, living, and being "just one of the guys"[56] stood as their triumph. That the white infantry soldiers treated them as they would any other combat soldier outweighed what in retrospect stood as the inevitable defeat of Germany. He thought back to Reisdorf, sitting around with tankers and doughs laughing at their awkward attempts to make pancakes as some soldier outside the unit snapped photos.[57] At some point they would go home to America winners, heroes, and most important, "just guys" like everyone else. While the end of the war changed the world, of more interest to them, William McBurney and "the guys" believed they had changed America.

From most accounts that reached Bates, the 761st fought like veteran tankers. While in Steyr, Bates reviewed unit statistics dating to October 1944: they had suffered nearly five hundred casualties, including thirty-six killed in action.[58] They had also lost more than a battalion's worth of fighting machines. Reports credited the 761st with 129,640 direct and indirect enemy casualties. Bates would take the number.[59] The men always surprised him. Their prowess under fire stood in the eight battlefield commissions. Bates knew more men deserved the honor, but they had given their lives.

The pragmatic Harrison knew the end of the war would dismantle what they had built together. Juanita and Ivan Jr. waited in Detroit, but these men with whom he shared the unimaginable would soon disband. At some point, the 761st would cease to exist. How could it all be over?

On May 8, the 761st remained in Steyr. Bates had little to celebrate, but the pageantry of the surrender fascinated him. He tugged his two majors—Ed Reynolds and Russ Geist, and headed to the other side of town. They looked for the site of the surrender. Bates had seen men, units, and towns surrender, but here he would witness an army and a nation capitulate. He hungered to learn what such an event entailed. The men watched "a great parade of German soldiers as they marched and drove into our area to surrender." The German officers ensured units stood organized and supervised, providing some relief for the Americans. "They came by the thousands, some in vehicles but most in horse-drawn carts."[60]

For Bates, after the spectacular German surrender, he turned his attention to the Russians. To his dismay, meeting with his Russian counterparts would occupy much of the day. Bates hesitated, but began a sad good-bye to Ed Reynolds. He, Long, Sanford, and Fields had a 4:30 P.M. departure the next day back to the States.[61] The army had ordered former prisoners of war sent home among some of the first following the German surrender.

Bates did not know what to expect in meeting Russian soldiers. He recalled the night a few weeks earlier when he bunked in the home of a professor from the University of Bonn. The scholar had a strong opinion of the Russians. He said someone would occupy Germany and hoped for Allied control. He predicted a Russian occupation would destroy what remained of his nation. He also thought the Americans should thank the Germans for preventing Russia from attacking the United States. Bates understood his reasoning but disagreed to himself. The professor also predicted that Germans and Americans would fight Russia together in the future. Bates pondered his prediction, but could not imagine the scenario.[62]

As he thought back to the elegant evening with the professor, he watched a Russian tank approach with twelve infantrymen. The Americans and Russians communicated rather well through their respective languages, combined with creative hand gestures. A German interpreter jumped in to assist but proved more of a hindrance than help.[63] Bates eyed the Russians. "They looked like dead-end kids with a couple of old men added." Their clothing appeared as a collection of "anything they could pick up."[64] The next steps especially with the Russians would prove arduous, but it seemed better than the hellish limbo of dragging his tankers across Germany waiting for a nation to implode.

Ivan Harrison knew he would never win a popularity contest with Bates. They had been together for a long time. Harrison knew Bates better than he knew Juanita and had spent more time with him. But Bates had developed his preferred circle that did not include Harrison. Ivan Harrison believed in Paul Bates and kept watch over him. With victory, he assumed the army would pull Bates from the unit. At that moment, it did not seem possible or fair, but he had been with a segregated outfit a long time. Once Bates left, Harrison felt confident he would command the 761st.

Most of Paul Bates's attention remained in Klingen-Muenster commanding Task Force Rhine, lauding their magnificent opening through the Siegfried Line. The remainder of the man clung to his pen and paper as well as the lifeline held by Taffy Rosen. Her promise pulled him through his darkness to war's end, with a strength and determination that surpassed his. She guided him through his months in medical limbo. Paul Bates's war was almost over before it began, a frightening fact. But it ended with Task Force Rhine. He had realized his destiny, linked forever to the 761st, but had no plan beyond what stood as their pinnacle. The weeks that followed Task Force Rhine proved psychological torture. He needed Taffy Rosen. He wanted to rest his head on her lap and cry out the pain of his years-long personal and professional war he shared with his men. He limped away a proud but damaged man.

Tankers of the 761st Battalion. (*Ellsworth G. McConnell Collection*)

William McBurney looked at the Russians. He turned and saw Teddy Windsor, whom McBurney felt saved his life each day in their tank. Though Windsor stood as a giant to his tank gunner status, McBurney could not wait to get home to his railroad flat on Madison Avenue and 117th Street and say, "Dad, it sure was hell, but they let me fly."

EPILOGUE

O N MAY 9, 1945, THE ARMY BEGAN TO DISMANTLE WHAT TOOK the men of the 761st Tank Battalion years to build, with the departure of Major Ed Reynolds, Captain John Long, Technician 5th Grade George Sandford, and Technician 5th Grade Freddie Fields. The army mandated that former prisoners of war stood among the first to return to the States. Other unit members left soon after. The battalion broke apart, as Ivan Harrison had predicted.

Most of the battalion's soldiers arrived home by 1946 and learned a cruel truth: They had not changed a nation. America had largely forgotten them, and most did not know of African American service on the battlefields of Europe. In the roar of postwar America, few cared. Some tankers chose to make their way in Europe. After years of training and months of fighting, many who returned to the United States felt lost. They sought the electrifying connection of the 761st. Most never found it again.

Bates, Harrison, and McBurney remained in Austria and Germany with the unit for several months. These men as well as many in the 761st lacked the "points" needed to return home immediately after the war. The army's personnel redeployment system awarded credits to soldiers based on one's time in a combat zone as well as combat involvement, among other qualifiers. The staff translated the 761st Tank Battalion's intense combat experience to a series of numbers.

The men's blitz across Europe had come at tremendous cost. The unit suffered thirty-six men killed in action, including three officers;

thirty-nine officers, 221 enlisted men fell wounded in action. Nonbattle casualties stood at nine officers and 192 men. The enemy captured four from the unit, but they returned unharmed. Total casualties pushed toward 50 percent, a hefty number for a relatively small outfit that fought alongside manpower and equipment behemoths like the 26th Infantry Division and the 4th Armored Division. The battalion lost seventy-one tanks, more than one and a half times its original allotment. November 1944 witnessed much of the carnage. The tankers, with no combat experience, faced a determined and capable enemy. The battalion lost twenty-two killed in action, two who later died of wounds; eighty-one wounded; and forty-four non-battle casualties. It lost fourteen tanks with another twenty damaged.

The army recognized the tankers for their sacrifice. It credited the unit with four campaigns: Northern France, Rhineland, Ardennes-Alsace, and Central Europe. The battalion elevated at least eight enlisted soldiers to the officer ranks with battlefield commissions. Bates stood certain more men would have received the coveted promotion had they not died in combat. The army also awarded eleven Silver Star and sixty-nine Bronze Star medals to the men of the 761st. The unit presented roughly three hundred Purple Hearts for combat wounds. Some men received more than one. Though the medals meant nothing to the dead and little to the disfigured, they acknowledged the contributions of the unit as a whole. In 1997 the army upgraded Staff Sergeant Ruben Rivers's second Silver Star to the Medal of Honor, recognition of Rivers's personal valor and a nod to the men with whom he fought.

Ivan Harrison understood what the unit had accomplished and soon after VE Day began the unit's bid for the Distinguished Unit Citation, an award created during the war that recognized units for a collective display of extraordinary heroism. It became the Presidential Unit Citation in 1966, though some knew it by this name during World War II. In a four-page summary with attached exhibits, Harrison detailed the unit's combat history and sacrifice from October 1944 to May 1945. In November 1945, possibly confident the army would approve the initial DUC request, he submitted for a second award, or an oak leaf cluster, for the unit's remarkable work as Task Force Rhine, opening the Siegfried Line so Allied forces could commence the final offensive across Germany.

The army turned down both of Harrison's submissions and suggested improvements, asking for higher headquarters endorsements.

The 71st Infantry Division, the unit to which the 761st attached after Task Force Rhine and a division that had not witnessed the heroic actions Harrison described, weighed in with a resounding "no" on the award. Harrison and others resubmitted and the denials continued. Future entries went nowhere, but that did not deter the war veterans from pursuing the matter. Like many smaller, independent outfits, the 761st Tank Battalion lacked a powerful advocate, like an infantry or armored division or even a well-respected general officer, for its cause. The dismantling of the unit did not help the quest.

After more than thirty years of pressing, President Jimmy Carter signed the citation. Army Secretary Clifford L. Alexander, Jr., who had worked with battalion veterans as early as 1953 for a unit reunion in New York City, presented the Presidential Unit Citation at a Fort Myer, Virginia, ceremony, April 20, 1978. Charles "Pop" Gates, then a retired lieutenant colonel, spoke on behalf of the unit. The final award stood as a single citation for all 761st actions from October 31, 1944, to May 6, 1945.

By the end of the war, soldiers and the army at large had heard of the 761st Tank Battalion. According to army historians writing at war's end, black soldiers clamored to join the unit, even if it meant more time abroad. The army's historians swept into occupied Germany to study and record its war-weary force for the benefit of the army's future. Many enduring works resulted, including "The Employment of Negro Troops," a history written by Center of Military History historian Ulysses Lee between 1947 and 1951 and published in 1966. Lee noted the 761st possessed unusually high morale for a black unit. He credited some of his information to Trezzvant Anderson's work on the 761st.

Anderson joined the 761st on May 25, 1945, to write the unit's history. He had spent what time he could with the tankers during the combat phase, making the move ideal for him and an army that may have seen promise it needed to capture. Anderson's talent lay in telling stories and the army had a significant one it needed him to recount. His resulting *Come Out Fighting* remains a very good version of events, especially as the unit fought across Western Europe, despite possible embellishments to better showcase the men. He included an extensive collection of photographs and little-known vignettes, like a photograph and detailed caption of the unit's orchestra. He printed two thousand copies in Austria for the men. *Come Out Fighting* is part unit history, part memoir, part marketing ploy, and part hero worship. Dave Williams's father wrote to Anderson, a letter Anderson saved, asking for six more copies, one for each of his children. He saw this as a "family heirloom." Anderson claimed his *Come Out Fighting* garnered interest in a Distinguished Unit Citation for the 761st, but Harrison had submitted the citation request less than two months after Anderson's official unit arrival.

Paul Bates relinquished command of the battalion in November 1945. Now-Major Ivan Harrison stood as its new commander, guiding it toward an eventual end. The *Baltimore Afro-American* reported on April 30, 1946, the army's decision to inactivate the unit. It also wrote that its members questioned the decision, given the "unit's wartime fighting record." The 761st reached its World War II close on June 1, 1946. On November 24, 1947, the army reactivated the 761st as a part of the regular army at Fort Knox, Kentucky, and again inactivated the battalion March 15, 1955.

Their camaraderie outlived the war. As William McBurney stated, "We just clicked." By 1947, a few 761st veterans began to talk about getting together. They formed the 761st Tank Battalion Veterans Association and gathered for their first reunion at the Carnegie Hotel in Cleveland, Ohio, in 1949. They elected Herman Taylor as their first president. Meeting each year in a different city, they remained close, even when faced with the challenges of segregation to find a suitable facility to host a reunion. One year even Dave Williams had trouble booking a hotel for the mixed-race association.[1]

The 761st's reunions reached a peak of several hundred veterans attending during the 1960s. With too few veterans remaining to continue the gatherings, the men and their families held their last reunion in 2011.

NOTES

INTRODUCTION: ORDER OF BATTLE

1. Interview with Dale Genius, local historian, Alexandria, Louisiana.

2. Stokes, "Lumbering in Southwest Louisiana," 3.

3. Genius interview. Population census numbers do not appear to support the numbers needed to build and run Camp Claiborne. Rapides Parish population stood at 65,455 in 1930. By 1940 it ticked up to 73,370. Numbers from installations brought the total easily to 400,000. Claiborne alone ran just under that number at its peak. The boom of incoming workers probably peaked just after the 1940 census and decreased after the war and before the 1950 census. United States Census Bureau, *Louisiana Population of Counties by Decennial Census: 1900 to 1990*. According to Hochschild and Powell: "The 1930 census marked the last stage of the period of racial reorganization; after that year, the Census Bureau perceived only three races (white, Negro, Indian) and five Asian nationalities for many decades. It no longer explicitly identified racial mixture, mixed parentage, the Mexican race, Hindoos, fractions of Indian blood, or other innovative categories. After 1940, it no longer used the term 'color' in conjunction with 'race.'" Hochschild and Powell, "Racial Reorganization and the United States Census 1850–1930." http://scholar.harvard.edu/jlhochschild/publications/racial-reorganization-and-united-states-census-1850-1930-mulattoes-half-br.

4. *New York Times*, January 12, 1942, 9, coverage refers to "Little Harlem."

5. Ibid.; Alexandria *Daily Town Talk*, January 12, 1942, 1; New Orleans *Times-Picayune*, January 12, 1942, 1.

6. *Town Talk*, January 13, 1942, 1.

7. *Louisiana Weekly*, January 17, 1942, 1.

8. Given the tremendous disparity in accounts of events, Lee Street became a lightning rod for some organizations to further their work for racial equality. The War Department in Washington dispatched members of its Inspector General Office to investigate the incident and sort out the facts. The final report from

Washington determined no one had died in the melee. This War Department declaration did not deter men like James B. LaFourche from using Lee Street to support the goals of the NAACP. Correspondence continued into 1943 between Truman K. Gibson, aide to the secretary of war, and LaFourche over NAACP actions that Gibson considered gross misrepresentations of the facts. LaFourche-Gibson, March 24, 1943; Gibson-LaFourche, March 27, 1943. Current lore continues to contradict. One Alexandria official maintains residents found the corpses of rotting soldiers under their homes, supporting local accounts of the day, but there is no official evidence.

9. Lee, *Employment of Negro Troops*, 32–33.

10. Hill, "Exploring the Life and History of the 'Buffalo Soldiers.'"

11. Bowers, Hammond, and MacGarrigle, *Black Soldier White Army*, 8.

12. Ibid.

13. Ibid.

14. Ibid., 10.

15. Ibid.

16. Buckley, *American Patriots*, 186.

17. Bowers, Hammond, and MacGarrigle, *Black Soldier White Army*, 13.

18. Edgerton, *Hidden Heroism*, 86; "Sgt. Henry Lincoln Johnson: Perhaps, the Most Tragic Hero of Them All," Examiner.com, May 26, 2013.

19. "Our Negro Soldiers' Brilliant War Record," *New York Times*, February 9, 1919.

20. "Honor Negro War Heroes; Colonel Roosevelt Sends Praise of Privates Johnson and Roberts," *New York Times*, June 28, 1918.

21. Goodwin, *No Ordinary Time*, 169.

22. Osur, "Black-White Relations in the U.S. Military 1940-1972." Letters from General Marshall to Senator Lodge and Judge Hastie, September 27, 1940, and December 1, 1941.

23. *Pittsburgh Courier*, February 7, 1942, into 1943, various editions.

Chapter One: Why Not Me?

1. Harris, *Harlem's Hellfighters*, 155, 223–239, 241, 255; Myers and Miles, *The Harlem Hellfighters*, 119–127.

2. McBurney. William McBurney visited the recruiter more than once. Thomas McBurney signed a Certification of Consent on May 22, 1942, one day after his son's eighteenth birthday. The original is in William McBurney's personnel military file.

3. William McBurney interviews 2012, 2013. Hereinafter "William McBurney."

4. *Evening World*, February 15, 1919, 4. *New York Tribune*, February 18, 1919, 1; Harris, *Harlem's Hellfighters*, 261.

5. Harris, *Harlem's Hellfighters*, 49.

6. *New York Times*, January 17, 1941, 10.

7. *New York Times*, January 12, 1942, 9.

8. Lives Lost, Pearl Harbor: 2, 403. US Navy Fact File.

9. Ferraraccio, *Battle of Wake Island*, historical presentation.

10. Walker, *Iron Hulls, Iron Hearts*, 26, 29.

11. Selective Service and Training Act of 1940. *Franklin D. Roosevelt: Proclamation 2425—Selective Service Registration*, September 16, 1940.

12. U.S. Department of State, *Lend-Lease and Military Aid to the Allies in the Early Years of World War II*; Lend-Lease Act, Lend-Lease bill, dated January 10, 1941. Records of the U.S. House of Representatives, HR 77A-D13.

CHAPTER TWO: SMOOTH AND TAFFY

1. Federal Writers Project, *Los Angeles in the 1930s*, 411.

2. Paul Bates's Western Maryland college records and 1931 class yearbook.

3. James E. Lightner, *A History of McDaniel College, 1866–2002*, McDaniel College, 2007, 290.

4. McDaniel Archivist, Barbara O'Brien.

5. Bates's college records.

6. *Gold Bug* newspaper issues, various, 1930–31; McDaniel archivist.

7. Western Maryland year book, 1931.

8. Emerson Auditory, Western Maryland (McDaniel) College records for Gwendolyn Mann. Interviews with Barbara O'Brien, McDaniel archivist; Interview with son, Baron Bates Hereinafter, "Baron Bates."

9. Emerson recommendations (Christina Zamon, Emerson archivist).

10. Western Maryland. Mann offer and acceptance.

11. Baron Bates.

12. Baron Bates.

13. Baron Bates recalled an outdoor dining set she ordered from an upscale New York retailer for the wooden shack the three shared south of Los Angeles.

14. Paul Bates's military personnel records.

15. Ibid.

16. Ibid.

17. Baron Bates.

18. Bates's military records.

19. Ibid.

20. Lee, 188–189.

21. Paul Bates military file.

22. Baron Bates.

23. Ibid.

24. Ibid.

25. Interview with Taffy (Rosen) Bates. Hereinafter, "Taffy Bates."

26. Ibid.

27. Ibid.

28. Rosen service "record" (card), National Personnel Records Center.

29. Taffy Bates.

30. Ibid.

31. Ibid.

32. Ibid.

CHAPTER THREE: THE CALL TO KNOX

1. William McBurney.

2. Kimball, and Emmet, eds., *The Complete Lyrics of Irving Berlin*, 165.

3. "Officers Stop Riot at Camp Upton. Negro Soldiers Clash with White Workmen. . . ," *New York Times,* September 14, 1917, 3.

4. "Negroes to March in Upton Parade," *New York Times,* February 18, 1918, 6.

5. Lee, *The Employment of Negro Troops*, 101.

6. "Camp Upton, New York," Special to the *New York Times*, November 29, 1941, 10. The paper seemed to carry a number of updates on Camp Upton, including insurance tallies.

7. Many CCC workers proved the poorest of the poor, and studies showed 70 percent of enrollees suffered from malnutrition. *CCC Facts*, Civilian Conservation Corps.

8. Mayer, *Nature's New Deal*.

9. William McBurney.

10. *New York Times*, July 5, 1942, page not available.

11. Magee, *Irving Berlin's American Musical Theater*, 213; Warner clipping in Berlin scrapbook.

12. Ibid.

13. Bergreen, "Irving Berlin: This Is the Army," National Archives *Prologue Magazine*, 28, no. 2 (Summer 1996), parts 1–4.

14. American Treasures of the Library of Congress, "God Bless America."

15. Hoffman, *Through Mobility We Conquer*, 260. In 1939, the U.S. Cavalry had two mechanized and twelve horse-mounted regiments. Herr was "determined mechanization would not take over his branch."

16. Cameron, *Mobility, Shock and Firepower*, 256.

17. Ibid., 234.

18. Gillie, *Forging the Thunderbolt*.

19. Cameron, *Mobility, Shock, and Firepower*, 261.

20. Ibid., 202.

21. Interview with John Weston, 2013; Anderson, *Come Out Fighting*, 3.

22. Army Institute of Heraldry, 758th Tank Battalion unit insignia files.

23. "New Fort Knox Trainees from Eight States," *New Journal and Guide*, April 25, 1942.

24. Anderson, *Come Out Fighting*, 3.

25. Ibid., 9.

26. Cameron, "Armor Combat Development 1917-1945."

27. Cameron, *Mobility, Shock, and Firepower*, 391. Staff Writer, M3 Lee/M3 Grant(Medium Tank M3) 1942. Military Factory, February 26, 2012.

28. Fort Knox Instructional Materials, May 19, June 23, 20, 1942.

29. FM 23-75 Basic Field Manual. War Department 37-mm Gun, April 16, 1940.

30. Zaloga and Laurier, *M3 and M5 Stuart Light Tank, 1940-45*, 3, 9. Attributed to the British 7th Armoured Division, 1941.

31. TM 9-726 Technical Manual Light Tank M3 (Stuart). War Department, July 15, 1942.

32. Cameron, *Mobility, Shock, Firepower*, 273–274.

33. Ibid., 275.

34. Ibid. Cameron interview.

CHAPTER FOUR: SHINY GOLD BARS

1. Anderson, *Come Out Fighting*, 5.

2. Ibid.; Ivan Harrison military files.

3. Anderson, *Come Out Fighting*, 5.

4. Ibid.

5. Wynn, *William Henry Hastie (1904–1976)*.

6. Oral History Interview with Judge William H. Hastie, Transcript. Harry S. Truman Library and Museum.

7. Biography, Sam Brown, 761st Tank Battalion Web site.

8. Companies carried lettered designations, A, B, C, and later D, corresponding to Able, Baker, Charlie, and Dog.

9. Ivan Harrison, Jr.

10. Ivan Harrison, Sr., military files. Letter from Joseph Beil's daughter, Roz Sell, to Ivan Harrison, Jr. "I am the daughter of the late Joseph Beil who worked for Campus Sweater and Sportswear Company based in Cleveland, Ohio. He started his sales career 'on the road' opening new accounts across Michigan and Indiana prior to WWII. He employed a driver named Ivan Harrison who traveled with him while my dad showed clothing samples to prospective customers. When WWII broke out, Mr. Harrison joined the army. He subsequently requested a letter of recommendation for officers' training school, which my father gladly and proudly provided." August 18, 2010.

11. Draft notice, Harrison military files, May 5, 1941.

12. Ibid. Headquarters 92nd Engineer Battalion, Special Order Number 6, January 10, 1942.

13. Harrison, Jr.

14. Camp Claiborne Historical Research Center.

15. Evangeline Parish Government Statistics.

16. Library of Congress Biographical Directory; "Know Southern History."

17. Stolz, "An Ardent Military Spirit"; "Know Southern History."

18. Stolz, "An Ardent Military Spirit," 1; Wynne, *On the Road Histories: Mississippi*, 36.

19. *Encyclopedia of the War of 1812*, 286.

20. Edwards, *A Melancholy Experience*, 30–32.

21. Library of Congress photograph of cars of construction workers parked along highway by entrance to Camp Claiborne, Alexandria, Louisiana; LOC, Alexandria, La., Dec. 1940. Construction workers' living conditions on camps Livingston, Claiborne, and Fort Beauregard.

22. Interview with Carlton Smith, transcribed (1974).

23. Anderson, "Complete Biography of Trezzvant Anderson."

24. Anderson, ibid., letter from Charlotte NAACP, 1942.

25. Anderson wrote of women with whom he had relationships, the first in England, later France, and then Germany. He saved letters from many after the

war. Anderson Papers. Anderson was married at the time of his enlistment. His papers do not mention his wife.

26. Army War College study, resulting memorandum, Army War College 1925 Memorandum on "The Use of Negro Manpower," October 30, 1925. Army War College, "Employment of Negro Manpower in War," November 10, 1925, FDR Library.

27. Anderson, "Biography."

28. OQMG memo to 761st, October 2, 1942.

29. Cruise memo to OQMG, November 2, 1942.

30. Ibid.

31. Ibid. The list of six mottos included: "Come out Fighting!" "Call on us," Ready and Able," "Fast and Furious," "Full of Fight," "Roll, tanks roll."

32. OQMG approval dated December 24, 1942.

CHAPTER FIVE: A GOOD TEMPO

1. Paul Bates letter to Taffy Rosen on work schedule, undated. (Hereinafter "Bates-Rosen.") Paul Bates tended to leave his letters undated. He might write the day of the week and the time, but no date. The family has kept them in order and the reader can approximate a date by the action he describes. Few of Taffy Rosen's letters to Paul Bates survived the war.

2. Enlistment Record, Theodore Windsor.

3. Harrison Military Files.

4. Anderson, *Come Out Fighting*, 24; Bates-Rosen undated.

5. Bates Military Files.

6. Bates-Rosen, undated.

7. "The Use of Negro Manpower," October, 30, 1925, Army War College. One example that is mentioned in the previous chapter.

8. Bates-Rosen, undated.

9. Ibid.

10. Bates-Rosen, undated.

11. Bates-Rosen, undated.

12. McConnell enlistment record.

13. Ibid., McConnell Honorable Discharge.

14. McConnell Family, 1930 U.S. Federal Census, 41-367, Sheet 10A April 17, 1930.

15. McBurney.

16. Horatio Scott Enlistment Record.

17. McBurney.

18. McBurney's Military Personnel File; McBurney.

19. McBurney.

20. Ibid.

21. Ibid.

22. Ibid.

23. Russell Guthrie interview. Hereinafter "Guthrie."

24. Ibid.

25. *Colliers*, April 14, 1942, 41.

26. TM 9-726, "Technical Manual Light Tank M3," 30.

27. Ibid.

28. Ibid.

29. Ibid., 33.

30. FM 17-30, "Armored Force Field Manual Tank Platoon," October 1942.

31. FM 17-32, "The Tank Company, Light and Medium."

32. FM-17-12, "Tank Gunnery."

33. Memorandum, Officers and NCOs Schools. Though the date is March 17, 1944, for the week March 20–25, the scheduling is indicative of the 761st with Bates running training and the appearance he is running the battalion, though he is not yet the commander.

34. Anderson, *Come Out Fighting*, 9; Lieutenant General Lesley McNair letter to Commanding General Third Army, March 14, 1943.

CHAPTER SIX: ORGANIZATION DAY

1. Event Program, April 1, 1943, Richard English Collection, Armistead Center, Tulane University, New Orleans (hereinafter "English Collection"; Event Program, hereinafter, "Program").

2. English official military record and collection of documents in English Collection.

3. Interview with English's son, Reginald J. English.

4. Photographs of Richard English, Armistead Center Collection; Anderson, *Come Out Fighting*, 7, 8.

5. "A Camera Trip Through Camp Claiborne," 1942, 1 (possibly a government public awareness publication).

6. English Collection. News clipping, "Racing Chatter" by Tom Wilson. English had another article about his father dated June 30, 1938, from the *St. Louis Post-Dispatch*. This article refers to Jim English as having been "one of the top jockeys in the country."

7. Reginald English.

8. English Military Files.

9. Ibid.

10. English Collection.

11. Ibid.

12. *Town Talk*, April 1, 1943, 1.

13. *Berkeley Daily Gazette*, April 1, 1943, 1.

14. Program; English Collection.

15. Ibid.

16. Ibid.

17. Ibid.

18. Institute of Heraldry Files, 761st Insignia and Motto, 1942.

19. Anderson, *Come Out Fighting*, 116.

20. Program; English Collection; Anderson, *Come Out Fighting*, 9, 116.

CHAPTER SEVEN: BIG-TIME MANEUVERS

1. *New York Times,* "Army's Day of Decision," June 12, 1946.

2. Zimmerman, *The Last and Largest Wargame Before World War II.*

3. Ibid.

4. Gabel, *The US Army GHQ Maneuvers of 1941,* 193.

5. NYT, "Few Claims are Made on Army in Louisiana," AP, September 23, 1941.

6. Zimmerman, *The Last and Largest Wargame Before World War II.*

7. Blumenson, *The Patton Papers: 1940-1945,* 42.

8. D'Este, *Eisenhower,* 271, 274–275.

9. Bates-Rosen, undated.

10. Anderson, *Come Out Fighting,* 9; Bates-Rosen undated.

11. *Times-Picayune,* April 13, 1943, 1.

12. Anderson, *Come Out Fighting,* 9; Army Ground Forces memo dated December 7, 1942. Includes roster for each of the three phases of the maneuvers. A number of units have been crossed out, some written in. The 761st Tank Battalion is typed in a slightly larger font at the bottom of the short list that includes the 85th Infantry Division. It is difficult to tell exactly when the AGF added the 761st. The unit is denoted as "(Cld)" for colored. The 758th Tank Battalion is crossed from the list and appears not to have carried the "colored" designator for the maneuvers.

13. "Thousands of Race Soldiers on Maneuvers in Louisiana," *Pittsburgh Courier,* April 17, 1943, 1.

14. Ibid., 1–4.

15. Ibid., 1.

16. McBurney.

17. "Soldiers Undergo Toughest Maneuvers In Louisiana," *Pittsburgh Courier,* April 24, 1943, 1.

18. Anderson, *Come Out Fighting,* 9.

19. Yale University Archivist, Yale Class of 1942, 25th Reunion volume.

20. Yale University Archivist, Catalogue of Officers and Graduates of Yale University, 1925–1954.

21. Unit Roster, National Personnel Records Center. Rosters for 758th showed full name of Barnes.

22. Williams, *Hit Hard,* 10–12. Williams's account of his personal experiences closely mirrors primary sources of the period.

23. Ibid., 86–87.

24. Ibid., 46.

25. Ibid., 85.

26. *Pittsburgh Courier,* April 24, 1943, 1.

27. Green, *How K-Rations Fed Soldiers and Saved American Businesses.*

28. Bates-Rosen, undated.

29. Bates-Rosen, undated.

30. Bates-Rosen, undated.

31. Bates-Rosen, undated.

32. "General Davis Lauds Efficiency of Soldiers," *Pittsburgh Courier,* May 8, 1943, 1.

33. Bates-Rosen, undated.

34. Bates memo, May 16, 1943. He was not yet the official commander, but would act as such until 5th Tank Group decided how it would handle the Wright situation.

35. "93rd Division Ready to Fight!" *Pittsburgh Courier*, May 15, 1943, 1.

36. Bates-Rosen, undated.

37. "The First Anniversary of the Illustrious 761st Tank Battalion," *Claiborne News*, April 8.

38. "Willis Rice Private U.S. Army: A 'Blue Star' Who's Going Somewhere, and who will Raise Hell for Our Side," *New Journal and Guide* September 12, 1942, 11. Several articles ran about Rice. *Yank* magazine reportedly wrote about him, too.

39. *Claiborne News*, various, mid-1943.

40. Guthrie.

41. *New York Times*, January 31, 1943, 7; Hastie Truman Library Oral History, January 5, 1972.

42. Hastie memorandum to General George C. Marshall, January 30, 1943, GCMRL/G. C. Marshall Papers.

43. Marshall to Hastie, January 21, 1943, GCMRL/G. C. Marshall Papers.

44. "Discrimination in Air Forces Caused Dr. Hastie to Resign from War Department," *Baltimore Afro-American*, February 2, 1943, 1.

45. "200 Colored Soldiers Mix in Stockton Riot," *Berkeley Daily Gazette*, April 1, 1943, 1.

46. "Citizens Say Negroes Did Not Incite Riot," *Pittsburgh Courier*, April 22, 1943, 1.

CHAPTER 8: THE CASE FOR TANKS

1. Bates military files.

2. Maiorino, *Leonardo Da Vinci*, 132.

3. Macksey and Batchelor, *Tank*, 7.

4. Humes, *Churchill the Prophetic Statesman*, 51–52.

5. Cameron.

6. PBS, *The Great War*, Resources: "World War I Casualty and Death Tables."

7. Order of Battle of United States Land Forces in the World War, 1931.

8. "America's Story," Library of Congress.

9. Axelrod and Clark, *Patton*, chapter 2, "Cadet, Soldier, Athlete, Swordsman."

10. Ibid., chapter 4, "The Great War and the New Weapon."

11. Stewart, ed., *American Military History Vol. II, The United States Army In a Global Era, 1917–2003*, chapter 2.

12. Cameron interview.

13. Ibid.

14. Cameron.

15. Ibid.

16. Patton, "Tanks in Future Wars," *Cavalry Journal*, May 1920.

17. Eisenhower, "A Tank Discussion," *Infantry Journal*, November 1920.

18. Samuels, *Doctrine and Dogma*, front matter, 2–4, 169.

19. MacArthur received the temporary rank of general in 1930 for the chief of staff position. He reverted to his then-permanent rank of major general in 1935, and retired in 1937. The Army recalled him in 1941.

20. Cameron, 49. In an interview Cameron emphasized that the infantry focused on its primary mission— the infantryman—and not on the tank, given its support role.

21. PBS, *The Great War:* "World War I Casualty and Death Tables."

22. Jackson, *The Fall of France*, 27, 43.

23. Gole and Coffman, *Exposing the Third Reich*, foreword.

24. Ibid., Appendix 1; Smith letter to Brigitta von Schell; *Truman Smith Papers*, introduction (finding aid).

25. Carruthers, *Panzer IV*, 26.

26. Gole and Coffman, *Exposing the Third Reich*, 170–171; *Truman Smith Papers*, introduction.

27. *Truman Smith Papers*, introduction.

28. Kowalsky, *Stalin and the Spanish Civil War*, chapter 15, "Soviet Tank Crews and Tank Instructors." Much of the information on Arman remains untranslated in Russian.

29. Axelrod, *Patton*, 64.

30. Ibid.

31. *Popular Science*, March 1931, 33.

32. Hoffmann, "A Yankee Inventor and the Military Etablishment," *Military Affairs*, February 1975, 12–18.

33. Ibid.

34. Ibid.

35. Rosen military file/card. Taffy Bates.

36. Orders to 761st from 5th Tank Group, September 6, 1943. Ref. GNGCT HQ Army Ground Forces letter dated, August 28, 1943, Richard English Collection.

CHAPTER NINE: AGGRESSORS IN THE WEST

1. Rail movement to Camp Hood, Texas Administrative, Order 1 dated September 7, 1943.

2. Anderson, *Come Out Fighting*, 9.

3. Citation General Orders No 10. 761st Tank Battalion, July 14, 1943.

4. Historical Record, 761st Tank Battalion (updated 1944), 2, ref AR 600-68, May 4, 1943.

5. Harrison military records, Promotion.

6. Harrison military records.

7. Interview, Wesley Edwards Duggan (Juanita's sister).

8. Interview, Pamela Harrison Collins (Ivan Harrison, Sr.'s daughter.)

9. Duggan.

10. Duggan.

11. Duggan; death certificate.

12. Ibid.

13. Ivan Harrison, Jr.; Duggan.

14. Interview with Herbert H. Hudgins.

15. Ibid.

16. *New York Times*, July 11, 1943, E3.

17. Taffy Bates.

18. Army Ground Forces memo, January 18, 1943, underscored dire personnel situation.

19. Rail Movement to Camp Hood, Texas, Administrative Order 1, September 7, 1943. Richard English Collection. A rear detail led by Captain Arthur L. Campbell, Jr., provided the final checks necessary to leave Camp Claiborne.

20. Interview with Louise Latimer; Interview with Baylor archivist.

21. Ibid., Baylor's *The Daily Lariat*, June 3, 1940, 4.

22. Louise Latimer; Autobiographical sheet, Philip Latimer.

23. Ibid.

24. Rail Movement to Camp Hood, September 7, 1943.

25. 5th Tank Group (L) memo, June 24, 1943.

26. English military files. Richard English established a literacy program at Camp Polk before the Army transferred him to the 761st.

27. English military files.

28. Bates-Rosen, September 17, 1943.

29. Pugsley, *Imprint on the Land*, 4, 6.

30. Ibid., 6.

31. Ibid., 7.

32. Ibid., 8, 147–149.

33. Sitton, *Harder Than Hardscrabble*, 195.

34. Pugsley, *Imprint on the Land*, 148.

35. Ibid.

36. Bates-Rosen, September 17, 1943.

37. Bates-Rosen, September 17, 20, 1943.

38. *Mad Tanker* (761) October 23, 1943, 1.

39. AGF-CG Tank Destroyer Center, undated, though observations made during October 1943.

40. Bates-Rosen, September 25, 1943.

41. Bates-Rosen, September 20, 1943.

42. Bates-Rosen, January 28, 1944.

43. Bates-Rosen, undated.

44. Rosen.

CHAPTER 10: BIG GUN, MORE STEEL

1. War Department letter, "Reorganization of Tank Battalion," October 27, 1942; Anderson, *Come Out Fighting*, 11; Bates-Rosen letter undated about receiving sixty medium tanks.

2. Anderson, *Come Out Fighting*, 13.

3. Anderson, *Come Out Fighting*, 15; Bates-Rosen undated, writes of 200 new, untrained soldiers and five officers.

4. TM 9-759 Medium Tank M4A3, August 4, 1942, 3. The weight of the tank without armament, fuel, or crew is recorded as 59,560 lbs.

5. TM 9-759, 6.

6. Author's observations inside the M4. Interviews with Dr. Robert S. Cameron and Armor Museum curator Arthur L. Dyer, Fort Benning, Ga.

7. TM 9-759, 5–6; FM 17-12 "Armored Force Field Manual, Tank Gunnery," April 22, 1943, 16, 19.

8. Anderson, *Come Out Fighting*, 9.

9. Ibid.

10. Bates-Rosen, undated.

11. Anderson, *Come Out Fighting*, 13.

12. Ibid.

13. Harrison, Jr.

14. Historical Record, 761st Tank Battalion, 1942–1944, 3.

15. Jefferson, *Fighting for Hope*, 137.

16. McBurney.

17. Interview with Army Judge Advocate General historian Frederic Borch.

18. Ibid.; McBurney.

19. FM 18-5, "Tank Destroyer Field Manual: Organization and Tactics of Tank Destroyer Units," 4, 39.

20. Cameron, *Mobility, Shock and Firepower*, 313, 316; Gabel, *Army General HQ Maneuvers of 1941*; Denny, *Evolution and Demise of U.S. Tank Destroyer Doctrine*, 11.

21. Gabel, *Seek, Strike, and Destroy*, 10.

22. Denny, *Evolution and Demise of U.S. Tank Destroyer Doctrine*, 11.

23. Gabel, *Seek, Strike, and Destroy*, 15; Denny, *Evolution and Demise of U.S. Tank Destroyer Doctrine*, 13.

24. Dunham, *Tank Destroyer History Study No. 29*, Army Ground Forces, 4, 11; Cameron, *Mobility, Shock and Firepower*, 406.

25. Zaloga and Laurier, *M18 Hellcat Tank Destroyer*, 6.

26. Cameron, *Mobility, Shock and Firepower*, 316.

27. Denny, *Evolution and Demise of U.S. Tank Destroyer Doctrine*, 29; *The Tank Destroyer History Study No. 29*, 7.

28. Denny, *Evolution and Demise of U.S. Tank Destroyer Doctrine*, 42.

29. Cameron, *Mobility, Shock, and Firepower*, 423; Roberts letter to Bruce, April 7, 1943, Bruce papers.

30. Gabel, *Seek, Strike and Destroy*, 36–37.

31. Ibid., 37–38.

32. Ibid.; Zaloga, *U.S. Tank and Tank Destroyer Battalions in the ETO 1944–45*, 14. Once in Europe, Patton's infantry divisions usually had a battalion of tank destroyers attached to them. In the end, they seem to have been employed however the division commander deemed fit.

33. "Army Applies Lessons Learned in Africa to Desert Training," War Department Release, December 3, 1942. The release outlines hardline approach to training.

34. *Training in the Ground Army 1942–1945, Study No.11*, 1948, 30, 42. This work published shortly after the war shows McNair's deep concern over training as well as the competency of his officers, as detailed regarding the 1941 Louisiana Maneuvers. The term "woeful" was used to describe what he saw in

1941; Graduation Address of Gen. McNair at U.S. Military Academy, January 8, 1943, McNair Speech file.

35. McNair, McNear, and McNeir Genealogies: (Supplement, 1955) 59.
36. The 808th Tank Destroyer Battalion, *Specialized Training.*
37. Ibid., *Firing by Ear Rather than Sight.*
38. FM 17-12, 11.
39. Guthrie; M4 Medium Tank: The Sherman Crew.
40. FM 17-12 Gunner Proficiency Tests, 83–97.

CHAPTER ELEVEN: FACE-OFF

1. Guthrie.
2. McNair letter, April 27, 1942.
3. Cameron interview.
4. Gabel, 21.
5. Anderson 13; Bates-Rosen undated.
6. FM 18-24, November 1944 *Tank Destroyer Pioneer Platoon.*
7. Harley-Davidson *Enthusiast* magazine, May 1943.
8. Ibid.
9. Guthrie.
10. Williams, *Hit Hard*, 120–121.
11. Ibid., 121.
12. Ibid., 87–89.
13. Ibid., 121.
14. Archer, *World History of Warfare*, 531.
15. Ibid.
16. Assorted and numerous letters to Judge William Hastie, Civilian Aide to the Secretary of War and his assistant, Chicago attorney Truman K. Gibson. (National Archives and Records Administration files.)
17. Bates-Rosen, undated.
18. Ibid.
19. Vernon, "Jim Crow, Meet Lieutenant Robinson." Vernon takes this from "A War Department report."
20. Referred to in ibid.
21. Gibson's signature title becomes Acting Civilian Aide. "Acting" disappears from his signature block by the end of the summer. The news media named him as the aide, such as one *Chicago Tribune* article. An undated Army release noted he had been named as acting civilian aide to War Secretary Stimson. The *Pittsburgh Courier* and the *Baltimore Afro-American* closely followed Hastie and Gibson and the post of the civilian aide.
22. Gibson's brief biography in his personal papers held at the Library of Congress, Washington, D.C.
23. Gibson-Isabelle Gibson, January 31 and 4, 1941.
24. Gibson-Isabelle Gibson, February 10, 1941.
25. LaFourche-Gibson, March 24, 1943; Gibson-LaFourche, March 27, 1943; Gibson-War Department Inspector General, April 12, 1943; Gibson-George Roudebush, Chief, Sedition Section, Department of Justice, May 21, 1943.

26. Gibson papers, LOC. Outline of three radio scripts, half-hour shows about "Negro Troops in the U.S. Army." Undated, though Hastie was the civilian aide at the time and Gibson still his assistant. Gibson official papers.

27. Gibson War Department correspondence regarding the making and release of "The Negro Soldier," such as April 12, 1944, letter from Mrs. L. M. Hillman of Terrell Junior High School, Washington, D.C. National Archives.

28. Minutes of Advisory Committee on Special Troop Policies, August 14, 1943. A draft of the pamphlet accurately outlines the grievances of black soldiers. Soldiers living on posts with discriminatory practices, as listed in the pamphlets probably did not see their grievances as trivial. Was Gibson out of touch or working for change within a system of discriminatory practices?

29. "Vance"-Gibson, undated, but after the 761st move to Hood.

30. Ibid.

31. Austin, Texas, Library, Austin History Center, 1.

32. Ibid.

33. Navy History and Heritage Command, Fact File, *Cook Third Class Doris Miller, USN.*

34. Ibid.

35. Ibid.

36. *New York Age,* the Sports World, November 27, 1943, 11.

37. Ibid.

38. Margolick, *Beyond Glory,* 9, 27, 129.

39. Ibid., 159–161; "Schmeling Stops Louis in Twelfth as 45,000 Look On," *New York Times,* June 20, 1936, 1.

40. Deford, "The Choices of Max Schmeling," National Public Radio, February 9, 2005.

41. *New York Times,* June 22, 1938.

42. Margolick, *Beyond Glory,* 289.

43. "Louis Defeats Schmeling by a Knockout in the First," *New York Times,* June 23, 1938.

44. Ibid.

45. Faulk, *Fort Hood,* 186–187.

CHAPTER TWELVE: LIEUTENANT JACK ROOSEVELT ROBINSON

1. Robinson personnel file and Army medical records; Rampersad, *Jackie Robinson,* 5, 46, 85–86.

2. Gibson and Huntley, *Knocking Down Barriers,* 12.

3. Rampersad, *Jackie Robinson,* 91, 93.

4. Gibson official papers.

5. Gibson official papers.

6. War Department memo on ending segregation on posts.

7. Vernon, "Jim Crow, Meet Lieutenant Robinson."

8. Bates-Rosen, undated.

9. Ibid., undated.

10. Robinson military files; Rampersad, *Jackie Robinson,* 100.

11. Robinson military files. On May 19, Lieutenant Leonard P. Taylor noted

Robinson as the assistant special services officer, the official title for the unit's morale leader.

12. McBurney; Robinson military files.

13. McBurney.

14. Ibid.

15. Ibid.

16. *Columbia* (Ohio) *Dispatch*. Gibson's 2002 reflections on his period at the War Department. The tone of this quote may seem to vary greatly with the Truman Gibson portrayed in this story. Gibson was a pragmatic man who worked behind the scenes for the greater good, that included an end to segregation. He was much more outspoken later in life, but his commitment to change never wavered.

17. War Department 1943 survey *The Negroes' Role in War: A Study of White and Colored Opinions*, July 8, 1943, revealed 25 percent of blacks supported segregation. Other studies showed numbers as high as 38 percent of black soldiers and 88 percent of white soldiers. For black soldiers taking the survey, it is possible they surmised if all sides are equal, segregation has its advantages. For example, one might believe a large group or unit of black soldiers has more power than a small number integrated in a white unit, not unlike a voting bloc or union. Gibson and others sought desegregation at the War Department for varied reasons, the most pragmatic being segregation required two systems, draining the Army resources that could be better directed in the war effort.

18. Bates-Rosen, undated.

19. Ibid., undated.

20. Anderson, *Come Out Fighting*, 15.

21. Robinson medical records.

22. William A. Cline interview, February 14, 1944 (hereinafter "Cline"). Vernon, "Jim Crow, Meet Lieutenant Robinson." Robinson court-martial transcripts, *United States v. Robinson* 1944 (hereinafter "Transcript"), 44.

23. Transcript, 43–45.

24. Bates-Rosen, undated.

25. Army Judge Advocate General historian, Frederic Borch.

26. Transcript, 4.

27. Robinson-Gibson letter. Jack Roosevelt Robinson wrote to Truman Gibson who now stood as the civilian aide to the secretary of war, the post Judge William Hastie vacated (in protest) at the end of January 1943.

28. Gibson-Robinson letter. Gibson was more vocal in later years about his interest in stopping racism. In the case of Robinson, he believed the process had to run its course before he or Washington intervened.

29. Cline interview, February 14, 2012. Cline had been trained as an artillery officer. At Camp Hood, the Army assigned him to Fourth Army Headquarters as a defense attorney and he was assigned the Robinson case.

30. Ibid.

31. Letter 5th Group to XIII Corps, July 24, 1944; Vernon, "Jim Crow, Meet Lieutenant Robinson."

32. Vernon, "Jim Crow, Meet Lieutenant Robinson."
33. Robinson's various correspondence regarding his request for medical reevaluation and discharge.
34. Record of Trial, Robinson, Jack R., August 2, 1944; other front matter before trial transcript.
35. Special Order Number 120, Headquarters XIII Corps dated June 10, 1944.
36. Transcript, 34–36.
37. Transcript, 38–40.
38. Transcript, 45.
39. Transcript, 45.
40. Transcript, 61–62.
41. Transcript, 61–62.
42. Transcript, 62–63.
43. Transcript, 70–80.
44. Robinson to Adjutant General, August 25, 1944.

Chapter Thirteen: Patton's Welcome

1. "Rundstedt Bares Invasion Defenses," *New York Times*, February 15, 1944, 1.
2. Anderson, *Come Out Fighting*, 15.
3. Interview with Taffy Bates; letter from Taffy Rosen to Paul Bates, lost. Rosen record card.
4. Anderson, *Come Out Fighting*, 17.
5. Bennett, *Don Bennett's War*, chapter 1, "Camp Shanks, New York." Written during nineteen-month recovery from wounds sustained in World War II.
6. Levine, "Remembering Camp Shanks."
7. Hudson River Valley National Heritage Area, Camp Shanks World War II Museum.
8. *Warships of World War II, Great Britain*, 1.
9. Guthrie.
10. Bates-Rosen, undated.
11. Judging from Trezzvant Anderson's letters, he seemed to find many friendly young women. The content of Anderson's letters to women is restricted by the archives holding them, but he did not appear to want for female companionship during his time (separate from that of the 761st) in England.
12. Guthrie.
13. Anderson, *Come Out Fighting*, 17. Some sources list the unit's arrival as October 9, others the tenth.
14. Anderson, *Come Out Fighting*, 21.
15. Ibid., 21.
16. Bates-Rosen, November 13, 1944. Paul Bates does not name Richard English, but identifies the officer as the Dog Company commander, English's position at the time. Bates rarely mentioned names in his letters.
17. Bates-Rosen, undated.
18. Williams, *Hit Hard*, 152.
19. Holtz, The Operations of Company C, 104th Infantry (26th Infantry Division) from Vic-sur-Seille to Albestroff, Eastern France, November 8–21, 1944 (Rhineland Campaign), 3. Hereinafter "Holtz."

20. Ibid., 5; Lorraine Campaign, as recounted by 26th Infantry Division Assistant G-3 Major William R. Porter, June 14, 1945, 2. Hereinafter "Porter."

21. Richard English papers – quote from news clipping.

22. Anderson, *Come Out Fighting*, 21. Either two accounts of the Paul speech were published or the paper and Anderson quoted different portions. Regardless, Paul's words to the black tankers were stirring and he won their trust.

23. Guthrie.

24. Guthrie. Some discussed sightings that cannot be verified.

25. Cameron.

26. Holtz, 4. Recollections of Patton's speech to the 26th as Holtz quoted.

27. Bates-Rosen, December 13, 1944.

28. Anderson, *Come Out Fighting*, 21. McBurney, Guthrie. E. G. McConnell recorded interview. The Patton visit and address quickly took on a mythic status with the men. It seems Anderson may have been present for the address. In the years following the war, judging from interviews and recorded oral histories, Patton's address had considerable impact on the men. It is one of the first events surviving members talk about. Patton seems to have had a positive and lasting impact on the 761st second only to Paul Bates; Williams, *Hit Hard*, 143.

29. Bates-Rosen, December 13, 1944.

30. Guthrie.

31. Williams, *Hit Hard*, 146–151.

32. Ibid., 151–152.

33. Ibid.

Chapter Fourteen: The Battle for Lorraine

1. Williams, *Hit Hard*, 158. Assistant S-3 officer, Russell Geist, November 7, 1944 (hereinafter "Geist").

2. Williams, *Hit Hard*. References to "D.J." can be found throughout.

3. Ibid., 159, 120–121.

4. Ibid., 162.

5. *Stars and Stripes*, Paris edition, various issues, October 1944. Quote, October 21, 1944.

6. Cole, *The Lorraine Campaign*, chapters 8, 9.

7. Gabel, *The Lorraine Campaign*, 19, 27; Cole, 157, 421, 499.

8. Ambrose, *Eisenhower*, 157.

9. Cole, *The Lorraine Campaign*, 166, 307, 313, 394.

10. Cooper and Ambrose, *Death Traps*, 35, 72.

11. Anderson papers.

12. Rudi Williams, "African Americans Gain Fame as World War II Red Ball Express Drivers," American Forces Press Service, February 15, 2002. U.S. Department of Defense News.

13. Headquarters, Third U.S. Army, Psychological Warfare branch G-2 Section, 8 A.M. November 9, 1944.

14. Anderson papers; correspondent's combat notebook.

15. Ibid.

16. Images of 761st taken November 5, 1944, by Signal Corps, National Archives.

17. English files. Trezzvant Anderson was an opportunist and knew a good story. Richard English kept at least one draft of Anderson's planned series on what Anderson considered a unit of historic firsts.

18. Holtz, 5.

19. Holtz, 6.

20. Williams, *Hit Hard*, 160.

21. Cole, *The Lorraine Campaign*, 293, 295.

22. S-3 Periodic Report November 7–8, Goldsmith. H Hour varied by unit, for example, the 2nd Battalion of the 101st jumped off at 0700. Barbour stood ready to support the 101st as directed; Bates also notes a 0700 commencement of the attack in his letter to Taffy Rosen, November 12, 1944.

23. Holtz, 4.

24. Geist, November After Action Report dated December 2, 1945, November 8 entry.

25. Williams, *Hit Hard*, 173.

26. Information on Rivers family from Census of 1940.

27. Medical Detachment Morning Report, November 9, 1944, reported Clifford Adams as seriously wounded and died of wounds (National Personnel Records Center).

28. Anderson, *Come Out Fighting*, 27–28; Williams, *Hit Hard*, 175.

29. Holtz, 8.

30. "History of a Combat Regiment 1939–1945: 104th Infantry" (hereinafter "History 104th"), 62–63.

31. Major John O. Dickerson, The Operations of the 2nd Battalion 101st Infantry (26th Infantry Division) in the Attack. Moyenvic, France, November 8–10, 1944 (Rhineland Campaign) (Personal Experience of a Battalion Operations Officer), 6.

32. Ibid., 17.

33. Ibid., 23.

34. Ibid., 25.

35. Ibid., 30–31.

36. June 19, 1945, Interview of Lieutenant Colonel James Nixon Peale, Jr., Commander, 3rd Battalion, 101st Infantry Regiment, 26th Infantry Division.

37. Ibid.

38. Dickerson, 21.

39. Ibid., 27.

40. Anderson, *Come Out Fighting*, 37.

41. Holtz, 7.

42. "History 104th," 64–65.

43. Williams, *Hit Hard*, 187.

44. Bates-Rosen V-mail, November 12, 1944. Headquarters Company Morning Report of November 9, 1944, reports Bates as "seriously injured: November 8."

45. Headquarters, 328th Infantry, Goldsmith, S-3 Periodic Report, November 7–8, 1944.

46. Reynolds-Bates.

47. Geist, November 8, 1944.

CHAPTER FIFTEEN: THE ORDEAL OF COMPANY C

1. Bates-Rosen V-mail, November 9, 1944.

2. Bates-Rosen V-mail, November 12, 1944.

3. Ibid.

4. Ibid.

5. Ibid.

6. History 104th, 64.

7. Geist, November 9, 1944.

8. Ibid.

9. Ibid.

10. Arrival of Lieutenant Colonel Hollis A. Hunt as commander and Major John F. George contained in Headquarters Morning Report, November 10, 1944. George became the S-3, initially. Anderson, p. 29, lists both men from 17th Armored Group. Taylor-Bates letter, December 22, 1944.

11. Taylor-Bates letter, December 22, 1944; Reynolds-Bates letter, December 1, 1944.

12. Geist, November 9, 1944.

13. Vogt, *Hitler's Last Victims*, 167; Bull, *World War II Infantry Tactics (2): Company and Battalion*, 45–47.

14. Geist, November 9, 1944.

15. Map; Geist, November 9, 1944.

16. Geist, November 9, 1944.

17. Ibid., Lorraine Campaign, 3rd Battalion 101st June 19, 1945, p. 6. Trezzvant Anderson, "GI Reviews 1944 Feats for Combat Units Used in Thick of Fighting in France," *Baltimore Afro-American*, March 24, 1945, credits Richard English and Dog Company with taking Salival "unassisted."

18. Baker Company Morning Report for November 10, 1944, listed King and Porter wounded November 9; Anderson, *Come Out Fighting*, 31.

19. Anderson, *Come Out Fighting*, 31.

20. Ibid.

21. Ibid., 32.

22. English Military Files, news article, possibly *Stars and Stripes*.

23. Interview with Reginald J. English.

24. Bates-Rosen, December 27, 1944.

25. Geist, November 9, 1944; Anderson, *Come Out Fighting*, 32.

26. Ibid., 32.

27. Geist, November 9, 1944; Anderson, *Come Out Fighting*, 34.

28. Turley (dated December 8, 1944), Coleman (dated December 8, 1944) Silver Star Citations; Anderson, *Come Out Fighting*, 34, 102. One news account in English's papers credits Turley with organizing crews from the burning tanks for their ultimate escape attempt.

29. Anderson, *Come Out Fighting*, 33.

30. Ibid.

31. Ibid., 34.

32. Ibid.

33. The Charlie Company Morning Report of November 12 finally reports the casualties, but lists men like Sam Turley as "missing and dropped from rolls." The action of November 9 "near Vic-sur-Seille" is mentioned. Charlie Morning Report of November 14 lists "1 officer 17 EM missing and should be deleted." Finally listed as Killed in Action. Americans began to learn of African American tanker combat deaths in "List First Tank Dead," *Chicago Defender*, December 16, 1944, 1.

34. Anderson, *Come Out Fighting*, 37. This message from Scott has become a bit of lore. Anderson quotes Scott's message to Crecy as from the hospital, "I'm okay, and I'll be back soon." The Morning Report dated November 11 reporting on November 10, lists seven wounded and Horatio Scott as killed in action. Since Scott was wounded November 9, it is possible he died of wounds November 10.

35. Geist, November 1944.

36. McBurney, Guthrie.

CHAPTER SIXTEEN: A STEP CLOSER TO GERMANY

1. History 104th, 64–65; Anderson, *Come Out Fighting*, 31.

2. Holtz, 10–11.

3. Ibid., 17.

4. Ibid., 20.

5. History 104th, 66.

6. Geist, November 10, 1944; S-3 104th November Report.

7. Lorraine Campaign, 3rd Battalion 101st Infantry Regiment 26th Infantry Division, June 19, 1945, 5.

8. Ibid.

9. Ibid.

10. Williams, *Hit Hard*, 195.

11. History 104th, 66.

12. 104th S-3 November Report.

13. History 104th, 67.

14. Ibid., 68.

15. Geist, November 10, 1944.

16. 104th S-3 November.

17. Geist, November 10, 1944.

18. *Lorraine Campaign, 26th Infantry Division 5 October 1944 to 13 December 1944*, dated January 17, 1945, 8 (hereinafter *Lorraine Campaign*).

19. Cole, *The Lorraine Campaign*, 335–336; Williams, *Hit Hard*, 194.

20. Cole, *The Lorraine Campaign*, 335–336.

21. "Tank Outfit Proves Mettle: Kills 200 Germans to Win Silver Star," *Pittsburgh Courier*, December 30, 1944, 1.

22. Geist, Daily S-3 Report, November 19–20, 1944.

23. Ibid.; *Lorraine Campaign*, 6; S-3 Daily Report 328th, November 19, 1945.

24. Williams, *Hit Hard*, 202, 205, 215.

25. The names of the tanks crews are spelled differently in various sources. "Jowers" and "Hillard" are from their enlistment records. "Robinson" is probably shown as such in his enlistment record, though hometowns do not match places of enlistment, common during this period.

26. Anderson, *Come Out Fighting*, 36.

27. Ibid.

28. Williams, *Hit Hard*, 210–211.

29. Anderson, *Come Out Fighting*, 36; Geist, November 19, 1944.

30. Williams, *Hit Hard*, 212.

31. Ibid., 214–215.

32. Ibid., 217. President Bill Clinton presented Rivers's family with the Medal of Honor, January 13, 1997. The citation reads: "For extraordinary heroism in action during the 15–19 November 1944, toward Guebling, France. Though severely wounded in the leg, Sergeant Rivers refused medical treatment and evacuation, took command of another tank, and advanced with his company in Guebling the next day. Repeatedly refusing evacuation, Sergeant Rivers continued to direct his tank's fire at enemy positions through the morning of 19 November 1944. At dawn, Company A's tanks began to advance towards Bougaktroff, but were stopped by enemy fire. Sergeant Rivers, joined by another tank, opened fire on the enemy tanks, covering company A as they withdrew. While doing so, Sergeant Rivers's tank was hit, killing him and wounding the crew. Staff Sergeant Rivers' fighting spirit and daring leadership were an inspiration to his unit and exemplify the highest traditions of military service."

33. Geist, November 19, 1944.

34. Ibid.

35. Geist, November 20, 1944.

36. Ibid.

37. Anderson, *Come Out Fighting*, 41.

38. Geist, November 21, 1944.

39. History 104th, 71.

40. Holtz, 17.

41. Proclamation 2629, November 1, 1944.

42. Holtz, 17.

43. Geist, November 24, 1944.

Chapter Seventeen: Village by Village

1. O'Dea, November Report.

2. Ibid.

3. Ibid.

4. Geist, November 25, 1944.

5. Bates-Rosen, December 27, 1944.

6. Anderson, *Come Out Fighting*, 100.

7. Geist, November 25, 1944.

8. Guthrie.

9. Guthrie. The Honskirch vignette is based on Russell Guthrie's recollection. The tanker interaction, while unconfirmed through other sources (there is a ver-

sion in *Come Out Fighting*), serves as a good example of teamwork under fire, something that happened in each engagement but is not recounted in official battalion sources.

10. 328th S-3 report, November 26, 1944, p. 1. Recommendation for Distinguished Unit Citation for the 761st Tank Battalion, dated July 25, 1945.

11. Geist, November 25, 1944.

12. 328th S-3 report November 26, 1944.

13. Anderson, *Come Out Fighting*, 41.

14. Geist, December 1, 1944.

15. Mitcham, *Hitler's Legions*, 362–363.

16. S-3 Daily Report 101st, December 2, 1944.

17. Ibid., 14–16.

18. Geist, December 1, 1944.

19. Geist, December 2, 1944.

20. *Lorraine Campaign*, 14–15.

21. Ibid.

22. Lorraine Campaign, 2nd Battalion, 101st Infantry Regiment, 26th Infantry Division, June 20, 1945, p. 16.

23. "Aachen Falls to First Army," *Stars and Stripes* October 21, 1944, 1.

24. Anderson, *Come Out Fighting*, 42. *The Order of Battle of the United States Army World War II European Theater of Operations*, Officer of the Theater Historian, Paris, France, December 1945, lists the 761st attached to the 26th Infantry Division October 29–December 12, 1944. Geist lists the change between the 26th and 87th as December 11.

25. Commendation to 761st, Headquarters XII Corps, December 9, 1944. "Tank Unit 24th Win High Praise," *Pittsburgh Courier*, June 2, 1945, 1.

26. Ibid.

27. Ibid.

28. Captain Garland Adamson, November Medical Detachment Report, dated November 29, 1944.

29. S-3 Periodic Report 328th, December 10, 1944.

CHAPTER EIGHTEEN: THE GERMAN COUNTEROFFENSIVE

1. Parker, *Battle of the Bulge*, 7.

2. Ibid., 342.

3. Ibid., 178.

4. Cole, *The Ardennes*, 35.

5. Ibid., 18, 48.

6. Parker, *Battle of the Bulge*, 345.

7. Cole, *The Ardennes*, 56–58.

8. Ibid., 73.

9. Ibid., 38.

10. Ibid., 67.

11. Ibid., 9.

12. Arnold, *Ardennes 1944*, 31.

13. Cole, *The Ardennes*, 180.

14. *Life at the Battle of the Bulge*, 1.

15. U.S. Army Armor School (Ray Merriam, ed.), *The Battle at St. Vith, Belgium, 17–23 December 1944: An Historical Example of Armor in the Defense*, 15. (The front as it stood the morning of December 16, 1944.)

16. Cole, *The Ardennes*, 53.

17. Ibid., 59–60.

18. Ibid., 96; Thompson, *The Ardennes on Fire*, 166.

19. Cole, *The Ardennes*, 85, 97.

20. Ibid., 97.

21. Ibid., 263–264; Parker, *Battle of the Bulge*, 122–124.

22. Cole, *The Ardennes*, 261–263.

23. Darby, *Dwight D. Eisenhower*, 53.

24. Frey and Kucher, *World War II as Reflected on Capital Markets*.

25. Darby, *Dwight D. Eisenhower*, 54.

26. Ibid., 60.

27. *Eisenhower: Early Career*. PBS, *American Experience*.

28. BBC History: *Field Marshal Bernard Montgomery*.

29. Beevor, "Freedom Sweeps Europe, But at What Cost?" *Guardian*, September 10, 2009.

30. *Eisenhower*, PBS, *American Experience*.

31. Ambrose, *Americans at War*, 136; Parker, *Battle of the Bulge*, 15, 32–33, 94, 98.

32. John S. D. Eisenhower, *Soldiers and Statesmen*, 69.

33. Ibid.

34. Ibid., 70.

35. Ibid.

36. Parker, *Battle of the Bulge*, 21–23, 37.

37. Ibid., 201.

38. *Southeast Missourian*, December 22, 1944.

39. Marshall, *Bastogne*, 8–9.

40. After Action Report for December 1944, 28th Infantry Division dated January 4, 1945, 5.

41. Marshall, *Bastogne*, 11.

CHAPTER NINETEEN: SERGEANT MCBURNEY'S WAR

1. Geist, December 16–20, 1944, dated January 1, 1944 (Geist erred on the year); Maintenance December Report (thirty-one tanks up at that time).

2. English Collection.

3. Geist, December 24, 1944. *The Order of Battle of the United States Army World War II European Theater of Operations*, Office of the Theater Historian, Paris, France, December 1945, lists the 761st attached to the 87th Infantry Division December 20–23, 1944; January 1–15, 1945; and January 26–February 1, 1945. The order of battle does not appear to match with Geist's account. For example, Geist, reattaches the units December 24. Geist states there was an attempt to have all the vehicles move together. This work typically sides with the account of the 761st S-3 since his view of operational information influences the actions of the unit; G-3 87th Infantry Division, December 22, 1944.

4. Geist, December 21, 1944.

5. Geist, December 15, 23, 24, 1944.

6. The Allied Counterattack, December 26, 1944–January 27, 1945, Captain Edward B. Krainik (1948–1949), 10 (hereinafter Krainik).

7. Geist, December 26, 28, 30, 1944.

8. Krainik, 12–13.

9. Krainik, 13, 14.

10. Geist, December 30, 1944.

11. Anderson, *Come Out Fighting*, 47.

12. Ibid.

13. Marshall, *Bastogne*, 109. The order, which came December 21 from VIII Corps, read: "hold the Bastogne line at all costs."

14. Cole, *The Ardennes*, 643–644.

15. Cole, *The Ardennes*, 325, 643–644.

16. Anderson, *Come Out Fighting*, 47; handwritten 761st log, possibly S-1.

17. Anderson, *Come Out Fighting*, 47.

18. Handwritten 761st report. McDowell and Private Allen Jones wounded January 2.

19. Anderson, *Come Out Fighting*, 49. These men would later receive battlefield commissions.

20. Cole, *The Ardennes*, 643–644.

21. S-3 Periodic Report 347th, January 1, 2, 1945

22. Anderson, *Come Out Fighting*, 47.

23. Ibid.

24. Williams, *Hit Hard*, 253.

25. Handwritten Report (S-1), January 4, 1945; Anderson, *Come Out Fighting*, 61.

26. Krainik, 10, 14.

27. S-3 Periodic Report 761st, January 3–4, 1945.

28. Handwritten 761st Report, January 3, 1945. Johnson died of wounds.

29. Krainik, 14.

30. Ibid., Olive-Drab, World War II Shoe Pacs, 1.

31. Anderson, *Come Out Fighting*, 30.

32. S-3 Periodic Reports for the period of the operation.

33. Richard C. Manchester, Personal Account, World War II Memoirs, 87th Infantry Division Legacy Association. Parker confirms the four lost tanks. Implied in 761st written report for January 4. Geist on January 7 notes Able has only two operational tanks.

34. Cameron. FM 17-25 Assault Gun Section and Platoon, September 8, 1944, 1.

35. Geist, January 7, 1945; S-3 Periodic Report 761st (Geist), January 7–8, 1945.

36. Robert J. Watson, Personal Account, *The Life of a Man Who Hated War—Curtis Shoup*, 87th Infantry Division Legacy Association.

37. Ibid. Shoup was posthumously awarded the Medal of Honor, dated July 25, 1945. The citation reads: "On 7 January 1945, near Tillet, Belgium, his company

attacked German troops on rising ground. Intense hostile machinegun fire pinned down and threatened to annihilate the American unit in an exposed position where frozen ground made it impossible to dig in for protection. Heavy mortar and artillery fire from enemy batteries was added to the storm of destruction falling on the Americans. Realizing that the machinegun must be silenced at all costs, S/Sgt. Shoup, armed with an automatic rifle, crawled to within 75 yards of the enemy emplacement. He found that his fire was ineffective from this position, and completely disregarding his own safety, stood up and grimly strode ahead into the murderous stream of bullets, firing his low-held weapon as he went. He was hit several times and finally was knocked to the ground. But he struggled to his feet and staggered forward until close enough to hurl a grenade, wiping out the enemy machinegun nest with his dying action. By his heroism, fearless determination, and supreme sacrifice, S/Sgt. Shoup eliminated a hostile weapon which threatened to destroy his company and turned a desperate situation into victory."

38. Mitcham, *Hitler's Legions*, 385–386.
39. Geist, January 7, 1945.
40. Geist, January 9, 1945.
41. Ibid.
42. Ibid.; Anderson, *Come Out Fighting*, 50; McBurney; Morning Report Charlie Company, January 10. Handwritten report, January 9, 1945.
43. Mitchell Kady, *87th Infantry Division Lost 1,310 Killed, 4,000 Wounded in Three Months of World War II*, Commentary, 87th Infantry Division Legacy Association.
44. Anderson, *Come Out Fighting*, 102. Williams's Silver Star citation is dated January 8; Williams, various.
45. Williams, *Hit Hard*, 291. Able Company Morning Report of January 16, 1945, reports loss of Williams on January 9, 1945.
46. Parker, *Battle of the Bulge*, 218–219, 260–261.

CHAPTER TWENTY: BATES'S RETURN

1. Geist, January 11, 1945; S-3 Periodic Report 347th, January 12–13, 1945.
2. Ibid.
3. "Tankmen Lauded for Valor in First Days of Combat," *Baltimore Afro-American*, December 30, 1944, 9. A number of black papers ran a version of this story. *Stars and Stripes* also seemed to choose the facts it reported, so this practice appears to extend beyond the black press.
4. *Baltimore Afro-American*, January 14, 1945; G-3 87th Infantry Division, January 14, 1945.
5. *Baltimore Afro-American*, January 20, 1945.
6. Geist, January 18, 1945.
7. Ibid., January 19, 1945.
8. Ibid., January 23, 24, 25, 1945.
9. Ibid., January 19, 1945.
10. Ibid., January 23, 24, 25, 1945.
11. Ibid., January 24, 25, 1945.
12. Ibid., January 22, 23, 24, 1945.

13. 761st Summary for Distinguished Unit Citation, dated July 25, 1945. Anderson, *Come Out Fighting*, 54.

14. Geist, January 18, 1945.

15. Order of Battle, January 26–February 1, 1945; G-3 17th Airborne reported 761st attached to 87th, February 26, 1945.

16. Geist, February 1, 1945; Anderson, *Come Out Fighting*, 53. Order of Battle states 761st detached from 17th Airborne January 27, attached to 95th Infantry Division February 2, 1945.

17. Geist, February 2, 1945.

18. Anderson, *Come Out Fighting*, 54.

19. Geist, February 7, 1945.

20. Anderson, *Come Out Fighting*, 57.

21. Ibid.

22. Taylor-Bates letter, December 22, 1944.

23. Geist, February 9, 1945.

24. Geist reports (Daily Report) February 8, 20, 1945, are just two examples. He refers to maintenance as well as training. The 95th Infantry Division G-3 daily reports for the period also report the ongoing maintenance efforts of the 761st.

25. Geist, Daily Report, February 19, 1945.

26. Geist, Daily S-3 log, February 17, 1945; Headquarters Morning Report, February 18, 1945. 761st Handwritten Report, probably S-1, notes this as February 16, 1945.

27. Bates-Rosen, November 12, 1944.

28. O'Daniels-Bates letter, November 26, 1944.

29. Ibid.

30. Leonard P. Taylor-Bates letter, December 22, 1944.

31. Major Charles Wingo letter to Leonard P. Taylor dated November 19, 1944.

32. Anderson, *Come Out Fighting*, 4. Confirmed by Kayin Shabazz, Roert W. Woodruff Library Research Center, Clark Atlanta University. Trezzvant Anderson's papers are also maintained there.

33. Wingo-Taylor letter dated November 19, 1944.

34. Wingo-Taylor letters (he refers to three); two are November 19 and November 30.

35. Bates-Rosen short note, undated. Probably a cover note to correspondence he had regarding the brooding Wingo.

36. Ibid.

37. Reynolds-Bates, December 1, 1944.

38. Ibid.

39. Phillips-Bates, November 28, 1944.

40. Bates-Rosen, December 19, 1944.

41. Bates-Rosen, February 17, 1945.

42. Bates-Rosen, February 19, 1945.

43. The 761st had detached from the 95th Infantry Division and joined XVI Corps, Ninth U.S. Army; Order of Battle; Geist, February 13, 1945. Order of Battle states the 761st remained with the 79th Infantry Division February

20–March 1, 1945. Geist reports 761st companies maneuvering in support of 79th units like the 79th Reconnaissance Troop and the 314th Infantry Regiment through March 4. Sometime during March 7 and 8, Geist reports the 761st reattaches to Third Army. The Order of Battle for the 103rd Infantry Division reports that the 761st attached to the division March 10 and remained until March 28.

44. Marshall, *Bastogne*, 116–117.

45. Narrative of Operations 103rd Infantry Division (hereinafter Narrative 103rd), 22, March 14, 1945.

46. Geist, March 13–14, 1945. G-3 103rd Reports, March 15, 17, 1945; Operations Instruction Number 70, 103rd Infantry Division, March 18, 1945. G-3 103rd, March 13, 1945.

47. Operations Instruction Number 71, 103rd Infantry Division, March 18, 1945.

48. Narrative 103rd, 29–30 (March 17–18); Geist, March 16, 17, 18, 1945.

49. Bates-Rosen, March 25, 1945.

50. Narrative 103rd, 32.

51. Ibid., 34.

52. G-3 103rd, March 19, 1945.

53. G-3 103rd, March 20, 1945.

54. Whiting, *West Wall*, 5–6, 114 ("Prelude to the Battle 1936–1944").

55. Ibid., 165.

56. Ibid., 66.

CHAPTER TWENTY-ONE: TASK FORCE RHINE

1. Geist, March 21, 1945. Narrative 103rd implies Task Force Rhine was assembled sooner and in operation by the evening of March 21; Anderson, *Come Out Fighting*, 65; Bates-Rosen, March 25, describes Task Force Cactus and Task Force Rhine, but gives no specific dates; Operations Instruction Number 72, 103rd Infantry Division, March 21, 1945, 8 pm.

2. Geist, March 21, 1945.

3. Anderson, *Come Out Fighting*, 7.

4. Ibid.

5. Ibid., 65; G-3 103rd, March 22, 1945; Operations Instruction Number 72, 103rd Infantry Division, March 21, 1845, 8 pm.

6. Geist, March 21, 1945.

7. Bates-Rosen, March 25, 1945.

8. Geist, March 21, 1945; G-3 103rd, March 22, 1945.

9. Anderson, *Come Out Fighting*, 71.

10. Geist, March 21–22, 1945.

11. Bates-Rosen, March 25, 1945.

12. Narrative 103rd, 38.

13. Geist, March 22, 1945.

14. Geist, March 22, 1945. Narrative 103rd states Task Force Rhine probably broke through the Siegfried Line in Reisdorf (p. 43); Bates-Rosen, March 25, 1945.

15. Bates-Rosen, March 25, 1945; G-3 103rd, March 23, 1945.

16. Ibid.

17. Geist, March 22, 1945; Bates-Rosen, March 25, 1945; G-3 103rd, March 23, 1945.

18. Geist, March 22, 1945; Anderson, *Come Out Fighting*, 73; Bates-Rosen, March 25, 1945.

19. Bates-Rosen, March 25, 1945.

20. Narrative 103rd, 40.

21. Geist, March 22, 1945.

22. Ibid.

23. Narrative 103rd, 40.

24. Geist, March 22, 1945; Bates-Rosen, March 25, 1945; Narrative 103rd, 38.

25. Bates-Rosen, March 25, 1945.

26. Bates-Rosen, March 25, 1945; Narrative 103rd, 43; Anderson, *Come Out Fighting*, 75.

27. Geist, March 22, 1945; Anderson, *Come Out Fighting*, 75.

28. Narrative 103rd, 42; Bates-Rosen, March 25, 1945.

29. Bates-Rosen, March 18, 1945.

30. Bates-Rosen, March 20, 1945.

31. Geist, March 22, 1945.

32. Bates-Rosen, March 25, 1945; Geist, March 23, 1945; Narrative 103rd, 40, 42.

33. Geist, March 23, 1945.

34. Narrative 103rd, 42–43; G-3 103rd, March 23, 1945.

35. Bates-Rosen, March 25, 1945.

36. Geist, March 23, 1945.

37. Ibid.

38. Bates-Rosen, March 23, 1945.

Chapter Twenty-Two: We Lived Through It

1. 103rd Daily Narrative, March 23, 1945, 44.

2. Anderson, *Come Out Fighting*, 76, boxed item and information that follows; I&E News Summary, March 24, 1945. Only the general's 103rd is mentioned in this action.

3. Bates-Rosen, March 27, 1945; Baron Bates. Baron kept a scrapbook of letters from his father to him as well as those to his mother. He kept various artifacts like a clipping from the local paper crediting Bates and the 761st for leading Task Force Rhine and accomplishing the mission. Oddly the paper covers the mission better than any of the operations or "3" reports.

4. Geist, March 28, 1945; Order of Battle 71st Infantry Division; Anderson, *Come Out Fighting*, 79; G-3 103rd March 28, 1945.

5. Geist, March 31, 1945.

6. "Tank Units Plunge Through Nazi Towns, Blaze Path for White Infantrymen," *Chicago Defender*, April 7, 1945, 1.

7. Bates-Rosen, March 27, 1945

8. Ibid.

9. Ibid.

10. Geist, 761st S-3 Report for April 1945, dated May 2, 1945.

11. 761 After Action Report dated April 1, 1945, signed by the adjutant Clarence T. Godbold. The 761st's effective strength March 31, 1945, was 34 officers, three warrant officers, and 662 men. They were shy just five officers and 22 enlisted men.

12. Bates-Rosen, March 29, April 12, 1945.

13. Though the 761st stood attached to the 71st Infantry Division effective March 28, 1945, the battalion journey of more than 100 miles was to find and meet its new division. During that time, Bates enjoyed several days of relative autonomy; Anderson, *Come Out Fighting*, 79.

14. Geist's daily report covering April 3–4 as just one example, shows just 13 of 50 tanks down. Of those 13, 6 would be operational within 24 hours. Of the 50 tanks, 13 were Stuarts with 37 mm main guns, the rest were Shermans divided mainly between 75mm and 76 mm guns.

15. Ibid.; Bates-Rosen, April 26, 1945.

16. 71st Infantry Division, 57; Mitcham (German Order of Battle), 447–448.

17. Bates-Rosen, April 2, 1945.

18. Bates-Rosen, April 12, 1945.

19. Geist, April 4, 1945.

20. Letter translation, 409th Infantry Division, March 24, 1945.

21. 47 Volksgrenadier, January 29, 1945.

22. Bates-Rosen, April 6, 1945.

23. Bates-Rosen, April 4, 1945.

24. Ibid.

25. Bates-Rosen, April 2, 3, 1945.

26. Bates-Rosen, April 5, 1945.

27. Bates-Rosen, April 6, 1945.

28. Bates-Rosen, April 5, 1945.

29. Geist, April 16, 1945.

30. Bates-Rosen, April 2, 1945.

31. Bates-Rosen, April 6, 1945.

32. Bates-Rosen, April 5, 1945.

33. Ibid.

34. Ibid.

35. Ibid.

36. Bates-Rosen, undated (7, final page of letter).

37. Ibid.

38. Bates-Rosen, April 17, 1945.

39. Ibid.

40. Geist, April 16, 1945.

41. Geist, April 19, 1945; Bates-Rosen, undated, 3.

42. Bates-Rosen, undated, 4.

43. Anderson, *New York Amsterdam News*, June 30, 1945, 2. *Atlanta Daily World*, June 27, 1945, 1. Aside from Anderson's accounts, a later "history" of the 71st Infantry Division reports the sacking of the castle. Bates never writes of

the incident, but wrote little of the unit at this time. He was also consumed with the POW status of his four men. Geist does not mention Neuhaus, but Geist did not mention much during April.

44. Bates-Rosen, April 21, 1945.

45. Geist, April 23, 1945.

46. Bates-Rosen, May 9, 1945.

47. Bates-Rosen, April 25, 1945.

48. Captain John W. Williams (Personal experience of the Battalion S-3), *The Operations of the 3d Battalion 5th Infantry (71st Infantry Division) in a River Crossing and the Establishment of a Bridgehead on the South Bank of the Danube River on 26-27 April 1942.* (Advanced Infantry Officers Course, 1948–1949), 7.

49. McMahon, *The Siegfried and Beyond*, 421, 392. Geist does not mention the incident. The tank companies are split among the infantry regiment. Geist is probably at the command post at this time.

50. McMahon, *The Siegfried and Beyond*, 396. Eddy was promoted to lieutenant colonel after the successful crossing.

51. Geist, April 27, 28, 29, 30, 1945.

52. Bates-Rosen, May 1, 1945; Headquarters Morning Report, May 1.

53. Guthrie.

54. Bates-Rosen, May 9, 1945.

55. Guthrie.

56. McBurney. Washington maintained interest in how the races faired in theater. One report from the inspector general regarding the European Theater quoted one black quartermaster as "hating to see the doughs walk." His unit would drive out of their way to help the infantry soldiers. Though he found some snags such as the forwarding of OCS applications, overall, "The racial attitudes of the men throughout the Theater appear to be excellent." March 31, 1945.

57. *New Journal and Guide*, Signal Corps Photo, April 14, 1945.

58. VE Day figures. Handwritten chart.

59. Ibid.

60. Bates-Rosen, May 9, 1945.

61. 761st S-2/S-3 Journal, May 8–10, 1945.

62. Bates-Rosen, April 13, 1945.

63. Ibid.

64. Ibid. Bates-Barrie Bates, May 12, 1945. Bates describes his surprised impression of the Russians to his young son.

EPILOGUE

1. In 1982, a group of 761st veterans returned together to the battlefields of the Lorraine and the Ardennes. Within ten years of the journey, the men who had remained close for half a century reached an unforeseen breaking point. Some of the tankers claimed a proud role in the liberation of the Nazi concentration camps at Dachau and Buchenwald. But many in the unit disagreed and said the events never occurred. The men fell into two factions, almost splitting the association. The camp connection attracted outside interest. A documentary film, *The*

Liberators: Fighting on Two Fronts in World War II, resulted. The work juxtaposes the African American experience with that of the Jewish people. Filmmakers took several unit members to Germany where they met with death camp survivors. It debuted on PBS on Veterans Day 1992. Tankers remained certain of their recollections of events. According to Baron Bates, one filmmaker called Paul Bates a racist for maintaining the unit had no involvement in camp liberation and had traveled nowhere near the two camps. Despite the controversy, the film garnered an Academy Award nomination.

Bitter division among the veterans continued. Though each side remains sure of its truth, no evidence of interaction with a concentration camp appears in the primary-source material studied for this book. The controversy made it to the floor of the U.S. House of Representatives, May 25, 1994. Texas congressman Greg Laughlin said, "On the day in question, April 11, 1945, the 6th Armored Division was operating under the command of the 20th Corps, and Buchenwald was located in that zone. On that same day, all four companies of the 761st Tank Battalion were attached to the 71st Infantry Division which was operating under the command of the 12th Corps. Official records indicate that the 71st Infantry Division, including the attached 761st Tank Battalion was fighting near Coburg, Germany, which is approximately 60 to 70 miles from Buchenwald." (*Congressional Record*, 103rd Congress, p. H4084.)

Army historians explain that many veterans have claimed concentration camp liberations over the years. The 761st situation stands as one of many from the war. Officials now credit the 71st Infantry Division with the May 4, 1945, liberation of a short-lived, smaller camp, Gunskirchen, one of the many subcamps of the Mauthausen concentration camp system in Austria. Given the 761st's official attachment to the division, tanker involvement stands possible. Much angst has taken place over the issue of camp liberation, but the controversy, a red herring of sorts, has nothing to do with the superb factual record of the 761st Tank Battalion.

BIBLIOGRAPHY

Evangeline Parish (La.) Government Statistics

Dillard University Archives

Fort Benning, Donovan Library Holdings
After-action Report for December 1944, 28th Infantry Division, dated January 4, 1945.
History of a Combat Regiment 1939–1945: 104th Infantry.
History of a Combat Regiment: The 104th Infantry.
Holtz, (Major) Werner. The Operations of Company C, 104th Infantry (26th Infantry Division) from Vic-sur-Seille to Albestroff, Eastern France, 8–21 November 1944 (Rhineland Campaign) 1947–1948.
Krainik, Captain Edward B. The Allied Counterattack 26 December 1944–27 January 1945 (1948–1949).
Lorraine Campaign, 26th Infantry Division 5 October 1944 to 13 December 1944, dated 17 January 1945.
Narrative of Operations 103rd Infantry Division, March 14, 1945.
The Operations of the 2nd Battalion 101st Infantry (26th Infantry Division) in the Attack. Moyenvic, France, 8–10 November 1944 (Rhineland Campaign) (Personal Experience of a Battalion Operations Officer) Major John O. Dickerson. Advanced Infantry Officer Course, 1947–1948.
Interview of Lieutenant Colonel James Nixon Peale, Jr., Commander, 3rd Battalion, 101st Infantry Regiment, 26th Infantry Division, June 19, 1945.
Lorraine Campaign, as recounted by 26th Infantry Division Assistant G-3 Major William R. Porter, June 14, 1945.

Williams, John W. Captain (Personal experience of the Battalion S-3). *The Operations of the 3d Battalion 5th Infantry (71st Infantry Division) in a River Crossing and the Establishment of a Bridgehead on the South Bank of the Danube River on 26–27 April 1945* (Advanced Infantry Officers Course, 1948–1949).

INSTITUTE OF HERALDRY, WASHINGTON, D.C.
758th Tank Battalion unit insignia original files, Army Institute of Heraldry.
761st Tank Battalion unit insignia, motto original files.

LIBRARY OF CONGRESS
America's Story.
Biographical Directory; *Know Southern History. Collection of Southern biographies, undated.*
Memorandum, Officers and NCOs Schools. Though the date, March 17, 1944, for the week March 20–25, the scheduling is indicative of the 761st with Bates running training and the appearance he is running the battalion, though he is not yet the commander.
Lieutenant General Lesley McNair letter to Commanding General Third Army, March 14, 1943.
Truman K. Gibson, Jr. papers, Library of Congress, Washington, D.C.

NATIONAL ARCHIVES, COLLEGE PARK, MARYLAND
26th, 87th, 95th, 79th, 103rd, 71st, infantry divisions and associated regiments daily operational summaries (G-3/S-3), also daily unit updates submitted by the 761st to the unit to which it was attached. Official correspondence, awards contained.
761st Collection—Daily operational reports, periodic operational summaries, monthly reports from battalion staff officers, medical reports, map overlays, stacks of internal coded messages from combat phase.
Army Ground Forces Collection papers.
Assistant Secretary of War papers (John McCloy).
G-3 103rd March 22, 1945; Operations Instruction Number 72, 103rd Infantry Division, March 21, 1845, 8 pm.
Army Maneuver Collection, including the Louisiana Maneuvers of 1941 and 1943.
Operations Instruction Number 71 103rd Infantry Division, March 18, 1945.
Operations regimental reports from the 104th, 101st, and 328th infantry regiments of the 26th Infantry Division.
Operations reports from the 409th, 410th, 411th infantry regiments of the 103rd Infantry Division.

Operations reports from the 5th, 14th, 66th infantry regiments of the 71st Infantry Division.

Papers of the Civilian Aide to the Secretary of War (Hastie, Gibson).

Periodic Reports from the 345th, 346th, 347th infantry regiments of the 87th Infantry Division.

Tank Destroyer Center papers.

NARA Enlistment records.

NARA Prisoner of war records.

NATIONAL PERSONNEL RECORDS CENTER, ST LOUIS

758th Tank Battalion Rosters.

761st Tank Battalion personnel records, partial records, Morning Reports, Muster Reports, Unit Rosters (to 1943). (Majority destroyed in 1973 fire.)

UNITED STATES CENSUS BUREAU

U.S. CENSUS RECORDS, 1920, 1930, 1940.

PERSONAL COLLECTIONS, PRIVATE ARCHIVES, OTHER

Trezzvant Anderson Collection, Robert W. Woodruff Library and Archives, Clark Atlanta University, Atlanta, Georgia.

Paul Bates Letters 1943–1945 courtesy of Mrs. Paul (Taffy) Bates.

Paul Bates Military File, National Personnel Records Center and Baron Bates.

Bates College Records, courtesy McDaniel College.

Collections for Paul Bates from Western Maryland/McDaniel College, Barbara O'Brien, McDaniel archivist.

Andrew Bruce papers, Military History Institute, Carlisle, Pa.

The Richard English Collection, The Armistead Center, Tulane University, New Orleans.

Ivan Harrison, Sr., Collection Courtesy Ivan Harrison, Jr. (military records, correspondence, letters, appointments, orders, promotions, etc).

Philip and Louise Latimer background information, Baylor University online archives.

Manchester Richard C., Personal Account, World War II Memoirs, 87th Infantry Division Legacy Association, undated.

Gwendolyn Mann letters, etc. Emerson College Archivist Christina Zamon.

William McBurney military records, National Personnel Records Center, St. Louis (NPRC).

Jack Roosevelt Robinson military personnel records, NPRC.

Truman Smith papers, Military History Institute, Carlisle, Pa.

Dave Williams information from Yale Archivist, Nancy F. Lyon.

SELECTED NEWSPAPERS AND PERIODICALS
Atlanta Daily World .
Baltimore Afro American.
Berkeley Daily Gazette.
Chicago Defender.
Chicago Tribune.
Claiborne News (post paper).
Colliers.
Columbia Dispatch.
Daily Lariat (Baylor).
Evening Independent (St. Petersburg, Fla.).
Evening World.
The Gold Bug (Western Maryland College).
Harley-Davidson "Enthusiast" magazine.
Louisiana Weekly.
Mad Tanker (761st internal sheet at Camp Hood).
New Journal and Guide.
The Times-Picayune.
New York Amsterdam News.
The New York Times.
New York Tribune.
Pittsburgh Courier.
Popular Science.
Southeast Missourian.
Sports World.
St. Louis Post-Dispatch.
Stars and Stripes.
Town Talk (Alexandria, La.).
Yank magazine.

INTERVIEWS
761st veterans' interviews—tape and transcript. Library of Congress, Washington, D.C.
Barron Bates.
Mrs. Paul (Taffy) Bates.
Frederic Borch, Army Judge Advocate General historian.
Dr. Robert S. Cameron, Army Armor Historian.
William A. Cline, February 14, 2012, transcript.
Wesley Edwards Duggan, youngest sister of Juanita Harrison.
Len Dyer, Army Armor curator.
The Richard English Family.
Dale Genius, Alexandria, La., Historian.
Truman K. Gibson interview (transcript).

Russell Guthrie.

Ivan Harrison, Jr.

Pamela Harrison Collins.

Judge William H. Hastie, Oral History Interview Transcript. Harry S. Truman Library and Museum.

Herbert H. Hudgins, paperboy at Camp Claiborne during the war.

Carlton Smith, transcribed 1974.

Louise Latimer.

Thomas G. Mangrum, World War II communications technician.

William McBurney.

Public education history office for the state of New York.

Kayin Shabazz, Archives Research Center, Robert W. Woodruff Library, Clarke-Atlanta University.

Elizabeth A. Vane, U.S. Army Nurse Corps Historian.

John Weston, 758th Tank Battalion.

Glenn Williams, Army Historian.

STUDIES AND REPORTS

Army War College study, resulting memorandum, Army War College 1925 Memorandum on "*The Use of Negro Manpower*," October, 30, 1925.

Army War College, "Employment of Negro Manpower in War," November 10, 1925, FDR Library.

Dunham, Lieutenant Colonel Emory A., *Tank Destroyer History Study No. 29*, Historical Section of the Army Ground Forces in 1946.

Training in the Ground Army 1942–1945, Study No.11, 1948.

McNair, James Birtley, McNair, McNear, and McNeir Genealogies: (Supplement, 1955) BCR (Bibliographical Center for Research) (March 11, 2010) Original publication, 1928, publisher unknown.

War Department 1943 survey *The Negroes' Role in War: A study of White and Colored Opinions*. July 8, 1943.

Robinson Court Martial Transcripts, *United States v. Robinson* 1944, Courtesy US Army.

Order of Battle of United States Land Forces in the World War, 1931.

The Order of Battle of the United States Army World War II European Theater of Operations, Officer of the Theater Historian, Paris, France, December 1945.

See also Mitcham below.

ARMY INSTRUCTION MANUALS

Fort Knox Instructional Materials, May 19, June 23, 20, 1942.

FM 23-75 Basic Field Manual. War Department 37-mm Gun, April 16, 1940.

TM 9-726 Technical Manual Light Tank M3 (Stuart). War Department, July 15, 1942.

TM 9-726 Technical Manual Light Tank M3, July 15, 1942.

FM 17-30, "*Armored Force Field Manual Tank Platoon,*" October 1942.

FM 17-32, "*The Tank Company, Light and Medium,*" August 2, 1942.

TM 9-759 Medium Tank M4A3, August 4, 1942.

TM 9-731B Medium Tank M4A2, January 13, 1943.

FM 17-12 Armored Force Field Manual, Tank Gunnery, April 22, 1943.

FM 18-5 *Tank Destroyer Field Manual: Organization and Tactics of Tank Destroyer Units, July 18, 1944.*

The 808th Tank Destroyer Battalion, *Specialized Training.*

Firing by Ear Rather than Sight.

FM 18-24 *Tank Destroyer Pioneer Platoon November 1944.*

"Use of Tanks," XII Corps, December 4, 1944.

Ford FE Information.

ONLINE AND MEDIA RESOURCES

Austin, Texas, Library, Austin History Center—History.

Autobiographical sheet, Philip Latimer. 761st Tank Battalion Web site.

BBC *History Field Marshal Bernard Montgomery.*

Bennett, Don Sr., *Don Bennett's War.* http://don.genemcguire.com/index.htm.

Brown, Sam: Biography, The Brown Family, 761st Tank Battalion Web site, 1982.

"*A Camera Trip through Camp Claiborne,*" 1942. (Possibly a government public awareness publication.)

The Coming of Camp Hood. Film. Updated 2012 by City of Killeen.

Deford, Frank. "The Choices of Max Schmeling." National Public Radio, February 9, 2005.

Eisenhower. PBS: *American Experience.*

Eisenhower: Early Career. PBS: *American Experience.*

English Collection. News clipping, "Racing Chatter" by Tom Wilson. English had another article about his father dated June 30, 1938, from the *St. Louis Post-Dispatch.* This article refers to Jim English as having been "one of the top jockeys in the country."

Ferraraccio, John, *Battle of Wake Island,* historical presentation, National Park Service, no year.

The Great War. PBS. Resources: "World War I Casualty and Death Tables."

Hudson River Valley National Heritage Area, Camp Shanks World War II Museum.

Life at the Battle of the Bulge: Photos from Hitler's Last Gamble. Life.com.

Navy History and Heritage Command, Fact File, *Cook Third Class Doris Miller, USN*. U.S. Navy Fact File.

U.S. Census Bureau. Louisiana Population of Counties by Decennial Census: 1900 to 1990.

Watson, Robert J. Personal Account, *The Life of a Man Who Hated War—Curtis Shoup*, 87th Infantry Division Legacy Association, undated.

Zimmerman, Dwight Jon. *The Last and Largest Wargame Before World War II: The Louisiana Maneuvers*, August 15, 2011 (Defense Media Network) http://www.defensemedianetwork.com.

BOOKS AND ARTICLES

Ambrose, Stephen E. *Americans at War*. University Press of Mississippi, 1997.

———. *Eisenhower: Soldier and President*. Touchstone Books, 1991.

Anderson, Trezzvant. *Come Out Fighting*.

Archer, Christian I., and John R. Ferris. *World History of Warfare*. University of Nebraska Press, 2008.

Arnold, James R. *Ardennes 1944: Hitler's Last Gamble in the West*. Osprey Publishing 1990.

Axelrod, Alan, and Wesley K. Clark. *Patton: A Biography*. Palgrave Macmillan, 2006.

Beevor, Antony. "Freedom Sweeps Europe, But at What Cost?" *Guardian*, September 10, 2009.

Bergreen, Laurence. *As Thousands Cheer: The Life of Irving Berlin*. Da Capo Press 1989.

———. "Irving Berlin: This Is the Army." *National Archives Prologue Magazine*, 28, no. 2 (Summer 1996).

Blumenson, Martin. *The Patton Papers: 1940–1945*. Da Capo Press, 1996.

Bowers, William T. William M. Hammond, and George L. MacGarrigle. *Black Soldier White Army*. Army Center for Military History, 1996.

Brown, Thomas J. *John Bell Hood: Extracting Truth from History*. Xlibris, 2012.

Buckley, Gail. *American Patriots: The Story of Blacks in the Military from the Revolution to Desert Storm*. Random House, 2001.

Bull, Stephen. *World War II Infantry Tactics (2): Company and Battalion*. Osprey, 2005.

Cameron, Dr. Robert S. "Armor Combat Development 1917–1945." *Armor* (September–October 1997).

———. *Mobility, Shock and Firepower: The Emergence of the U.S. Army's Armor Branch, 1917–1945*. Center of Military History, 2008.

Carruthers, Bob. *Panzer IV: The Workhorse of the Panzerwaffe*. Coda Books, 2012.

CCC Facts, Civilian Conservation Corps.

Cole, Hugh M. *The Ardennes: The Battle of the Bulge*. Center of Military History, 1965.

———. *The Lorraine Campaign*. Center of Military History, 1993.

Cooper, Belton Y., and Stephen A. Ambrose. *Death Traps: The Survival of an American Armored Division in World War II*. Presidio Press, 2007.

Darby, Jean. *Dwight D. Eisenhower*. Lerner, 2004.

Denny, Major Bryan E. *The Evolution and Demise of U.S. Tank Destroyer Doctrine in the Second World War*. Master's thesis, U.S. Army Command and General Staff College, Fort Leavenworth, 2003; BiblioBazaar, 2012.

D'Este, Carlo, *Eisenhower: A Soldier's Life*. Henry Holt, 2002.

Edgerton, Robert B. *Hidden Heroism: Black Soldiers in America's Wars*. Basic Books, 2001.

Edwards, Michael J. "A Melancholy Experience: William CC Claiborne and the Louisiana Militia 1811–1815." Ph. D. dissertation. University of New Orleans, 2011.

Eisenhower, Dwight D. "A Tank Discussion." *Infantry Journal*, November 1920.

Eisenhower, John S. D. *Soldier and Statesman: Reflection on Leadership*. University of Missouri Press, 2012.

Encyclopedia of the War of 1812. edited by David Stephen Heidler and Jeanne T. Heidler. ABC-CLIO, 1997.

Erenberg, Lewis A. *The Greatest Fight of Our Generation: Louis v. Schmeling*. Oxford University Press, 2006.

Faulk, Odie B. and Laura B. *Fort Hood the First 50 Years*. F.W. Mayborn Foundation, 1990.

Federal Writers Project. *Los Angeles in the 1930s: The WPA Guide to the City of Angels*. Works Project Administration.

Ford, Lacy K. *Deliver Us from Evil: The Slavery Question in the Old South*. Oxford University Press, 2009.

Frey, Bruna S., and Marcel Kucher. *World War II as Reflected on Capital Markets*. University of Zurich, Elsevier Economics Letters, July 6, 1999.

Gabel, Christopher R. *The Lorraine Campaign: An Overview*. Combat Studies Institute, U.S. Army Command and General Staff College, 1985.

———. *Seek, Strike, and Destroy: U.S. Army Tank Destroyer, Doctrine in World War II*. Fort Leavenworth, KS: U.S. Army Command and General Staff College, 1985.

———. *The U.S. Army GHQ Maneuvers of 1941*. Center of Military History, 1991.

Gabel, Richard. *The Army General HQ Maneuvers of 1941.* Center of Military History, 1991.

Gillie, Mildred Hanson. *Forging the Thunderbolt: History of the U.S. Army's Armored Forces, 1917–45.* Military Service Publishing, 1947.

Gole, Jenry G., and Edward M. Coffman. *Exposing the Third Reich: Colonel Truman Smith in Hitler's Germany.* University Press of Kentucky, 2013.

Goodwin, Doris Kearns. *No Ordinary Time: Franklin & Eleanor Roosevelt: The Home Front in World War II.* Simon & Schuster, 1994.

Green, Hardy. "How K-Rations Fed Soldiers and Saved American Businesses." Bloomberg, February 20, 2013.

Hamm, Charles. *Irving Berlin: Songs from the Melting Pot: The Formative Years, 1907–1914.* Oxford University Press, 1997.

Harris, Stephen L. *Harlem's Hellfighters: The African-American 369th Infantry in World War I.* Potomac Books, 2003.

Hill, Walter. "Exploring the Life and History of the 'Buffalo Soldiers.'" *The Record* (National Archives), March 1998.

Hochschild, J. L., and B. M. Powell. "Racial Reorganization and the United States Census 1850–1930: Mulattoes, Half-Breeds, Mixed Parentage, Hindoos, and the Mexican Race." *Studies in American Political Development* 27, no. 1 (2008).

Hofmann, George. F. *Through Mobility We Conquer: The Mechanization of the U.S. Cavalry.* University Press of Kentucky, 2006.

———. "A Yankee Inventor and the Military Establishment, The Christie Tank Controversy." *Military Affairs*, February 1975.

Humes, James C. *Churchill the Prophetic Statesman.* Regnery History, 2012.

Ivy, Lenora A. "A Study in Leadership: The 761st Tank Battalion and the 92nd Division." Master's thesis, U.S. Army Command and General Staff College, 1995.

Jackson, Julian. *The Fall of France: The Nazi Invasion of 1940.* Oxford University Press, 2003.

Jefferson, Robert F. *Fighting for Hope: African American Troops of the 93rd Infantry Division in World War II and Postwar America.* Johns Hopkins University Press 2008.

Jones, Terry L. *The Louisiana Journey.* Gibbs Smith, 2007.

Kaidy, Mitchell. *87th Infantry Division Lost 1,310 Killed, 4,000 Wounded in Three Months of World War II.* Commentary, the 87th Infantry Division Legacy Association, undated.

Kimball, Robert, and Linda Emmet, editors. *The Complete Lyrics of Irving Berlin.* Knopf, 2001.

Kowalsky, Daniel. *Stalin and the Spanish Civil War*. Columbia University Press, 2004.

Lee, Ulysses. *The Employment of Negro Troops*. Army Center for Military History, 1966.

Lenton, H.T. and J. J. Colledge. *Warships of World War II*. 2nd rev. ed. Ian Allan, 1973.

Levine, David. "Remembering Camp Shanks." *Hudson Valley*, August 16, 2010.

Macksey, Kenneth, and John H. Batchelor. *Tank: A History of the Armoured Fighting Vehicle*. Scribner's, 1970.

Magee, Jeffrey. *Irving Berlin's American Musical Theater*. Oxford University Press, 2012.

Maiorino, Giancarlo. *Leonardo Da Vinci: The Daedalian Mythmaker*. Pennsylvania State University Press, 1992.

Manchester, William, and Paul Reid. *The Last Lion: Winston Spencer Churchill*. Little, Brown, 2012.

Margolick, David. *Beyond Glory: Joe Louis vs. Max Schmeling and a World on the Brink*. Alfred A. Knopf, 2005.

Marshall, S. L. A. *Bastogne: The First Eight Days* (US Army in Action Series) (reprint) Center of Military History. Original printed by Infantry Journal Press, 1946.

———. *The Siege of Bastogne*. Parts 1–4. U.S. Army, 1945.

Mayer, Neil M. *Nature's New Deal: The Civilian Conservation Corps and the Roots of the American Environmental Movement*. Oxford University Press, 2007.

McMahon, Gerald. *The Siegfried and Beyond: The Odyssey of the 66th Infantry Regiment and its Companions in Arms (Also goes under " ... the Odyssey of a Wartime Regiment, the 71st Infantry Division)* published by the 71st Infantry Division, 1993.

McWilliams, Carey. *Southern California: An Island on the Land*. Duell, Sloan, & Pearce, 1946.

Mitcham, Samuel M. Jr. *Hitler's Legions: The German Army Order of Battle, World War II*. Stein & Day, 1985.

Morton, Louis. *Germany First: The Basic Concept of Allied Strategy in World War II*. Army Center for Military History, 1960.

Mussolini, Benito. *My Autobiography with "The Political and Social Doctrine of Fascism."* Dover, 2012.

Myers, Walter Dean, and Bill Miles, *The Harlem Hellfighters: When Pride Met Courage*. HarperCollins, 2009.

Myler, Patrick. *Ring of Hate: Joe Louis vs. Max Schmeling: The Fight of the Century*. Arcade, 2005.

Osur, Alan M., Major, Ph.D. "Black-White Relations in the US Military 1940–1972." *Air University Review* Nov.–Dec. 1981.

Parker, Danny S. *Battle of the Bulge: Hitler's Ardennes Offensive.* Da Capo Press, 2004.

Patton, George C., Jr. "Tanks in Future Wars." *Cavalry Journal*, May 1920.

Phelps, Stephen. *The Tizard Mission: The Top-Secret Operation That Changed the Course of World War II.* Westholme, 2012.

Pugsley, William S. *Imprint on the Land: Life Before Camp Hood 1820–1942.* Prewitt & Associates, 2001.

Rampersad, Arnold. *Jackie Robinson: A Biography.* Ballantine, 1997.

Roberts, Randy. *Joe Louis: Hard Times Man.* Yale University Press, 2010.

Samuels, Martin. *Doctrine and Dogma: German and British Infantry Tactics in the First World War* (Contributions in Military Studies). Praeger, 1992.

"Sgt. Henry Lincoln Johnson: Perhaps, the Most Tragic Hero of Them All." May 26, 2013, *Examiner.com.*

Sitton, Thad, ed. *Harder Than Hardscrabble: Oral Recollections of the Farming Life from the Edge of the Texas Hill Country.* University of Texas Press, 2003.

Stewart, Richard W., general editor. *American Military History Vol. II, The United States Army in a Global Era, 1917–2003.* U.S. Army Center for Military History, 2005.

Stokes, George Alvin. "Lumbering in Southwest Louisiana: A Study of the Industry as a Culturo-Geographic Factor." Ph.D. dissertation, Louisiana State University, 1954.

Stolz, Joseph E. III. "An Ardent Military Spirit: William C.C. Claiborne and the Creation of the Orleans Territorial Militia." Ph.D. dissertation, University of New Orleans, 2009.

"Tank Unit with Patton Proves Mettle in Battle." *News Journal and Guide*, December 9, 1944, C20.

Thompson, Timothy J. *The Ardennes on Fire: The First Day of the German Assault.* Xlibris, 2010.

Tomblin, Barbara Brooks. *G.I. Nightingales: The Army Nurse Corps in World War II.* University Press of Kentucky, 2001.

U.S. Army Armor School (Ray Merriam, ed.). *The Battle at St. Vith, Belgium, 17–23 December 1944: An Historical Example of Armor in the Defense.* Merriam Press Military Monograph 5. 5th edition. January 2012.

Vernon, John. "Jim Crow, Meet Lieutenant Robinson, a 1944 Court Martial." *Prologue Magazine,* National Archives, 2008.

Vogt, Herbert R. *Hitler's Last Victims*. Xlibris, 2008.

Walker, Ian. *Iron Hulls, Iron Hearts: Mussolini's Elite Armoured Divisions in North Africa*. Crowood, 2012.

Whiting, Charles. *West Wall: The Battle for Hitler's Siegfried Line*. History Press Limited, 2007.

Williams, David J. *Hit Hard*. Bantam, 1983.

Wynn, Linda T. *William Henry Hastie (1904–1976)*. Tennessee State, undated.

Wynne, Ben. *On the Road Histories: Mississippi*. Interlink Publishing Group, 2007.

Zaloga, Steven J. *U.S. Tank and Tank Destroyer Battalions in the ETO 1944–45*. Osprey, 2013.

Zaloga, Steven, and Jim Laurier. *M3 and M5 Stuart Light Tank, 1940–45*. Osprey, 1999.

———. *M18 Hellcat Tank Destroyer 1943–1997*. Osprey, 2013.

ACKNOWLEDGMENTS

I N 2005 MILITARY OFFICER MAGAZINE ASKED THAT I WRITE AN article on the 761st Tank Battalion for its Black History Month issue in February 2006. I informed the editor that if the unit was worth a story, the magazine was doing a disservice to the men, pigeon-holing them by race. The 761st Tank Battalion has a fabulous and in many ways timeless story. The value of this unit and its men exceeds an article and surpasses what this book conveys.

I have written *The Black Panthers: A Story of Race, War, and Courage* mainly from the primary sources of the period—the as-it-happened reports, letters, news articles, and the like. I have tried to write it through the men's eyes, the lens of 1942–1945. The book tells the story of a remarkable unit during an equally remarkable time. These men fought for their country like millions of other Americans. I hope the facts speak for these combat tankers and the people that cared about them.

I would like to thank Michael Neff, director of Algonkian Writers Conferences, for insisting I needed to write this book, as I sat bewildered on a train bound for New York to pitch another written work. I cannot say enough about the public and private archives that struggle to keep their doors open for the seekers of the seemingly obscure information and morsels that can make a character or a story come alive. This includes the National Archives, College Park, Maryland; the National Personnel Records Center, St. Louis; the Robert W.

Woodruff Library, at Clark Atlanta University; and Tulane University's Armistead Center, New Orleans. University archivists Barbara O'Brien at McDaniel College (Western Maryland) and Christina Zamon at Emerson College proved especially helpful. Nancy Lyon, the archivist at Yale University as well as Baylor University, provided valuable information. Thanks go to Guy Nasuti at the Military History Institute, Carlisle, Pennsylvania. The interlibrary loan program through the public library system proved invaluable. Thank you to the city of Alexandria, Virginia, for participating in this worthwhile network. Thank you to Bonnie Henning at the Institute of Heraldry for sharing a rich history of unit insignia.

Many thanks to the people within the Department of the Army. Fort Benning, Georgia, which is now home to both the U.S. Army Infantry and Armor centers, opened its doors to me. Armor Museum curator Len Dyer shared his knowledge and the army's vast tank collection. Fort Hood historian Richard Powell, whom Hood lost for budgetary reasons, helped with the Camp Hood portion of the story. Alexandria, Louisiana, historian Dale Genius shared his knowledge as well as little-known artifacts from now-closed Camp Claiborne.

The historians whose doorsteps I have darkened have been as helpful as they have been patient. I marvel at their knowledge and understanding of history within and beyond their specialties. Alexandria, Louisiana, historian Dale Genius shared his knowledge as well as little-known artifacts from now-closed Camp Claiborne. Fred Borch, now historian for the army's Judge Advocate General School in Charlottesville, Virginia, is as gifted and thorough a historian as he is a lawyer. Thank you to Dr. Robert S. Cameron, the U.S. Army's armor historian and author of the riveting as well as rollicking *Mobility, Shock, and Firepower: The Emergence of the US Army's Armor Branch, 1917–1945*. He understood my work and supported me any way he could. Glenn Williams, a senior historian at the Army's Center of Military History, Washington, D.C., probably rues the day he picked up the phone and found me on the other end. Glenn underscores the value of Army historians. Though his specialty lies in the eighteenth century he can discuss World War II, the Civil War, the War of 1812, and the best on the Baroque music scene, or most any topic in accurate detail. Glenn, a truly selfless and kind gentleman and scholar, helped me with this project, probably at the cost of his own. He remains a great and trusted friend who kept me from losing hope as well as my sanity.

There would be no book without the unit and its tankers. At this point, seventy years later, there would be no book without their families. William McBurney remains my shy, but optimistic teen and it has been a privilege to talk with him. Russell Guthrie retains the energy of that sixteen-year-old who falsified his age to enlist. They were kind enough to talk from a World War II period perspective.

John Weston, a member of the first group of black tankers in history, lent great insight, and retired U.S. Army Colonel Aaron Dotson shared his memories of Warren Crecy. Lillian "Torchy" McConnell, widow of tanker E.G. McConnell, shared her collection of images. Louise Latimer shared her memories of husband Philip. The English, Crecy, Dade, McBurney, and Guthrie families helped and supported me where they could.

I would have been nowhere without the Bates and Harrison families, specifically Baron Bates and Ivan Harrison, Jr. They opened their parent's lives to me and hung with me through the journey. We discovered unknown aspects of their parents lives. These finds proved thrilling for me and probably unnerving for them, but they continued to trust me and helped with access in many areas.

There is nurse and poet Mrs. Paul Bates, the name she prefers to be known by. She appears in this book as Taffy or Helen Rosen. She is as beautiful and outspoken as the day she volunteered for the Army Nurse Corps. She has retained the strength and resilience she took with her when she left home at seventeen. Mrs. Bates opened her home to me, and trusted me with Paul Bates's letters that span much of the war. Without her gracious support there may have been no story. She remains my heroine on many levels, and I am sorry I could not write more in this book on this remarkable woman. She could have refashioned herself in any way she wanted, but chose a future with Paul Bates, making his life all the brighter. Sitting close with Mrs. Bates and reading her poetry aloud to her remains one of my most poignant experiences.

Thanks also to Bruce H. Franklin of Westholme Publishing for believing in this unit and this work and taking a chance on me, and his associates, Noreen O'Connor-Abel, Trudi Gershenov, Paul Dangel, John Hulse, and Mike Kopf.

To my Rudy Schulz, a retired U.S. Army lieutenant colonel whose father was firing back at the Allies as a German child soldier of sixteen, I have put you through hell. Thank you for being the stable one.

Finally, I have to thank all the men of the 761st, those still with us, those taken from us in battle, and those who left us in the years after the war. We have spent nearly two years together living, training, and fighting more battles across Europe than can be recounted here. You allowed me to be a part of your unit throughout the journey. Sam Turley, it is as if I watched you sacrifice yourself outside Morville. If I had to point to a Medal of Honor-worthy action, yours was it. You saved a company and quite possibly the battalion. All of you already know how much you mean to me.

INDEX